WITHDRAWN FROM
OHIO UNIVERSITY

PAPERS FROM THE 4th ICHL

AMSTERDAM STUDIES IN THE THEORY AND HISTORY OF LINGUISTIC SCIENCE

General Editor
E. F. KONRAD KOERNER
(University of Ottawa)

Series IV – CURRENT ISSUES IN LINGUISTIC THEORY

Advisory Editorial Board

Henning Andersen (Copenhagen); Raimo Anttila (Los Angeles)
Tomaz V. Gamkrelidze (Tiflis); Klaus J. Kohler (Kiel)
J. Peter Maher (Chicago); Ernst Pulgram (Ann Arbor, Mich.)
E. Wyn Roberts (Vancouver, B.C.); Danny Steinberg (Honolulu)

Volume 14

E. C. Traugott, R. Labrum, S. Shepherd (eds.)

Papers from the
4th International Conference
on Historical Linguistics

PAPERS
from the
4th INTERNATIONAL CONFERENCE
on
HISTORICAL LINGUISTICS

Edited by

Elizabeth Closs Traugott
Rebecca Labrum & Susan Shepherd

AMSTERDAM / JOHN BENJAMINS B.V.

1980

© Copyright 1980 – John Benjamins B.V.
ISSN 0304 0763 / ISBN 90 272 3501 5

No part of this book may be reproduced in any form by print, photoprint, microfilm or any other means, without written permission from the publisher.

ACKNOWLEDGMENTS

Preparation of these proceedings has been made possible by a grant from the Dean of Humanities and Sciences, Stanford University. For this we wish to express our profoundest gratitude and appreciation.

Many thanks are also due to Alice Branch and Randa Mulford, who typed the manuscript of this book, to Susan Blum, who helped compile the indexes, and to Richard Dasher, who did the art work.

Elizabeth Closs Traugott
Rebecca LaBrum
Susan Shepherd

Stanford, December 1979

TABLE OF CONTENTS

Acknowledgments v

Preface 1

Eugene Holman:
    Typology as Instigator and Regulator of Linguistic Change . . 7

Lyle Campbell:
    Explaining Universals and Their Exceptions 17

Sarah Grey Thomason:
    Continuity of Transmission and Genetic Relationship 27

John S. Justeson and Laurence D. Stephens:
    Chance Cognation: A Probabilistic Model and Decision
    Procedure for Historical Inference 37

William M. Christie, Jr.:
    Redundancy as Explanation in Historical Linguistics 47

Michael Shapiro:
    The Structure of Meaning in Semiotic Perspective 53

Flora Klein:
    Pragmatic and Sociolinguistic Bias in Semantic Change . . 61

Martin B. Harris:
    The Marking of Definiteness: A Diachronic Perspective . . 75

Marianne Mithun:
    A Functional Approach to Syntactic Reconstruction 87

Carol F. Justus:
    Implications of Pre-Complementizers with Hittite šak-/šek-
    'Know' 97

Anders Ahlqvist:
    On Word Order in Irish 107

Marit Christoffersen:
    Marked and Unmarked Word Order in Old Norse 115

Marinel Gerritsen:
   An Analysis of the Rise of SOV Patterns in Dutch 123
Frank Jansen:
   Developments in the Dutch Left-Dislocation Structures and
   the Verb-Second Constraint 137
Theodora Bynon:
   From Passive to Active in Kurdish via the Ergative
   Construction 151
Alice C. Harris:
   On the Loss of a Rule of Syntax 165
W. J. Pepicello:
   The Development of Accusative-Infinitive Constructions .. 175
Mario Saltarelli:
   Syntactic Diffusion 183
Michael Canale, Raymond Mougeon, and Edouard Beniak:
   Infinitival Complements to Verbs of Motion in Ontarian .. 193
   and Quebec French .. ..
Geoffrey C. Horrocks:
   Verb Compounds in Greek: The Elimination of a Transfor-
   mational Rule 199
Robert K. Herbert:
   The Role of Perception in Restructuring and Relexicaliza-
   tion: Two Case Histories 211
Robert J. Jeffers and Arnold M. Zwicky:
   The Evolution of Clitics 221
Joseph H. Greenberg:
   Circumfixes and Typological Change 233
Richard D. Janda:
   On the Decline of Declensional Systems: The Overall Loss of
   OE Nominal Case Inflections and the ME Reanalysis of -es as
   his 243
Emily Klenin:
   Conditions on Object Marking: Stages in the History of the
   East Slavic Genitive-Accusative 253
Janine K. Reklaitis:
   Reduction of Case Markers in Lithuanian: Data for
   Discussion 259
Max W. Wheeler:
   Analogy and Inflectional Affix Replacement 273

Henning Andersen:
Russian Conjugation: Acquisition and Evolutive Change .. 285

Marilyn May Vihman:
Sound Change and Child Language 303

Yakov Malkiel:
The Fluctuating Intensity of a 'Sound Law' 321

Roger Wright:
Linguistic Reasons for Phonetic Archaisms in Romance .. 331

Dieter Wanner and Thomas D. Cravens:
Early Intervocalic Voicing in Tuscan 339

John Reighard:
The Transition Problem: Lexical Diffusion vs. Variable
Rules 349

James Milroy:
Lexical Alternation and the History of English: Evidence
from an Urban Vernacular 355

Martha Laferriere:
Pragmatic Features and Phonological Change 363

Alice Wyland Grundt:
Tonal Accents in Basque and Greek 371

Carol W. Pfaff:
Acquisition and Development of "Gastarbeiterdeutsch" by
Migrant Workers and Their Children in Germany 381

Johanna Nichols:
Pidginization and Foreigner Talk: Chinese Pidgin Russian .. 397

Paul Kiparsky:
Concluding Statement 409

Index of Names 419

Index of Languages 429

Index of Subject Matter 433

PREFACE

The studies in this volume are revised versions of a large number of the papers presented at the Fourth International Conference on Historical Linguistics, Stanford, 26-30th March 1979. The total program is printed below. An asterisk indicates that the title alone was read *in abstentia*.

March 26th. Morning Session.

General theory.   Chairwoman: Anna Giacolone Ramat
 (U of Pavia)

*Roger Lass (Edinburgh U). "Functional non-explanation in historical linguistics".

E. F. Konrad Koerner (U of Ottawa). "The neogrammarian doctrine: breakthrough or extension of the Schleicherian paradigm? A problem in linguistic historiography".

Michael Shapiro (U of California, Los Angeles). "The structure of meaning in semiotic perspective".

Pedro Beade (York U, Ontario). "Metarules revisited".

John S. Justeson (U of South Carolina) and Laurence D. Stephens (Stanford U). "Chance cognation: a probabalistic model and decision procedure for historical inference".

Wayne O'Neil (MIT). "Literacy and language change".

Carol Wollman Pfaff (Freie Universität Berlin). "Acquisition and development of Gastarbeiterdeutsch by migrant workers and their children in Germany".

March 26th. Afternoon Session.

Typology, universals, and word order change.   Chairman: Luís V. Aracil (U of Barcelona)

    Eugene Holman (U of Helsinki). "Typology as instigator and regulator of linguistic change".

    Lyle Campbell (SUNY Albany). "Historical explanation of universals".

    Joseph H. Greenberg (Stanford U). "Circumfixes and typological change".

    Carol Justus (U of California, Berkeley). "Implications of precomplementizers with Hittite 'know'".

    Anders Ahlqvist (University College, Galway). "On word order in Irish".

    Marit Christoffersen (U of Bergen). "Marked and unmarked word order in Old Norse".

    Marinel Gerritsen (Royal Dutch Academy of Sciences). "An analysis of the rise of SOV patterns in Dutch".

    Frank Jansen (Moller Institut, Netherlands). "The survival of the 'fittest' Dutch left-dislocation; a case study in grammaticalization".

March 27th. Morning Session.

Cliticization and the development of definiteness.   Chairman: Charles-James N. Bailey (Technische Universität Berlin)

    *Cynthia L. Allen (Australian National U). "Generalization of syntactic rules: a case study".

    Robert J. Jeffers and Arnold Zwicky (Ohio State U). "The evolution of clitics".

    Flora Klein (Georgetown U). "Differential pragmatic and sociolinguistic exploitation in semantic change".

    Martin Harris (U of Salford). "The marking of definiteness: a diachronic perspective".

Nominal classifiers, case marking.

> *Janine E. Reklaitis (U of Illinois at Chicago Circle). "Reduction of case markers in Lithuanian: data for discussion".
>
> Hansjakob Seiler (U of Cologne). "Universal operational dimensions and language change".
>
> Carol Lord (U of California, Los Angeles). "The evolution of object markers in Benue-Kwa".
>
> Emily Klenin (Harvard U). "Conditions on object marking".
>
> Richard Janda (U of California, Los Angeles). "On the decline of declensional systems: the reanalysis of -es as *his* and the overall loss of OE nominal inflections".

March 27th. Afternoon Session.

Sound change.   Chairman: M. Chidananda Murthy
                                           (Bangalore U)

> *Witold Mańczak (U of Cracow). "Irregular sound change due to frequency".
>
> Alice Wyland Grundt (San Francisco). "Tonal accents in Basque and Greek".
>
> Steven N. Dworkin (Arizona State U). "Phonotactic awkwardness and lexical loss".
>
> Ernst Pulgram (U of Michigan). "Greek *phi* in Latin-Romance".
>
> Roger Wright (U of Liverpool). "Linguistic reasons for phonetic archaisms in Romance".
>
> Gregory K. Iverson (U of Iowa). "On the role of markedness in rule morphologization".
>
> William M. Christie, Jr. (U of Arizona). "Redundancy as explanation in language change".

March 27th. Evening Session.

Colloquium on the relevance of sociolinguistics to historical linguistics.

> Moderator: Charles A. Ferguson (Stanford U)

Panelists: Charles-James N. Bailey (Technische Universität Berlin). "The role of language development in a theory of language".

Martha Laferriere (MIT). "Pragmatic features and phonological change".

Sarah Grey Thomason (U of Pittsburgh). "Continuity of transmission and genetic relationship".

Peter Trudgill (U of Reading). "On the rise of the creoloid".

March 29th. Morning Session.

Opacity, perception, reanalysis.   Chairwoman: Maria Tsiapera
(U of North Carolina)

Robert K. Herbert (Michigan State U). "Misperception in reanalysis and relexicalization; two case histories".

Jean-Marie Hombert (U of California, Santa Barbara). "The role of perception in sound changes".

Marianne Mithun (SUNY Albany). "A functional approach to syntactic reconstruction".

J. Peter Maher (Hamburg U and NE Illinois U). "Concrete to abstract? The localist theory of case, perfective *up* etc".

Josh Ard (U of Wisconsin-Milwaukee). "A diachronic explanation of conditions on transformations".

Michael Canale, Raymond Mougeon, and Edouard Beniak (OISE, Toronto). "Infinitival complements to verbs of motion in Ontarian and Quebec French".

Alice Harris (Harvard U). "On the loss of a rule in syntax".

March 29th. Afternoon Session.

Analogy, diffusion.   Chairman: Peter Trudgill
(U of Reading)

Mario Saltarelli (U of Illinois, Urbana). "Syntactic diffusion".

Joan Bybee-Hooper (SUNY, Buffalo). "Morphophonemic change: paradigm-internal and paradigm-external motivation".

Denis Dumas (U of Québec à Montréal). "Quebec French lengthening consonants: an interesting split".

Yakov Malkiel (U of California, Berkeley). "The fluctuating intensity of a 'sound law'".

John Reighard (U de Montréal). "The transition problem: lexical diffusion vs. variable rules".

Luise Hertrich Hathaway (U of Illinois at Chicago Circle). "Sound change and lexical diffusion on a social basis".

Dieter Wanner and Thomas D. Cravens (U of Illinois at Urbana). "Early intervocalic voicing in Tuscan".

Jim Milroy (Queen's U, Belfast). "Lexical alternation and the history of English: evidence from an urban vernacular".

March 30th. Morning Session.

Transitivity, ergativity.　　　　Chairman: Hreinn Benediktsson
　　　　　　　　　　　　　　　　　　　　　　　(U of Iceland)

　　*Theodora Bynon (SOAS). "From passive to active in western Iranian via the ergative construction".

　　W. J. Pepicello (Temple U). "The development of accusative-infinitive constructions".

　　Bernard Comrie (USC). "Inverse verb forms in Chukchee: the comparative-historical evidence".

　　Paul J. Hopper (SUNY, Binghamton). "Some discourse origins of ergativity".

Verb and AUX systems.

　　*Karen J. Neff (Hofstra U). "On the development of tense from aspect".

　　Maria Tsiapera (U of North Carolina). "Language change: the labial and $eu\bar{o}$ verbal system in Greek".

　　Geoffrey C. Horrocks (U of London). "Verb compounds in Greek: the elimination of a transformational rule".

　　Max W. Wheeler (U of Liverpool). "Analogy and inflectional affix replacement".

Susan Steele (U of Arizona). "Constraining change by changing the constraints".

March 30th. Afternoon Session.

Language acquisition and   Chairman: Hansjakob Seiler
language change.   (U of Cologne)

*James Bynon (SOAS). "The baby register and diachrony: the evidence from Arabic and Berber".

*Emmanuel N. Kwofie (U of Lagos). "Second language acquisition and linguistic evolution".

Marilyn May Vihman (Stanford U). "Sound change and child language".

Henning Andersen (U of Copenhagen). "Russian conjugation: acquisition and evolutive change".

John Ohala and Mel Greenlee (U of California, Berkeley). "Phonetically motivated parallels between child phonology and historical sound change".

Meryl E. Solberg (MIT). "Ontogenesis and change".

Johanna Nichols (U of California, Berkeley). "Pidginization and foreigner talk: Chinese Pidgin Russian".

Paul Kiparsky (MIT). Closing statement.

Abstracts of all papers are available in Language and Language Behavior Abstracts, Supplement No. 3, 1979.

The first papers in this volume focus on general theoretical and methodological issues. Subsequent papers focus on pragmatic, semantic, syntactic, lexical, morphological, phonological, and phonetic changes, in that order. The volume ends with two papers on the changes found in simplified registers, followed by Paul Kiparsky's review of the conference and of the field.

E.C.T.
R.L.
S.S.

TYPOLOGY AS INSTIGATOR AND REGULATOR OF
LINGUISTIC CHANGE

EUGENE HOLMAN
University of Helsinki

From the standpoint of traditional typology, contemporary Finnish presents a bewildering picture.* Superficial scrutiny of its morphological processes conveys the impression of a straightforward and consistently realized, if somewhat idiosyncratic, agglutination, e.g. talo 'house' ~ taloa 'idem pS'[1] ~ talosta 'elS' ~ taloja 'pP' ~ taloista 'elP'; kuva 'picture' ~ kuvaa 'idem pS' ~ kuvasta 'elS' ~ kuvia 'pP' ~ kuvista 'elP', etc. This impression is quickly vitiated, however, when one considers the intricacies of patterns such as yö 'night' ~ yötä 'idem pS' ~ yöstä 'elS' ~ öitä 'pP' ~ öistä 'elP'; nuoli 'arrow' ~ nuolta 'idem pS' ~ nuolesta 'elS' ~ nuolia 'pP' ~ nuolista 'elP'; tuoli ~ 'chair' ~ tuolia 'idem pS' ~ tuolista 'elS' ~ tuoleja 'pP' ~ tuoleista 'elP'; rae 'grain' ~ raetta 'idem pS' ~ rakeesta 'elS' ~ rakeita 'pP' ~ rakeista 'elP', in which the techniques of agglutination, symbolism, and fusion (Sapir 1921;127ff.) coexist in uneasy alliance. Furthermore, the existence of directed movement away from agglutination towards symbolism and fusion is attested to by comparison of the situation prevailing in the supradialectal standard language with the situations of both the rapidly developing colloquial koiné (cf. Paunonen 1976a) and of many innovative provincial dialects, in which paradigms containing forms such as *patã* 'pot' ~ *patta* 'idem pS' ~ *paðã* 'gS' stand in contrast to the standard pata ~ pataa ~ padan.

Korhonen (1969) has written extensively on the background of an analogous movement in Lappish, and Čerkasskij (1965) is a treatment of the same phenomenon with respect to the Turkic languages. This kind of 'homotrophy' may, of course, be due to mere chance; certainly the number of ways in which a syntagm consisting of superordinate lexical morpheme and subordinate relational morpheme could be internally organized is severely limited. Consequently, the number of options by which transition from one type of morphological process to another could be effected should be correspondingly small. Nonetheless, the fact that this movement, after a long period of typological stability, should be taking place in the languages concerned with such rapidity and, for the most part, in the wake of factors traceable to the collective influence wielded by what in themselves were relatively minor short term modifications in the surface structure of syntagms, appears to suggest that we are dealing with a more or less generally valid strategy of resolving the conflicts inherent in agglutinative organization, rather than with a fortuitous pattern of change.

In this presentation we shall be concerned with an analysis of this movement in terms of the former assumption from the perspective provided by a functionalist interpretation of the concept of linguistic type.

A logical consequence of the functionalist view that 'la langue est un système de moyens d'expression appropriés à un but' (*Thèses* p. 5) is that the traditional concept of linguistic type must be extended so as to entail entire internally consistent patterns of systemic organization, rather than be limited to the characteristics of one or a few subsystems selected at random and analyzed in isolation, if it is to be of use in providing insights into the recurrent modes of behavior that appear to be associated with the functioning and gradual reorganization of languages in time. In accordance with this view, the existence of linguistic types should be understood in relation to and as a consequence of the dualistic ontology of language as abstract structure and concrete substance in mutual interaction with both each other, and with constantly changing extralinguistic objective and subjective reality. If languages are understood to be both abstract hierarchies of heterogeneous invariants which participate in various types of interdependent relations for a specific purpose within culturally established norms, as well as physically manifested internally structured acoustic signals, the material characteristics of which are determined by the organization of the abstract language system embodied in them, against the background provided by the neurophysiological, articulatory, and perceptual capabilities of their human users, then many characterstics of linguistic organization in general, and of specific patterns of mutually consistent organizational strategies in particular, follow deductively.

Hierarchical organization implies coordinated interaction between both the units which are functionally equivalent in terms of the overall entity, and between the various strata of the system as a whole in the interaction of the system with its environment. The inseparable existence of and constant interaction between abstract invariance and concretely manifested variance means that a language can never be a completely determinate entity, but rather must be constantly undergoing reorganization, in accordance with which those factors of its physical manifestation consistent with the dominant traits of its abstract organization will stand a greater chance of being recycled into it, and thus of forming the basis for the recreation of its structure, than will those corresponding to poorly integrated or non-integrated features. This, in turn, amounts to attributing to a language system an inherent ability to optimalize itself qualitatively by the reinforcement resulting from the unconscious preference by its speakers of some as opposed to others of the variants arising during the normal course of everyday language use.

Now optimalization within a hierarchical organization entails movement of the system as a whole towards organizational and material characteristics which are mutually in harmony with and supportive of one another (cf. Lange 1966: 62ff.). Hence, the necessary consequence of systemic organization is a specific mode of relating to and being influenced by the various factors ultimately determining the physical form to be assumed by the material embodiments of the components of the system. This, in turn, means that the concept of type of linguistic organization is not and cannot be limited to the classification or characterization of the strategies preferred by specific languages for expressing isolated concepts or for constructing syntagms. Instead, the traits of the particular strategy of linguistic organization dominant in a specific language should be evidenced in the material characteristics of most of the heterogeneous elements interacting with one another in their functioning as a system, since it is these characteristics which form the paradigmatic basis for its optimalization (cf. Mel'nikov 1969).

Let us now proceed to an exemplification of these claims.

All languages must contain signs for the expression of both lexical and relational concepts, as well as strategies for constructing syntagms of the two. However, the techniques by which these two classes of signs enter into relationships with one another while nevertheless retaining enough material characteristics to ensure their unequivocable differentiation varies from language to language.

Among the conceivable strategies are amalgamation, subordination by affixation, or mere juxtaposition, with no constraints excluding the utilization of some or all of these strategies to different degrees within the same language. Optimalization of a language system in respect to any one or specific combination of these strategies would entail the posing of several constraints on the material characteristics of the morphemes involved. As an illustration of this, let us construct a model of the framework within which subordination by affixation could optimally be realized from the standpoint of the extraction of information from the speech signal by its users.

Before the content of a message can be extracted, it must go through several information processing stages, of which phonic encoding is the first. The phonic system may be visualized as a complex filter, the input to which is an incoming acoustic signal, and the output from which is a chain of discrete units, exhibiting structural characteristics relevant to the abstract invariants constituting the different levels of structure of the linguistic system in question, and thus to the further analysis of the signal grammatically, semantically, and pragmatically. Hence, in addition to serving as the basis for the encoding of the speech continuum into discrete units, the phonic system also provides the means for a very strong preprocessing of it.

This means that speech perception, although obviously a function of the phonic system in question, is not a simple function of its informational output, but rather should be understood as depending upon specific properties of the speech signal itself, such as contrast with its immediate environment and internal organization. It is no accident that the ideal syllable shape is CV, nor that all languages appear to exhibit different restrictions on the sounds and sound combinations allowed to appear in word initial, word internal, and word final position. These constraints provide the acoustic signal with a certain amount of statistically predictable structure as entities both contrasting with their environment and possessing internal cohesion; they serve as reference points to which the incoming speech continuum may be related.

Bearing in mind that subordination by affixation involves a linear relation between two functionally different linguistic signs, it is understandable that the undisturbed grammatical functioning of languages making primary use of this organizational strategy would be greatly facilitated by any means that would enhance the auditor's ability to isolate words as units and segment them unambiguously into their superordinate and various subordinate components.

For this reason natural concomitants of this organizational strategy are relatively large inventories of positive and negative border signals. The presence of specific items from the phonic inventory, fixed patterns of word stress, sharp restrictions on the segments allowed to appear at the beginning as opposed to within or at the ends of syntagms, vowel harmony, assimilation limited to the most transparent instances of amalgamation, and an overriding tendency to avoid such innovations which would lead to alterations in the surface manifestation of morphemes greater than such which could be mapped onto each other by a simple algorithm, indicate in themselves the presence of boundaries between syntagms and their components, or, on the contrary, the absence of such boundaries, and thus provide a framework within which subordination by affixation could optimally be realized. In languages making primary use of this organizational strategy specific aspects of the surface structure of morphemes and syntagms, both in regard to their immediate surroundings in the stream of speech and as internally cohesive units, are thrust into prominence and consequently serve a crucial role in determining both the manner in which a perceived speech signal will be interpreted and evaluated against established structure and, in the long run, the course which will be taken by the system in its gradual optimalization.

This type of organizational strategy involves a complex coordinated interplay between many levels of linguistic structure. Once it has come into a position of dominance, it appears to be particularly stable and resistant to disruption (cf. Serebrennikov 1963).

What factors, then, may be alluded to in order to explain its rapid degeneration after a long period of dominance in Finnish, Turkic, and other languages?

In languages making primary use of subordination by affixation both the syntagm and its constituent morphemes form a highly integrated *Gestalt* in which the presence or absence of specific phonic characteristics in specific positions mirrors unambiguously the relation of the constituent in question both to the surrounding speech signal and to the transmission of lexical as opposed to relational information. This means that in languages of this type, a considerable proportion of the information needed for grammatical encoding is overtly marked in the speech signal.

The everyday functioning of such a language system will give rise to situations in which this condition is violated, and the phonic characteristics normally imbued

with an iconic function will, exceptionally, only have
their constitutive and differentiating functions. For example, Finnish has a large inventory of consonant complexes, but there are severe restrictions on where these may
occur. All complexes may appear at the border between the
first and second syllables (e.g. vihko 'notebook', helppo
'easy'), but very few are allowed to appear at the border
between the second and third syllables in primitive morphemes (e.g. lusikka 'spoon', ullappa 'open sea'). With the
exception of recent loans and, in some lects, of forms resulting from recent apocope and syncope (mnä 'I' cf. minä;
snō '(s)he says' cf. sanoo, etc.; talðsans 'in his/her
house' cf. talossansa, juǫ veť 'drink water!' cf. juo vettä,
etc.), none are permitted at the beginning or end of syntagms. Consequently, the presence of complex consonantism
in the speech signal conveys information bearing on the relation of the sequence being processed to both its surroundings and to the grammatical information being transmitted by it.

When these conditions are violated as a result of
either the interaction of the system with the physiological
and psychological capabilities of its users, or of extrasystemic contact, the language is faced with the problem of
adapting to these contingencies in a manner that will do
the least amount of damage to its signalling mechanisms.
In some cases, specifically where the phonic characteristics of the words in question serve as indices of their
extrasystemic origin or of their affective functioning,
indexicality takes precedence over iconicity, a normal sequence of events in the life and functioning of sign systems (cf. Anttila 1978:46f.). In other cases, specifically
those that arise as a result of the establishment in the
system of the reflexes of forms which, although once in
conformity with its regularities, have, through the inexorable working of natural phonetic change (e.g. $^+pän\ddot{a} > {}^+p\ddot{a}$
≡ pää 'head'), or because of the inevitable conflicts
arising between semantics and etymology (e.g. lihava 'fat'
= liha 'meat' + {augmentative suffix}), become modified in
such a manner as to violate one or several of its recurrent
patterns, the signs in question have no recourse to their
extrasystemic or pragmatic indexicality. The only way they
can be dealt with short of doctoring them so as to readapt
them to the patterns of the system is by overtly marking
either them or the signs with which they commonly associate, in a manner clearly indicating exception to the norm.
While this would amount to a short term modification of the
system to accommodate a contingency, the introduction into
the system of marked and unmarked variants that this involves is in complete opposition to its entire *raison*

d'être, the maintenance of a 1:1 relationship between form and function, and thus constitutes the seeds of its destruction.

This is well exemplified by an examination of the manner in which certain Finnish affixes have developed. Due to exigencies of space, I must restrict the pertinent data to the barest minimum.

The overwhelmingly dominant phono-morphological pattern in both contemporary Finnish and its immediate progenitors, early and late proto-Finnic, consists of a bisyllabic $C_0^1V_1^2C^3V$ sequence, bearing main stress on the initial syllable and no stress on the second one. When appearing as the superordinate member of a syntagm to which various derivational, inflectional, and pragmatic relational morphemes have been subordinated, the resultant syntagm exhibits, in addition to the initial main stress, secondary stress on the third and every subsequent odd numbered syllable save the last, but no stress on any intervening even-numbered syllables.

In early proto-Finnic the signs of the partitive case and of the present participle were $^+$-*ta* ~ $^+$-*tä* and $^+$-*pa* ~ $^+$-*pä* respectively. By the late proto-Finnic period they existed in the strong and weak variants $^+$-*ta* ~ $^+$-*tä* ~ $^+$-*δa* ~ $^+$-*δä*, and $^+$-*pa* ~ $^+$-*pä* ~ $^+$-*βa* ~ $^+$-*βä* (Kangasmaa-Minn 1968). The distribution of these variants was such that when the sign occurred in conjunction with morphemes conforming to the dominant bisyllabic CVCV sequence, it was in the weak grade, otherwise it occurred in the strong grade, e.g. $^+$*sanoβa* 'say Pp-a'[2], $^+$*sanottaβa* 'idem Pp-p' contra $^+$*jōpa* 'drink Pp-a', $^+$*jōttapa* 'idem Pp-p'; $^+$*itkeβä* 'cry Pp-p'; $^+$*itkettäβä* 'idem Pp-p' contra $^+$*sōpä* 'eat Pp-a', $^+$*söttäpä* 'idem Pp-p'; $^+$*kalaδa* 'fish pS' contra $^+$*māta* 'land pS', $^+$*lihaβata* 'fat pS'; $^+$*küläδä* 'village pS' contra $^+$*ōtä* 'night pS', $^+$*ikäβätä* 'boring pS'. The number of allophones had thus increased to four for each of the signs concerned, the distribution and form of which, although at least partially motivated by phonetic factors, also served a semiotic function as indices of the structural irregularity of the forms to which they were attached.

Subsequent development of the language has led to both the quasi-bisyllabification of many of the late proto-Finnic monosyllabic roots, e.g. $^+$*pä* ≡ pää 'head' > *peä* > *piä* (cf. Holman 1979); $^+$*tē* > tie 'road' > *tiä* (cf. Holman 1977), as well as to the spread of the unmarked form to trisyllabic roots ending in a vowel, e.g. ikävätä 'boring pS (archaic)' ~ ikävää 'idem (unmarked)'; juottapa 'drink

Pp-p (archaic)' ~ juottava 'idem (normal)' (cf. Kangasmaa-Minn 1968:111 f.). Additionally, there exist a few doublets with different semantic function, e.g. syöpä 'cancer' contra syövä 'eat Pp-a', käypä 'valid' contra käyvä 'go etc. Pp-a'; juopa 'gap' contra juova 'drink Pp-a'.

Restricting ourselves to the partitive singular, we see that the end result is a situation in which the correct form of the inherited affixed partitive can only be determined by several opaque and often contradictory rules, e.g. tuoli 'chair' ~ tuolia, but nuoli 'arrow' ~ nuolta; vesi 'water' ~ vettä but kipsi 'cast' ~ kipsiä and lapsi 'child' ~ lasta, etc., with the consequence that in many forms of popular speech the partitive singular is, wherever possible, expressed by prolongation of the vowel of the second syllable, e.g. mehu 'juice' ~ mehū, lato 'barn' ~ latō, presumably on the basis of the model provided by kala 'fish' ~ kalaa, kylä 'village' ~ kylää (cf. Paunonen 1976a: 134), or, alternatively, in dialects which do not differentiate between long and short vowels in unstressed syllables, by prolongation of the intervocalic consonant, e.g. mehu ~ mehhu, lato ~ latto, kala ~ kalla. (Forms utilizing both strategies also occur, e.g. mehu ~ mehhū, lato ~ lattō, kala ~ kallā.)

These strategies, which, incidentally, leave a large residue of forms which cashed in on their contiguity with a dental consonant and thus have t as their partitive marker, e.g. hevonen 'horse' ~ hevosta, käsi (<<^+käte) 'hand' ~ kättä, varsi (<<^+varte) 'handle' ~ vartta, etc., result in the partitive singular having at least ten different surface manifestations in many lects. Historically, the motivation for each modification is relatively straightforward; from the standpoint of the present-day language, however, in respect to suffixation the lexicon is divided up into over eighty mutually exclusive although partially overlapping classes consisting of 'constellations of allomorphs', the interparadigmatic and intraparadigmatic relations of which are extremely complex. The members of these constellations are in many cases incapable in themselves of indicating unequivocably either the case form in question or the inflectional class to which the lexical stem belongs. This becomes clear only when a specific form is perceived in relation to the other allomorphs of the same lexical item (Paunonen 1976b).

The developments which we have discussed here are typical examples of the type of conflict arising in a language utilizing subordination by affixation and of the manner in which it is often resolved. It exemplifies the manner in which specific patterns of linguistic organization affect the entire stratification of language by bringing specific types of situations into prominence. In doing so, they influence the nature of the short term solutions selected to deal with contingencies arising in the everyday functioning of language which, as they accumulate, provide the paradigmatic basis for both the breakdown of the pattern responsible for their having been brought into existence, and its replacement by another.

NOTES

*I would like to take this opportunity to thank Farrell Ackerman and Martti Nyman for reading an earlier version of this paper and offering many suggestions for its improvement

[1] In accordance with established practice in Finno-Ugric linguistics underlining indicates that the quoted form is in the orthography of the language in question. Finnish orthography may, for the purposes of this article, be regarded as approximating a taxonomic phonemic transcription. Forms in italics represent a coarse phonetic transcription. The grave accent over a vowel represents a prolongation intermediate between monomoric short (indicated by the vowel sign itself), or bimoric long (indicated by a macron). The abbreviations used for indicating the morphological form of a word are the following: p = partitive, el = elative, g = genitive; S = singular, P = plural. Thus pS = 'partitive singular', etc. Cf. note 2.

[2] For verbal stems the following abbreviations are used: P = present, p = participle, -a = active, -p = passive. The abbreviations for nominal stems are the same as in footnote 1. Note that pP = partitive plural; Pp = present participle.

REFERENCES

Anttila, Raimo. 1978. "The acceptance of sound change by linguistic structure". In *Recent developments in historical phonology* 43-55. Ed. by Jacek Fisiak. The Hague.
Čerkasskij, M.A. 1965. *Tjurkskij vokalizm i singarmonizm*. Moscow.
Holman, Eugene. 1977. "The diphthongization of Finnish long mid vowels as part of a homeostatic process". In *Papers from the Conference in General Linguistics. Lammi 22-23.9.1977. Suomen kielitieteellisen yhdistyksen julkaisuja* 1-15. Turku.
_____. 1979. "The Eastern Finnish diphthongization of long compact vowels and its diachronic implications". *Soviet Finno-Ugric Studies* 15.18-25.
Kangasmaa-Minn, Eeva. 1968. "Suffiksaalisesta astevaihtelusta". *Mémoires de la Société Finno-ougrienne* 145.110-16.

Korhonen, Mikko. 1969. "Die Entwicklung der morphologischen Methode im Lappischen". *Finnisch-ugrische Forschungen* 37.203-362.
Lange, Oskar. 1966. *Ganzheit und Entwicklung in kybernetischer Sicht.* Berlin.
Mel'nikov, G.P. 1969. "Jazykovaja stratifikacija i klassifikacija jazykov". In *Edinicy raznyx urovnej grammatičeskogo stroja jazyka i ix vzaimodejstvie* 116-25. Moscow.
Paunonen, Heikki. 1976a. "Idiolectical variation in Helsinki urban speech". *Linguistics* 183. 125-40.
____. 1976b. "Allomorfien dynamiikkaa". *Virittäjä* 80.82-107.
Sapir, Edward. 1921. *Language. An introduction to the study of speech.* New York: Harcourt, Brace and Co.
Serebrennikov, Boris A. 1963. "O pričinax ustojčivosti aggljutinativnogo stroja". *Voprosy Jazykoznanija* 12.1.46-56.
Thèses. 1929. In *Travaux du Cercle Linguistique de Prague* 1.5-29.

EXPLAINING UNIVERSALS AND THEIR EXCEPTIONS

LYLE CAMPBELL
State University of New York, Albany

0. *Introduction.* The goal of research on linguistic universals has been to establish features common to human languages and to understand principles which may explain them. Establishing and understanding universals is taken as a major goal of linguistic theory. In this paper I will attempt to characterize strategies for investigating linguistic universals. The main purpose of this paper is to show that universals and their exceptions may be fully explained only when the role of 'external' (sociocultural) factors is taken into account.

1. *Research programs.* The main research program for establishing universals has been the cross-linguistic search of the world's languages. Universals found in this way have been classified as:

1) *absolute* (or unrestricted): all languages exhibit the trait (e.g., all languages have vowels),

2) *statistical* (near-universals): with greater than chance frequency languages tend to exhibit the trait (e.g., languages tend to have nasals with greater than chance frequency); and

3) *implicational*: if a language exhibits some trait X then it will also have another trait Y (that is, the presence of X implies the presence of Y) (e.g., contrastive nasalized vowels imply the presence of non-nasalized vowels in the language) (cf. Greenberg 1975).

As Greenberg (1975) has pointed out, such universals establish a typology which is useful in their cross-linguistic investigation. The role of typology in the investigation of universals will help us to understand better the historical explanations and violations of universals to be considered below.

Absolute universals imply two types, one of languages exhibiting the trait and the other of logically possible languages without the trait, predicting that the second type will have no real examples. For example, the universal that all languages have vowels implies two types, one of languages with vowels and the other of languages with no vowels, indicating that no language exists of the second logically possible type.[1] Statistical universals imply two types of languages where most languages are of one type while the other type has very few. Implicational universals may be the most interesting; they establish three types, one type which has both traits (one trait implied by the presence of the other), another type with only the unimplied trait, and a third logically possible type which has only the implied trait, which the universal predicts will have no real examples. For example, the implicational universal that the presence of uvular stops implies the presence of velar stops in a language ([q] ⊃ [k]) establishes three types, languages with both [q] and [k], languages with only [k] but no [q], and logically possible but supposedly non-existent languages with only [q] but no [k].

A research strategy for testing universals cross-linguistically seeks examples of languages exhibiting the traits of the logically possible types which are predicted by the universals to exhibit no real examples. For example, in the first case, the universal that all languages have vowels could be tested by seeking examples of languages which have no vowels; that is, examples of languages of the type predicted not to exist by the universal. Similarly, one can test the implicational universal that [q] implies [k] by seeking languages of the type predicted not to exist - languages with [q] but no [k].

2. *Explanations*. The program for investigating universals, as discussed so far, is to establish a hypothesis based on cross-linguistic investigation and then to test it by seeking examples of the type of languages that the typology of the universal predicts do not exist. But the discovery that something does or does not occur cross-linguistically does nothing to 'explain' the universal. Nevertheless, most universals do have explanations - explanations stemming from constraints on human speech production and perception, i.e., physical and psychological explanations. I call these 'internal' explanations. Discussions of 'naturalness', 'phonetic motivation', 'unmarked' elements, and 'universals' have all involved internal explanations. For example, intervocalic voicing of obstruents is 'natural' (phonetically motivated) because limitations of human muscle control tend toward continued vibration of

the vocal cords in the environment between vowels. The
frequent lowering of quality of nasalized vowels stems
from the altered perception of vowel height with nasalization (Ohala 1974a). This perceptual fact would appear
to explain the universal that the presence of nasalized
high vowels implies also the presence of nasalized nonhigh
vowels, that is:

$$\begin{bmatrix} V \\ + \text{ high} \\ + \text{ nasal} \end{bmatrix} \supset \begin{bmatrix} V \\ - \text{ high} \\ + \text{ nasal} \end{bmatrix}$$

A second research strategy for the investigation of
universals, then, seeks the internal explanations, the
physical and psychological factors which explain why certain traits should be found universally in human language.

3. *External factors*. So far I have attempted only to
characterize strategies for investigation of universals,
suggesting the coupling of cross-linguistic investigation
with internal explanations. This research program is complicated, however, by 'external' factors. By external
factors I mean factors outside the structure of language
per se and outside the structure of the human organism,
involving such things as language contact and borrowing,
social evaluation of linguistic variables (involving prestigious and stigmatized speech forms), linguistic play,
literacy, mass communication, political decree, etc. The
'natural' and 'universal' aspects of language are for the
most part determined by internal factors, factors stemming
from the limitations and potentials of human speech production and perception. However, naturalness and universals are frequently complicated by external factors,
factors outside the language but imposed on the language
from outside for sociocultural reasons. The investigation
of linguistic universals will be enhanced by an understanding of the different effects of internal and external factors in language development.

Perhaps the role of external factors in research on
universals is best understood through some examples. I
begin with universals of color terms (Berlin and Kay 1969,
Berlin and Berlin 1975). Since this example involves a
case where language and culture are relatively directly related in more or less obvious ways, it should perhaps
occasion less surprise to discover that sociocultural factors may cause violations of color universals. From this
case of more direct involvement of culture in language
universals it is not such a big step to the externally motivated exceptions of more firmly linguistic universals.

Briefly, the original Berlin-Kay hypothesis about color universals was that all languages seem to place the foci of their color labels at basically the same locations on the color chart, and that the encoding of color terms is not random, but follows implicational universals. All languages contain terms for black and white; if a language has three basic color terms, then it has in addition red; if four terms, then either green or yellow, if five terms, then both green and yellow; if six terms, then in addition to these others it will contain a term for blue; if a language contains seven terms, then brown; if eight or more, then purple, pink, orange, grey, or some combination of these is possible. Schematically this is:

$$\begin{matrix} \text{black} \\ \text{white} \end{matrix} \rightarrow \text{red} \begin{matrix} \nearrow \text{green} \rightarrow \text{yellow} \searrow \\ \searrow \text{yellow} \rightarrow \text{green} \nearrow \end{matrix} \rightarrow \text{blue} \rightarrow \text{brown} \rightarrow \begin{bmatrix} \text{purple} \\ \text{pink} \\ \text{orange} \\ \text{grey} \end{bmatrix}$$

(For revisions, see Berlin and Berlin 1975.)

The proposed universal that the foci of basic color terms coincide for all people is due to internal factors, to universals of human perception. Nevertheless, exceptions have been found (McNeill 1972) where the foci of basic colors do not correspond to the universal foci as predicted, but to the color of some natural object of considerable cultural importance to the speakers of those languages. For example, in Pukapukan colors match parts of important tubers; in the older Japanese system they match those of indigenous plants used for dyes. Do these exceptions constitute true counterexamples to the proposed universals of color? Probably not. When only internal factors (here visual perception) play a role in color terminology, the foci match the expectations of the proposed universals. However, languages (and cultures) can choose to modify such universals for external cultural reasons. For cultural reasons, these languages chose to violate the universals to make the colors match culturally salient objects of their universe. Without an understanding of the role of internal motivation of the universals and the potential of externally motivated exceptions to them, we would find it difficult to explain the facts of color terminology, why the color foci are so extremely widespread and nearly universal, and why the few exceptions to the otherwise universal foci exist.

This example may help us to understand exceptions to more common linguistic universals. The universal that languages which have [q] (uvular or post velar stops) by implication also have [k] (velars) seems always to hold

true except in some languages of different genetic families
in an area of the Northwest Coast. Languages from the
northern part of Vancouver Island to the mouth of the Columbia River share a diffused sound shift [k] > [č] due to
areal influence. These languages for a period of time had
[q] and [č], but no [k] (until new [k]'s were later developed) (Sapir 1926, Kinkade 1973, Kinkade and Powell 1976).
Areal pressure and borrowing are important external factors. We might safely predict that the shift of [k] to [č]
in a language with [q] could not take place when only internal factors play a role, that changes controlled only
by internal factors do not violate universals, though external factors are not so restricted, and may in fact lead
to the violation of some universals. It is important to
recognize the difference between changes induced by internal factors and those induced by external factors. Otherwise we might be tempted to reject some potential universal,
well motivated by internal factors, upon discovery of an
externally motivated exception. In this case, if we were
to reject the universal upon finding an externally induced
exception, we would find it difficult to explain why these
languages so soon developed new /k/. That is, it seems
that the universal has explanatory value useful in accounting for the rapid development of new sounds which bring the
languages back into line with the expectations of the universal. What seems important is not that the universal
has for a short period of time what appear to be counter-
examples, but that the exceptions are due to areal pressure
(external factors), and in this example were shortlived.

A second example is the change of Proto-Algonquian
[*a·] to a nasalized vowel in Eastern Algonquian, due to
contact with Iroquoian languages (Goddard 1965, 1971,
Sherzer 1972). This example would seem to violate the
historical universal that nasalized vowels originate only
in the context of nasal consonants (i.e., VN > ṼN > Ṽ)
(Ferguson 1963). However, this exception has an external
origin, from areal diffusion, and therefore the universal
should not be rejected on this basis alone.[2]

Another kind of example also comes from the Northwest
Coast. Languages of several families in one linguistic
area lack primary nasals. In the Nootkan family, Nitinat
and Makah have changed Proto-Nootkan nasals to corresponding voiced stops. Not only is this a rare and unusual
change, it violates the otherwise near-universal (statistical universal) that languages do not lack primary
nasals, and moreover, that languages usually do not lack
primary nasals while containing voiced stops. Nevertheless,

Nitinat and Makah belong to that linguistic area of the Northwest Coast which lacks primary nasals, and the nasals were lost due to areal pressure (Haas 1969a, 1969b). (Perhaps if it were not for the languages of this linguistic area, the universal would be absolute.)

Since many phonological universals appear to have explanations determined by internal factors, perhaps the most productive strategy for research on universals is to investigate the perceptual and articulatory potentials and limitations of man which sharply limit the range of candidates for universals, and to couple this research with the traditional cross-linguistic approach to universals. Then perhaps the internal reasons for a trait's universality (or near-universality) need not be abandoned just because some speech community for external reasons of whatever sort chooses to modify the expected through external intervention.

4. *Universals and the problem of separation of levels.* It is usually assumed, at least implicitly, that while universals hold true at the phonemic (underlying) level, that allophonic rules are of much less consequence, since they only involve phonemes in restricted contexts. This, too, can occasion problems in the interpretation of universals. For example, Greenberg (1970) shows that implosion is favored for labials in the glottalic series. This explains why Proto-Mayan and many modern Mayan languages have /bʕ, t', k', q'/ (bʕ = imploded). However, the Cholan-Tzotzilan and Yucatecan subgroups added the allophonic rule:

$$bʕ \longrightarrow p' / \_\_ \begin{cases} \text{sonorant} \\ \text{fricative} \end{cases}$$

(p' = ejective (glottalized))
(see Campbell 1973)

At this stage one would perhaps ask why [bʕ] became [p'] in this environment, but one would presumably not cite these Mayan languages as violations of Greenberg's universal, since at the underlying level they still conform. However, later an externally motivated change took place in which [p'] (which had been only allophonic) took on expressive value and came to be used onomatopoetically in forms for, for example, 'break, drip, stumble, burst', etc., which lacked the conditioning environment of the allophonic rule. At this stage /p'/ had to be considered part of the underlying form of such words. At this point the languages could be said to violate the spirit of the universal favoring implosion for glottalic labials, a violation brought on in part by the exploitation of the allophonic variant for expressive or onomatopoetic purposes. However, except for the separation of levels, one might ask why these languages were not exceptions to the universal already upon addition of the allophonic rule instead of later, when the resultant sound was projected into new environments for external reasons?

A somewhat different but related example illustrates both the problem of levels and externally motivated exceptions to universals. In Pipil, a Nahua (Aztec) language of El Salvador, there is a rule which devoiced final sonorants:

$$\begin{bmatrix} l \\ w \\ y \end{bmatrix} \longrightarrow \begin{bmatrix} \ɬ \\ \ẇ \\ \ẏ \end{bmatrix} / \underline{\quad} \#$$

Several languages of Mesoamerica have such a rule. For a language to have voiced /l/ generally with a voiceless [ɬ] finally violates no universal, certainly not the near-universal that [ɬ] ⊃ [l]. However, the Teotepeque dialect of Pipil has only voiceless [ɬ], no voiced [l]. However, Teotepeque Pipil is very nearly extinct, with no fully competent speakers remaining. In the process of language death, learning of the obsolescing language is characterized by both overgeneralization and undergeneralization. The remaining Teotepeque Pipil speakers (whose dominant language is Spanish) have failed to learn the rule of final sonorant devoicing correctly; [y] and [w] are now voiced in all environments, including finally (undergeneralization), while [ɬ] is now voiceless in all environments, not just finally (overgeneralization). Teotepeque Pipil with only voiceless [ɬ] would seem to violate the usually expected [ɬ] ⊃ [l], but the violation with only voiceless [ɬ] is explained by the external fact of imperfect learning in the situation of language death.

5. *Internal and external considerations in other areas of language*. While the purpose of this paper is to consider universals and their exceptions, it is important to point out that the internal and external factors involved in the explanation of universals are also involved in the explanation of natural rules, natural sound changes, and exceptions and unnatural rules and changes. (For more details, see Ohala 1974a, 1974b, Campbell 1976, in press.)

For example, Finnish has a well-known phonological rule:

$$t \longrightarrow s/\_\_\_ i\ \#\ \text{(see Paunonen 1973 for details)}$$

This rule is fairly general but does not apply to the past tense forms of these few verbs:

    piti (past of *pitä* - 'to hold') (never **pisi*)
    veti (*vetä* - 'to pull') (never **vesi*)
    kuti (*kute* - 'to spawn') (never **kusi*)
    kynti (*kyntä* - 'to plow') (never **kynsi*)

The rule does not apply to these verbs for an external reason: to avoid pernicious homophony with the following:

    pisi   'urinated' (obscene)
    vesi   'water'
    kusi   'urinated' (obscene)
    kynsi 'fingernail, scratched' (verb *kynsiä* 'to scratch')

It is easy to see why the rule was violated in these cases to avoid otherwise embarrassing past tenses.

That external factors may complicate natural sound changes should be clear from the Nitinat-Makah and Eastern Algonquian cases presented above. In general it can be said that sound changes induced by internal factors are natural and regular, and that unnatural changes and exceptions to natural changes typically have external motivation (see especially Campbell 1976).

6. *Conclusions*. One conclusion is inescapable, that at least some universals may have exceptions due to external factors. It seems clear from these examples that both internal and external explanations of universals and their exceptions must be taken into account in the investigation of universals. This may raise more questions than it answers, but they are questions that must be considered if the role of universals in linguistic theory is to be meaningful. For example, we need to ask, can any universal be violated by external intervention or only certain ones? It would seem that some universals are too central to communicative needs of language to be violated. For example, it is difficult to imagine a language suppressing all its vowels due to external factors. If some internally motivated universals can be violated by external factors, then which ones are they and under what conditions may they be violated, and how long may the violation persist before the universal brings the language back into expected equilibrium? Perhaps the most important question is how do we

distinguish between a proposed but false universal and a true universal that happens to have an external exception? In examples such as those presented here, the external factors are apparent because the history of the languages of these illustrative examples is reasonably clear. However, many exceptions will probably occur in cases where the history is not clear, and the interpretation as true counterexample vs. externally motivated exception will not be clear. This and other problems are fundamental and crucial to the explanation of universals and to future research in universals.

NOTES

[1] Of course, it is possible to conceptualize absolute universals as implicational universals of a trivial sort, where the knowledge of something as a language implies the existence of the trait. For example, the absolute universal that all languages have vowels may be thought of in the form, if language, then vowels (Language ⊃ V).

[2] Recent work shows that nasalization of vowels may develop in glottal environments and spontaneously on low vowels without the nasal consonant required in the early formulation of the universal. Though these considerations may seem to weaken this example's full strength as an externally motivated exception to the universal, it still appears true that nasalization in this case is due to Iroquoian contact. It is not the example, then, that is weakened, but the universal concerning the origin of nasalization of vowels. In any event, this example illustrates in principle how external factors may complicate the understanding of universals, regardless of whether the actual example ultimately holds up.

REFERENCES

Berlin, Brent and Elois Ann Berlin. 1975. "Aguaruna color categories". *American Ethnologist* 2.61-87.
Berlin, Brent and Paul Kay. 1969. *Basic color terms: their universality and evolution*. Berkeley: University of California Press.
Campbell, Lyle. 1973. "On glottalic consonants". *IJAL* 39.44-6.
_____. 1976. "Language contact and language change". In *Current progress in historical linguistics*, 181-94. Ed. by William Christie. Amsterdam: North Holland.
_____. In Press. "The psychological and sociological reality of Finnish vowel harmony". In *Issues in vowel harmony*. Ed. by Robert Vago. Amsterdam: John Benjamins, B.V.
Ferguson, Charles A. 1963. "Assumptions about nasals". In *Universals of language*, 42-7. Ed. by Joseph H. Greenberg. Cambridge: MIT Press.

Goddard, Ives. 1965. "The Eastern Algonquian intrusive nasal". *IJAL* 31.206-20.
_____. 1971. "More on the nasalization of PA *a· in Eastern Algonquian". *IJAL* 37.139-45.
Greenberg, Joseph H. 1970. "Some generalizations concerning glottalic consonants, especially implosives". *IJAL* 36.123-45
_____. 1975. "Research on language universals". *Annual Review of Anthropology* 4.75-94. Ed. by Bernard J. Seigel.
Haas, Mary. 1969a. *The prehistory of languages*. Janua Linguarum (Series Minor, 57). The Hague: Mouton.
_____. 1969b. "Internal reconstruction of the Nootka-Nitinat pronominal suffixes". *IJAL* 35:108-29.
Kinkade, M. Dale. 1973. "The alveopalatal shift in Cowlitz Salish". *IJAL* 39:224-31.
Kinkade, M. Dale and J. Powell. 1976. "Language and the prehistory of North America". *World Archaeology* 8.83-100.
McNeill, N.B. 1972. "Colour and colour terminology". *Journal of Linguistics* 8.21-33.
Ohala, John. 1974a. "Experimental historical phonology". In *Historical linguistics II: theory and practice*, 353-89. Ed. by John M. Anderson and Charles Jones. Amsterdam: North Holland.
_____. 1974. "Phonetic explanation in phonology". In *Papers from the parasession on natural phonology*, 251-74. Ed. by A. Bruck, R. Fox, M. Lagaly.
Paunonen, H. 1973. "On free variation". *Suomalais-ugrilaisen Seuran Aikakauskirja* 72.285-300.
Sapir, Edward. 1926. "A Chinookan phonetic law". *IJAL* 4.105-10.
Sherzer, Joel. 1972. "Vowel nasalization in Eastern Algonquian: an areal-typological perspective on linguistic universals". *IJAL* 38.267-8.

CONTINUITY OF TRANSMISSION AND GENETIC RELATIONSHIP

SARAH GREY THOMASON
University of Pittsburgh

0. *Introduction.* In the context of historical linguistics pidgin and creole studies have, from their inception, served to focus attention on the criteria to be used in establishing genetic relationships of languages. Schuchardt argued that a creole is a Mischsprache and must therefore be considered to have multiple ancestors. This view is now being echoed by some modern scholars. Some pidgin/creole specialists, carrying Schuchardt's line of reasoning to an extreme, have even suggested that the whole question of genetic relationship is empty—that the traditional approach to linguistic evolution should simply be abandoned because pidginization and creolization are so pervasive that no such thing as 'normal' (internally motivated) diversification, from one parent to two or more daughter languages, exists.[1] Other linguists, notably Weinreich, believe that *the* criterion for genetic relationship is 'the existence of cognates in the basic morpheme stock, with parallelism in allomorphic alternations as a powerful supplement' (1958:376). On this criterion, as Weinreich observes, a typical pidgin or creole would be grouped genetically with its vocabulary-base language,[2] and grammatical features derived from other languages would be treated as borrowings and/or substratum residue. Most linguists would probably disagree with Weinreich about the absolute priority of the lexicon (if I graft Russian lexical morphemes onto my English grammar, am I speaking Russian?), and the most common approach is still the one advocated by Meillet and Hall: languages are genetically related if and only if they have 'systematic correspondences in all aspects of language structure' (Hall 1958:368). They then go on to claim that the creoles they are considering must be classified genetically with their vocabulary-base languages on this traditional criterion (Hall 1958:370f.; Meillet 1921: 85, cited by Weinreich 1958:375).[3] Neither scholar has much to say about the general problem of applying the cri-

terion to pidgins and creoles, except to doubt that there are any languages which are too 'mixed' to classify genetically. Few linguists have accepted Schuchardt's basic position--that pidgins and creoles don't fit into the standard genetic picture--*and* then gone on to try to reconcile the facts of pidgin/creole structure and development with the traditional genetic model. The most systematic attempt in print is Whinnom's distinction between primary hybrid languages, which can be classified genetically, and secondary and tertiary hybrids, which cannot (1971:111).[4]

Two questions are really at issue here. First, do pidgins and creoles in fact pose a challenge to the standard model of genetic relationship? And second, if they do, is the standard model thereby rendered valueless?

1. *The challenge of pidgins and creoles to genetic linguistics*. The answer to the first question is certainly yes, as the arguments of Schuchardt and succeeding generations of scholars show. The response to this challenge offered by Meillet and Hall is far from adequate, because they (though only Hall explicitly) insist that, to be unclassifiable genetically, a language must have exactly half of its basic features from one source and half from another or others (Hall 1958:370). This would mean that any slight shift from such a perfect mix would immediately permit us to classify the language genetically. It is hard to see how this criterion could be applied usefully. Even aside from the impossibility of demonstrating a perfect structural balance in Hall's historical sense (how would one weigh a pronoun system from source A against a dominant word order pattern from source B, for instance?), this approach seems to me to miss the point of genetic classification. A language is a means of communication, not merely a list of features. A claim of genetic relationship is not a claim about the number of traits acquired from one source as opposed to another; rather, it is a claim about the history of a speech community.[5] When we say that language B is a changed later form of language A, we certainly do not mean that all of B's lexicon and grammar were inherited from A. We do, however, mean that A speakers passed their language on to their linguistic descendants, and those descendants to their descendants, and so on, until enough changes accrued in A to necessitate calling it a new language, B.[6]

Of course the linguistic features of a language constitute the evidence we use to establish a claim of genetic relationship, and in the magnificently documented (relatively speaking) history of the IE family we have found, time and again, that the histories of the splintering speech communities are reflected in the bundles of features that occur in the linguistic subgroups. But this does not mean that it is methodologically or theoretically valid to use feature-counting *instead of* the historical criterion--continuity of transmission--as the primary criterion of genetic relationship. On the contrary: to arrive at a reasonable theory of the position of pidgins and creoles vis-à-vis the genetic model, I think we must rehabilitate Meillet's own conviction that 'the relationship of languages results uniquely from the continuity of the feeling of linguistic unity' (1921:81; translation mine)--or, to put it more precisely (since it is the facts of transmission that count, not the speakers' intuitions), the continuity of transmission.

Before outlining the form such a theory might take, however, I should consider the question of whether it is worth developing at all. That is, to return to the second question raised above, should we not rather forget about the standard genetic model and conclude, with Bailey, that '...creoles and the utility of the wave model make family trees obsolete' (1973:33), because (among other things) probably '...every system or node on a family tree should have at least two parents' (1973:20)? Bailey's position is an extreme one, since for him the term 'creole' applies, in effect, to all languages: any language that has undergone moderate to extensive foreign interference is to be called a creole, and he believes (as do I) that no living language is likely to have entirely escaped significant foreign interference throughout its history. Among the many implications of his view for historical linguistics, I will concentrate on just one here.

The family tree model of linguistic diversification, for all its oversimplification of historical reality, is an absolute prerequisite for the application of the comparative method in the reconstruction of prehistoric linguistic states. As soon as we admit two parents for a given language, we make it impossible to use that language in carrying out comparative reconstruction, since we have no principled way of deciding which parts of its structure to compare to which set of 'half-sister' languages. In fact, in this framework, whatever historical reality *is* embodied in the results of comparative reconstruction vanishes.

But look at the actual results of comparative reconstruction. In spite of the fact that both the assumption of clean splits and the assumption of post-split independent changes are demonstrably false (because dialects

diverge gradually into separate languages, often during a
period of continuing interdialectal communication, and
drift produces similar changes in related languages), the
comparative method has been one of the most successful
tools of any in the historical sciences for investigating
unattested prehistory. Where its results can be checked,
most notably in the Romance subfamily of IE, we find that,
although what we reconstruct is not the actual proto-language, Latin, it is a reasonably close approximation of
that proto-language. It is certainly true that Slavic
traits borrowed into Rumanian, for instance, will be set
apart as unanalyzable residue after we have reconstructed
Proto-Romance, and that we will have to look outside of
Romance for their historical source. But the presence of
developments outside the direct genetic line is surely an
insufficient reason for abandoning the family tree, and
with it comparative reconstruction, as long as we can reasonably expect to be able to separate most externally motivated changes from internally motivated ones. I think we
can, and this takes us back to the notion of continuity of
transmission.

2. *Normal transmission, synchronic feature clusters, and
genetic relationship*. The case of Proto-Romance suggests
that, where the transmission of a language within its
speech community is normal in the sense described above,
its structure as a whole will reflect its genetic heritage
and permit successful comparative reconstruction of a single proto-language; and if a language's structure as a
whole, grammar and lexicon, is mostly derivable from a single source, then we can assume continuity of transmission.
For example, as with most speech communities undergoing
territorial expansion, the Vulgar Latin community absorbed
a great many speakers of other languages, and some changes
in the developing Romance languages no doubt originated in
the imperfect learning of these populations as they shifted
to Latin/Romance. The end products, however, are clearly
basically Latin in origin, and this fact argues for an essential continuity of transmission from Latin to the modern
Romance languages. That is, the speakers of Vulgar Latin
in, say, Spain must have been sufficiently accessible to
the indigenous population that the people shifting to Latin
had a model they could, and ultimately did, imitate suc-
cessfully during the process of shift. This sketch is not
meant to imply that the process was either simple sociolin-
guistically or rapid historically. In particular, the
early stages of the process quite possibly saw much heavier
substratum interference than the later stages did, since
the continuing presence of original Latin speakers would
presumably have enabled the shifting speakers to arrive at

an increasingly interference-free version of Latin/Romance during the inevitable period of widespread bilingualism. Similarly, although Rumanian speakers came under cultural pressure from neighboring Slavs, and as a result borrowed heavily from Slavic, there is no linguistic or historical reason to suppose that any break occurred in the transmission of Rumanian from one generation to the next--that any generation of Rumanian children somehow failed to acquire the whole language of their older peers and parents.

A corollary of the view that continuity of transmission is *the* criterion for establishing genetic relationship of languages is that a language whose history shows a discontinuity in transmission cannot be classified genetically. Such a language would be one that arose neither through the transmission from parents and peers to children in ordinary first-language acquisition nor through a combination of that process plus simultaneous successful shift (via bilingualism) of some other population. The typical well-known pidgins and creoles, on all of the popular origin theories, seem to me to fall into this category.

Weinreich has remarked that 'to use relative continuity or discontinuity of transmission as a *criterion* [for genetic relationship]...would probably be unwise, since past circumstances of transmission cannot easily be reconstructed' (1958:375). I think the attitude reflected in this comment explains in large part the fact that most linguists concerned both with pidgins and creoles and with genetic relationship have turned to the ahistorical criterion of synchronic feature clusters. In languages not generally classed as creoles whose external histories are well attested, continuity of transmission and clusters of inherited features point to the same genetic conclusion. But where the external history of a language is not known, the only possible approach to establishing genetic relationship is to assume that synchronic clusters of features result from a past history of normal transmission. This approach has proved successful with reasonably closely related languages all over the world, but it provides unambiguous results only when hypothesized sister languages share the great majority of their grammatical and lexical structures. Where significant portions of a language's structure come from some source(s) other than the putative genetic one, then we must suspect a discontinuity in transmission. A discontinuity is particularly likely if there is a marked discrepancy in the extent to which different parts of the language's structure match the hypothesized parent language, since with normal transmission changes in the morphology and syntax, for instance, should more or less keep pace with changes in the basic vocabulary (see Thomason (forthcoming) for an argument on this point with respect to the Na-Dene hypothesis).

Weinreich was absolutely correct, of course, in saying that the circumstances of transmission cannot be definitely reconstructed for unattested periods, and in any case there will inevitably be borderline cases--cases where the transmission was semicontinuous, as well as cases where the relative weight of grammar and vocabulary derived from the genetic source is in doubt. Continuity of transmission is no more clear-cut as a criterion than feature-counting is; its advantage over feature-counting is that it is a historical criterion. Nevertheless, if we compare known instances of normal genetic development with known instances of non-genetic development (especially creoles), we may eventually be able to arrive at a clearer picture of the extent to which discontinuity of transmission correlates with diversity in the historical sources of a language's structures.

A start has been made in this direction. Space restrictions do not permit me to give details of relevant cases here, but, in contrast to familiar cases of normal transmission like that of Proto-Romance and its daughter languages, important cases of discontinuity in transmission include the Caribbean creoles, which arose under pathological social conditions when enslaved Africans shifted abruptly--and unsuccessfully--to insufficiently available European target languages; and Pitcairnese, an English-based creole in the formative period of which the English of the original nine English-speaking men was not passed on as a whole to the children born to the original thirteen Polynesian women. In addition to these clear cases that show a sharp break in the transmission of a vocabulary-base language, there are a number of interesting borderline cases--cases in which, even when the language's external history is rather well known, the transmission may or may not have been normal, and the resulting language's linguistic structures may or may not be derived mostly from a single source. In one particularly striking instance, Afrikaans, the transmission process was bent (rather than broken) in the early years of Cape Colony Dutch, because many children were learning the language from servants and slaves who probably knew little Dutch (Valkhoff 1966).

In other borderline cases, for example Middle English dialects of the Danelaw and Norse from the ninth century until about 1150, the languages involved are so closely related that many of the resulting structures could be from either source language. Moreover, limited intercommunication may well have been possible even between monolingual speakers of the two languages, so that there is no need to assume any sharp break in transmission (in either direction) during a process of gradual anglicization of the Norse population's speech. A third type is the semicontinuous transmission that characterizes the most extreme cases of borrowing, as in some dialects of Asia Minor Greek (cf. Dawkins 1916). Here, speakers of the borrowing language are gradually shifting to another language whose speakers exert continual heavy cultural pressure on them. The shifting population's language may be riddled with borrowed lexical and grammatical features to the extent that learners' acquisition of the borrowing language as a whole may be in doubt.

3. *Conclusion*. The major proposal in this paper, then, is that continuity of transmission in a speech community should be regarded as criterial for the establishment of genetic relationship between languages, because the notion of genetic relationship is historically vacuous unless it is based on some notion of continuity. When a language evolves through a continuous history of normal transmission, the great majority of its lexical and grammatical structures are derived from its single parent language. This fact is a corollary to a definition of genetic relationship based on continuity of transmission, since 'normal transmission' means either ordinary first-language acquisition or a combination of this with successful second-language acquisition (in cases of language shift).

Where lexical and grammatical source languages are genetically and/or typologically distant, pidgins and historically abrupt creoles (i.e., those that most likely did not develop through nativization of stable pidgins) can be shown to have arisen through a discontinuity in the transmission of their vocabulary-base languages, because, unless decreolization has led to later convergence, there will be a marked discrepancy between the pidgin's or creole's lexical fit and its grammatical fit with its vocabulary base language. Too many of the nonlexical structures will be derived from some source(s) other than the vocabulary-base language, e.g., the substrate/adstrate languages or universally unmarked categories. These languages have no genetic affiliations: they are unclassifiable.

The criterion of normal transmission cannot always be applied unambiguously. The existence of borderline cases points to a need for a much more cautious, and more rigorous, application of the traditional tests of genetic relationship. Before claiming that we have proved two languages to be genetically related, we must do much more than point to some probable cognate sets. In particular, extensive lexical and grammatical correspondences must be established before we can begin even to exclude clear-cut instances of abnormal transmission from a hypothesized language family. It may be impossible to exclude borderline cases, especially those of the English/Norse type; but, if we do include them in carrying out comparative reconstruction, their presence will probably cause little distortion in the results of reconstruction.

One result of emphasizing normal transmission as a criterion of genetic relationship will be that the verdict on many hypotheses of distant relationship, especially where the languages are close geographically, will of necessity be 'not proven'. If two languages are so distantly related as to have lost most of their shared inherited structures, then it is likely to be impossible to prove that one or both of them did *not* arise through a process of creolization. I am not suggesting that historical linguists should stop investigating distant genetic relationships, but only that they should beware of this inherent source of indeterminacy.

NOTES

[1] Bailey 1973 seems to be espousing this basic position. Several speakers at the 1975 International Conference on Pidgins and Creoles in Honolulu also expressed such a view during discussion.

[2] Probable exceptions are Chinook Jargon and Russenorsk, whose basic lexicons come from two or more languages.

[3] There is still little agreement among specialists as to the relative amounts of IndoEuropean grammars, on the one hand, and African (Chinese, Melanesian, etc.) and/or universal grammar, on the other, in pidgins and creoles with European vocabulary-base languages. I am not concerned here to evaluate the substance of the arguments, except to remark that all sides are arguing in the absence of sufficient typological evidence about the various substrate languages, and that extensive decreolization in the Caribbean has surely added many European features since the creoles' formative period.

[4] Thomason and Kaufman (forthcoming) also addresses the general question, arguing--as Whinnom (1971) does--that pidgins and creoles should not be classified genetically at all. Our reasoning differs from Whinnom's, however, and we would disagree with some of his conclusions. The question of normal transmission is emphasized neither in Whinnom nor in Thomason and Kaufman. In fact, Whinnom's elaborate biological analogy is essentially asocial and therefore, in my opinion, it cannot constitute a realistic model of what goes on in language change.

[5] I am using the term 'speech community' in its more general meaning and not in contradistinction to 'language community', either in the sense of Silverstein 1972 or in the sense of Bailey 1973.

[6] Some scholars would not agree that B is a different language from A unless A has diversified into at least two daughter languages, so this may be an oversimplified outline of the outcome of normal transmission.

[7] All the cases mentioned in these two paragraphs are discussed in detail in Thomason and Kaufman (forthcoming).

REFERENCES

Bailey, Charles-James N. 1973. *Variation and linguistic theory*. Arlington, Va: Center for Applied Linguistics.

Dawkins, R.M. 1916. *Modern Greek in Asia Minor*. Cambridge: University Press.

Hall, Robert A., Jr. 1958. "Creolized languages and 'genetic relationships'". *Word* 14.367-73.

Meillet, Antoine. 1921(1958). "Le problème de la parenté des langues". Repr. in his *Linguistique historique et linguistique générale*, 76-101. Paris: Champion.

Silverstein, Michael. 1972. "Chinook Jargon: language contact and the problem of multi-level generative systems". *Lg.* 48.378-406, 596-632.

Thomason, Sarah G. Forthcoming. "Morphological instability, with and without language contact". In *Historical morphology*. Ed. by Jacek Fisiak. The Hague: Mouton-De Gruyter.

Thomason, Sarah G., and Terrence Kaufman. Forthcoming. *Language contact, creolization, and genetic linguistics*.

Valkhoff, Marius F. 1966. *Studies in Portuguese and creole*. Johannesburg: Witwaterstrand University Press.

Weinreich, Uriel. 1958. "On the compatibility of genetic relationship and convergent development". *Word* 14.374-79.

Whinnom, Keith. 1971. "Linguistic hybridization and the 'special case' of pidgins and creoles". In *Pidginization & creolization of languages*, 91-115. Ed. by Dell Hymes. New York: Cambridge University Press.

CHANCE COGNATION: A PROBABILISTIC MODEL
AND DECISION PROCEDURE FOR HISTORICAL INFERENCE

JOHN S. JUSTESON
University of South Carolina
and
LAURENCE D. STEPHENS
Stanford University

0. *Introduction.* 'Is it valid to count similar morphemes in two languages, leaving aside all consideration of cognates, and use this as a method of determining genetic relationship?' asked Fairbanks (1955:117), adding, 'The idea of such a comparison is a shock to the comparativist.' The answer, of course, is yes, and no one is shocked so long as the method yields a substantial number of sound-meaning resemblances. As Greenberg (1957:34ff) argues, apart from violations of the arbitrary relation between sound and meaning (e.g. sound symbolism) and the independence of meaningful forms, a hypothesis of historical relationship is required to explain sound-meaning resemblances sufficiently in excess of chance. In some cases, particularly in long-range comparisons, it is by no means obvious when the excess is sufficient. In such cases, without the determination of fairly regular phonological correspondences, one must evaluate a hypothesis of historical (including genetic) relationship by applying the statistical theory of hypothesis testing; such evaluation requires precise formulation of the probability distribution of the random variable K of the number of apparent cognates arising by chance--'chance cognates'. We present a solution to this problem based on combinatorial modelling of the principles of arbitrariness of the sound-meaning relation and the independence of meaningful forms.

Among the few earlier attempts to solve this problem, the models by Collinder (1948) and Cowan (1962) were undermined by fundamental misunderstandings of both the theory of probability and the methodology of statistical inference.

However, Cowan's is still the only attempt to quantify the effect of word length on the likelihood of chance cognation.

Swadesh (1954) attempted to estimate the probability of chance cognation directly from the phoneme inventories of the languages being compared. A rigorous estimate would require so much information concerning positional and transitional phoneme frequencies that it is seldom feasible, so simplifying assumptions are required. Bender's (1969) empirical estimates show that the overall effect of Swadesh's simplifications was to overestimate the probability of chance cognation.

Later Swadesh (1956) adopted an essentially combinatorial method. He counted the number of phonetic resemblances in the n^2 pairs of items from a pair of word lists having n items each; for r such resemblances the binomial estimate for the proportion of chance cognates is r/n^2. Swadesh devised no test for statistical significance of an excess of apparent cognates over the number expected by chance. Such a test requires a demonstration that the proportion of phonetic resemblances among the semantically matching words is significantly larger than among the semantically different words. The crucial insight is that the number of phonetically similar forms shared by the two lists, irrespective of meaning, is needed to determine whether the number of similar forms which agree in meaning exceeds the number that would be expected by chance.

1. *The combinatorial model.* In the hypothetical word lists of Figure I, the words for 'fire' are quite similar. There are no other apparent cognates, but the word for

	air	animal	earth	fire	man	moon	plant	sun	water	woman
1.	tin	krak	hoh	<u>mom</u>	apuh	wa	pur	kat	<u>lip</u>	atah
2.	pad	dap	kah	<u>mam</u>	rab	gur	<u>lib</u>	nal	dug	ba

A hypothetical language comparision
FIGURE I

'plant' in the second list resembles the word for 'water' in the first. Since the lists share two phonetically similar words, might it be coincidental that one of them agrees also in meaning? To answer this we need to know how many ways the words in list 2 can be assigned to meanings to get at least one apparent cognate with list 1; and what proportion this represents of the total number of ways the words in that list might be assigned. Since 18.9% of the assignments give at least one apparent cognate, there is no evidence here for historical relationship.

This combinatorial approach makes possible an explicit calculation of the probability that the number K of chance cognates is exactly k, given the overall number of phonetic resemblances. The parameters of this distribution are the number n of items on a list of semantically equivalent forms for each language; and the number r of forms on one list that are phonetically similar to forms on the other. Equations (1)-(1b) give the probability distribution, expected value, and variance of the random variable K:

(1) $$P\{ k \mid n,r \} = \frac{r!}{k!n!} \sum_{j=0}^{r-k} (-1)^j \frac{(r-k-j)!}{j!(n-k-j)!}$$

(1a) $E_{n,r}(K) = r/n$

(1b) $\text{Var}_{n,r}(K) = \frac{r}{n} \left(\frac{n-1}{n} + \frac{r-1}{n(n-1)} \right)$

The theoretical distribution (1) is confirmed by tests against the most substantial and reliable data available for the empirical distribution of chance cognates (Bender 1969); the fit is excellent (cf. Table I).

k	Strict Criteria		Extended Criteria	
	Expected	Observed	Expected	Observed
0	557.14 (558.08)	563	508.24 (509.59)	519
1	69.43 (67.65)	62	110.51 (108.09)	97
2...r	3.42 (4.27)	5	11.25 (12.31)	14
	$r = 4$	$\hat{r} = 4.00$	$r = 7$	$\hat{r} = 6.87$
	$\chi^2 = 1.5867;\ p = .452$		$\chi^2 = 2.5516;\ p = .279$	

Distribution of Chance Cognates[1]
TABLE I

Distribution (1) is closely approximated by the Poisson distribution

(2) $$P\{ k \mid n,r \} \approx e^{-r/n} \frac{(r/n)^k}{k!}$$

with mean and variance r/n,[2] accounting for the fit of Bender's data to a Poisson distribution.[3] Our Poisson estimates are in parentheses in the table.

2. *Bias*. Statistical assessment of apparent cognation can be biased if discovery procedures are not explicitly modelled. Crucial procedures are (i) the selection of criteria for phonetic similarity (and also semantic similarity, see section 4) and (ii) the definition of the data base. Our procedures control for this bias.

(i) Criteria for phonetic resemblance are normally determined after the recognition of possible cognates; the criteria adopted are those that yield the most convincing case. Without explicitly modelling the power of the investigator to select the results, statistical assessment is biased against the hypothesis of chance. However, in altering the criteria for phonetic similarity one alters the number of overall phonetic resemblances, and these in turn determine the number of chance cognates according to distribution (1). If the incidence of apparent cognates is due to chance, the likelihood of getting the number actually attained is unaffected when assessed by this distribution (see Figure II).

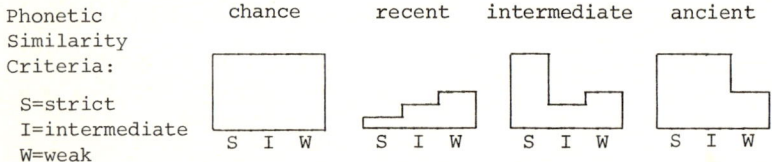

Likelihood function with varying phonetic criteria
FIGURE II

This flexibility in selecting the criteria for resemblance can be turned to advantage in testing for historical relationship. For greater time depths, with more intervening phonological change, weaker criteria for phonetic resemblance are needed to pick up the actual cognates between languages.[4] For ancient relationships, the value of the likelihood function should be high under strict criteria but lower for weak criteria which do register the effects of the presence of legitimate cognates. For more recent relationships, the likelihood function should be low under strict criteria; under weaker criteria it should rise slightly, an effect of a fair proportion of spurious apparent cognates.

(ii) The major interest in distant genetic comparison has been in finding more distant relatives of IE, and less commonly, other language families. Most comparativists have a knowledge of IE basic vocabulary, so any prima facie case for IE relationship results from what amounts to a comparison of IE basic vocabulary with that of all other languages that are the object of linguistic inquiry. This 'search-till-success' method is readily modelled by a geometric distribution on the number l of languages compared with IE, where p^* is the likelihood of the result as it would be assessed were the comparison between a pair of languages only:

(3) $\quad P\{ p^* \leq \alpha$ for the first time after l comparisons $\} = \alpha(1-\alpha)^{l-1}$

(3a) $\quad E_\alpha(L) = \dfrac{1}{\alpha}$

(3b) $\quad Var_\alpha(L) = \dfrac{1-\alpha}{\alpha^2}$

The probability that at least one of the languages examined will yield a pairwise result as unlikely as α is:

(4) $\quad P\{ p^* \leq \alpha$ at least once after l comparisons $\} = 1 - (1-\alpha)^l$

Letting $\alpha = \hat{p}_k$, an average estimate for the probability that $K \geq k$ chance cognates, Table II gives the values of k for which the number of languages one expects to compare exceeds 500--an estimate for the number of distinct language families in the world--and the number of apparent cognates needed to reject chance association of a language family with IE at the 5% and 1% levels of significance between lists of 100 words each.

Phonetic Similarity Criteria	$E_k(L) > 500$	$1-(1-\hat{p}_k)^l \leq \alpha$	
		$\alpha=.05$	$\alpha=.01$
Strict	3	4	5
Extended	4	5	6
Weak	8	12	14

Apparent Cognates Required for IE Relationship[5]
TABLE II

3. *Simultaneous mass comparison.* As Greenberg (1957:42-3) notes, multiple agreement on the same semantic item across several languages gives greater support to a hypothesis of historical relationship among the languages sharing this agreement. Indeed,

(5) $\quad P\{k \mid l,n,r\} = \dfrac{r!}{k!(n!)^{l-1}} \sum_{j=0}^{r-k} \dfrac{[(n-k-j)!]^{l-1}}{j!(r-k-j)!}$

(5a) $\quad E_{l,n,r}(K) = r/n^{l-1}$

(5b) $\quad \text{Var}_{l,n,r}(K) = \dfrac{r}{n^{l-1}} \left(\dfrac{n^{l-1}-1}{n^{l-1}} + (r-1)\dfrac{[n^{l-1}(n-1)^{l-1}]}{n^{l-1}(n-1)^{l-1}} \right)$

so the number of chance cognates across l languages decreases exponentially with l. Bender's data also confirm distribution (5) (see Table III).

	Chance Cognates k	Strict Criteria Expected	Observed	Extended Criteria Expected	Observed
	0	1328.23	1327	1324.76	1326
$l = 3$	$1...r$	1.77	3	5.24	4

$\hat{r}_2 = 13.07$ $\quad\quad\quad\quad\quad\quad\quad \hat{r}_2 = 38.67$
$\chi^2 = 0.8559;\ p = .350 \quad\quad \chi^2 = 0.2946;\ p = .587$

Empirical Confirmation of Distribution (5) [Poisson estimate][6]
TABLE III

4. *Multiple phonetic and semantic resemblances.* As the criteria for phonetic resemblance are weakened it becomes more likely that a single form on one list will resemble more than one on another. This obviously increases the probability of getting a chance cognate for that item, and the expected number of chance cognates rises accordingly. The same argument holds as criteria for semantic agreement are relaxed. In both cases, multiple resemblances alter the combinatorial model.

Items on the first list which phonetically resemble an item i on the second may be grouped into sets S_i of phonetically similar items. Letting $\rho(A)$ be the number of members of set A, and $T_{i,j}$ the set of items common to S_i and S_j:

(6a) $\quad E_{n,r,\{S_i\}}(K) = \dfrac{1}{n} \sum_{i=1}^{r} \rho(S_i)$

(6b) $\quad \text{Var}_{n,r,\{S_i\}}(K) = \sum_{i \le r} \dfrac{\rho(S_i)[n-\rho(S_i)]}{n^2} + 2 \sum_{j \ne k} \left(\dfrac{\rho(S_j)\rho(S_k)}{n^2(n-1)} \right)$

$$-\frac{2}{n(n-1)}\left(\rho(T_{j,k})[\rho(T_{j,k})-1]+\frac{\rho(T_{j,k})[\rho(S_j)+(S_k)]}{\rho(S_j)\rho(S_k)}\right)$$

The distribution is approximated by a Poisson distribution with mean as in (6a).[7]

For a general idea of the behavior of this distribution, consider a special case. Suppose that there are t items in each set, that none of the sets overlap, and that the total number tr of resemblances is less than n. This distribution

(7) $\quad P\{k \mid n,r,\{S_i\}\} = \frac{t^k k!}{k! n!} \sum_{j=0}^{r-k} (-1) \frac{(n-k-j)!}{(r-k-j)!} \frac{t^j}{j!} \simeq P\{k \mid n, tr\}$

has a mean of tr/n, which is just t times the expected value of formula (1) for cases without phonetic similarity sets. Thus we can expect the number of chance cognates to increase approximately in proportion to the average size of the similarity sets.

The identical formulation applies for semantic similarity sets and indeed for cases that combine multiple semantic similarities and multiple phonetic similarities. Letting S_i^s be the semantic similarity set for item i and S_i^p its phonetic similarity set, one takes $S_i = S_i^s \times S_i^p$ in the formulas above.

The effect of phonetic similarity sets on probability assessments is illustrated by a now-famous comparison between the verbal subject markers of PIE and one comparable set from Lake Miwok (LM) (see Figure III). Assuming four

	1 sg.	2 sg.	3 sg.	1 pl.	2 pl.	3 pl.
PIE	*-m(i)	*-s(i)	*-t(i)	*-mes	? *-te	*-nt(i)
LM	-m	-s	∅	-maš	-toš	-p

A Distant Morphological Comparison
FIGURE III

potential phonetic similarities out of six items, the likelihood that all would agree in meaning is .0028. However, the PIE form *$t(i)$ would be considered similar to LM $toš$ if it and not *te had been in the corresponding position; one LM form is similar to two PIE forms. For this case the probability of getting four apparent cognates doubles to .0056.

5. *Two noncombinatorial factors.* (i) In the distributions

presented here it is assumed that all phonetic resemblances weigh equally in assessing the probability of chance cognation. However, the chance of resemblance in six or more units between two items is minuscule, even with weak criteria.[8] Between morphologically simple items, almost any such agreement is a prima facie case for historical relationship; this implies borrowing unless there is significant agreement among the far commoner short items. (To test the latter, pairs similar across many phonemes must be removed from the test lists and apparent cognation assessed on this reduced list of short similarities.) In the case that morphologically complex items are similar, direct comparison would violate the principle of independence of forms which the distribution requires; for valid statistical treatment, independence must be restored by dissociating these elements and testing the agreement of the constituents separately.

(ii) Apparent cognates between two languages may show a statistically significant concentration in one domain of the lexicon. When the likelihood of chance cognation is tested within that set alone (as in the LM/PIE comparison above), statistical assessment is biased against the hypothesis of chance if the group compared is one of several comparable groups, such as one of several declensional classes. To compare two languages under these circumstances, apply formula (4) with the parameter l set to the total number of pairs of comparable groups (which clearly may exceed the number of languages involved).[9] Even ignoring the significance level for the observed number of apparent cognates, the number of phonetic similarities concentrated within a category might be thought significant; this must be tested through a Swadesh-type phoneme frequency approach.

6. *Interpretation of results*. If the assessed probability p_k is high, chance resemblance is one hypothesis sufficient to explain the number of apparent cognates; but the number of true cognates can be so low that p_k is high for historically related pairs of languages. Thus, sound linguistic arguments for relationship take precedence over high p_k values.

If p_k is low, there are still nonhistorical alternatives to chance whenever the sound-sense relation is not arbitrary or when meaningful forms are not phonetically independent. Lexical sound-symbolism should have only minor statistical effects, but within small closed sets the violations can have strong effects which must be analyzed statistically. For example, typological study of morphological affixes distinguishing person and number reveals numerous disturbances of both the arbitrariness and independence principles. Among the more well-known regularities we point to the tendency of morphological affixes to be short, to involve the less marked phonemes of the language, to have a nasal consonant in the first person, and to have dental or alveolar consonants in other persons; furthermore, singulars and plurals are often not independent in the same person. In these and in many other respects, the LM and PIE systems are typical.

7. *Summary*. This paper presents and tests probability distributions governing the number of apparent cognates that appear by chance in language comparison; provides controls on biases typically associated with research in which phonological correspondences are not established; quantifies the gradual increase in the number of chance cognates expected as one searches ever more widely for related language families; quantifies the dramatic decrease in the likelihood of chance cognation under mass comparison and its rapid increase when criteria for phonetic or semantic similarity are weakened to the point that many items on one list are similar to more than one on another; and provides practical procedures for testing the hypothesis of chance against alternative hypotheses concerning the basis for apparent cognation.

NOTES

[1] Bender does not report the parameter r; it is estimated by $\hat{r} = n^2 \hat{p}$.

[2] The accuracy of the Poisson approximation is excellent and should be used for large n. Explicit computation of (1) is not feasible for large n, so in the test of the exact distribution against Bender's data the 99-word list was divided into three more manageable 33-word lists. By tripling the sample size, this also increased the power of the test. Bender's results under his weak criteria could not be tested since he does not report the data necessary to make this division.

[3] The fit of (2) to Bender's data is excellent for the strict and extended criteria on the 99-word list as well. It cannot be tested for his weak criteria since there only he took phonetic similarity to be a transitive relation. For example, under the weak criteria English *all* resembles Navaho *ʔałco*, *ʔałco* resembles Georgian *qvela* which in turn resembles Amharic *hullu* and Remo *gulay* which resemble each other. In Bender's weak counts, each of these was taken to resemble all the others, giving ten pairs of apparent cognates rather than five. This procedure produces abnormally high numbers of language pairs with a high number of apparent cognates and lowers somewhat the number with

REDUNDANCY AS EXPLANATION IN HISTORICAL LINGUISTICS

WILLIAM M. CHRISTIE, JR.
University of Arizona

Redundancy is one of those features of language that we all heard about in our first linguistics courses and then left alone. We may have renewed our acquaintance with it as we have ourselves had occasion to teach beginning linguistics, but for the most part we have left it in the shadows with no clear place in linguistic theory. I would like to bring redundancy out of the shadows and examine the place it might take in linguistic theory and the tasks it might perform for us.

Redundancy in language has been sufficiently neglected that we need first of all to define precisely what it is we are talking about. It is not, in fact, an obvious common feature of the sentences we usually dissect in our various investigations. We generally confine ourselves to sentences that are pared down to the minimal essentials. For example, Lakoff's well known sentences, *Seymour sliced the salami with a knife* and *Seymour used a knife to slice the salami*, both signal the instrumental function in simple, single ways, one with *with*, the other with *use*. But I think that the sentence type added to the set by Chomsky is in fact more common in everyday language use. In *Seymour used a knife to slice the salami with*, the instrumental function is signaled twice, that is, redundantly, by both *use* and *with*. We can use this example to define just what we mean by redundancy. At some level of structure there is an element of instrumentality that is represented at some other level of structure by *use* and/or *with*. Instrumentality, *use*, and *with* are 'elements' on different levels. For the purposes of this paper, I wish to leave the term 'element' maximally undefined. It may be a lexical item, a relation, or whatever. If we consider the production of sentences, we find that instrumentality is an element in a sequence that constitutes a message to be transmitted. *Use* and *with*, on the other hand, are elements in a sequence that transmits this message. In this particular example, the formulation I have just offered is simply another way of expressing the old observation that we do not speak in deep structure. We can now define redundancy as the provision in the transmission sequence of multiple cues (elements) to represent some single element in the corresponding message sequence. Note that message sequence and transmission sequence are relative terms. For example, what was the transmission sequence in the example just mentioned may be treated as the message sequence in analysis of redundancy at the phonological level.

There is another aspect to redundancy that I want to mention here in order to exclude it from our consideration. It is possible to have partial redundancy within a single level in terms of mutual expectations of elements. For example, at some level in the phonology, an initial [Cy] cluster will inevitably be followed by [u] in my speech. The specific features of that vowel are, in that environment on that level, completely redundant. They are fully predictable within that level. To some extent this sort of refundancy may interlock with the other type we are considering, but it can also be treated independently. However, for our present purposes I want to look only at redundancy as a type of relationship *between* levels of structure.

Now that we have been properly introduced to redundancy, just what can it do for us? At least two things, as I see it. First, it can provide an explanation for certain phenomena in historical linguistics. Second, it can provide a type of test for the adequacy of our grammatical models, whether synchronic or diachronic. The historical explanation will be considered first.

It should be clear from the foregoing discussion that a full consideration of redundancy pushes us strongly in the direction of a functionalist approach to language. Such an approach confronts us at once with the fact that language is a communications system. In the face of this fact, historical linguistics presents a special problem, for any change in the language system raises the possibility of a disruption of communication. If the cues in some transmission sequence are altered, the receiver may correlate some incorrect message sequence with the received transmission sequence — a breakdown in communication. The question facing the historical linguist, then, is this: How is communication maintained in the face of language change? The question is, of course, not new. The gradualist view of sound change was an attempt to answer just such

a question. If sounds change gradually, in imperceptible
steps, hearers will not be able to detect the shifts in
the sounds, and there will thus be no disruption of communication. There are, of course, a number of serious problems with this view. In the first place, some sound
changes are not and in fact cannot be gradual. Further,
there is fairly frequent interaction among members of different dialect groups. Although one dialect may have
undergone a sound change which has not occurred at all, or
progressed only slightly, in the other dialects, communication still need not be disrupted. Finally, one would be
hard put to describe syntactic change as gradual in the
same sense as phonological change. Some other hypothesis
will have be offered, and redundancy is our prime candidate.

Consider how redundancy can explain sound change.
First, we may take phonemes to be the message elements and
their features to be the transmission elements. For this
we will have to include both distinctive and nondistinctive
features. At one stage in the history of a language certain features are distinctive and others are not. At this
stage the nondistinctive features are free to change without any danger of disruption in the communicative system.
However, shifts in categorization (not in the sounds
themselves) may occur, through which certain features that
were previously nondistinctive become distinctive, while
certain previously distinctive features may become nondistinctive. At this point, the originally distinctive
features are free to change, again without a disruption in
the process of communication. The net result is the possibility of a complete change in the articulatory and auditory characteristics of the phonemes without any threat of
a disruption of communication. Note that this change can
be general or restricted to certain environments. Redundancy can handle both cases equally well. What is essential in the process is that at each stage the phoneme be
represented redundantly by a set of features, some distinctive and some not, the latter being the ones that are free
to change.

Many examples of language change become somewhat
clearer if viewed in this light, especially some that seem
rather improbable. For example, Andersen's (1973) treatment of the so-called *tetak* dialects handles that rather
improbable development in terms essentially similar to the
ones I am proposing here. Another example, drawn from the
history of English, may make the whole matter somewhat
clearer. The Great Vowel Shift (GVS) is sufficiently familiar that it can be taken as an illustration without giving

all the details. Note that I am not proposing an explanation of why such a change occurred, but rather of how it could have occurred at whatever rate without impairing communication. At some stage of late Middle English we can assume a relationship between the long and short vowels, such that they are essentially identical except for the feature of length. Since this feature suffices to keep the long and short vowels distinct from each other, members of either set are free to change features other than length, so long as the necessary distinctions are maintained within each set. (In fact, of course, there was some merger, but that is not essential for our present purposes.) Given this freedom, the long vowels acquired an added phonetic feature of height, at first totally nondistinctive. Note that it does not matter in the least whether this feature was acquired gradually or abruptly. In the case of the GVS it was probably gradual, but in other sound changes that we might have discussed it could well have been abrupt. The important point is that in no case would this shift in the nondistinctive feature set affect communication. Following this feature shift, a perceptual shift occurs. The height distinction (however one wants to mark it) comes to be perceived as distinctive, while the length distinction ceases to be so treated. We are now very close to our Modern English system. All that is still wanting is the subsequent change in the phonetic characteristics of length to the present pattern, in which length varies also according to phonetic environment. These length features are, of course, free to change because they are no longer distinctive.

The foregoing may seem not only unexceptionable, but even a bit too obvious and dull. But it has implications that are often ignored. If we accept the importance of redundancy in this process, if we allow it to perform this service of explaining the GVS (as it rather clearly does), then we must grant it a place in our grammatical models. However, such a place may be difficult to provide. Note that each case of functional redundancy that we describe requires as a part of it the postulation of two distinct levels of structure. As we increase the number of observed cases of functional redundancy, we increase the likelihood that we will need to recognize an increasing number of levels of structure. Of course, many of the cases will be found to operate between the same two levels. But there will be an uncomfortable number of cases in which the same sequence will serve as a transmission sequence for one example but as the message sequence for another.

Consider the English passive. I have observed elsewhere (Christie 1977) that the passive construction is

signaled redundantly in the syntax with two distinctive
elements, the passive component of the verb and the optional *by* phrase. But in one of its uses the passive construction itself is one of the two redundant cues for the thematization of the goal, the other cue being the sentence
initial position of the goal. Consider the following sentences.

    1. Fourteen different forks he ate with at our
supper yesterday.

??2. Fourteen different people the cake was eaten
by last night.

    3. Fourteen different varieties of bugs he played
with on that trip.

?4. Fourteen different varieties of bugs he was
bitten by on that trip.

Thematization of a nonsubject NP is clearly permissible in
most cases, but it becomes very strange in a passive because the surface subject of the passive is already thema-
tized. Thus the passive and sentence initial position are
redundant cues in a transmission sequence for goal thematization in a message sequence. But in a different pairing
of message and transmission, the passive construction itself is a part of a message sequence that is redundantly
cued in another transmission sequence by the *be-en* verb
form and the *by*-agent. We thus have here at least tentative evidence for three structural levels in an area where
fewer are normally posited.

    This is not to say that redundancy must be the major
determining factor in the structure we assign to a grammar.
It is not that powerful. My point is a more limited one.
It is useful to have around when we do diachrony. But if
we admit it there, our synchronic descriptions will have to
make a place for it as well. And that place will, to some
degree at least, affect the overall structure of the grammar we have to construct.

REFERENCES

Andersen, Henning. 1973. "Abductive and deductive change". *Lg*. 49.765-93.
Christie, William. 1977. "Some multiple cues for juncture in English". *General Linguistics* 17.212-22.

THE STRUCTURE OF MEANING IN SEMIOTIC PERSPECTIVE

MICHAEL SHAPIRO
University of California, Los Angeles

The conception of language as a system of signs has been a part of linguistic thought since at least the time of the Stoics. Nonetheless, very little of practical consequence has ensued therefrom, despite the efforts of such major modern theoreticians as de Saussure, Hjelmslev, and Jakobson. To the small extent that investigators have made substantive attempts at couching their analyses of linguistic structure in explicitly semiotic terms, the study of synchrony has perhaps fared better overall than that of diachrony. What I would like to do here is sketch a theory of meaning that subsumes linguistic change and makes overt reference, moreover, to change as an aspect of continuity. This theory will be explicitly semiotic in terminology and purport, relying in all essential respects on the thought of the American philosopher-scientist Charles Sanders Peirce (1839-1914), whose theory of signs (or 'semiotic') constitutes the richest body of knowledge about and source of insight into the conceptual foundations of sign systems. Owing to the widespread unfamiliarity with Peirce's leading ideas, my task will of necessity include a rehearsal of some of the staples of Peircean semiotic and other pertinent aspects of his philosophy that illuminate the problem of meaning and meaning change.

'A sign stands *for* something *to* the idea which it produces or modifies' (1.339--such references are to Peirce 1965-66 by volume and paragraph number), says Peirce, and in this description of the sign situation its three essential elements stand out in relief. Peirce's 'sign' (or 'representamen') corresponds to the Augustinian signans, his 'something' (or 'object') to signatum, his 'idea' (or 'interpretant') to the Thomistic understanding of meaning as a psychic entity. A sign's status as a triadic relative is emphasized by Peirce when he terms the mutable conditions obtaining between the components of a sign its *fundamenta relationis* (3.638). A true (i.e. 'non-degenerate') sign necessarily partakes of this triadicity, and it is just the third member of the triad, the interpretant, that makes a true sign what it is. Moreover, the interpretant of a sign proper is itself a sign (2.303), and the particular character of the originating sign's fundamentum relationis is diagrammed by that of its interpretant: 'A sign therefore is an object which is in relation to its object on the one hand and to an interpretant on the other in such a way as to bring the interpretant into a relation to the object, corresponding to its own relation to the object' (8.332). Thus the relations between signans and signatum which give rise to Peirce's fundamental trichotomy of icon, index, and symbol must be mirrored in the interpretant of a true sign.

This latter division, which depends on the relation between sign and object, is of particular importance to my topic, since all linguistic elements are symbols in the Peircean sense of this multipurpose word. While an icon is defined as 'a sign of which the character that fits it to become a sign of the sort that it is, is simply inherent in it as a quality of it' (Peirce 1976:242); and an index defined as 'a sign which is fit to serve as such by virtue of being in a real relation with its object' (ibid.); Peirce proposes to define 'the technical designation *symbol*', following Aristotle (among other logicians), as 'a sign which is fit to serve as such simply because it will be so interpreted', or owing to the fact that 'it determines the interpretant sign' (Peirce 1976:243). Despite their great utility and ability to fulfill functions that genuine signs cannot, icons and indices are degenerate (in the mathematical sense). A pure icon is independent of any purpose and is capable of asserting nothing. 'If it conveys information, it is only in the sense in which the object that it is used to represent may be said to convey information. An *icon* can only be a fragment of a completer sign' (Peirce 1976:242). A pure index is likewise incapable of asserting anything; it 'simply forces attention to the object with which it reacts and puts the interpreter into mediate reaction with that object, but conveys no information' (ibid.).

Thus it is symbols--despite the indirectness of their signification--that are the species of sign capable of constituting linguistic discourse. 'The most characteristic aspect of a symbol is its aspect as related to its interpretant; because a symbol is distinguished as a sign which becomes such by virtue of determining its interpretant' (Peirce 1976:260). Here we note the full power of Peirce's definition as it applies to the notion that language is a symbolic system. And if we accept Jakobson's statement that 'everything language can and does communicate stands first and foremost in a necessary, intimate connection with meaning and always carries semantic information' (1972:76), we are forced to the conclusion that all linguistic phenomena must ultimately be comprehended as instantiations of symbolicity. The semiotic perspective articulated by Peirce encompasses symbols as the epitomical signs, and 'language is an example of a purely semiotic system' (Jakobson 1971:703). In order to make progress in the exploration of meaning, it thus appears we must probe the ontology of the symbol.

The successful investigation of semiosis, including symbols, cannot proceed, however, without taking due account of Peirce's three categories, which he called Firstness, Secondness, and Thirdness. Firstness subsumes things that are termed Firsts and is defined by Peirce as 'the mode of being of that which is such as it is positively and without reference to anything else' (in Hardwick 1977:24). Secondness (which subsumes Seconds) is 'the mode of being of that which is such as it is, with respect to a second but regardless of any third' (ibid.). And Thirdness (into which category fall Thirds) he defines as 'the mode of being of that which is such as it is, in bringing a second and third into relation to each other' (ibid.). There is a hierarchical relationship between the categories, a relation of inclusion along a unidirectional gradient of increasing complexity which has Thirdness encompass Secondness and Firstness, Secondness encompass Firstness, and Firstness in its unalloyed state be a pure simplex.

It is Thirdness that figures most prominently in the structure of a semiotic system such as language. Whereas Firstness is fundamentally a quality of feeling or a mere possibility and Secondness 'the experience of effort, prescinded from the idea of a purpose' (Hardwick, 25), Thirdness alone informs the notion of mediation or representation; that is to say, precisely the triadic relation that obtains between sign, object, and interpretant (cf. Hardwick, 31). Thirdness is generality governing lawlike change and transformation, which distinguishes it from Firstness, the possibility of a single unitary and immutable quality. Thirdness is accorded functional prominence in the Peircean concept of the interpretant. Since it is the interpretant that is indispensable to the integrity of the sign relation, semiosis—and, consequently, meaning—are ineluctably contingent on Thirdness via the role of the interpretant: 'every genuine triadic relation involves meaning, as meaning is obviously a triadic relation'

(1.345).

The categorial framework of Firsts, Seconds, and Thirds provides (in addition to other advantages) a way of understanding the different, seemingly incompatible aspects of meaning to which linguists have been attuned traditionally. To begin with the perceived 'ungraspability' (Lyons 1977) of meaning which has led some students to relegate the concept to the status of a 'pre-theoretical term' (ibid.: 1), we can now correctly judge this property to be inherent and highly necessary as the systematically built-in quotient or margin of inchoateness which allows meaning to subsist and to change. Firstness of meaning is tantamount to infinite regress, which is actually the inherent potential of an infinity of translatable signata indispensable to the fulfillment of new communicative needs as they arise in the course of cultural growth. The relation between sign and object cannot, of course, remain ultimately inchoate, and the mediational or interpretative system which comprises semantic structure comports an element of Secondness, of what Peirce terms 'brute reaction' between actual meanings as they are differentiated from each other, in the imposition of pragmatically definite choice that language makes on the potentially infinite continuum of reference. Simple reaction as represented by selection (the segmentation of the semantic continuum) does not complete the picture, however. This role is reserved for Thirdness, manifested in the rule or law, the patterning and coherence, which facilitate understanding between speakers through the system of interpretants that places practical communicative limits on infinite regress, thereby creating the condition of structure in meaning. Peirce himself puts it tellingly: 'Reality is compulsive. But the compulsiveness is absolutely *hic et nunc*. It is for an instant and it is gone.... The reality only exists as an element of the regularity. And the regularity is the symbol. Reality, therefore, can only be regarded as the limit of the endless series of symbols' (1976:261).

Symbols by their very nature, while producing an endless series of interpretants that are themselves symbols, tend towards definiteness, towards interpretants that are continually more determinate than their antecedents. Growth--a tendency to become determined via interpretation --inheres in the structure of the symbol as its fundamental definiens. That is why Peirce goes so far as to assert that 'a symbol is an embryonic reality endowed with power of growth into the very truth, the very entelechy of reality' (1976:262). (So much for truth-conditional semantics!)

The structure and development of tropes is particularly suited to an illustration of the teleological nature of symbols. The dynamic or life cycle of tropes (perhaps more aptly to be called their 'life spiral') typically involves the lexicalization of an initially living metonymy or metaphor (by what Stern 1931:390 calls adequation)(see Shapiro and Shapiro 1976). This aspect is especially common to the diachronic accretion of terminology in a specialized (e.g. scientific) sector of the vocabulary. As Quine has it, 'the neatly worked inner stretches of science are an open space in the tropical jungle, created by clearing tropes away' (1978:162). To take an example from the idiom of contemporary sports, specifically basketball in America, within the last decade an expression—*back door*—has entered common parlance to describe a maneuver whereby one of the offensive team's players (without the ball) manages to penetrate unnoticed behind the opposing team's defenses close enough to the basket to attempt an unobstructed short shot (usually a layup). When this play first came into existence, its linguistic designation was patently metaphorical (cf. *getting in through the back door*). Both the play and the expression, indeed, arose spontaneously, by chance, as instantiations of the 'brute force' of Secondness. But as the play spread and grew in frequency, it ceased to be the spontaneous result of chance configurations in game situations. It became what is known as a set play, that is a maneuver planned and perfected in practice sessions, designed to take its place among the stock of plays in a team's repertoire or 'play book'. At this crucial point, the metaphor had largely lost its figural status, having become a term. Now, *back door* became a deriving base for terminological exfoliations such as *to go back door*, *to back door*, *to pull a back door* (*play*), etc. Indeed, here we can legitimately speak of a lexicalization of the original trope. In a Peircean perspective, this is the predicted teleological result of the very ontology of a symbol. In its status as the epitomically indeterminate sign, the symbol is defined by its preeminent power of growth and development, of determining itself increasingly, of making its meaning more concrete (=clear, not non-abstract) by engendering successive interpretants with which it maintains a semantic affinity along a gradient simultaneously synchronic and diachronic.

What is particularly significant about the playing out of this preordained development in terminology is the semiotic connection between the gradual attenuation of indeterminacy and the concept embedded in the word *term* itself. The end result of the growth of symbols is precisely the etymologically veridical *term*(*inus*)!

Linking this process to Peirce's pragmatistic conception of habit as the ultimate logical interpretant (cf. Fitzgerald 1964;170 & passim), we can see with clarity that the intellectual, rational core of habit presupposes a concomitant loss of the spontaneous, the emotive quotient of sign function. In the Peircean idiom, we have here a progression away from the emotional interpretant toward the final interpretant, viz. a mental habit subtending a habit of action. An immediate morphological parallel that suggests itself is lexicalization in affective (expressive) formations. In a language as replete with diminutives and hypocoristics as Russian, it is common to observe the transition of an original expressive derivation into the category of terms broadly conceived (i.e. neutral substantives with no affective meaning). A word such as *nosok* 'sock, spout, toe (of footwear or hose)' shows an (incomplete) effacement of the historically primary meaning 'little nose' via an intermediate stage involving figuration, whereby the protruberance characteristic of a nose is transferred onto objects occupying the same position vis-à-vis an anchoring mass. Hardly an isolated example in Russian, it has, moreover, analogous counterparts in many other languages.

But the power of a symbol does not stop with the demise of a trope or the eclipse of affective meaning resulting from fading and lexicalization. The entombed history of the linguistic sign can always be disinterred--by poets, or by those who recur to the poetic function for aesthetic effect in an otherwise discursive context (such as that of advertising slogans). Thirdness, with its definitional *esse in futuro*, always teleologically transcends the limitations of Secondness, of the here and now.

The telos of the symbol, its teleological thrust, is not confined to this kind of sign; it is only most prominent therein. For signs are entelechies (Peirce 1976:229), and entelechy is just 'the third element...which brings things together...the element which is prominent in such ideas as Plan, Cause, and Law' (ibid., 295-96).

We thus come to the notion that linguistic semiosis necessarily presupposes the involvement of the most important member of the semiotic triad, the interpretant, whose role is defined by the only fallible mode of inference--abduction. This definition accords perfectly with the essential nature of the symbol and with symbolicity. Collocated within the matrix of Peirce's categories and his pragmaticism, semiotic fallibilism renders change in meaning understandable as an inalienable part of the sign situation and, consequently, as an aspect of semantic continuity assuring interpretability across discontinuous generations. What is even more important, change itself becomes an ontological component of linguistic meaning and the nature of meaning. A semiotic perspective thus leads without fail to the position that synchronic grammar (including lexis) cannot be validated without recourse to diachrony: every structure incorporates a dynamic. Or as Roman Jakobson put it (1971:562), 'when the time factor enters into such a system of symbolic values as language, it becomes a symbol itself'.

REFERENCES

Fitzgerald, John J. 1964. *Peirce's theory of signs as foundation for pragmatism*. The Hague: Mouton.
Hardwick, Charles S. (ed.). 1977. *Semiotic and significs: the correspondence between Charles S. Peirce and Victoria Lady Welby*. Bloomington: Indiana University Press.
Jakobson, Roman. 1971. *Selected writings, II: word and language*. The Hague: Mouton.
_____. 1972. "Verbal communication". *Scientific American* 227:3.72-80.
Lyons, John. 1977. "Basic problems of semantics". Plenary report to the Twelfth International Congress of Linguists, abstracts, 1-3. Vienna: Interconvention.
Peirce, Charles S. 1965-6. *Collected papers*. Ed. by Charles Hartshorne and Paul Weiss (vols. 1-6) and Arthur Burks (vols. 7-8). Cambridge, Mass.: Harvard University Press. 2nd printing (8 vols. in 4).
_____. 1976. *The new elements of mathematics, IV: mathematical philosophy*. Ed. by Carolyn Eisele. The Hague: Mouton.
Quine, W.V. 1978. "A postscript on metaphor". *Critical Inquiry* 5.161-2.
Shapiro, Michael and Marianne Shapiro. 1976. *Hierarchy and the structure of tropes*. Bloomington: Indiana University Press.
Stern, Gustaf. 1931. *Meaning and change of meaning*. Bloomington: Indiana University Press.

PRAGMATIC AND SOCIOLINGUISTIC BIAS
IN SEMANTIC CHANGE

FLORA KLEIN
Georgetown University

0. Language change seems to pose a dilemma for structural models which define the value of linguistic units by their mutual relations with other members of a larger 'system'.* While this view accounts well for stability, it makes it difficult to envision change and in particular the transition between successive stages or systems.

Sociolinguistic theory portrays change as effected by progressive, *socially mediated biases* in favor of, or against, particular linguistic features (Weinreich, Labov, and Herzog 1968; Labov 1972, Chapter 7). This paper supports the view that, where semantic systems are postulated, one must also consider the likelihood of shifts in the predominant *pragmatic strategies* or 'norms' of actual use (Coseriu 1967; García 1975:503). I further emphasize the possibility of *interaction* between these two kinds of bias, suggesting at least one type of situation likely to lead to the reinterpretation of pragmatic preferences as social norms.

These views are illustrated in a reconstruction of some key aspects of a change from one semantic system to another--namely, the systems which may be postulated as underlying the currently different usage of the third-person oblique clitics *le*, *la*, and *lo* in different varieties of Spanish. Assuming that, in principle, the pragmatic and sociolinguistic biases which brought about the change may have been similar to biases observable at present, my arguments are based on observation of present-day speech and supported by preliminary samples recorded in an ongoing investigation in various parts of Castilla--the general area in which the change occurred. For the most part, however, the developments in question seem to have taken place recently enough for more direct investigation (roughly, from the Middle Ages). My proposals are therefore intended as working hypotheses, or theoretically motivated bases for re-examination of pertinent data, both historical and current.

1. In the great majority of the Spanish-speaking world, apparently including most of Spain itself, the use of the clitics *le*, *la*, and *lo* responds to an etymological distinction of case, as shown in Figure I. But in the vernacular

	Dative	Accusative	
		fem.	ILLAM > *la*
	ILLI > *le*	masc.	ILLUM
		neuter	ILLUD > *lo*

Origin of Spanish 3rd person oblique clitics
FIGURE I

of a large area of northwestern and central Spain (apparently comprising the greater part of Castilla la Vieja and adjoining areas to the South, including Madrid) the use of *le*, *la*, and *lo* does not reflect the object's case-role, but seems to be based instead on characteristics of the object itself, which I call *referential* characteristics. The utterances listed under (A) and under (B) in Figure II illustrate consequent differences in actual usage, with respect to the messages in the English glosses.

	A. Case-distinguishing usage	B. Caseless (Referential) usage	C. Traditional terms for individual referential uses
i	*Lo* conocí en la mili	*Le* conocí en la mili	'leísmo' for (masculine) animates
	'I met *him* in the army'		
ii	*Le* dieron un cargo oficial	*Le* dieron un cargo oficial	
	'They gave *him* an official post'		
iii	*La* conocí en una fiesta	*La* conocí en una fiesta	
	'I met *her* at a party'		
iv	Su novio *le* dió una sortija	Su novio *la* dió una sortija	'laísmo'
	'Her fiance gave *her* a ring'		
v	*Lo* compramos de segunda mano	*Le* compramos de segunda mano	'leísmo' for (masculine) inanimates
	'We bought *it* second-hand (e.g. the car=masc.)'		

vi *Le* cambiamos la   *Le* cambiamos la
    tapicería   tapicería
        'We changed the upholstery on *it*
        (e.g. the car=masc.)'

vii *Lo* tomamos con las   *Lo* tomamos con las
    comidas   comidas
        'We take *it* with our meals
        (e.g. wine=masc.)'

viii Hoy día *le* añaden de   Hoy día *lo* añaden de   'loísmo'
    todo   todo
        'Nowadays they add all kinds of
        things to *it* (e.g. to wine=masc.)'

FIGURE II

Note, first, that overt differences in usage occur in some contexts but not in others. Thus column (C) lists traditional terms for the individual referential uses (under B) which differ from their case-distinguishing counterparts (under A). It should be noted, too, that the various individual uses—and in particular, the innovative 'referential' uses—are not equally accepted. At present only one referential use is accepted as 'standard', as a regional alternative to its case-distinguishing counterpart—namely so-called 'leísmo', or the use of the etymological dative *le* in an accusative context, when it refers to a masculine animate (as in (Bi)). As I show in Klein (in press), the privileged status of leísmo for masculine animates is manifest in measures of acceptance and of sociolinguistic distribution, both in generally caseless areas and in case-distinguishing areas as well, though of course not to the same degree in each. As an example, compare the sociolinguistic distribution of the three most frequent referential uses (leísmo for masculine animates, for masculine inanimates, and laísmo) in the caseless province of Valladolid (in Figure III) and in the case-distinguishing province of Logroño (in Figure IV).

2. The historical question, then, is how did the usage exemplified under (B) in Figure II, and the social preferences described above, develop from the original system depicted in Figure I? Traditionally, the change has been regarded as extending distinction of gender at the expense of distinction of case, in the direction of a system such as that diagrammed in Figure V. The developments in this direction have been viewed as spearheaded by an increasing tendency to 'extend' the dative *le* into accusative contexts,

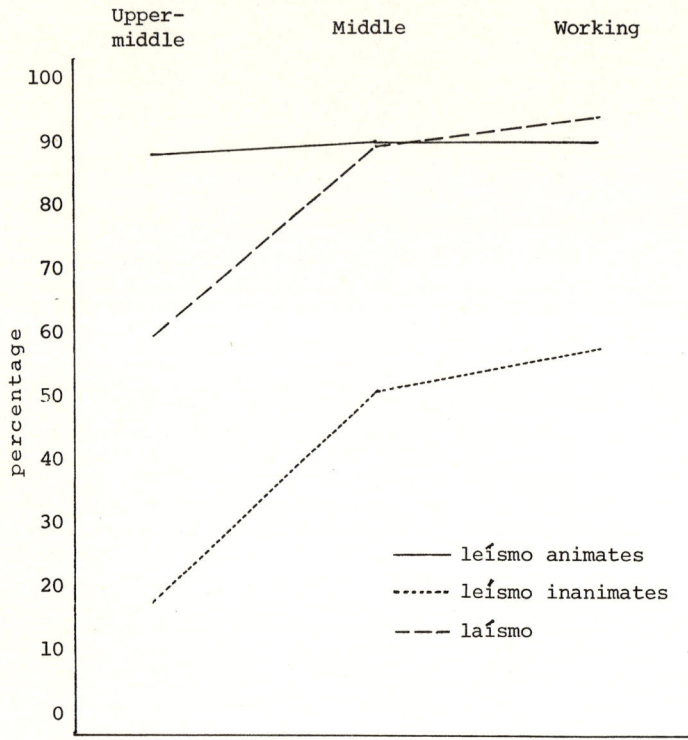

	leísmo animates			leísmo inanimates			laísmo		
	Total N	N le	% le	Total N	N le	% le	Total N	N la	% la
Upper-middle	34	30	88%	28	5	18%	22	13	59%
Middle	108	93	90%	38	19	50%	18	16	89%
Working	58	52	90%	51	29	57%	18	17	94%

Frequency of leísmo for masculine animates, leísmo for masculine inanimates, and laísmo in Valladolid men as a function of social class

FIGURE III

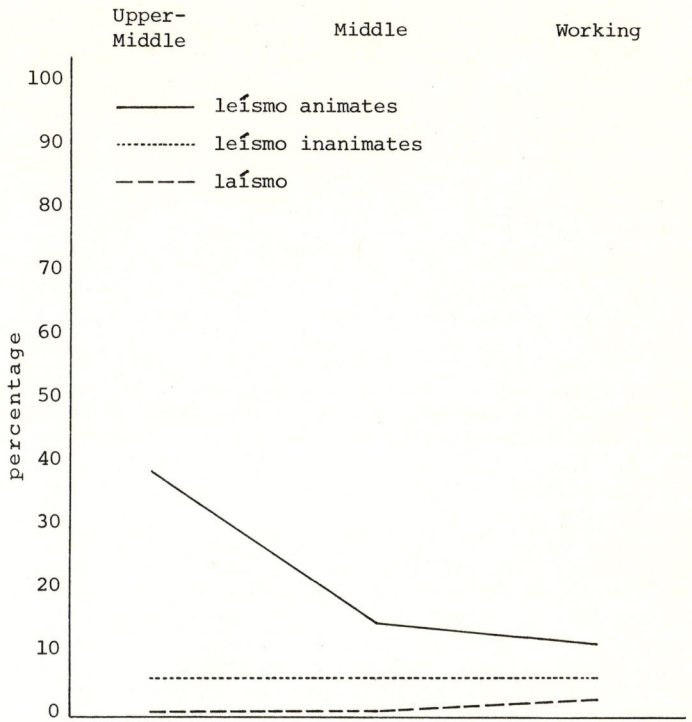

	leísmo animates			leísmo inanimates			laísmo		
	Total N	N le	% le	Total N	N le	% le	Total N	N la	% la
Upper-middle	13	5	38%	20	1	5%	6	0	0%
Middle	36	5	14%	44	2	5%	16	0	0%
Working	54	6	11%	41	2	5%	45	1	2%

Frequency of leísmo for masculine animates,
leísmo for masculine inanimates, and laísmo in
Logroño men as a function of social class
FIGURE IV

feminine *la*
masculine *le*
neuter   *lo*

Caseless (Referential) System
FIGURE V

leading to the eventual reanalysis of the opposition of *le* vs. *lo* as indicating masculine vs. neuter, rather than dative vs. accusative. Each of these tendencies is attributed, in turn, to 'analogy' with similar distinctions or synchretisms in other areas of the language.

Among other problems, however, this account shares a theoretical weakness common to many appeals to analogy-- namely, failure to furnish a principled motive for the allegedly analogous treatment of the various elements in question. These elements traditionally are left unanalyzed --and this includes, of course, the clitics themselves, as well as case and gender.

At present, the semantic analysis of the clitics proposed by Erica García has contributed substantially toward clarifying some of these central issues. In the first place García analyzes the clitics *le*, *la*, and *lo* as 'deictics', defining deixis as 'an *instruction to the hearer* to find the (clitic's) referent' (García 1975:65, my emphasis). Further, she demonstrates that the accusative vs. dative opposition signals difference in the relative degree of contribution of the object to the event expressed by the verb, with the lowest degree of contribution expressed by the accusative (*lo/la*) and a relatively higher contribution by the dative (*le*).

Determining that the two cases differ in meaning, and identifying their meanings, makes it possible to understand their actual distribution in case-distinguishing dialects, as reflecting plausible pragmatic exploitations of the meanings posited. In particular, and most importantly for our present purposes, it makes it possible to explain *as a consequence of the case-system* itself (and in particular of its relative nature) the tendency to 'extend *le*' into the accusative's domain. As García's analysis predicts, such 'extensions' occur when the object is described as relatively active: e.g. when it is animate, and/or the subject of an infinitive, or the object of a verb which implies the object's activity (e.g. *ayudar* 'help', *dirigir* 'direct', etc.).

Yet even with this explanation for their occurrence, the 'extensions of *le*' in case-distinguishing usage do not suffice to explain the development of caseless leísmo. For any such explanation would depend crucially on the association of *le* with masculine antecedents. Yet, at least in present-day case-distinguishing usage, this association does not seem to be nearly as strong as traditional observations suggest.

This can be seen in Figure VI, which shows the frequency of *le* as a function of the antecedent's gender and number and of its referent's animateness, in a sample of rural speech from the case-distinguishing Castilian area of Soria. All occurrences of *le*, *la*, and *lo* are counted which refer to masculine or feminine logical third persons, and which occur in single-object utterances--the latter being the situation in which 'extensions of *le*' are most frequent.[1]

			N *le*	N *la*	N *lo*	%*le*
Masculine	Sg	An	45	0	81	36%
		Inan	9	0	123	7%
	Pl	An	28	0	68	29%
		Inan	7	0	77	8%
Feminine	Sg	An	7	36	0	16%
		Inan	0	71	0	0%
	Pl	An	19	31	0	38%
		Inan	1	34	0	3%

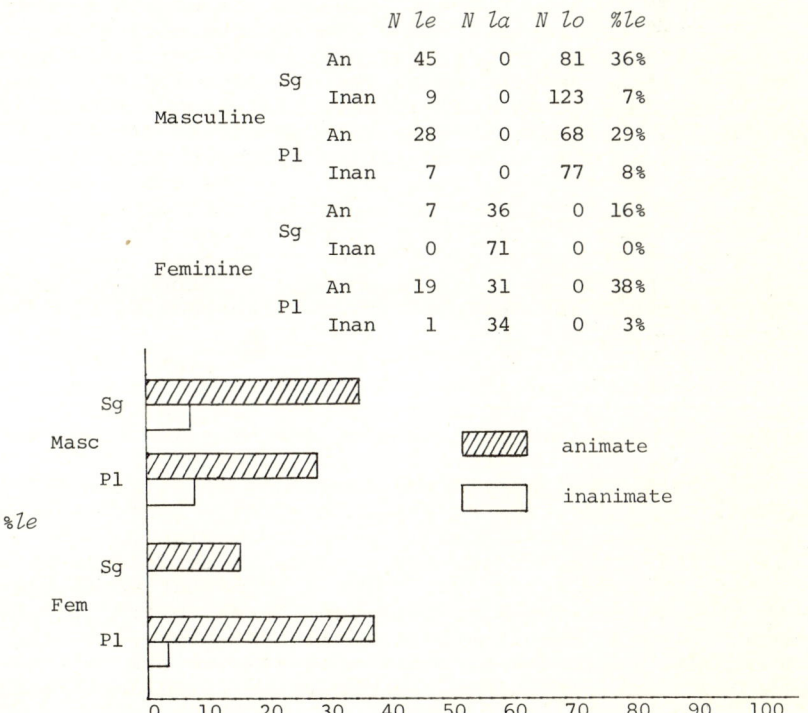

Percentage of *le/s* in rural sample from Soria as a function of the object's gender and animateness

FIGURE VI

The results support García's analysis of case (and traditional observations) inasmuch as *le* is much more frequent with animate than with inanimate objects. On the other hand the alleged correlation of *le* with masculines is supported only in part: it holds for inanimates (where it is not predicted), but for animates only in the singular. In the plural, *les* is more frequent for feminines than for masculines; hence if animate objects are considered as a whole, the percentage of *le/s* is very similar for both genders (33% for masculines, 30% for feminines).

3. Why, then, has it so generally been observed that 'extensions of *le*' refer predominantly--if not almost exclusively--to masculines? Perhaps because the correlation seems to hold to some extent. It should be noted, too, that masculine antecedents are about twice as frequent as feminines, so that innovations may simply be more noticeable in reference to masculines than to feminines. To a considerable extent, however, one may suspect this observation of being an artifact of a non-structural approach to the question. For traditional treatments typically are concerned with frequencies of the non-etymological, caseless uses, considered individually and without regard to whether they reflect usage that is caseless overall, or not.[2] Now, if case-distinguishing usage is considered together with caseless (the latter being the usage whose development we are trying to explain), then certainly *le* will be found to refer predominantly to masculines. For one of the features of caseless or referential usage is precisely that in it *le* is 'masculine', rather than dative, and accordingly the feminine is *la*--irrespective of 'degree of activity'.

This is evident if we consider a sample of caseless speech, recorded by rural speakers of the province of Valladolid. Applying the same criteria as we did with the sample from Soria we get the results shown in Figure VII. We see that in Valladolid the frequency of *le* does differ markedly as a function of the antecedent's gender, and that this difference is especially pronounced with animate referents (and with plurals, for reasons to be discussed presently). Now it seems that this is just what we should expect of a caseless usage, both considered in itself and as compared to the results obtained in case-distinguishing Soria. If, following García's analysis, we assume that in case-distinguishing usage the choice of *le* reflects a relative degree of activity on the part of the object, then the one characteristic of the object itself which must be expected to correlate with higher frequency of *le* is animateness. On the other hand in caseless usage the situation

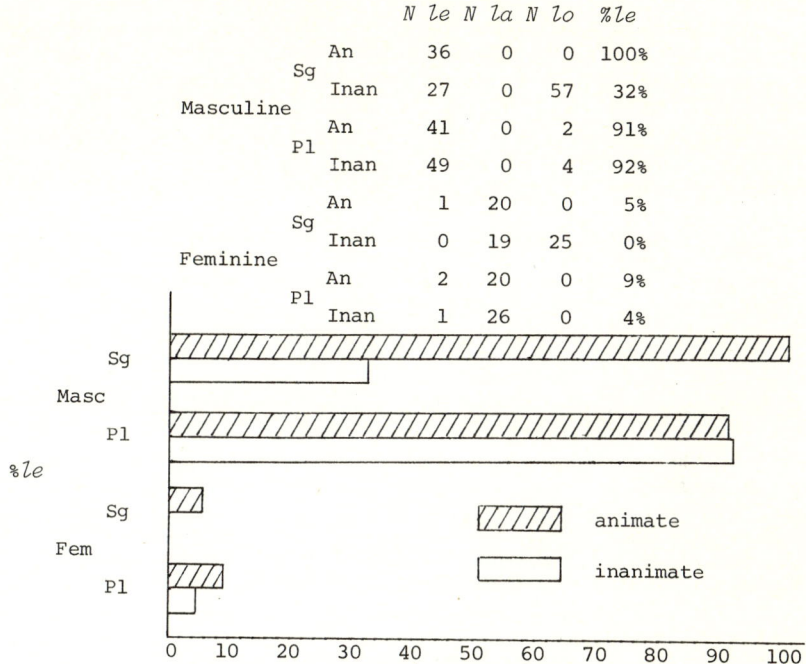

Percentage of *le/s* in rural sample from Valladolid as a function of the object's gender and animateness

FIGURE VII

should be quite different: where case-role is not a factor, it is plausible that clitic choice should be relatively more sensitive to characteristics of the object itself--i.e. to what I call 'referential' factors. Among them we may expect the object's gender to be important--especially with animate objects, where it can reflect a real-world difference of sex.[3]

4. The data from Valladolid, however, also reflect another referential factor which may be suspected of influencing the development of a referential system of clitic use. As Figure VII shows, among masculines there is a sharp drop in the frequency of *le*, relative to the alternative *lo*, when the object is both inanimate and singular. What this reflects is the influence of another referential characteristic of importance in caseless usage, in that it largely determines the occurrence of *lo*, as opposed to *le* or *la*. This is the discreteness of the object. Thus, in caseless usage

nondiscrete objects are much more likely to be cliticized by *lo* than discrete objects. As examples (1) and (2) show, clitization by *lo* occurs regardless of the linguistic gender of the antecedent, or of its relative proximity in the discourse:

(1) (antes) s'encendían con paja, pero duraba mucho la paja. Pero ahora, esta paja larga *lo* metes y a la media hora no hay nada

'formerly they burned straw, but the straw lasted a long time. But now, this long straw (fem.) you put *it* (*lo*) in and in a half-hour there's nothing left'

(2) Por ejemplo, hiervo el agua, *lo* tengo hervido en una botella, toos los días *lo* hiervo. Y luego na más es templar*lo*.

'For instance, I boil the water (fem.), I keep *it* (*lo*) boiled (non-fem.) in a bottle, every day I boil *it* (*lo*). And then I just have to warm *it* (*lo*).'

Figure VIII shows the frequency of *lo* in the singular inanimates of the Valladolid rural sample as a function of the object's discreteness and linguistic gender.

		Total N	N *lo*	%*lo*
Masculine	Discrete	28	6	21%
	Non-Discrete	56	50	91%
Feminine	Discrete	14	3	21%
	Non-Discrete	26	21	81%

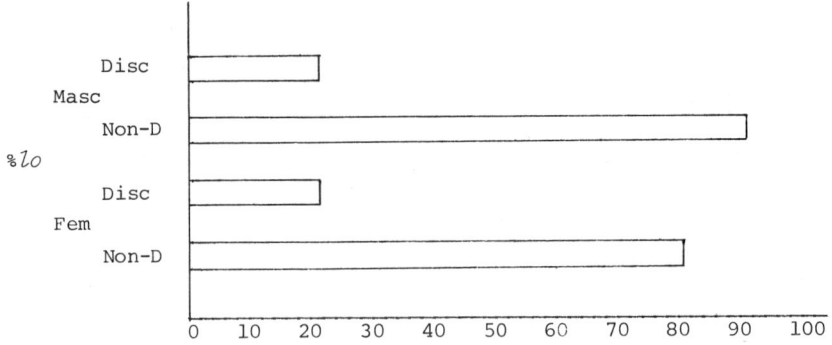

Frequency of *lo/s* in Valladolid rural sample as a function of object's discreteness and linguistic gender
FIGURE VIII

In Klein 1979 I argue for the synchronic analysis of this use of *lo* as an extended exploitation of 'vague reference', effected by the neuter (see Mariner 1973). Briefly, since the only neuter substantives in Spanish are just the so-called indefinite pronouns, in fact neuters never refer to a specific nominal antecedent, by its gender and number, as do masculines and feminines. Now, conventional neuters seem to utilize 'vague reference' in a negative sense, to avoid referring precisely; accordingly, they correlate with antecedents which either are non-substantive (examples (3) and (4)), semantically indefinite (5), or at least not present in the immediate context.

(3) *Lo* dicen pero no *lo* creo

'They say *so* but I don't believe *it*'

(4) Es inteligente pero no *lo* parece

'He/she is intelligent, but doesn't seem *so*'

(5) Todo nos *lo* quitaron

'Everything they took *it* away from us'
(='They took everything from us')

The 'referential' neuters of Valladolid, however, seem to exploit 'vague reference' directly, to suggest entities otherwise described contextually as (relatively) vague in themselves, insofar as their boundaries are not precise. Such entities, therefore, can be specifically identified in the immediate context, without contradiction.

It also happens to be plausible that this manner of using the neuter should occur just where we find it, in northwestern Spain. For it turns out that a similar use of neuters to refer to so-called 'masses' has been noted in neighboring dialects. They are described as the currently scattered and isolated remnants of Astur-Leonés—the Ibero-Romance dialect which prevailed throughout this area until Medieval times, when it was progressively supplanted by Castilian (e.g. Hall 1972).

More important for our present purpose, however, is the influence which this 'mass neuter' may be presumed to have exerted on the development of an exclusively neuter clitic, and of the referential system of clitic use. For the main referential difference between conventional and 'mass' neuters is that the latter have antecedents which are both nominal and present in the immediate context. Hence, with 'mass neuters' the referent of *lo* can readily be recognized, and it can be recognized as an entity of a certain kind (an imprecisely delimited entity), as opposed to entities not of this kind (precisely delimited entities). This reinforces the referential nature of the opposition--provided of course that entities 'of other kinds' are referred to by forms distinct from *lo*. The initial formal support for the opposition 'vague' vs. 'precise reference' in the clitics would then have been found with feminine objects--i.e. through the opposition of instances such as (6) vs. (7):

(6) La leche *lo* guardamos

   'The milk (fem.) we keep *it* (*lo*)' =
   'We keep the milk'

(7) La casa *la* guardamos

   'The house (fem.) we keep *it* (*la*)' =
   'We keep the house'

For in the case-distinguishing system only the feminine is formally distinct from the neuter.

Yet this opposition could not be entirely consolidated without extending it to the masculine as well, and here the only candidate for a form distinct from *lo* would be *le*. It is at this point, I believe, that the observed 'extensions of *le*' into traditionally accusative contexts would take on importance. Of course, the eventual reinterpretation of *le* as masculine would be facilitated to the extent that pre-existing 'extensions of *le*' were associated more strongly with masculines, and especially with a type of object which presumably correlates highly with 'discreteness'--namely animates.

As the traditional treatments observe, once *le* becomes the clitic form for masculines, the masculine is left with no distinction of case. It then is natural that case should be lost in the feminine as well. But I would stress that the extension of *le* to refer to all discrete masculine objects, in all circumstances, at the same time must have further reinforced the referential character of the emerging oppositions. Thus, as *le* comes to be interpreted as 'masculine', it ceases to be appropriate for reference to feminine objects, under any circumstances.

The main difference between this reconstruction and the traditional view is, then, that the present proposal gives relatively more importance to the *development of oppositions based on reference*, rather than simply to the loss of case. This shift in emphasis is based on the finding that caseless Castilian speech has a referential neuter. In this respect it resembles, both semantically and formally, dialects locally prior to Castilian. Thus, inasmuch as the spread of caseless uses appears to follow closely on the heels of the progressive expansion of Castilian, this view of the developments also suggests a precipitant for their inception, which is plausible on the face of it and empirically verifiable in any event.

5. It thus appears that the current caseless vernacular represented, at least, by our rural Valladolid sample (and quite possibly by the local middle class as well: see Figure III) can be regarded as manifesting the system in Figure V--*if* the neuter (*lo*) is analyzed as signalling 'vague reference', as opposed to 'precise reference' expressed by the masculine and feminine. But how, then, do we explain the special social status enjoyed by leísmo for masculine animates, as compared to other referential uses? This is one of many questions which requires further research. In approaching it, however, one should keep in mind a circumstance of potential sociolinguistic importance: namely, that the use of *le* for masculine animates constitutes the *intersection* of the more prominent and *referentially obvious pragmatic biases* of the case-distinguishing system, on the one hand, and of the referential system, on the other. Since case distinction favors *le* for animates (see Figure VI), while referential usage favors *le* for masculines (see Figure VII), this appears to be a natural area for adaptive compromise between the two.[4]

NOTES

*This research was supported in part by a grant from the American Philosophical Society.

[1] In case-distinguishing usage, reference to a logical second person favors the dative (García 1975: Chapter 7). With a female interviewer, therefore, it strongly prejudices the results in favor of a correlation of *le* with feminine.

[2] Under these conditions different dialects can only be distinguished (statistically) through geographic provenience. To my knowledge, only García and Otheguy (1977) have utilized geographic provenience as an independent variable with respect to this particular issue. Interestingly, their results coincide with mine insofar as the influence of the object's gender is much greater among informants from Madrid (a caseless area) than it is among those from case-distinguishing Latin America (1977:5). Since García and Otheguy's findings are based on responses of educated informants to the written language (questionnaires), they might be expected to be more homogeneous than mine, since normative prescription has long condemned the use of *le* for feminines in accusative context (Real Academia 1974:205).

[3] In fact if the results for rural Valladolid are stated as a function of natural gender (sex), the difference is categorical: 100% *le* for males, 100% *la* for females (Klein 1979).

[4] (Andersen 1974:22). The intriguing question here is whether (and to what extent) this adaptive principle ever informed an actual Spanish vernacular, or whether it was primarily an 'abduction' performed by prescriptive grammarians--and consequently incorporated into some formal styles, the usage of non-native speakers (including peninsular bilinguals), etc. The history (and geographic provenience) of normative recommendations on this question suggests that the latter may well have been the case (see Cuervo 1895:219f.).

REFERENCES

Andersen, Henning. 1974. "Towards a typology of change: bifurcating changes and binary relations". In *Historical linguistics II: theory and description in phonology*, 17-60. Ed. by John M. Anderson and Charles Jones. Amsterdam: North Holland.

Coseriu, Eugenio. 1967. *Sistema, norma, y habla. Teoría del lenguaje y lingüística general*. Madrid: Gredos. 2d Edition.

Cuervo, Rufino José. 1895. "Los casos enclíticos y proclíticos del pronombre de tercera persona en castellano". *Romania* 24.95-244.

García, Erica C. 1975. *The role of theory in linguistic analysis: the Spanish pronoun system*. Amsterdam: North Holland.

_____, and Ricardo Otheguy. 1977. "Explaining dialectal variation: a test for linguistic theory". Paper delivered at the Twelfth International Congress of Linguistics. Vienna, Austria.

Hall, R.A. Jr. 1972. "'Neuters', mass-nouns, and the ablative in Romance". In *Readings in Romance linguistics*. Ed. by James M. Anderson and Jo Ann Creore. The Hague: Mouton.

Klein, Flora. 1979. "Neuterality, or the semantics of gender in a dialect of Castilla". Paper delivered at the Ninth Linguistics Symposium on Romance Languages. Georgetown University, Washington, D.C.

_____. In press. "Factores sociales en algunas diferencias lingüísticas en Castilla la Vieja". *Papers: Revista de Sociología*.

Labov, William. 1972. *Sociolinguistic patterns*. Philadelphia: University of Pennsylvania Press.

Lapesa, Rafael. 1968. "Sobre los orígenes y evolución del leísmo, laísmo y loísmo". In *Festschrift Walter von Wartburg*, 523-51. Ed. by K. Baldinger. Tübingen.

Mariner, Sebastián. 1973. "Situación del neutro románico en la oposición genérica". *Revista española de lingüística* 3.23-38.

Real Academia Española. 1974. *Esbozo de una nueva gramática de la lengua española*. Madrid: Espasa-Calpe.

Weinreich, Uriel, William Labov, and Marvin I. Herzog. 1968. "Empirical Foundations for a Theory of Language Change". In *Directions for historical linguistics: a symposium*, 97-188. Ed. by W.P. Lehmann and Yakov Malkiel. Austin: University of Texas Press.

THE MARKING OF DEFINITENESS:
A DIACHRONIC PERSPECTIVE

MARTIN B. HARRIS
University of Salford

Within recent grammatical tradition, there has been a deep-rooted tendency to treat definite articles and personal pronouns as wholly distinct categories, generally discussed quite separately with respect to their morphology and syntax. Such separate treatment has been the norm despite the fact that in one of the languages on which traditional grammatical analysis has most often been based, namely Latin, there are particularly clear reasons for regarding definite articles and certain personal pronouns, those of the third person, as a single unitary category. This traditional view has not however remained unchallenged. Within the last decade or so in particular, a number of suggestions have been made to the effect that definite articles and some or all personal pronouns should be regarded as differing exponents of a single underlying category, either by deriving pronouns from articles (Postal 1966, Querido 1969) or articles from pronouns (Sommerstein 1972). I have myself advanced elsewhere (Harris, forthcoming) the view that certain problems involved in the adoption of either of these proposals can be avoided by suggesting that every noun phrase should be positively or negatively marked with respect to a certain feature, which we will, following convention, call 'definiteness'. The surface realization of this feature may take the form either of a definite article or of a personal or anaphoric pronoun depending on the remaining semantic features of the NP in question. It would not, I think, be unfair to claim that, despite the apparent lack of agreement on how to represent the position within a formal linguistic description, there would now be widespread acceptance among theoretical linguists of the view, supported by morphological and syntactic evidence from a variety of languages and language families, that definite articles and third person personal pronouns should be regarded as syntactically conditioned variants of one and the same underlying element or feature.

This approach within general linguistic theory, and
within synchronic descriptions of particular languages,
is, despite certain honorable exceptions (e.g., Bello and
Cuervo 1970), unfortunately not yet generally reflected
within pedagogical grammars or in diachronic analyses of
the morphology and syntax of the categories in question.
The present paper summarizes briefly a view developed more
fully elsewhere (Harris, forthcoming), that an integrated
view of the diachronic development of definite articles,
third person pronouns, anaphoric pronouns and certain demonstratives in Romance provides a coherent, economic and
intuitively satisfying analysis of a variety of developments previously seen as wholly or partly distinct. It
continues by examining the position in several other Indo-
European languages, before passing to the situation in
certain African languages and to the general conclusions
drawn from analyses of parallel grammatical categories in
such languages by Greenberg and others. The paper concludes by returning briefly to the evolution of Romance.
No further reference will be made to pronouns of the first
and second persons.[1] Let us turn, then, to the position
in Romance. The time-honored description of the situation
in Classical Latin (CL) asserts simply that the language
had no definite articles and no true third person pronouns.
In the latter case, however, the language could when necessary have recourse to a form borrowed from the paradigm of
a Latin demonstrative, namely is, ea, id, discussed
further below.

For our purposes, we shall need to reformulate this
description somewhat. Briefly, we may say that the semantic feature [+ definite] - which we take to have both par-
ticularizing and anaphoric functions — is frequently combined with other features, such as grammatical person,
demonstrativeness (proximity), etc., and that such bundles
of features, in Latin as elsewhere, were normally marked
overtly in surface structure. Definiteness alone, however,
was not explicitly marked in CL, either as a determiner
or as a pronoun, unless intolerable ambiguity would result.[2] In practice, we may say that such ambiguity is not
likely to occur in the determiner slot, where the first
reference to any non-unique noun may be taken, generally
speaking, to be [- definite] and all subsequent references
to be [+ definite], and where the potentially 'determined'
noun is necessarily itself present. Neither is ambiguity
likely to result in the case of third person subject pronouns, given that the fact that the subject is third person
is clearly marked by a verbal desinence (or by the absence
of such a desinence) and that a third person verb form is
not normally used unless the identity of the subject is
known.[3]

In the case of direct and indirect objects, however, given that a verb form in Latin was marked for person and number in respect of the associated subject NP but not in respect of any other NPs within the sentence as a whole, there was clearly a need, at times at least, for a form to indicate a third person direct or indirect object, just as the oblique cases of the non-third person personal pronouns were in fact normally present in surface structure. The fundamental position in CL, then, was that the normal exponent of definiteness was zero, regardless of whether this feature would have surfaced concomitantly with a noun, i.e. as a determiner, or as the sole exponent of an NP, i.e. as a third person or anaphoric pronoun. Where, however, intolerable ambiguity might ensue - as with certain oblique pronominal uses - or where a particular emphatic or adversative effect was sought, forms were available to be pressed into service, forms from the paradigm of the anaphoric is, ea, id. This particular paradigm had no future in Romance, however, and its functions, including those under discussion here, were in due course taken over by the remote demonstrative ille in the spoken language.

It is not part of our purpose here to review once again the fascinating expansion of the use of derivatives of ille in Romance. Suffice it to say that when definiteness came increasingly to be overtly marked in Vulgar Latin (VL) and Romance, it was ille that in every case came to serve as the exponent of this particular element of meaning, no distinction being made between 'articles' and 'pronouns'. In those languages, such as Spanish, where determiners and the corresponding pronouns continue in general to be only minimally differentiated, the position has remained largely unchanged to this day. In French, on the other hand, where determiners and pronouns have come, largely for phonological reasons, to be fairly systematically distinguished, the same fundamental unity is somewhat obscured at a superficial level by the wide degree of allomorphy within the definite article/third person pronoun/anaphoric pronoun paradigm. In sum, then, in Romance data entitle us to claim that definite articles, third person pronouns and anaphoric pronouns are best treated as a single category, at least to the same extent as demonstratives or possessives are so treated. In languages such as VL and Spanish, where determiners and pronouns sharing the same value are not in general formally distinguished, definite articles and third person pronouns may well form a coherent morphological paradigm. Where determiners and pronouns are differentiated, as in French, more complex allomorphic variation may be expected.

The Romance data also highlight two other interesting points. First, the evidence of CL reminds us that a language may well in general not mark overtly the category definiteness which is under discussion here, in either of its two principal guises; and secondly, when a language which had not previously marked definiteness overtly comes to do so, or when the original exponents of definiteness have become for whatever reason unsatisfactory and need to be replaced, then recourse will generally be made to the remote demonstrative for the new forms required (cf. Greenberg 1977:102). As Greenberg observes, there are 'numerous well documented cases' to support this point. The reason seems to be that, within a demonstrative system, binary, ternary or whatever, it is the remote member which, when occasion warrants it, serves also as the unmarked form. An unmarked demonstrative is one where the distinction of proximity which in general characterizes demonstratives is neutralized; and a demonstrative minus its proximity marker is really nothing other than an alternative exponent of definiteness in the sense in which that term is used here. Languages are sometimes said to have a special form serving as an unmarked demonstrative in this sense (cf. note 11 below). Such is the case with the CL demonstrative is, referred to earlier. Our analysis, however, suggests that this form is best described as the marker of definiteness in these relatively few instances where definiteness was overtly marked. Had is survived, it would surely have been the source of both definite articles and third person pronouns in Romance.

In VL, as we have seen, definiteness came generally to be marked overtly in surface structure. The obvious exponent, however, is, was probably for phonological reasons not destined to survive in Romance, so the language had to look elsewhere. The remote demonstrative ille, coming as we predict to serve also as the unmarked member within the demonstrative system (while of course retaining, at first, its marked value also) came ipso facto to be the obvious - though not, for a long while, the undisputed - candidate for the role of definite article or pronoun in Romance.

The position we have described in Romance is paralleled to a remarkable degree in the evolution of various branches of Germanic, including English. Broadly speaking, we may say that OE had a paradigm $s\bar{e}$, $s\bar{e}o$, ð æ t, which served as the more remote of a two-term demonstrative system, opposed to the forerunner of modern *this*.[4] It was, not unexpectedly, also pressed into service as an anaphoric pronoun, and in due course as a definite article; and, significantly, was 'not infrequent ... as a personal pronoun' (Baugh & Cable 1978:58). In other words, it was used both as a remote demonstrative and also as the marker of definiteness, both as a determiner and as a pronoun. The overlap in usage between remote demonstrative and anaphoric pronoun/definite article parallels exactly the usage of i l l e in VL.[5] OE differs from VL, however, in that although *sē*, *sēo*, *ðæt* could also be used as third person personal pronouns (like i l l e), the principal exponents of this category (*he*, etc.) came from a different source. This different source was none other than a second demonstrative stem. Furthermore, when the original feminine singular form was replaced - possibly by virtue of homonymic clash with the masculine - it seems virtually certain that it was from the feminine definite article/anaphoric pronoun *sēo* that modern *she* derives. Equally, the plural forms *they*, *them* etc. - borrowed, most unusually for personal pronouns, from outside the dialect in question - come from Scandinavian forms which had as one of their functions that of unmarked demonstrative in the source language. The position is much the same in the modern language. *That/those* have a variety of functions in addition to that of remote demonstrative. In many varieties of English, *that/those* are commonly used as anaphoric pronouns, alongside such forms as *the ones* ('those I bought' vs. 'the ones I bought'). In some dialects, *that* is used for standard *it*, either systematically or in certain specific cases (e.g., with weather verbs); and in many non-standard varieties of British English, the plural forms *they* and *them* serve both as demonstratives and as personal pronouns, in alternation with or to the exclusion of *those*, but leaving *these* unscathed ('back in they days', 'give me them books').[6] In English, then, throughout its history, the links between remote demonstratives, anaphoric pronouns, third person pronouns, and definite articles are at all times very close, a fact which superficial allmorphic variation should not be allowed to obscure. Basically, all the exponents the semantic category [+ definite] (the full paradigms of *the*, *he* and *that* when not opposed to *this*) are in complementary distribution in English, although there is a certain amount of free variation at times. The pattern, in fact, is strikingly similar in synchronic terms to that in French (*le*, *il*, *celui*), where the earlier formal unity of these now diverse paradigms is of course common knowledge.

So much then for English. If we turn now to the position in late common Slavonic, as attested in Old Bulgarian and Old Russian, we find once again a very similar picture. the earliest attested marker of definiteness was a postposed element -И, cognate with Latin i s, found in particular - though not exclusively (Vaillant 1948:113) - with adjectives, and identical in form with the oblique cases of the third person and anaphoric pronoun, the masculine singular accusative of which was also -И. It is interesting to observe that once again we find that the same form can be used to mark definiteness regardless of whether the surface realization is as a determiner or as a pronoun, and the parallels both with Latin i s and OE sē are immediately striking. Furthermore, already in late common Slavic, alternative forms were available to serve in tonic positions, -И being invariably enclitic, these forms being drawn from the (suppletive) paradigm of Tъ. This Tъ, differentiated both from Cь and from OHъ, the proximate and remote demonstratives respectively, was primarily used 'to refer to what has been mentioned or is known of, and to provide for the anaphoric -И its nominative and emphatic forms',[8] i.e., in effect as an unmarked demonstrative. What then more natural source for the new postposed definite article which emerged in Middle Russian, gradually to replace - И in this role as the latter came to lose its independent status, being reinterpreted as part of the declension system of adjectives (Vaillant 1942:12)? Once again we have one form serving as a third person/anaphoric pronoun and as a definite determiner. At that stage, the parallel with, for example, *el* (*él*) in contemporary Spanish is striking. It is interesting to note, however, that this new definite article has not survived in modern standard Russian, the language thus being in this respect parallel to CL, although postposed articles from the same source are found in certain north Russian dialects and elsewhere, e.g., in Bulgarian. Nevertheless, derivatives of Tъ do survive in the standard language, a reduplicated form reminiscent again of VL (e.g., i s t e i p s e, etc.) giving тот 'that' and a prefixed form этот reminiscent of e c c e i s t e giving 'this', to the virtual exclusion of derivatives of Cь.[9] (We pass over here the expressive or emphatic particle -то, derived from the same source, since its current distribution clearly places it outside the scope of the present discussion). The older remote demonstrative OHь does however survive to give the modern nominative forms of the third person pronouns. The links between remote demonstratives on the one hand, and anaphoric/third person pronouns and definite articles on the other, are thus clearly apparent at several stages in the development of late common Slavonic to contemporary Russian.

Let us now turn to the position in certain non Indo-European languages, basing our analysis on Joseph Greenberg's recent paper 'How does a language acquire gender markers?' (Greenberg 1978). We shall not be concerned here with the derivation of definite markers from remote demonstratives, simply noting once again that Greenberg sees demonstratives as 'the normal source of [the] definite article' (1978:75; on p. 77, Greenberg talks felicitously of demonstratives becoming 'bleached of deixis by anaphoric uses'). Nor are we surprised to observe, in the Gurma group of Voltaic, that the definite article and its equivalents 'match synchronically not the demonstratives of these languages, but the verb subject and object pronouns' (*loc cit*). Greenberg continues, 'This does not exclude the diachronic possibility that they come from earlier demonstratives which, on the one hand, developed into pronouns and on the other, into articles', and draws his readers' attention to French which, as we have seen, shows, like all the other Romance languages, precisely the shared origin of definite articles and personal pronouns alluded to by Greenberg.[10] Rather we shall examine briefly the sequence that he establishes whereby (remote) demonstratives become Stage I (definite) articles, Stage II (non-generic) articles and finally Stage III articles, noun markers often serving to subdivide nouns into gender classes.[11] Basically, a Stage I article corresponds very closely to that of English, serving to identify a particular item or items, howsoever these may be particularized in the mind of the language user. (Let us note at this stage that Italian (p. 66) and Rumanian (p. 76) are both mentioned by Greenberg as having an article of this type). Stage II articles include 'both definite determination and non-definite specific uses' but also 'generally include instances of non-referential use' (p. 62). A Stage II article 'is usually the lexical citation form' and 'heavily predominates in text' (p. 63). Finally, Stage III articles are found when 'the máss of common nouns now only have a single form ... the former article is a pure marker which no longer has any synchronic connection with specificity' (p. 69). Such articles serve to mark genders in those languages where they were originally subject to agreement in respect of this category; otherwise they are simply markers of nominality on all, or most, common nouns.

It is the aim of the concluding part of this paper to show that the Romance languages, in particular French, are continuing to develop in exactly the way which the sequence outlined by Greenberg would have us expect. Italian and Spanish are probably best viewed as having Stage I articles, beginning to develop towards Stage II - there are certainly non-anaphoric uses of the article in both these languages - but only tentatively in comparison with their more precocious sister. Here, in French, we seem to have a situation in which the language is nearer to Stage III than Stage II. Let us however examine the criteria for a Stage II article first. Essentially, the French definite article has all the functions of a Stage II article consistent with the presence in the language of a quite separate indefinite article, the very existence of which element prevents the emergence of a canonical Stage II article as discussed by Greenberg. Once this point is borne in mind, we soon observe that the definite article has gone well-beyond the original semantically motivated uses as the marker of anaphora. Indeed, as I have argued elsewhere (e.g., Harris 1978:74-6, Harris, forthcoming) the *le/la/les* paradigm (in addition to and, perhaps increasingly, instead of its semantically marked functions), is now the unmarked member of the set of determiners, chosen when no other determiner is semantically motivated. Essentially, then, the minimal NP in contemporary French is Det + N, *le/la/les* being chosen if no other determiner is appropriate. We note that the principal exceptions to this rule are almost exactly those discussed by Greenberg (1978:64-8); for example, with proper names, with other determiners, in certain locative and temporal constructions and in compounds based on the genitive construction.

All of this may lead one to the view that allowance having been made for the indefinite article in Romance we are dealing with a clear instance of a Stage II article. There is a further point, however, that the number and gender of a typical NP in contemporary French are now generally marked solely by the form of the preposed determiner. This is because the postposed elements which originally served to mark these categories in French and which still survive elsewhere in Romance have now been lost, whereas this is not so with respect to the preposed determiners which varied and still vary for number and gender in an absolutely orthodox way.

Greenberg mentions (1978:56) certain West Atlantic languages in which original class-marking prefixes came to be replicated by suffixed definite articles. In Wolof, for example, the original prefixes have been largely lost, being replaced by 'suffixed class markers which can in certain constructions still be separated from the noun and which function as a definite article', whereas in Fula the suffixes are now only class markers.[12] It would appear, bearing in mind that French is replacing suffixes by prefixes rather than vice-versa, that French is somewhere between Wolof and Fula on this particular developmental path. The *le/la/les* paradigm is certainly used to mark gender and number in place of an earlier system of suffixes. On the other hand, it is only one of a set of mutually exclusive determiners, all of which are marked for gender and number.[13] Equally, *le/la/les* is certainly not always used with the full value of a definite article, but it is still the most frequent marker of non-pronominal anaphora in the contemporary language. As Greenberg notes, 'the line between Stage II and Stage III is somewhat arbitrary' (p. 69). Clearly, however, a powerful piece of evidence that a Stage III situation is emerging would be the creation of a new (Stage I) definite article in a language. I submit once again the view I have propounded elsewhere (Harris 1977, forthcoming), that this is just the value of *ce, cette, ces* (without *-ci* or *-là*, of course!) in the contemporary language. Just as a language replaces a weakened demonstrative, so too a Stage II and even more a Stage III article will tend to be replaced, normally by 'weakening' another demonstrative, the whole chain of events consequently starting once more. Spanish and Italian, however, their gender + number marking systems being largely intact and their articles only gradually moving from Stage I to Stage II, have no need as yet for a new article. An exact parallel in a modern Aramaic dialect was drawn to my attention by Helmut Lüdtke and is mentioned by Greenberg (1978: 59).

Our conclusions, then, are simple. Remote demonstratives may develop into, or come to function additionally as, markers of anaphora, whether pronominally or adjectivally (i.e., as determiners). Allomorphic variation between third person pronouns, anaphoric pronouns, and definite articles will be language specific, tending to obscure a deeper and more fundamental unity.

Definite articles created from demonstratives in this way will tend to be used with a growing range of values, exactly as Greenberg suggests, with the possibility in the end of their semantic devaluation to the point where they become mere noun markers, with or without the additional function of marking number + gender. Finally, demonstratives and/or articles will tend to be renewed, the whole cycle being constantly repeated. It is our claim that virtually every stage in this process, illustrated from a variety of languages, can in fact be clearly seen in the history of one single Romance language as it has developed from Latin, namely French.

NOTES

[1] There are a number of reasons, both functional and formal, for wishing to treat first and second pronouns as a group distinct from the categories under examination here. These are fully surveyed in Bello and Cuervo (1970), chapters XIII and XIV, where the close links between articles and third person pronouns are discussed.

[2] It follows from this same point that, when definiteness was combined with another feature which either was clearly marked elsewhere in the structure (e.g., the grammatical person of the subject of the verb) or was recoverable from the context (e.g., certain possessives), such combinations of features were likewise not overtly marked in surface structure. As soon as another not otherwise recoverable element of meaning, such as emphasis, was added, then overt marking was of course necessary.

[3] Note that if the identity of the subject is not known, the use of a third person pronoun will not in fact solve the problem. If we contrast 'he came' with *venit*, for example, in neither case do we out of context know who came, although it is true that the English sentence, unlike the Latin one, tells us the sex of the subject.

[4] The systems in OE and modern German are very similar. The basic opposition in German is between *dieser* and *der* (near and remote), the latter form serving also as definite article, and as an anaphoric pronoun. The form serving exclusively as a remote demonstrative, *jener*, has a much more limited distribution.

[5] In addition, the separation between *that* (remote demonstrative) and *the* (definite article) in modern English is highly reminiscent of the divergence of *aquel* and *el* in Spanish. However, the parallel is not absolute, in that the anaphoric pronoun is *that* in English but *el* in Spanish. Such a divergence merely reinforces the view that in certain languages the functional distinction between pronoun and determiner is often sufficient to lead to formal variation (here English parallels French), whereas in other languages (e.g., Spanish) this is not in general the case.

[6] An accurate synchronic description of the position in dialects such as these (limiting ourselves to the plural forms only) would in our view be that the demonstrative system is as follows:

near	remote
these	they or them (depending on dialect)

The remote demonstrative serves also as the unmarked form (e.g., 'Them as came yesterday'). The personal pronouns are identical - allowing for possible allomorphy - with the remote demonstratives. If we ignore for a moment the fact that VL had a three-fold demonstrative system, and simply substitute i s t i for *these* and i l l i for *they/them*, the parallel is striking, only the non-pronominal definite usage (the definite article) being excluded from the scope of *they/them* in English but included within the scope of i l l i in VL.

⁷-И clearly still had considerable freedom of distribution in Old Slavonic, cf. Vaillant 1942: 7, 11.

⁸Translated from Vaillant 1948: §93 'Тъ ...... ordinairement réfère à ce qui a été dit ou qui est connu, et qui fournit a l'anaphorique И "lui" ..... son nominatif et ses formes insistantes'.

⁹The reduplication is very possibly due to the simple form having been used, for a while at least, as an 'article', as we have seen.

¹⁰Sapir (1965:72), talking of the Fogny dialect of Diola, tells us that the definite particularizer [kila] 'finds its most frequent use as a subject/object noun substitute. It also functions, however, as an adjective that stresses a definite noun. Here it acts as a demonstrative without indicating location ... [It] regularly and frequently substitutes for ..... the [personal] pronoun [ɔ]'. The parallelism of the distribution of [kila] with that of i l l e in VL is striking.

¹¹Greenberg (1978:61) notes that a definite article 'develops from a purely deictic element which has come to identify an element as previously mentioned in discourse. Such a use is often an additional function of an element which is also a pure deictic, but sometimes there is a particular demonstrative which has assumed this as its basic function. The source deictic is most often one which points to location near the third person rather than the first or second person, e.g., Latin i l l e '. Our earlier analysis suggests rather that CL had a particular demonstrative, i s , which was purely anaphoric in value, and that when this was lost in VL, it was then that the remote demonstrative i l l e which took over this function in addition to its earlier demonstrative value. (Eventually, of course, it was restricted to this newer function, replacement demonstratives being created in VL.) It should be noted also that 'a purely deictic element which has come to identify an element as previously mentioned in discourse' *is*, within the terminology adopted here, a personal/anaphoric pronoun and/or definite article, i.e., a marker of definiteness.

¹²The clitic personal pronouns in Fula remain however largely identical to these suffixes (Stennes 1967:101). In the case of disjunctive (independent) pronouns, essentially the same suffixes are added to the 'independent pronoun morpheme [kan-]' (*op cit*:106).

¹³French would, if our analysis is correct, thus diverge from the 'predominant tendency' in demonstrative constructions, which 'is to add the article to the noun redundantly ..... Sometimes, when the article is not on the noun, it is added to the demonstrative' (Greenberg 1978:65).

REFERENCES

Baugh, Albert C. and Thomas Cable. 1978. *A history of the English language*, London: Routledge, Kegan Paul. 3rd Ed.

Bello, Andrés and Rufino J. Cuervo. 1970. *Gramatica de la lengua castellana*, Buenos Aires: Editorial Sopena. 8th Ed.

Greenberg, Joseph H. 1977. "Niger-Congo noun class markers: prefixes, suffixes, both or neither". *Studies in African Linguistics*, Supplement 7. December 1977, 97-104.

_____. 1978. "How does a language acquire gender markers?" In *Universals of human language*. Ed. Joseph Greenberg, Charles Ferguson and Edith Moravcsik. Stanford University Press.

Harris, Martin B. 1977. "Demonstratives, articles, and third person pronouns in French: changes in progress". *Zeitschrift für Romanische Philologie* 93, 3/4: 249-61.

_____. 1978. *The evolution of French syntax: a comparative approach*. London: Longman.

_____. (forthcoming) "The marking of definiteness in Romance". In *Historical Morphology*. Ed. by Jaček Fisiak. The Hague: Mouton.

Postal, Paul M. 1966. "On so-called 'pronouns' in English". In *Monograph Series on Language & Linguistics*, 19. Ed. by F.P. Dinneen. Washington, D.C.: Georgetown University Press.

Querido, Antonio A.M. 1969. "Anaphore et deixis". *Canadian Journal of Linguistics* 14.91-107.

Sapir, J. David. 1965. *A grammar of Diola-Fogny*. West African Language Monographs, 3. Cambridge: Cambridge University Press.

Sommerstein, Alan. 1972. "On the so-called definite article in English". *Linguistic Inquiry* 3. 197-209.

Stennes, Leslie H. 1967. *A reference grammar of Adamawa Fulani*. African Language Monograph No. 8, African Studies Centre, Michigan State University.

Vaillant, André. 1942. "L'article en vieux slave". *Revue des études slaves* 20. 5-12.

_____. 1948. *Manuel du vieux slave, I: Grammaire*. Paris: Institut d' Etudes Slaves.

A FUNCTIONAL APPROACH TO
SYNTACTIC RECONSTRUCTION

MARIANNE MITHUN
State University of New York, Albany

0. *Introduction.* Often, related languages which are quite similar phonologically and morphologically exhibit a surprising degree of syntactic diversity. While the protophonology may be easily reconstructable, and easily justified in terms of established articulatory tendencies, the strange arrays of syntactic differences appear unrelatable as a set. Without shared retentions, syntactic reconstruction by the comparative method is impossible. A different approach to syntactic reconstruction is demonstrated here. The development of seemingly disparate syntactic differences among related languages is traced to a multidimensional drift arising from unstable conditions in the parent. The method is functional in orientation. It aims at uncovering and explaining syntactic change as a necessary response to reconstructable disequilibrium.

The Northern Iroquoian languages present the problem described above. Phonologically and morphologically they are quite similar, yet they exhibit myriad subtle but pervasive differences in their syntactic constructions, particularly in the areas of organization of discourse. Some have special markers for emphasis, some for definiteness, some for specificity, some for contrast. In cases where semantically analogous constructions exist in several languages, the markers are often not cognate from one language to the next, so the similarities cannot be attributed to a common inheritance from the parent language.

1. *General characteristics of the family.* The Iroquoian family consists of a Southern branch, represented solely by Cherokee, and a Northern branch. The first subbranch to diverge from Northern Iroquoian was Tuscarora-Nottoway. Sometime later, another subbranch, Huron-Wyandot, left the group. Most of the remaining group subsequently

became known as the Five Nations, now Mohawk, Oneida, Onondaga, Cayuga, and Seneca.

Certain grammatical characteristics of the protolanguage can be hypothesized on the basis of resemblances among the daughter languages. Words were of three morphlogical types: particles, nouns, and verbs. Both nouns and verbs could function syntactically as predicates, nominals, or adverbials, since they contained pronominal referents to their subjects and/or objects. The results could be very 'verby' sentences.

Tuscarora (1) Neyoʔnehswá:ʔnyeʔ   wè:rih   ʋ̀:wʋ̀:to:t
              it-cloud-around it-mean-s will-it-rain
              'Clouds mean rain'.

Wyandot (2) Hoteʔyɛʔa:ha: hatinda:reʔ
            they-siblings-are they-live
            'Several brothers and sisters were living together'.

Mohawk (3) Skáthne   tettyateraʔné:kv
           together they-2-each-other-beside

           akohsá:tvs   tetyateʔserehtahnhutérhaʔ
           one-straddles   it-links-what-drags

           wahshakoyaʔtaninú:tvʔ
           he-them-body-hitched
           'He hitched two horses side by side with a wagon harness'.

Because of the multiple syntactic functions of the word classes, the syntactic roles of constituents could not be inferred solely from their morphological categories. Some assistance was provided by the pronominal prefixes on the nouns and verbs, which indicate the person, gender, and number of their arguments, but this could only distinguish subjects from objects of different persons, numbers, or genders. Word order might be thought to offer a clue, but in Northern Iroquoian, constituents are ordered according to discourse function. New information tends to appear sentence initially. Without morphological clues, unambiguous case marking, or syntactically based word order, it could be difficult to decipher who did what to whom. The situation is further complicated by the possibility of constituents which are themselves clauses. No subordinating markers can be reconstructed for the parent language. In fact, it is difficult to determine whether subordination was distinct from simple concatenation of independent clauses. All of the modern languages contain constructions which are translated into English complex sentences, but actually consist of strings of clauses.

Tuscarora	(4)	*Wahratshṳ̀:nṍ:tiʔ*	*wáhraʔw*
		he-was-glad	he-came
		'He was glad that he had come'.	
Wyandot	(5)	*Kari:wá:yṍt*	*aʔki:yṹʔ*
		it-is-certain	would-I-you-two-kill
		'I am certain to kill both of you'.	
Mohawk	(6)	*I:kehreʔ* *tho*	*yá:keʔ*
		I-it-want there	there-would-I-go
		'I want to go'.	
Tuscarora	(7)	*Waʔktshá:riʔ* *hè:nı́:kv:*	*yerohkhwéhsthaʔ*
		I-it-opened that	one-uses-it-for-hay
		tshvʔ *yvkwaʔnvhsṹ:tiʔ*	
		just we-house-built	
		'I opened up the barn we had just built'.	
Wyandot	(8)	*Na:ruré̜:haʔ* *yarŏtatḗtraʔ*	*skwaʔrá:haré̜t*
		now-he-it-found it-wood-lies	it-hollow-is
		'Then he found a hollow log'.	
Mohawk	(9)	*Eʔ* *ká:yvʔ* *onṍ:yaʔ*	*yohoʔthı́:yeʔ*
		there it-lies it-stone	it-sharp-edged-is
		'There lies a stone with a sharp edge'.	

Is there a semantic feature inherent in subordination which cannot be expressed otherwise? Anthing stated in a complex sentence can be stated in a series of simple sentences with appropriate coreference relations. However, distinctions of information organization, emphasis and backgrounding, and presupposition simply cannot be presented as elegantly in a series of concatenated simple sentences as in complex ones. As seen above, some distinctions of the relative importance of lexical items to discourse were expressed by focus fronting in Northern Iroquoian. The relative importance of clauses and the identification of the case roles of constituents could be difficult to express and interpret, however. This basically unstable condition, that of perceptual difficulty in decoding, set the stage for divergent drifts in the daughter languages.

2. *Tuscarora*. Apart from a coordinating conjunction, Tuscarora has one primarily syntactic marker. It is the particle *haʔ*, which emphasizes the constituent following it. It carries no distinction of definiteness or specificity, and precedes generics, proper or common nouns, specific or nonspecific, definite or indefinite nominals, although no definiteness distinction is made in Tuscarora. The particle may precede any morphological type of constituent, particle, noun, or verb, but the constituent is

always one which is functioning syntactically as an argument. It never precedes the main predicate of a sentence.

Since Tuscarora constituent order is largely a function of focus relations, this additional emphatic device might seem marginally useful. The particle *ha?* is extremely frequent in Tuscarora discourse, however, occurring many times in almost any long sentence. The reason is clear. The fact that the particle precedes only nominals solves a major decoding problem for the language. Constituents preceded by *ha?* are immediately identified as arguments rather than predicates. The longer and more confusing the sentence, the more likely the emphatic marker.

The distribution of the emphatic, before syntactic nominals only, permits the overt marking of another type of construction: subordination. Sentential arguments can be identified as nominals, not independent clauses, by the presence of *ha?*. In sentences like (4), the particle may optionally precede the second clause, but the more complex a sentence is, the more likely the particle is to appear.

The acquisition of a subordination marker also permitted the elaboration of adverbial arguments. Without subordination, the cooccurrence of two events at one time or in one place must be established by two separate assertions, each specifying the time or place of that event, plus appropriate coreference relations between them. When subordination can be overtly marked, however, the adverbial can be backgrounded.

(11) *O:nv   yoθatho?ṽho:t   ha?   ò:nv nakara?thehá:?nyv?*
     then   it-night-divides   then so-she-climbing-was
     'It was midnight when she came up the stairs'.

(12) *Neyo?nvtá:kv   ha?   kṽ?   yé?rv?   nekarv?no?náhrhv*
     it-door-open   right   she-sits   it-logs-has
     'The door was open to the log house she was in'.

The overt marking of nonpredicates permitted still another type of importance ranking of information: relativization. Tuscarora constructions translated with English relative clauses often consist of simple strings of clauses with no apparent connection beyond the possible coreference of their arguments, as in (7). The overt subordination of one of the clauses, however, permits backgrounding of that information.

(13) *Ṽ:tsi ha?   royatká:yv: wahroyé:nv:?*
     one   he-slow-was   it-him-caught
     'It caught the one that was slow'.

No formal distinction between restrictive and non-restrictive relatives is obligatory in Tuscarora, but two devices have developed to specify something akin to restrictiveness. The first involves the overt statement that the portion of the group or general set referred to possesses a certain characteristic, as in (14).

(14) Thwé:ʔn waʔkrî:yoʔ haʔ tî:waʔθ   katá:kreʔ
     all   I-them-killed   so-it-amounts they-dwell
     'I killed all those alive in the universe'.

The second device exploits a specific morpheme -vt- which adds the meaning 'that particular...'. When it is suffixed to nominals which are followed by overtly subordinate relatives, the result is restrictive.

(15) Káhneʔ   rayehsú́:teh haʔ Tóm   rayá:θv   wahshé:kvʔʔ
     who   he-person-spec   Tom   he-is-called   you-him-saw
     'Which Tom did you see?'

     Haʔ   rayehsú́:teh   otá:ʔnakv: throʔnè:nvʔ
           he-person-spec   it-town-in   there-he-lives
     'The one who lives in town'.

The possibility of marking off clauses as subordinate permits still another distinction of communicative value: that accomplished by clefting. One constituent is focussed by fronting. The rest of the sentence is backgrounded by subordination to presupposition.

(16) Tá:ko:θ   haʔ wahú́:kri:k
     cat   it-bit-me
     'It was a cat that bit me'. (What bit me was a cat.)

The emphatic function of the particle haʔ permitted the development of syntactic devices in another direction. When it is combined with the focus-fronting mechanism, multivalue contrasts can be expressed, as in (17). One pair of constituents is contrasted initially, the other following haʔ.

(17) Wí:rv:n   wahrá:kvʔ haʔ tsí:r tisnvʔ Tsyán wahrá:kvʔ
     William   he-it-saw   dog   and   John   he-it-saw

     haʔ tá:ko:θ
          cat
     'William saw a dog, but John saw a cat'.

A second combination of these two emphatic devices is used to indicate that the information content of a constituent is especially high, because it is unexpected. A shift in topic can be marked by simultaneous focus-fronting plus the haʔ emphatic, as in (18).

(18) <u>Ha?</u>   na?tahskwá:wi: thweθkǔ?rv? hé?thoh
     he-him-animal-gave so-it-settled there
   ronǔ:θkwarv?
   him-toad
   'As for the man he had given the animal to, he got a wart'.

Tuscarora has, then, developed a fairly intricate set of mechanisms for ranking the communicative value of the elements of discourse, all of which are expressed with the particle ha?. The change can be easily understood in terms of a response to a decoding difficulty: that of identifying the case roles of constituents. The possibility of distinguishing arguments from predicates led to the marking of subordination, permitting sentential complements, relative clauses, sentential adverbials, and clefting. At the same time, the original emphatic function of the particle, when combined with the focus fronting in the language, permitted the expression of multivalue contrasts and shifts in topic.

3. *Wyandot*. Wyandot contains a different set of syntactic particles and devices for distinguishing the relative communicative importance of constituents. The problem of identifying the syntactic roles of constituents was solved with the acquisition of a definite marker (n)de, probably derived from a deictic pronoun. This optional definite particle, which may precede any type of nominal constituent, indicates that the referent of the nominal is identifiable to the hearer. Since the definite marker never precedes the main predicates, it has acquired the secondary function of identifying arguments.

(19) Ahu:jû?   <u>dŏ</u>:re:dih
     it-him-killed   the-one-starves
     'He died of starvation'.

Wyandot developed two mechanisms for identifying sentential arguments. For one, the particle, which had come to mark the argument status of verbs, was exploited to signal the nonpredicate status of clauses.

(20) Ndi? ada?ura:?di? <u>de</u>   ri:ju?   du:gu:kwa?
     the-I I-am-able   the I-it-kill   the-smallpox
     'I can kill the smallpox'.

The other complementizer is the demonstrative (n)dae? 'that', a not unusual development in languages in general. A clause containing the demonstrative is followed by a clause identifying its referent.

(21) Ata:wɑ́tõʔ   *daeʔ*   daõhsanõkerataʔ
    it-impossible that the-one-body-retains-what-used-to-
                                                        be
    'It is not possible to retain the old ways'.

As in Tuscarora, the particle which had come to signal
the argument status of constituents came to mark the subordination of adverbials.

(22) *Danoneré:dara:hahs*   kari:wɑ́yõht ne ndi awajé:da:õʔ
    the-someone-me-trap-s it-certain now the-I it-me-grabs
    'If I get into a trap, it always gets hold of me'.

The definite marker signals the dependence of the following clause.

Relativization is not necessarily overtly marked in
Wyandot. Modification is often accomplished simply by a
series of juxtaposed clauses, as in (8). As in Tuscarora,
the particle which distinguished arguments from predicates
can be used for marking the dependence of relatives.

(23) Nẽ   yẽhãõʔ   de   yawí:nõ
    now she-said the   she-pretty

    dehiwé:y   *nahõmẽnẽhtiʔ*...
    the-he-her-spouse the-he-person-young
    'Then the young woman spoke to the young man, her
    husband...'

Restrictiveness is not obligatorily expressed, but
two devices for marking restrictiveness do exist in the
language. One involves the overt assertion of the restriction, as in Tuscarora. The head of the relative clause is
a quantifier.

(24) Tahomãtihcẽʔ   tiwɑ́ʔ
    there-they-them-killed   so-it-amounts

    utijaʔtõtaʔndiʔ
    their-bodies-are-fastened
    'Then they slaughtered those who had gotten caught'.

The other involves a combination of the definite marker
nde and the demonstrative. The definite marks the subordination of the relative clause and the demonstrative
contributes specificity.

(25) Nẽ   unẽʔu:tih   *daeʔ*   *dekwayuwɑ́:nẽh*
    now   she-her-combs that   the-she-is-large
    'Then she combed the hair of the eldest'.

Once restrictiveness could be expressed along with
focus, clefting became possible. The clause which ex-

presses the presupposed property is backgrounded by the
subordinating particle. The nominal identifying the referent is focussed by fronting. The demonstrative, which
contributes restrictiveness, supplies the feature of uniqueness.

(26) *Ndaeʔ ndeʔ tawakó:taʔ ahti:cróga*
    that the it-began they-it-made
    'These are the ones who made the first beginning'.

Although the Wyandot definite marker resembles the
Tuscarora emphatic in marking nominalization and subordination, it is nearly opposite in its primary meaning.
The definite indicates that what follows is identifiable,
or old. The emphatic signals the importance of what follows. For this reason, its total set of functions is not
congruent with those of the Tuscarora emphatic. It cannot
indicate contrast or shift of topic. For multivalue contrast, a temporal deictic was exploited.

(27) *I:cɛ́hskɛ̃ʔnã̆ʔ ndeʔsa tiju nɛ̃̆ʔ diʔ trŏ́di*
    you-small the-you this now the-I much

    nɛ̃ ndi yeyuwá:nɛ̃
    now the-I I-large
    'You are very small, while I am very large'.

This temporal deictic was also extended to a topic shifter.

(28) *Nɛ̃ daeʔ nŏmáʔdeʔ da:nŏ:nɛ̃ʔ*
    now that the-next the-bear
    'Now the next one was the bear'.

A remedy for the same weakness in the system can be
seen to have provided the basis for the development of devices for ranking constituents according to their communicative value in discourse, as in Tuscarora. The marking
of nominalization led to the marking of subordination in
complements, relatives, and cleft constructions. The
choice of a definite marker instead of an emphatic for
this purpose affected the subsequent development of these
devices, however. Different markers had to be adopted for
the needs still to be filled, the demonstrative for restrictiveness, and the temporal deictic for contrast.

    4. *Mohawk*. Information ranking devices in Mohawk
follow still different patterns. Cognate to the Wyandot
definite particle is the Mohawk *ne*. It occurs optionally
before any type of nominal constituent, including proper
names and possessed nominals. The particle indicates that
the referent of the following nominal is identifiable. As
in Wyandot and Tuscarora, the development of a prenominal

particle provided a solution to the problem of distinguishing arguments from predicates.

Instead of indicating subordination by marking clauses as arguments, however, Mohawk acquired a subordinating marker from a different source. A particle *tsi*, generally translatable as 'as', was exploited to indicate the co-reference relations between clauses in complex constructions. The particle now signals the dependence of the clause which follows it.

As in the parent language, relativization can be accomplished by simple juxtaposition. Restrictiveness is not necessarily distinguished. Two devices have arisen, however, to mark restrictive relatives. For one, the restrictiveness is overtly asserted with a quantifier.

(29) Akwé:ku   ronvhé:yu   <u>tsi</u>   <u>niká:yv</u>   ne
     all   they-died-have   as   so-they-lie   the

   ruwá:kv
   they-him-seen-have
   'All who have seen him are dead'.

The other is based on a specific marker, *nè:ne*.

(30) <u>Nè:ne</u> ǔska <u>nè:ne</u>   yáh   tha?tehó:ka   <u>nè:ne</u>
     that   one   that   not   is-he-fast   that

   katsi?nuwáksv   wahoyé:na?
   it-creature-evil   it-him-caught
   'The monster caught the one that was slow'.

In addition to these particles, Mohawk also contains a contrastive demonstrative *né:?e*. It shows that an argument contrasts with expectation. It was this feature of contrast which was exploited for clefting. The constituent which identifies the possessor of the property is fronted for focus, as in Tuscarora and Wyandot. Its uniqueness, or contrast with all other possible referents, is expressed by the contrastive particle.

(31) Shawátis   <u>né:?e</u>   wahahwistandhsko?
     John   that   he-money-stole
     'John is the one who stole the money'.

When the contrastive particle is combined with the focus fronting device, multivalue comparisons are possible.

(32) Otsi?tvhokú:ha   <u>né:?e</u>   tehatí:tvs   tánu?
     birds   that   they-fly   and

   kǔtsu <u>né:?e</u>   rutá:wvs
   fish   that   they-swim
   'Now birds fly, while fish, on the other hand, swim'.

Now while Tuscarora used the contrastive marker combined with focus fronting to indicate topic shift, and Wyandot simply exploited the temporal for this purpose, Mohawk used a new topic shifter: *na:ʔa* (despite its similarity to *ne:ʔe* no cognate relationship is yet establable):

(33) ...tánuʔ   <u>naʔ</u>   ne   wahshakóryoʔ   ne   roʔnistóha
         and   that the   he-her-killed the his-mother
'...and as for him, he killed his mother'.

5. *Conclusion*. All of the languages developed devices for the overt marking of subordination, but the devices are not based on cognate forms. There is not even correspondence among the sets of functions performed by each syntactic marker from one language to the next. Tuscarora has developed overt marking of all types of subordination as well as emphasis and contrast, by means of a single particle *haʔ*. Wyandot has developed sets of constructions based on three particles: one marks definiteness, complementation, and sentential adverbials, another complementation, and in concert with the definite, clefting, while a third indicates shift in topic. Mohawk has a still larger repertoire of such primarily syntactic particles, whose functions are congruent neither to those in Tuscarora nor to those in Wyandot. One marks definiteness and nominalization of words, another subordination of complements and adverbials, a third restrictiveness of relatives, a fourth contrast and clefting, and a fifth, shift in topic. Forms and functions are neither cognate nor congruent.

These divergent states can be understood in terms of therapeutic developments set in motion by an unstable situation in the parent: the indecipherability of constituent roles. Each language developed a cure from material already present in the language. The features of a construction they abstracted when choosing a marker for it varied, prompting different choices of markers. The secondary features of the markers chosen affected the subsequent syntactic development of each language.

IMPLICATIONS OF PRE-COMPLEMENTIZERS WITH HITTITE ŠAK-/ŠEK- 'KNOW'

CAROL F. JUSTUS
University of California, Berkeley

0. *Introduction.* Between the goal of establishing a homogeneous image of human language and the heterogeneous fact of actual data lies a chasm.* In the search for universals of grammar and typological variants of these universals, language data of particular synchronic states offer variation in form that appears to refute claims of regularity and unity. Phonological approaches to variation are well known (e.g. Weinreich, Labov and Herzog 1968; Andersen 1973). Comparable studies in syntax, on the other hand, are few (Wolfram 1976, for example). Questions concerning generalizations about word order patterns as valid universal and typological statements about language have been raised (Watkins 1976; Campbell and Mithun 1978, for example). Lack in understanding the systematic nature of variation in syntax may well lie at the basis of attacks on word order typology as a model for the study of syntactic change. The purpose here is to suggest how variation among complementizer mechanisms associated with sentential objects of Hittite šak-/šek- 'know' is consistent within a homogeneous view of language.

Generative-transformational syntax has proposed systematic universal categories of syntax. To discuss change in the surface as well as deep structure of languages, we need, in addition to universal categories, an understanding of the variants subject to change and their interrelationships. With Greenberg's (1966) revolutionary study of implicational universals and Lehmann's application of these as a measure of the extreme ends of a continuum from languages which are verb final (OV) in structure to languages which are verb initial (VO), syntactic studies in fact have a framework for measuring orderly variation in the system. In this context I turn to a single language structure in search of further clarification of universals and their typological variants. Assumed is that synchronic variation

is the raw data for historical linguists, and that the
variants, rather than the universals, are of primary concern in plotting language change. The universal system
furnishes the skeletal structure to be enlivened by an understanding of how particular language variants relate to
it and to each other.

1. *The problem.* The early IE language Hittite, an OV language with postpositions and prenominal modifiers, but with
sentence initial or preverbal qualifiers, has verb complement constructions which both precede and follow the verb.
Analysis of such constructions with Hittite 'know' shows
formal irregularities in clausal structure to be twofold:
irregularities in order, and irregularities in type of
clausal cohesion. Cohesion of clauses dependent on *šak-/
šek-* varies thus:

(a) semantically, depending on case relation between clause
and verb;

(b) depending on whether the entire clause as abstract idea
functions as object (NP --> S) or whether a single noun
with modification is object (NP --> NP + S); and

(c) whether the object is conceived as animate or inanimate.

In English similar data might fall into a paradigm based on
complementizer mechanism:

(1a) I know the name of the king.

(1b) I know *that* the king had a personal god.

(1c) I know *what* the king saw in his dream.

(1d) I know *where/when* he lost his speech.

Here clauses with *that*, *what*, and *where/when* introduce constituents comparable in function to the object in (1a), *the
name of the king*. Correspondingly, Hittite *šag/k-* 'know'
has *kuit* 'relative marker',[1] *kuwapi* 'where/when', while
that counterparts are often, as shown in (2a-d) below, simply asyndetically preposed to the main clause:

(2a) apun=   wa memian   UL šekkueni[2]
     that-acc-ptc matter-acc not know-1p

     'We are not acquainted with that matter'.
                           (XXII 70 Vs 37-8 (Th. 49))

(2b) kinun=wa= z nuwa sal.meš SU.GI [(punuškiz)]zi UL
     now- ptc-ptc yet old-women   asks-3s   not

šaggaḫḫi
know-1s

'I do not know that she is consulting the old women'.
(I 16 III 68f.(Th. 52))

(2c) nu kaš   *kuit* memai   n= *at* zik   šakti
ptc this-one-nom what speak-3s ptc-it you-nom know-2s
'You (will) know what this one says'.
(XXXV 148 Rs III 12 (Th. 70))

(2d) *kuwapi*=wa paiši ammuk=ma=wa= tta le   šaggaḫḫi
where -ptc go-2s I-   ptc-ptc-you let-not know-1s
'I do not want to know where you are going'.
(KBo V 9 II 44f. (Th. 77))

Verb complement clauses such as (2b) and its variants will concern us here.

    Just as English uses variant complementizer mechanisms:

(3a) I know the king lost his speech.
(3b) I know *that* the king lost his speech.
(3c) I know *it, that* the king lost his speech.
(3d) I know. The king lost his speech.
(3e) *That* the king lost his speech, I know.

so does Hittite:

(4a) Compare here (2b), above, with (3a): asyndetic juxtaposing.
(4b) [*I*]*ŠTU* É.GAL^{LIM}=ya= war=at=kan *kuit* para udaš
from palace-   ptc-ptc-it-ptc that prev. brought-3s
nu= war=aš=mu=   kan *UL* ŠÀta
ptc-ptc-it-to-me-ptc not heart-3s-past
'I am not aware that anything was brought out of the palace'.   (XIII 33 II 10-2 (Th. 75))

(4c) *memiyan*=   ma • *kuin*=   pat daiškit   n= *an UL*
matter-acc-ptc what-acc-ptc set-forth-3s ptc-it not
šaqqaḫḫi
know-1s
'But I do not know what matter he was advocating'.
(XXIII 91,16 (Th. 64))

(4d) KUR ^{uru}Alašiya=wa ammel nu= war=at QA[T]AMMA šak
     land   Alašiya-ptc of-me ptc-ptc-it the-same know-2s-imper.

'Likewise recognize (that) the land of Alašiya is mine'.
                                        (XIV 1 Rs 88 (Th. 90))

(4e) apaš=   wa ammel nu= war=an šak
     that-one-nom-ptc of-me ptc-ptc-him know-2s-imper.

'Recognize that one, that he is mine (on my side)'.
                                        (VIII 81 Vs II 8 (Th. 98))

(4f) nu šekkir ^{d}UTU^{ŠI}= wa INA KUR ^{uru}Taggašta uizzi
     ptc knew-3p Sun-King-ptc into land Taggašta comes-3s

'They knew (that) the Sun was coming into the land of Taggašta'.
                                        (KBo V 8 I 6 (Th. 59))

Whereas (3e) with preposed *that* clause is highly marked in English, Hittite (4f) with postposing is a stylistic variant of (4a). Comparable postposed variants of (4b) are usual with *kuit* 'that' (Friedrich 1960:163), but preposed complements (4b-e) represent the Hittite norm. These usages are consistent with word order differences (such as basic SVO versus SOV order, prepositions instead of postpositions) among constituent orders harmonic with the ends of the continuum VO and OV, and inconsistencies in between (Lehmann 1978:15-23; Justus 1978:169-222).

The point of variation lies with (3c) versus (4d-e); where Hittite has -*at* (neuter-inanimate) and -*an* (common gender), English has only neuter *it*. To parallel Hittite usage one would expect English constructions like 'I know him/her, (that) he/she has lost his/her speech'. Otherwise, both languages use asyndeton as in (3a), (4a), and (4f). Such constructions in English have been analyzed as 'that' deletion, but in IE tradition as parataxis, and variously interpreted as incomplete subordination (Justus, to appear). In both languages, the complementizer proper (*that/kuit*) is a form related to the relative or demonstrative, but itself a frozen form without anaphoric or cataphoric function, and without productive distinctions for case, number or gender. Compare (2c) above: 'what...it' (*kuit...at*: neuter), and (4c) 'what matter...it' (*memiyan kuin...an*: common gender), where *kuit* and *kuin* have cataphoric function, -*at* and -*an*, with main clause positions as object of 'know', anaphoric reference to the preposed noun constituent. These phoric usages contrast with complementizer *kuit* usage (4b).

While sentences like (3c) are restricted in English, sentences like (4d) are productive in Hittite. Example (4e), on the other hand, represents a rare variant of the sort one might consider a scribal error in contexts such as (5) below. Important here are -at and -an (4d-e) and their relation to relative clauses (4c). Suffice it then to notice the range of cohesive strategy between main clause and object clause: (a) asyndetic juxtaposition; (b) complementizer (kuit/that); (c) specialized use of anaphora which I call pre-complementizer (-at, -an/it).

2. *The Hittite system.* I will now sketch for Hittite the productive processes of anaphora, quite aside from any role of the pronoun in complementation. Next, I will show that certain philological problems have an explanation, once we understand that neither neuter -at nor common gender -an were originally designed as part of a system of noun class deixis that included (endophoric) reference to grammatical constituents, but were rather part of a semantically based system that differentiated animate and inanimate nouns. Finally I conclude that third person anaphora, as nonuniversal, is a likely variant in the process of syntactic change, and that its development in Hittite is harmonic with its inconsistency in OV patterning.

In Hittite, common gender nouns and pronominals generally refer to animate nouns, neuter genders to inanimates. Consistent with this system, ḫaššuš 'king' is referenced by common gender -an, uddar/uttar 'word, matter' by neuter -at. But certain asymmetries exist. For example, keššar 'hand' (neuter) occurs beside kešseraš (common gender). More importantly, beside uttar 'word' is memiaš 'word, speech' (common gender). The Hittites may well have conceived of a universe in which an inanimate result of speaking (uttar) contrasted with an animate capacity for speech (memiaš). Compare Muršiliš' speech (memian) loss. In any case, the language codes a neuter-abstract uttar beside a common-abstract memiaš. Otherwise Hittite abstract nouns belong to the old IE heteroclitic r/n stem class. As such they form a phonologically defined subclass of the neuter. Compare Hittite watar, wetenaš 'water'; Greek hudōr, hudatos 'water'; Latin iter, itineris 'journey'. As a separate class, then, abstract nouns did not exist, but formed a derivational subclass. No corresponding pronominal form distinguished them from neuter inanimates where they belonged by virtue of the r/n suffix.

However, grammatical constituents (whole clausal ideas) lacked both r/n suffix and any semantic relation to animate or inanimate classes. Yet pre-complementizer -at

often refers, as well, to the entire *that*-clause. Compare
(4d) as opposed to (4c) and (4e). In (4d) -*at* refers to
the fact that Alašiya is on the king's side, the entire
clause. In (4c) -*an* resumes the relative nouṅ *memiyan*
(*kuin*), while (4e) is ambiguous: 'Recognize that one (who)
is on my side' or 'Recognize (that) that one is on my
side'. Compare now the philologically difficult -*an* varying with -*at*:

(5) kaša alwanzineš   antuḫšiš ... man=an [SAL= m]a

    see   bewitched-nom man-nom   if-him woman-ptc

    iyan   ḫarzi   n= *an*   zik   ᵈUTUuš   šakti

    treated has-3s ptc-him you-nom Sungod-nom you-know

    (Variant for n= *an*   : n=   *at*)

                  ptc-him   ptc-it

    'See! Here is a bewitched man.... If a woman, on the
      other hand, has treated him, you, O Sungod, will know
      (notice) him'.   (KBo XII 126 I 12f. (Th. 105))

A bewitched man is treated either by a man (omitted...) or
a woman for the bewitchment. Here -*an* ambiguously refers
to the entire clause, or simply to the bewitched man. The
variant text, however, replaces -*an* with neuter -*at*. Compare now a clear use of -*at* with reference to an entire
clause:

(6a) kaša= wa   *ANA* ᵈWi[š]uriyanti ḫuwappi   SALni

    look!-ptc to   goddess-W.-d/l evil-d/l woman-d/l

    SISKUR.SISKUR peškimi nu= za   zik ᵈUTUuš   kutruwaš

    offerings   give-1s ptc-ptc you Sungod-nom witness-

       eš   uizzi=   *at* ša [nnai ku]watqa n= *at*

    nom be-imp-2s happen-3s-it hides-3s   somehow ptc-it

    EGIRan   zik nepi[šaš] ᵈUTUuš   šak

    afterward you of-heaven Sungod-nom know-2s-imper.

    'Look! You be witness, O Sungod, that I give offerings
      to Wišuriyanta, the evil woman. Should she somehow
      hide it, you, O Sungod of heaven, remember it'.
                  (KBo XV 25 Vs 34-7 (Th. 96))

Here -*at* twice refers to the fact of the giving of the of-
ferings: *uizzi*=*at*; n=*at*.

    Usages such as (6b) seem to foreshadow English 'fact
(that)':

(6b) *UL*= wa šakti   Upelluri *memiyan*= a= wa= ta *UL*
      not-ptc you-know U.-voc   word-acc-ptc-ptc-you not
      kuiški udaš   *UL*= war=*an* šakti ^{d}Kumarbiš=wa...
      someone brought not-ptc-it you-know K.-nom- ptc
      D^{LIM}in $D^{meš}$aš IGIanda šamnait
      god-acc gods-d/l against created-3s

> 'Don't you know, Upelluri? Has no one brought you word? Don't you know that Kumarbi created a god (to rise up) against the gods?'
> (XXXIII 101 30ff. (Th. 102-103))

Here *memiyan* is ambiguously concrete 'fact' or abstract 'that' referring to Kumarbi's creation of the new god. The extension of both animate 'speech' and inanimate 'word' to abstract 'matter' allows grammatically separate noun classes to function syntactically in the same way. Neuter -*at* or common -*an* thus both have a grammatical basis as pre-complementizers: -*at* refers to inanimate-abstract *uttar*, while -*an* refers to animate-abstract *memiaš*, similar to English 'it, that' or 'fact that'. Grammatical constituents themselves, apart from a functional equivalence to *uttar* and *memiaš*, have no semantic basis for neuter or common gender agreement. I suggest that the hesitation between -*at* and -*an* referring to a grammatical constituent results from the rise of a new semantic noun class which can no longer be derivationally derived by means of the heteroclitic suffix. The semantic extensions of *uttar* and *memiaš* result from the pressure of this new class to reshape the basis for deictic reference. An earlier animate-inanimate contrast thus is changing to accommodate, in addition, a noun class based on the feature abstract.

As often in language, relative and verb complement constructions share structural ambiguities. Compare the object of *tarueni* 'we tell' in (7):

(7) kuiš   šagaiš   kišari ta LUGALi SAL.LUGAL=ya
     what=nom omen-nom occurs ptc king-to queen-   and
     tarueni
     we-tell

> 'We will tell the king and queen what omen occurs'.
> (KBo XVII 1 IV 9 (Raman 1973:26; 28-30))

Here the preposed *kuiš* (relative adjective) plus *šagaiš* (relative noun) 'what omen' without anaphoric referent in the main clause represents a variant of the relative constructions in (2c) and (4c), above. Relative constructions have counterparts without *kuiš* as well (Justus 1976:234):

(8a) DINGIR^(meš) ḫumanteš HUR.SAGi taruppanteš nu= za=
    gods   all-nom mountain-on assembled-nom ptc-ptc-
    kan LUGALun duškeškanzi
    ptc king-acc welcome-3p
    'All the gods (who are) assembled on the mountain
      welcome the king'.   (XXIX 1 III 3-4)

(8b) ^mTamnaššun=a ḫušwantan *IṢBATU*   š= an ^(uru)Hattuša
    T.-acc-ptc   alive-acc they-seized ptc-him   H.-to
    uwatet
    brought-3s
    'Tamnaššu (whom) they seized, he brought to Ḫattuša'.
                                           (KBo XXII 2 Rs 9)

Here the modifying clause is preposed: 'All the gods assembled on the mountain, (they) welcome the king', or 'The Tamnaššuš they seized, he took to Ḫattušaš'. Complement clauses without complementizers thus parallel modifying clauses without relative markers (cf. (2b) above).

Not only do relative and verb complement constructions share the complementizer base (*kuit*) and usages of anaphoric enclitics, then, but both can be asyndetically preposed without any overt marker of the noun relation. I suggest here that it is the OV nature of Hittite that accounts for the generally preposed character of subordinate clauses; but more interestingly, the inconsistency of its OV character accounts for the innovating use of pre-complementizers beside older asyndetic preposing and *kuit* as complementizer. Hesitancy between common gender *-an* and neuter *-at* as (anaphoric) pre-complementizers indicates that earlier stages did not use phoric reference for relating grammatical constituents. To the degree that third person pronominals occurred, they agreed with noun classes based on semantic animacy, and were inadequately differentiated to refer to abstract textual constituents. One might thus say that the pre-complementizers augment a system which had no third person pronoun, but juxtaposed relative clauses before the head noun, object clauses in noun position before the verb. They provide thus new mechanisms for endophoric reference (Halliday and Hasan 1976:33, 306).

The consistently OV Japanese lacks third person pronouns as do many languages. It has no relative pronoun, but preposes relative clauses asyndetically before the head noun (Kuno 1978:86-90, 127-30, 137; cf. Lehmann 1978:22f). It further lacks clefting constructions that require such pronominals ('*It* was his speech that the king lost', '*It* was obvious that the king had lost his speech' beside 'That the king lost his speech was obvious'). One recalls here that reconstruction of anaphoric pronouns is problematic in IE (Lehmann 1974:17f; 320f.). If one considers the lack of a third person pronoun to be harmonic with other relics of OV structure in IE such as postpositions or the genitive and ablative of comparison, as well as with asyndetic preposing of subordinate constructions, then Hittite pre-complementizers are disharmonic with a consistent OV state. Like wise disharmonic are other IE means for forming complement constructions (cf. infinitives, verbal nouns and 'that' equivalents). I conclude that Hittite pre-complementizers represent a variant, beside asyndetic preposing, harmonic with the fact that the language is (no longer) as consistently OV as Japanese. Beside structures harmonic with OV languages and the mirror image structures harmonic with VO languages, then, one can also identify correlates of inconsistent states as mechanisms of change. I have suggested that pre-complementizers have such a function.

NOTES

*Data for this study form part of a larger work which will appear as part of the ongoing publication, Kammenhuber (1973--) sub *šak-/šek-* 'know'. References to hand copy editions of the cuneiform text, *Keilschrifttexte aus Boghazköi* (KBo) and *Keilschrifturkunden aus Boghazköi* (without prefix = KUB) appear here, as well as number reference to *Thesaurus* (Kammenhuber 1973--). Further bibliography appears with the *Thesaurus* (or other) discussion of the passage.

[1] Hittite *kuit*, in addition to uses as a frozen form (complementizer 'because, that', cf. Friedrich 1960: §323 and 324, p.163; and as interrogative, cf. *ibid.* §286, p.147), forms part of the declensional system of the relative, e.g. sg. common *kuiš*, acc. *kuin*, neut. nom.-acc. *kuit* (*ibid.* §119, pp.68f.). Indirect questions are often formed with the conjunction *mān* 'whether' (*ibid.* §333, p.167), reserving *kuit* for complement and relative use. This is certainly true of clauses dependent on *šak-/šek-* 'know'. Translations 'that, what, which, because' for *kuit* are thus context dependent.

[2] Words in capital letters represent logographic writings resulting from the fact that the cuneiform system of writing was borrowed by the Hittite scribes from its use to write Akkadian (a Semitic language), a writing system in turn borrowed from the Sumerians. Italicized capitals indicate Akkadograms, plain capitals Sumerograms. Thus *UL* stands

for the Akkadian word for 'not', which in Hittite would be phonetically *natta*. The abbreviation *ptc.* = particle.

REFERENCES

Andersen, Henning. 1973. "Abductive and deductive change". *Lg.* 49. 765-93.
Campbell, Lyle, and Marianne Mithun. 1978. "Syntactic reconstruction; priorities and pitfalls". Ms.
Friedrich, Johannes. 1960. *Hethitisches Elementarbuch. I. Teil. Kurzgefasste Grammatik*. Heidelberg: Winter. 2nd ed.
Greenberg, Joseph H. 1966. "Some universals of grammar with particular reference to the order of meaningful elements". In *Universals of language*, 73-113. Ed. by Joseph H. Greenberg. Cambridge, Mass: MIT Press. 2nd ed.
Halliday, M.A.K., and Ruqaiya Hasan. 1976. *Cohesion in English*. London: Longman.
Justus, Carol F. 1976. "Relativization and topicalization in Hittite". In *Subject and topic*, 213-45. Ed. by Charles N. Li. New York: Academic Press.
_____. 1978. "Syntactic change: evidence for restructuring among coexistent variants". *JIES* 6.107-32.
_____. To appear. "Hittite *ištamaš-* 'hear': some syntactic implications". Münchener Studien zur Sprachwissenschaft.
Kammenhuber, Annelies. 1973--. *Materialen zu einem hethitischen Thesaurus*. Heidelberg: Winter.
Kuno, Susumu. 1978. "Japanese: a characteristic OV language". In *Syntactic typology*, 57-138. Ed. by Winfred P. Lehmann. Austin: University of Texas Press.
Lehmann, Winfred P. 1974. *Proto-Indo-European syntax*. Austin: University of Texas Press.
Raman, Carol F. Justus. 1973. *The Old Hittite relative construction*. Unpublished dissertation, University of Texas.
Watkins, Calvert. 1976. "Towards Proto-Indo-European syntax: problems and pseudo-problems". In *Diachronic syntax*, 305-26. Chicago: Chicago Linguistic Society.
Weinreich, Uriel, William Labov and Marvin Herzog. 1968. "Empirical foundations for a theory of language change". In *Directions for historical linguistics*, 98-188. Ed. by Winfred P. Lehmann and Yakov Malkiel. Austin: University of Texas Press.
Wolfram, Walt. 1976. "A-prefixing in Appalachian English". NEH lecture series: Language Variation in America, 1976 Linguistic Institute.

ON WORD ORDER IN IRISH

ANDERS AHLQVIST
University College, Galway

The main purpose of this paper is to give readers interested in typology and language universals a very brief guide to the work that has been carried out to investigate the history of Irish word order, which is usually VSO, as in the other Insular Celtic languages (Schmidt 1969). VSO order is consistent in the language of the Old Irish glosses as found especially in the great collections of Würzburg (Wb.), Milan (Ml.), and St. Gall (Sg.) which form the main corpus (cf. Stokes and Strachan 1901-3) for our knowledge of Classical Old Irish. A typical example is:

(1) *beoigidir in spirut in corp in fecht so*
    vivifies the spirit the body the time this
    'the spirit now quickens the body'. (Wb. 13^{d}7)

VSO order also applies when there is a cleft sentence, as in

(2) *is deidbir ha áigthiu ar is do thabirt díglae*
    it-is proper his fearing, for it-is to give punish-

    berid in claideb sin
    ment he-carries the sword that
    'reasonable it is to fear him, for it is to inflict punishment'. (Wb. 6^{a}13)

In the above examples, the clefted element is introduced by a copula, or rather, as I have argued elsewhere (1972), the copula serves to transform the clefted constituent into a predicate, thereby turning it, syntactically speaking, into the equivalent of a verb. Morphologically, on the other hand, it can be either a noun or, as exemplified in (2) an adjective (*deidbir*) or an adverbial phrase (*do thabirt díglae*). This remains the basic pattern down to the present day. On the other hand, it has long been known (see Wagner 1977, 208[10] for references) that in Old Irish poetry and other early sources, a compound verb may be split into two parts so as to leave the preverb at the beginning of the sentence and the main part of the verb at the end, as in

(3) no-m- choimmdiu -coíma
     me [the] Lord   cherishes
     'the Lord cherishes me'. (Sg. 205)

This state of affairs, which is susally described as tmesis, is well attested in other older IE languages. More recently, Bergin made the important discovery that in the oldest material simple verbs may also be found at the end of the sentence. Bergin states that, in this case,

> when the verb does not stand at the head of its clause, particularly when it follows its subject or object, it takes the dependent form, that is, a simple verb has the conjunct ending and a compound verb is in the prototonic form. (Bergin 1938: 197; cp. Binchy 1943:204-5)

For an example of such a prototonic form, see:

(4) is   tre   fír   flathemon
     it-is   through [the] justice of-[the]-ruler

     mortlithi (mórslóg no)   márlóchet
     plagues (great-hosts or) [and] great-lightnings

     di doínib   dingbatar
     from persons   are-kept
     'it is through the justice of the ruler that plagues and great lightnings are kept from the people'. (AM §12)

For a possible, but uncertain, example of the simple verb with conjunct ending, see (5) below.

Subsequently, scholars such as Watkins (1963) and Meid (1963) have made use not only of the final position of the verb in these cases, but also of Bergin's formulation of the distribution of forms in clause-initial and -final verbs, in order to attempt an explanation of why Classical Old Irish has separate absolute and conjunct endings. The former are found only in simple verbs if these are not preceded by a conjunct particle (cf. *beoigidir* and *berid* in (1) and (2) above), and the latter usually everywhere else (cf. (3) -*coíma* above). Controversy about this dichotomy is still rife: most historical linguists will know of Watkins' and Meid's fairly similar views on this matter, independently arrived at though they were; Boling's (1977) and Cowgill's (1975; 1975a) rather different views have not met with universal approval either. On this occasion, I can do no more than draw attention to McCone's (forthcoming) important article, in which he tries to deal with the problem in terms appropriate to a 'typical late Indo-European type' of language rather than in the almost Indo-

Celtic framework inherent in Meid's and Watkins's proposals. It is also worth noting that a useful guide to the philological and linguistic problems involved has been provided by Greene (1977); this gives a good overview of the material. One example of verb-final order, however, which he does not mention, is to be found in

(5)   *is*   *tre*   *fír*   *flathemon*
    it-is through [the] justice of-[the]-ruler

cech comarbe con   *a*   *chlí*   *ina*
every heir CONNECTIVE his house-post into-his

chainorbu   *clanda*
fair-inheritance plants
'it is through the justice of the ruler that every heir plants his house-pose in his fair inheritance.'
(AM §16)

Here the editor restores *clanda* at the end either to make it conform to Bergin's Law for a simple verb *clandaid*, or (and this seems somewhat more likely to me) to make it possible for the full verb form to be a compound verb in tmesis: *con- ... -clanda*. However, it must be noted that what the mss. have is *clandas* (i.e., a relative form: 'who plants'). In his criticism of the work of those he describes as 'Bergins Nachfolger' (Wagner 1967:301), Wagner quite correctly, I think, describes *clanda* as one of several forms that 'beruhen auf m. E. unzulässigen Textveränderungen, deren Begründung in den Anmerkungen nicht stichhaltig ist (Wagner 1977:229)'. On the other hand, it seems to me that Wagner goes too far when he argues that archaic Old Irish material with verb-final clauses is totally artificial, used by poets as a stylistic device (1967; cf. 1977:209-12). It is quite possible that this order is in fact a relic of an earlier period of the language when verb-final order was more common. Whereas I am of the opinion that Wagner's views on word order in Old Irish etc. are required reading for all those interested in these matters, it seems to me likely that we are in at least some cases dealing with genuine survivals. In this, I agree with Mac Coisdealbha's main conclusion that

> apart from an historically archaic language stratum A), represented by Bergin's rule in the strict sense, a further intermediate stratum B) can be inferred which, for syntactical reasons, cannot for the moment be seen as representing a natural stage in the spoken language developing ... to ... classical Old Irish (Mac Coisdealbha 1976:314).

In other words, he suggests that a number of the difficulties encountered in dealing with archaic Irish material may be accounted for by considering some of it to be the output of people who knew of the existence of the earlier pattern but were unable to apply its rules correctly because they were, themselves, speakers of a language with the same pattern as Classical Old Irish.

At this point, it will be useful to return to *Audacht Morainn* (or Morann's Testament'), for here we probably have a specimen of archaic Old Irish so early that it gives us some idea of the earlier system. At this early stage Old Irish was still a language in which verb-final position was unmarked, as it almost certainly must have been in Celtiberian. As Schmidt puts it: 'der archaische Charakter der Bronze von Botorrita zeigt sich syntaktisch in der B[asic] O[rder] OV' (1975:55). The description of a portion of AM as a fairly unitary specimen of genuinely archaic Old Irish is based on Kelly's analysis of the structure of the text, in which he suggests that

> the earliest strata of the text are Section 3 (the first part of the *Is tre fír flathemon* series, i.e., §§12-21) and Section 5 (the first part of the *Admestar* series, i.e., §§32-46). In these sections alliteration is rigidly applied and the syntax is archaic, with verb in final position (§§12-18, 20-1, 43, 44) and absence of *ocus* (7). The subject matter is in no way technical; both sections list the principal ingredients of peace and prosperity in a rural community. These two sections are to a certain extent complementary, though it is noteworthy that §§18, 19, and 20 deal with the same subjects, in the same order, as §§36, 37, and 38 (Kelly 1976, xliv).

In this material, as elsewhere in Irish, the copula is always in initial position (i.e., not preceded by an element other than a conjunction or a particle): cp. *air is* 'for it is' and *nicope* 'will not be' (§§32; 45-6); the introductory words *is tre fír flathemon* 'it is through the justice of the ruler' (§§12-21) and also (as it seems to me) the zero-form before *cech* in §16 (I would translate: 'it is through the justice of the ruler that everyone is an heir who, together with his house-post, plants into his own inheritance') and §19 *robbi* (I would translate: 'it is through the justice of the ruler that abundance can pertain to every tall high corn').[1] The only other sentence initial verbs here are the imperative *Apair* 'tell' (§§12; 32) and the subjunctive *Ad-mestar* 'may he estimate' (§§32-46), which may be described adequately in Dressler's terms when he state that 'Das Verbot der Anfangsstellung gilt also weder für Frage- oder Befehls- und Aufforderungssätze (1969:3)'. The latter is of course what one is dealing with in this case. In this context, it is appropriate to recall Watkins's recent warning to the effect that one must not equate '*unmarked* with *normal* and *marked* with *non-normal'* (1977:452). The injunction given in the word *Ad-mestar* was of course part of normal language. As far as the copula is concerned, it seems to me that the tmesis (cf. (3) above) of preverb and verb may offer a clue as to how the copula in Old Irish came to be associated with sentence initial position. Just as a preverb, being unstressed before the main part of the verb, would occur at the beginning of the sentence if separated from its verbal predicate, so the copula, having changed from a full word to an unstressed particle, would be placed in that same position in relation to its nominal or adverbial predicate. Note in this context that the cleft sentence is already fully developed in AM. This could have encouraged the establishment of an order Copula + Predicate + Subject (if nominal rather than pronominal) parallel to the order Copula + Predicate + (Non-) Relative Clause of cleft sentences. This may well have contributed, in the end, toward making the order Predicate (whether verbal or nominal) + Subject first the unmarked, and subsequently the normal order in Irish. At the same time, it must be borne in mind that some scholars, such as Mac Cana (1973:111-2) and Dressler (1969:19), have produced evidence for an SVO pattern like that of English. However, I am not quite sure how one should treat their examples in terms of markedness. It seems more likely than not that the majority of Mac Cana's examples are examples of unmarked order, whereas Dressler's single example looks to me more like a cleft sentence with deleted initial copula. However, I leave it to readers to decide for themselves whether an intermediate stage SVO really was required in the evolution of the language. I also leave to them the important question of whether, with Wagner (1969) and others, one must assume that a non-IE substratum played a role in the establishment of what is now, and for more than a thousand years has been, the normal word order pattern of Irish.

Finally, I should like to quote what Greene has had to say in conclusion of his Bonn lecture (1977:32):

> Many such problems exist, and they cannot be solved on the basis of theories about the development of the Irish language, still less on the basis of theories about Indo-European. The grammar of Archaic Irish envisaged by Thurneysen and Binchy can be written only when a corpus of evidence has been made available by the philological procedures appropriate to such a task. It is a sobering thought that we have not yet available a grammar of Middle Irish, another period of the language where contemporary manuscripts are lacking, although here the preceding and the following stages of the language are adequately known and described; as has been suggested above, many of the philological difficulties which Strachan found in the

study of Middle Irish are present, and to an even more formidable degree, in the task of elucidating the considerable mass of material which we call Archaic Irish. However, we may agree with Binchy that future scholars who decide to cultivate this rugged terrain are certain to reap a goodly harvest (Greene 1977:32).

To this it must now be added that the imminent publication, as I write these lines (28.3.1979), in six large volumes, of the collected diplomatic edition (Binchy 1979) of the Old Irish legal material will provide invaluable resources for this important endeavour.

NOTE

[1] The last two instances involve matters of philological interpretation, which I hope to discuss properly elsewhere.

REFERENCES

Ahlqvist, Anders. 1972. "Some aspects of the copula in Irish". *Éigse* 14.269-74.
AM = Kelly 1976.
Bergin, Osborn. 1938. "On the syntax of the verb in Old Irish". *Ériu* 12.197-214.
Binchy, D.A. 1943. "The linguistic and historical value of the Irish Law Tracts". *Proceedings of the British Academy* 29.195-228.
_____. 1979. *Corpus Iuris Hibernici* I-VI. Dublin: Institute for Advanced Studies.
Boling, Bruce. 1972. "Some problems of the phonology and morphology of the Old Irish verb". *Ériu* 23.73-101.
Cowgill, Warren. 1975. "The origins of the Insular Celtic conjunct and absolute verbal endings". In *Flexion und Wortbildung*, 40-70. Ed. by H. Rix. Wiesbaden: L. Reichelt.
_____. 1975a. "Two further notes on the origin of the Insular Celtic absolute and conjunct verb endings". *Ériu* 26.27-32.
Dressler, Wolfgang. 1969. "Eine textsyntaktische Regel der idg. Wortstellung". *KZ* 83.1-25.
Greene, David. 1977. "Archaic Irish". In *Indogermanisch und Keltisch*, 11-33. Ed. by K.H. Schmidt. Wiesbaden: L. Reichelt.
Kelly, Fergus. 1976. *Audacht Morainn*. Dublin: Institute for Advanced Studies.
Mac Cana, Proinsias. 1973. "On Celtic word order and the Welsh 'abnormal' sentence". *Ériu* 24.90-120.
Mac Coisdealbha, Pádraig. 1976. *The syntax of the sentence in Old Irish*. Bonn: Ph.D. dissertation.

McCone, K.R. (forthcoming). "Pretonic preverbs and the absolute verbal endings in Old Irish". *Ériu* 30.
Meid, Wolfgang. 1963. *Die indogermanischen Grundlagen der altirischen absoluten und konjunkten Verbalflexion*. Wiesbaden: Otto Harassowitz.
Schmidt, Karl Horst. 1969. "Die Stellung des Keltischen innerhalb der indogermanischen Sprachfamilie, historisch-vergleichend und typologisch gesehen". *KZ* 83.108-23.
_____. "Der Beitrag der keltiberischen Inschrift von Botorrita zur Rekonstruktion der protokeltischen Syntax". *Word* 28.51-62.
Stokes, Whitley and John Strachan. 1901-3. *Thesaurus Palaeohibernicus*. London: Cambridge University Press.
Wagner, Heinrich. 1959. *Das Verbum in den Sprachen der britischen Inseln*. Tübingen: Max Niemeyer.
_____. 1967. "Zür unregelmassigen Wortstellung in der altirischen Alliterationsdichtung". In *Beiträge Pokorny*, 289-314. Ed. by W. Meid. Innsbruck: Institut fur Sprachwissenschaft.
_____. 1977. "Wortstellung im Keltischen und Indogermanischen". In *Indogermanisch und Keltisch*, 204-35. Ed. by H. Schmidt. Wiesbaden: L. Reichelt.
Watkins, Calvert. 1963. "Preliminaries to a historical and comparative analysis of the syntax of the Old Irish verb". *Celtica* 6.1-49.
_____. 1977. "Towards Proto-Indo-European syntax: problems and pseudo-problems". *Indo-European Studies* III, 437-67. Harvard: Department of Linguistics.

MARKED AND UNMARKED WORD ORDER IN OLD NORSE

MARIT CHRISTOFFERSEN
University of Bergen

0. *Introduction.* The task of establishing a PIE word order has proved to be difficult, especially because of the diverging evidence provided by the daughter languages. We will probably have to look for different word order patterns even in PIE, as is the case in the daughter languages.

Even when studying one single language a few sentences from one text are not sufficient to establish the different word order patterns of that language, be it a so-called dead language or a language in use today. Texts representing a particular style may show predominance of a certain word order pattern, even if this pattern is marked within the system of that language as a whole. We should be aware of the dangers of drawing too extensive conclusions from small corpora, especially when we do not know the communicative function of the word order patterns of the language in question.

From a syntactic point of view, far too little work has been done on the medieval Scandinavian manuscripts. In this paper, I will present the syntactic patterns of the main clause in one medieval document, The Law of Magnus Lagabœte (AM 60 qv., pp. 21b-81b (abbreviated ML)), and make some brief comparisons with Modern Norwegian.

In my discussion, I will use the terms 'marked' and 'unmarked' word order. These terms are synonymous with what Kiefer calls 'basic order':

> A word order is referred to as basic if it can stand without any presuppositions as to what should be considered as being already known... (Kiefer 1970:140)

In the same sense Fourquet uses the term 'neutral':

> Lorsque plusieurs ordres sont possibles, il est généralement

> un qui apparaît comme l'ordre *neutre*, celui qu'on emploie en
> l'absence d'intention particulière ... On pourra distinguer
> ici un ordre neutre et un ordre plus ou moins expressif
> (Fourquet 1938:23f).

There is, in my opinion, no obligatory correlation between unmarked order and the most frequent order in one single text. Thus, the unmarked order cannot be inferred simply by counting. Yet, in a corpus consisting of main clauses with no adverbial modifiers at any level, there probably will be a correlation between the most frequent and the unmarked order in most cases.

1. *Historical overview*. Although I am well aware that many scholars deserve mention in a complete list of important work on Scandinavian philology, I am in this brief survey forced to limit myself to a few of those whose work seems to be of importance for my purpose here. These scholars have, at least to some extent, discussed the more general rules for word order in Old Scandinavian.

In the article 'Verbets stilling i sætningen i det norrøne sprog,' written five years before the publication of his *Syntax*, Marius Nygaard argues for SVO as the unmarked word order in ON. That is, he maintains--in opposition to Braune (1894:39ff)--that the natural position of the verb (V) in Old Norse prose is after the subject (S), even if the opposite order (VS) might be as frequent as SV. Braune on his part seems to be of the opinion that S in first position implies topicalization of the subject. Nygaard holds that nothing special is needed to bring the subject into the first position, but something is needed to get it out of that position (1900:215). In other words, he maintains that the subject in Old Norse has become what Li and Thompson (1976) would call a 'grammaticalized topic'. The SV order has become a formal arrangement and the subject in first position no longer really represents any sort of topicalization. The unmarked pattern according to Nygaard is thus SVO.

On the other hand, Andreas Heusler is, like Braune, impressed by the majority of the VSO structures in the sagas and is inclined to conceive the VSO pattern as the unmarked one because of its frequency. He says that it is used 'so häufig, dass man darin die aisl. Normalstellung sehen könnte' (1950:173). Heusler seems to postulate that a development has taken place in Old Icelandic, from SVO being the unmarked pattern to VSO being unmarked: 'Hier ist der Hauptfall von *bewegter* Stellung, die zur *gewohnten* geworden ist' (1950:173). Heusler thus looks upon the VSO as the normal word order pattern in Old Icelandic, but he admits that a new paragraph seldom starts with a VSO structure.

In 1941, Paul Diderichsen presented his doctoral dissertation *Sætningsbygningen i Skaanske Lov*. Diderichsen incontestably laid the foundations of the structural or formal description of the Danish and Scandinavian sentence structure, although he was not fully aware of the typological implications of the different patterns of ordering. He discusses the implications of looking at SV or VS as what he calls the 'habitual' order of the main clause (1941:54f), and concludes by considering the VS order to be the 'habitual' one, since there is often, in Old as well as Modern Danish (and Norwegian), a constituent other than S in front of V, thus modifying the SV order to XVS. Diderichsen's term 'habitual' order corresponds to frequent order, which is not necessarily synonymous with unmarked order. Diderichsen too would have agreed that the VSO structure--with no constituent in front of the V--is marked in Norwegian and Danish. Although he does not use our terminology, Diderichsen seems to hold that in Old Danish, the subject has not yet become a grammaticalized topic: in choosing the VS pattern as the 'habitual' one, he states that he is aware that this viewpoint affords a topicalized subject no different status than topicalized object (1941: 79).

3. *Typological characteristics*. The SOV hypothesis of Old Germanic represented by the Proto-Germanic runic inscriptions has a long tradition, and is still held by Lehmann in his various works and by Antonsen 1975, the latter basing his percentages for Northwest Germanic on 34 runic inscriptions, many of them incomplete. The most recent contributions to the debate are Lehmann 1978 and Ureland 1978.

On the other hand, Friedrich 1975 argues for an SVO hypothesis for Proto-Indo-European, and in fact, as Larsson already showed in 1931:37, there are many examples of the SVO order even in the Proto-Nordic inscriptions. Counting the word order patterns in the 35 examples in Krause 1971: 133f, Ureland shows that there are 8 clauses introduced by V, 15 verb-second and 12 verb-last, thus providing supporting evidence for the SVO hypothesis for early North Germanic.

In Old Norse, to take a specific example, given the three constituents *maðrinn* (S), *át* (V), *eplit* (O), only *maðrinn át eplit* 'the man ate the apple'--the SVO structure--can be considered neutral in Kiefer's sense. The VSO structure: *át maðrinn eplit*, communicates something besides the cognitive content, even if it is, as we have already said, extremely frequent in the sagas; and the OVS structure *eplit át maðrinn* is interpreted as a topicalized structure. The VOS pattern *át eplit maðrinn* is not acceptable, but not for typological reasons, since *át þat maðrinn* 'ate that the man' probably would pass.

But the SOV pattern *maðrinn eplit át* in main clauses is unacceptable for typological reasons. Further evidence for the SVO character of Old Norse is that the language is dominantly prepositional. The order between the relative clause and the antecedent is head plus modifier. The order between the nominal head and the adjective varies, whereas it is always modifier plus head in Modern Norwegian. The order between the noun and the genitive is mostly head plus genitive, while the order in Modern Norwegian varies in this respect (cf. Greenberg 1963 for these typological characteristics of SVO languages). In fact it might look as if Old Norse was more strongly VO than is Modern Norwegian. I must agree with Friedrich when he rejects the assumption that language types evolve along continuous and irreversible lines, and states that 'a linguistic system can oscillate indefinitely between the margins of two (or more) ideal types ...' (1975:3).

There can be no doubt about Old Norse, like Modern Norwegian, being VO. However, as we have seen, scholars do not fully agree upon which order deserves to be called unmarked, the SVO structure or the VSO structure. As we know, it is the order between V and O that has the greatest typological significance, not least because there are languages that do not have subjects, and others, like Old Norse, which do not always realize the subject explicitly. In Old Norse there can never be more than one element in front of V: 'le verbe ne se trouve jamais au delà de la seconde place' (Fourquet 1938:208). A consequence of this rule is that when S is first, V has to come next, and when O is first, V will come next and then S will follow. Old Norwegian, like Modern Norwegian, is verb-second in Vennemann's terms (1974:361). Fourquet (1938) finds no testimony of verb-last structures in Old Scandinavian, nor does my corpus contain evidence for such structures.

4. *Evidence from the Law of Magnus Lagabœte.* Finally, I will give a survey of the main trends in the word order patterns represented by the Law of Magnus Lagabœte, which consists of approximately 2500 main clauses.

As in Modern Norwegian, it seems clear that the SVO structure needs no particular motivation in Old Norwegian. It does not carry any sign of being contextually motivated, and it communicates nothing but the cognitive content of the clause. Yet this order is by no means the most frequent in this Old Norwegian Law text. Only 443 clauses actually have this structure, and this must be due primarily to the very special purpose of communication that this law text serves. The majority of the sentences are of the kind: 'If a man kills ... then ...'. When a conditional clause is preposed, the word order in the rest of the main clause is modified to Adv V S, according to the internal rules of word order in Old Norwegian, but the SVO order dominates in the main clauses without adverbial modifiers.

Among the 443 examples of subject-introduced clauses, there are no exceptions to the SVO order; but in sentences with complex verb forms, the order varies. Adverbs and objects may occupy the position in front of the non-finite verb, or they may be placed behind it. This fact is in my opinion not at all due to typological factors, but rather to rhythmical ones.

In Old Norse, direct objects, indirect objects, predicatives or the non-finite verb may be topicalized, causing the word order in the rest of the main clause to become (T)VS. There is never more than one element in front of V. ML has a total number of 127 clauses with topicalized direct object, indirect object, predicative or non-finite verb, and S is usually in third position, although it may occur later. The latter order is relatively rare in this text.

288 main clauses have initial V. I will insist here on the VSO order being marked in Old Norwegian, as it is in Modern Norwegian. In Modern Norwegian the VSO order is used in questions and in what we might call question-formed conditional clauses. In Old Norse this order was used with these two functions also, but it incontestably had a less restricted use at that stage of the language. After the conjunction *ok* 'and' (linking two main clauses) the VSO order is almost obligatory. However, VSO occurs even if there is no conjunction. In this case, I hypothesize, the word order still functions as a context marker, expressing the speaker's point of view that the content of the V-initiated clause is closely linked to what has been said before. Usually there is a common reference in the V-initiated clause and the immediate context; that is, there is what Halliday and Hasan (1976) call 'cohesion' between clauses. It is extremely unusual, in this corpus at least,

not to find a common reference in the V-initiated clause and its immediate context. Clauses introduced by V thus have a signal of being parts of a whole. By contrast, S-introduced clauses do not have this signal, although they of course may also be parts of a larger context (a narrative, for example). In this sense, clauses introduced by V are marked for contextual motivation, while clauses introduced by S are unmarked.

As an alternative to the VSO structures we sometimes find VOS with the same degree of communicative markedness, and I think that the word order here is due to factors of rhythm and weight. Factors of rhythm and weight do in fact modify the fairly rigid word order pattern of Modern Norwegian too, in particular the order between a sentence-modifying adverb and a light object. Thus, the VOS order is not likely to be found when the S and the O are of approximately the same physical weight. The internal order between the main constituents V and O is not modified by these factors in any case. VOS as a variant of VSO does not exist in Modern Norwegian. Norwegian of today has lost another grammatical feature possessed by Old Norwegian, namely the possibility of placing direct objects in front of a non-finite verb.

I have already mentioned that the majority of main clauses in this text are introduced by an adverbial phrase or a conditional clause. I have not yet examined this part of the corpus in detail, but the clauses normally have the word order Adv V S, although for the same reasons as I have sketched above, objects, adverbs and non-finite verb forms may precede the subject.

5. *Conclusion.* We have at least three levels or parameters (see Enkvist 1976:5ff) that interact in constituting the word order pattern at this stage of Norwegian:
   1. Affinity to a linguistic type, VO or OV.
   2. Expression of the communicative functions of the clause, usually bound to the introductory constituent.
   3. Modifications caused by the principles of weight and rhythm, which in particular affect the word order of the clause after the V. These principles function in Old Norwegian and to some extent in Norwegian today.

REFERENCES

Antonsen, Elmer H. 1975. *A concise grammar of the Older Runic inscriptions*. Tübingen.
Braune, Wilhelm. 1894. *Zur Lehre von der deutschen Wortstellung*. Forschungen zur deutschen Philologie. Leipzig.
Diderichsen, Paul. 1941. *Sætningsbygningen i Skaanske Lov*. Copenhagen: Ejnar Munksgaard; and *Acta Philologica Scandinavica* 15.1-252.
Enkvist, Nils Erik. 1976."Prolegomena to a symposium on 'The interaction of parameters affecting word order'". In *Reports on text linguistics: approaches to word order*. Ed. by Nils Erik Enkvist and Viljo Kohonen. Åbo.
Fourquet, Jean. 1938. *L'ordre des éléments de la phrase en germanique ancien*. Paris: Belles Lettres.
Friedrich, Paul. 1975. *Proto-Indo-European syntax*. Journal of Indo-European Studies, Monograph No. 1. Butte, Montana.
Greenberg, Joseph H. 1963. "Some universals of grammar with particular reference to the order of meaningful elements". In *Universals of language*. Ed. by Joseph H. Greenberg. Cambridge, Mass.: The M.I.T. Press.
Halliday, M.A.K. and Ruqaiya Hasan. 1976. *Cohesion in English*. London: Longman Group.
Heusler, Andreas. 1950. *Altisländisches Elementarbuch*. Heidelberg: Winter, 4th ed.
Kiefer, Ferenc. 1970. "On the problem of word order". In *Progress in Linguistics*. Ed. by Manfred Bierwisch and Karl E. Heidolph. The Hague: Mouton.
Krause, Wolfgang. 1971. *Die Sprache der urnordischen Runeninschriften*. Heidelberg: Winter.
Larsson, Carl. 1931. *Ordföljdstudier över det finita verbet i de nordiska formspråken*. 1. Uppsala Universitets Årsskrift. Uppsala.
Lehmann, Winfred P. 1974. *Proto-Indo-European syntax*. Austin: University of Texas Press.
_____. 1978. "A shift in the syntactic type of Early North Germanic and its phonological effects". In *The Nordic languages and modern linguistics* 3. Ed. by John Weinstock. Austin: University of Texas Press.
Li, Charles N. and Sandra Thompson. 1976. "Subject and topic: a new typology of language". In *Subject and topic*. Ed. by Charles N. Li. New York: Academic Press.
Nygaard, Marius. 1900. *Verbets stilling i sætningen i det norrøne sprog*. Arkiv för norkisk filologi 1900.
_____. 1905. *Norrøn syntax*. Kristiania: Aschehoug.
Ureland, P. Sture. 1978. "Typological, diachronic, and areal linguistic perspectives of North Germanic syntax". In *The Nordic languages and modern linguistics* 3. Ed. by John Weinstock. Austin: University of Texas Press.
Vennemann, Theo. 1974. "Topics, subjects and word order: from SXV to SVX via TVX". In *Historical linguistics I*. (Proceedings of the First International Conference on Historical Linguistics). Ed. by John M. Anderson and Charles Jones. Amsterdam: North Holland.

AN ANALYSIS OF THE RISE OF SOV PATTERNS IN DUTCH

MARINEL GERRITSEN
Royal Dutch Academy of Sciences
Institute of Dialectology

1. *Introduction.* There is no general agreement about the surface word order of Proto-Indo-European: SOV, SVO and even VSO have been suggested.* But there does seem to be agreement that the surface word order in the Germanic languages developed or is developing from Proto-Germanic SOV to SVO, probably via VSO. Vennemann's (1974a:80,82 and 1974b:16) suggestion, that certain SOV patterns in German, Dutch and other Western Indo-European languages (e.g. SOV in dependent clauses and SVfOV in main clauses in compound tenses) have to be considered remnants of the old SOV phase, is still cited and has been implicitly accepted in recent articles on syntactic change (e.g. Stockwell 1977, Givón 1977). But in fact only the history of English has been examined to test the validity of these statements; and in English they are apparently well documented now. However, Vennemann's suggestion has not yet been tested with regard to the development of surface word order in the other Germanic languages. In this paper, his hypothesis that the SOV order in Germanic languages such as Dutch and German represents the same development as that in Old English will be contested. Seven modern Germanic languages will be considered: English, Swedish, Norwegian, Danish, German, Frisian and Dutch. As far as I know, Swedish, Norwegian and Danish have followed the same general lines as the history of word order in English. By c. 1400 the SVO order was well established, although in some of the Nordic languages SOV sometimes occurred in relative clauses as late as the 17th century (Canale 1976, Traugott 1972 for English and Haugen 1976, Ureland 1976, Wessén 1970 for the Nordic languages). The history of German, Frisian and Dutch is quite different. From two dissertations in German which were written under the supervision of Behaghel in the 1920's, we know a good deal about German word order in the period between 1300 and 1600. It is apparent from the

counts of Hammarström (1923) and Maurer (1926) in natively composed chronicles, charters and chapbooks, that between 1300 and 1400 there were more main clauses in SVO order in compound tenses and dependent clauses than in the Heliand, which was written in the 9th century and is considered representative of the German of that time. This development from SOV to SVO is in line with the development of word order in English and the Scandinavian languages. However, Behaghel's pupils encountered a decrease of exbraciated constituents from about 1450 on, and consequently an increase in the SOV orders; thus it is apparent that the change in the word order of German from 1450 -1600 did not coincide with the developments in English and the Scandinavian languages. Maurer's and Hammarström's data from about 1600 indicate that the sentence structure of Current New High German was well established at that time.

The development of word order in Frisian and Dutch has never been closely studied. Consequently, the history of word order in these languages is less well known than that of German. From general syntactic studies on Middle Frisian and Middle Dutch from about 1300 on, it appears that approximately the same word order development occurred in Frisian and Dutch as in German (see Fokkema 1948 for Frisian, and Albering 1934, Allard 1937, Van Ginneken 1938, Van der Kallen 1938, Ornée 1955, Pulles 1950, Stellinga 1954 for Dutch).

It is clear from these works that SVO did not take over in three of the seven Germanic languages under discussion: German, Frisian and Dutch. Nevertheless, it is not clear to what extent these three languages had developed an SVO pattern before they became more firmly SOV languages. While it is usually mentioned that SVO sentences occur in certain texts from the Middle Ages, it is almost never reported what percentage of all the sentences (with at least a subject, object and verb) are SVO. Likewise, objects are rarely specified as nominal or pronominal.

In the remainder of this paper I will examine more closely the extent to which Middle Dutch adopted SVO patterns. I have restricted myself to Dutch simply because it is my mother tongue. It is not yet possible to say that the results of my investigation into the changes in word order in Dutch also apply to German and Frisian. For that, far more detailed studies of German and Frisian are needed. However, I suspect that the German and Frisian word order development is in keeping with the statistics for Dutch which will be reported in the next section.

2. *Word order development in Dutch.* Both SOV and SVO are found in the surface structure of Current Dutch. All dependent clauses--except some concessives and conditionals--with S, V and O can occur only in SOV order. Declarative main clauses in simple tenses have SVfO or XVfSO and those in compound tenses SVfOV or SVfSOV (see Table I). Modern Dutch matches the word order of Old English with the excep-

	Relative clauses	Subordinate† clauses	Declarative main clauses
simple tense	SOVf	SOVf	SVfO XVfSO
compound tense	SOVfV SOVVf	SOVfV SOVVf	SVfOV XVfSOV

In this and subsequent Tables:
† = All subordinate clauses except some conditionals and concessives which occur from the earliest sources on in VSO.

Word order of S, V and O in Current Standard Dutch
TABLE I

tion of the stronger verb second character of Modern Dutch. Vennemann's inference that the SOV orders were remnants of an old SOV phase is therefore very plausible, but mistaken, as is evident from the counts of Middle Dutch prose from c. 1275, *Het Limburgse leven van Jezus* (caput 1-100) in Table II.[1] It appears that all the sentence types which

	Relative clauses	Subordinate† clauses	Declarative main clauses
simple tense	SVfO 35 46% SOVf 41 54%	SVfO 60 67% SOVf 30 33%	SVfO 143 42% XVfSO 196 58%
compound tense	SVfVO 7 ⎱ 22% SVVfO 4 ⎰ SOVfV 24 ⎱ 78% SOVVf 15 ⎰	SVfVO 13 ⎱ 28% SVVfO 4 ⎰ SOVfV 25 ⎱ 72% SOVVf 19 ⎰	SVfVO 37 46% ⎱ 62% SVfOV 43 54% ⎰ XVfSVO 26 52% ⎱ 38% SVfSOV 24 48% ⎰

Word order of S, V and O in Middle Dutch prose from c. 1275,
Limburgse leven van Jezus (caput 1-100)
TABLE II

can occur only in SOV order in Current Dutch can occur also in SVO order in Middle Dutch. Among dependent clauses, this SVO tendency is stronger in subordinate clauses than in relative clauses and, for both dependent clause types, SVO occurs significantly more frequently in simple tenses than in compound tenses. Nearly half of the main clauses with compound tenses and beginning with a subject have the SVO order with the finite verb (Vf) directly before the non-finite one, and in over half of the main clauses in compound tenses beginning with an element other than a subject, the non-finite verb stands before the object.

The data from Table II indicate that in Middle Dutch the SVO order was most common in declarative main clauses,[2] less so in subordinate clauses and least common in relative clauses. This hierarchy is in keeping with the one Canale (1976) found for the word order development of English from SOV to SVO. Vennemann (1974b), Stockwell (1977) and Givón (1977) have argued that the natural word order drift follows the paradigm SOV → VSO → SVO. Although the word order change from SOV via VSO to SVO has been verified for a number of languages, the intermediate phases have not been so clearly substantiated in the Germanic languages. The data for Middle Dutch in Table II does not strongly confirm them, but may nevertheless be somewhat stronger than the data for English. The declarative main clauses in compound tenses beginning with *any* constituent other than the subject, often a topicalized constituent, occur in Middle Dutch in XVfSOV order and slightly more frequently in XVfSVO order. These orders to a great extent match the output of stage b) and the input of stage c) that Stockwell suggests as transitional in the sequence of changes between Gmc SOV and MnE (X)SVO (1977:296) (Stockwell's v is here replaced by Vf for consistency):

(a) SO(V)Vf → VfSO(V) by Comment Focusing

(b) VfSO(V) → XVfSO(V) by Linkage or Topicalization

(c) TVfX(V) → SVfX(V) by Subject = Topic

(d) SVfX(V) → SVfVX by Exbraciation

(e) Subordinate Order → Main Order by Generalization (or, at least, elimination of whatever difference existed).

The main clause order in Current Dutch which is XVfSOV or SVfOV appears to reflect sequence (c).

There are other possible traces of the intermediate VSO phase: the occasional occurrence of inversion in Middle Dutch dependent clauses that begin with a constituent other than the subject (see e.g. Allard 1937, Van der Kallen 1938, Van Ginneken 1938); the occasional occurrence of inversion without fronting of another constituent in conjunctive clauses (see e.g. Van den Berg 1971, Weijnen 1971); and the fact that the dependent clauses omitted in this survey--concessive and conditional dependent clauses--occur from the earliest sources on in VSO. Apparently the intermediate phases between SOV and SVO proposed by

Stockwell can be traced more clearly in the development of Middle Dutch than in that of English.

The word order of other elements is bound up with the SVO and SOV order. A statistical analysis similar to that of Canale (1976) has been carried out to trace to what extent the order of elements other than S, V and O conformed to the SVO direction in Middle Dutch. Following Canale's procedure, a distinction has been made between VP, NP, and other patterns, and between four clause types: main, subordinate, relative and conjunctive clause. Since Canale's study showed that the order of NP and other patterns is usually independent of the clause in which they occur, I made no division into types of clauses for the statistical analysis of NP and other patterns. While these aspects of Canale's paradigm were reduced, some refinements were introduced for VP patterns. For all types of clauses a differentiation was made between VP patterns occurring in simple tense sentences and those occurring in compound tense sentences. For simple tenses the VP patterns were counted according to the finite verb and for compound tenses according to the non-finite verb. By this standard the SOV patterns in main clauses and conjunctive clauses in complex tenses are in fact less characteristic of SOV than Table IV indicates, since Vf and V are often separated. (A count based only on Vf, however, produces the reverse and less interesting effect, because the deviation from the simple tenses is neglected.) Because of Canale's observation that the first constituents to exbraciate have the fewest ties with the V, two other refinements were introduced: first, direct objects, predicate nouns and predicate adjectives were distinguished from each other, although Canale classifies all of these under the general category object. Also, I distinguished between PP's and adverbs belonging to the VP and those belonging to the Predicate Constituent. It was assumed that among members of VP the direct object would be the first to adopt an SVO position, since it is least 'bound' to the verb, after that the predicate noun and last the predicate adjective. Further, it was assumed that the Predicate Constituent patterns (e.g. Place and Time PP's) would turn more quickly to SVO than the VP patterns would.

The results of the counts, based on Caput 1-12 of *Limburgse leven van Jezus*, are presented in Tables III, IV, V and VI. Percentages which rely on too little data (fewer than 5 examples according to my subjective standard) are put in parentheses. If 50 examples of the same word order pattern were found and no counterexample was found, no further examples of that pattern were counted. The different patterns are ordered so that those which should change most quickly to SVO are at the top of the table, those which should change next are under that and so on.

	Main Clause		Conjunctive Clause		Subordinate Clause†		Relative Clause	
	N	%	N	%	N	%	N	%
SOV patterns								
PP_{PP}pred.C-Vf	3	17%	0	0%	1	14%	0	0%
PP vp -Vf	1	3%	0	0%	1	16%	1	25%
Nom.Obj.-Vf	0	0%	2	13%	4	27%	6	67%
Nom.IO. -Vf	0	0%	-	-	2	29%	0	0%
Pred.Noun-Vf	0	0%	0	0%	1	(100%)	5	45%
Pred.Adj -Vf	0	0%	1	16%	5	71%	3	(100%)
Pron.IO -Vf	0	0%	-	-	1	(100%)	2	(100%)
Pron.Obj.-Vf	0	0%	0	0%	1	(100%)	5	100%
Adv pred.C -Vf	16	59%	3	23%	5	100%	5	100%
Adv vp -Vf	0	0%	1	(33%)	1	(100%)	-	--
VSO patterns								
Vf-$_{PP}$PPpred.C.	15	+83%	13	+100%	6	+86%	7	+100%
Vf- vp	28	+97%	13	+100%	5	+83%	3	75%
Vf- Nom.Obj.	61	100%	13	87%	11	*73%	3	*33%
Vf- Nom.IO.	5	100%	-	--	5	*71%	1	*(100%)
Vf- Pred.Noun	15	100%	7	100%	0	(0%)	6	*55%
Vf- Pred.Adj.	5	100%	5	84%	2	*29%	0	(0%)
Vf- Pron.IO.	10	100%	-	--	0	(0%)	0	(0%)
Vf- Pron.Obj.	6	100%	5	100%	0	(0%)	0	0%
Vf- Adv.pred.C	11	41%	10	77%	0	0%	0	0%
Vf- Adv.vp	1	(100%)	2	(67%)	0	(0%)	-	-

VP-patterns in simple tense sentences
(counted according to the finite verb)
TABLE III

In this and subsequent tables:
+ = Structures which never occur in Current Dutch
* = Structures which occur to a lesser extent in Current Dutch
( ) = Too few data (fewer than 5 examples to my subjective standard)

Canale's implicational hierarchy would be confirmed by an increase in the percentages from the top down in the SOV column and a decrease in the VSO column. My data are generally meager, but they do corroborate this hierarchy. For example, data in Table VI (NP patterns) and Table V (other patterns) provide the clearest confirmation of the hierarchy. With respect to the VP patterns, the counts of

SOV PATTERNS IN DUTCH

	Main Clause		Conjunctive Clause		Subordinate Clause†		Relative Clause	
	N	%	N	%	N	%	N	%
SOV patterns								
PP$_{PP}$pred.C -V	2	25%	0	0%	0	0%	1	25%
vp -V	4	33%	0	0%	2	28%	2	20%
Nom.obj. -V	5	45%	8	38%	3	50%	8	89%
Nom. IO. -V	0	(0%)	2	(100%)	-	-	-	-
Pred.noun-V	0	(0%)	0	(0%)	0	0%	0	(0%)
Pred.adj.-V	1	(100%)	2	(100%)	1	(100%)	1	(100%)
V - aux	0	0%	2	9%	13	46%	24	59%
Pron.IO. -V	5	100%	3	(100%)	-	-	5	100%
Pron.Obj.-V	4	100%	1	(100%)	5	100%	5	100%
Adv.$_{pred.C}$-V	5	83%	5	(100%)	3	100%	8	100%
Adv.$_{vp}$-V	-	-	-	-	1	(100%)	1	(100%)
VSO patterns								
V - PP$_{PP}$pred.C	6	+75%	6	+100%	3	+(100%)	3	+75%
V - vp	8	+66%	8	+100%	5	+72%	8	+80%
V - Nom.Obj.	6	*55%	13	*62%	3	*50%	1	*11%
V - Nom.IO.	1	*(100%)	0	(0%)	-	-	-	-
V - Pred.noun	2	*(100%)	4	*(100%)	-	-	3	*(100%)
V - Pred.adj.	0	0%	0	(0%)	0	(0%)	0	(0%)
aux - V	18	100%	21	91%	15	54%	17	41%
V - Pron.IO.	0	0%	0	(0%)	-	-	0	0%
V - Pron.Obj.	0	0%	0	0%	0	0%	0	0%
V - Adv.$_{pred.C}$	1	17%	0	(0%)	0	0%	0	0%
V - Adv.$_{vp}$	-	-	-	-	0	(0%)	0	(0%)

VP-patterns in compound tense sentences
(counted according to the non-finite verb).
TABLE IV

SOV	N	%	VSO	N	%
NP-P	0	0%	P-NP	+50	100%
Adv.-Adj.	6	100%	Adj.-Adv.	0	0%
comp.-stand.	3	(100%)	stand.-comp.	0	0%

Other patterns
TABLE V

the conjunctive, subordinate and relative clause also roughly support the hierarchy. Only the order of AUX and non-finite verb seems to move more quickly into the VSO order than predicted by Canale's hierarchy. According to my data AUX + V ought to be found between the PP's and the nominal object, not after the nominal object. The data

SOV

Rel. clause - N	0	0%
PP - N	0	0%
Proper name-Common name	4	22%
genitive - N	28	37%
adjective - N	50	100%
numeral - N	6	100%
possesivum - N	50	100%
demonstrativum - N	50	100%

VSO

N - Rel. clause	50	100%
N - PP	6	100%
Common name-Proper name	14	78%
N - genitive	47	63%
N - adjective	0	0%
N - numeral	0	0%
N - possesivum	0	0%
N - demonstrativum	0	0%

NP patterns
TABLE VI

for main clauses in complex tenses are also usually in line with the predictions, but for main clauses in simple tenses the PP's and adverbs disturb the overall SVO patterns of this type of sentence. This is probably due to the frequent sentence initial PP's and adverbs, which occur more often in simple than in complex tenses (cf. Table II).

The different types of clauses in Tables III and IV are arranged so that an increase of SOV patterns would be predicted from left to right. Thus, from left to right there should be an increase in the percentages in the SOV column and a decrease in the percentages in the VSO column. In spite of scarcity of data, this prediction is confirmed for nearly all the patterns except the PP's: relative clauses retain the SOV order longer than subordinate clauses do; subordinate clauses longer than conjunctive; and conjunctive clauses slightly longer than main clauses.

My tables indicate, on the one hand, that Canale's implicational hierarchy of the changes in word order from SOV to SVO is rather well corroborated for Dutch, and this makes it more plausible too that Middle Dutch developed from an SOV language. On the other hand, the results also point to the fact that the surface structure of Middle Dutch was more characteristic of SVO than is that of Current Dutch. The structures marked with an * in Tables III and IV are ungrammatical in Current Dutch. We are dealing here with absolute differences between Middle and Current Dutch, and these absolute differences indicate that the SVO word order was more common in Middle Dutch than in Current Dutch. Remember that the influence of SVO in Middle Dutch did not extend to pronominal objects. They were always--except in main clauses and conjunctive clauses in simple tenses--before the main verb. Traugott (1972) has indicated that the place of the pronominal object served as a kind of threshold for the development of SVO in English. The loss of the preverbal position of pronouns in English was directly correlated to the loss of SOV. According to my data Middle Dutch never crossed that threshold.

Besides the absolute differences some scalar differences can also be noted, thanks to the recent counts of spoken Current Dutch by Jansen (1978), which allow for a comparison between Current and Middle Dutch. These scalar differences are marked with a + in the Tables. They concern only the VP patterns, and point again to the greater SVO character of Middle Dutch. According to Jansen, only 30% of the Predicate PP's in subordinate and relative clauses come after the V in Current Dutch. In main and conjunctive clauses they follow the V only in compound tenses. On the other hand, 88% follow the V in my Middle Dutch text. The same is true for VP PP's. In Jansen's counts only 26% came after the V, and in my data 79%.

Another indication of the rise of SOV in Dutch is the fact that Current Dutch requires postposition-like elements in some clauses where Middle Dutch required prepositions. Compare in (1) the Middle Dutch with Kersbergen's (1936) translation in Current Dutch.

(1) Middle Dutch: en ghinc met hastecheiden *op* den berghe
'and went with speed *up* the mountain'

Current Dutch: en ging met haast de berg *op*
'and went with speed the mountain *up*'

I hope it has been clear in this brief space that up to the Middle Ages Middle Dutch was developing in an SVO direction like English and the Scandinavian languages, but that it returned to SOV after that time. I have already mentioned that a rough and very general description of Frisian and German seems to conform to the development sketched for Dutch. The question then arises why it is that in those languages the SVO tendency did not develop further; these languages ultimately acquired even more SOV characteristics than they had had about 1300.

3. *Possible reasons for the rise of SOV.* The rise of SOV patterns in German and Frisian has been attributed to an external cause--the imitation of Latin patterns (see e.g. Behaghel 1932, Fokkema 1948). In principle this could also be valid for Dutch. But it seems to me on the whole unlikely that the rise of SOV could be due to the influence of Latin. First, it has not been demonstrated that the word order of Latin was SOV (Ebert 1978:43). Even if this *could* be demonstrated, it is improbable that those SOV patterns influenced the rise of SOV in German, Dutch and Frisian, since it is doubtful that a 'nearly' dead language like Latin could influence the syntactic structure of a spoken language in a period like the Middle Ages when the majority of the people were illiterate. The influence of Latin is also questionable on the grounds that SOV developed far away from Italy, the center of Latin learning. The influence of Latin would be more plausible if the 'SOV area' had surrounded that center. Finally, the borrowing of Latin patterns seems to be an even more implausible explanation for the development of SOV in Frisian and Dutch than in German because of the internal structure of those languages. The Middle German case system had not been as weakened as those of Middle Dutch and Middle Frisian, and so German resembled Latin more than Frisian and Dutch. Borrowing Latin patterns is more improbable for Dutch and Frisian than for German, since reordering of constituents in Dutch and Frisian was more likely to lead to ambiguous sentences than it would in German.

It should be clear from the discussion above that I do not believe that the rise or perhaps better the return to SOV in Dutch, Frisian and German is especially due to the influence of Latin. At the same time, however, an internal or external cause is needed to explain the rise of SOV, because changes from SVO to SOV are usually unnatural (Li 1977:xiii). Moreover the rise of SOV in Frisian, German and Dutch is counter to the general rule that innovations are first introduced in main clauses and later spread to subordinate clauses, a rule which is the stronger since it is in keeping with a recent proposal in general syntactic theory (cf. Lightfoot's (1976) interpretation of Emonds' structure preserving hypothesis).[3]

Explanations for the rise of SOV present evident problems. Perhaps it would help to turn the question around. Both SVO and SOV structures were present in Middle Dutch at the same time and SOV predominated in the long run. Why is it that SVO did not take over in Dutch? Dutch main clauses never went beyond phase c) of Stockwell's hypothesized transitional sequences between Germanic SOV and

Modern English (X)SVO. In other words, exbraciation did not continue. Were the motivations for exbraciation which Stockwell puts forward for English, and which led to a reinterpretation of English as an SVO language, not also present in Dutch, Frisian and German? I have surveyed this question briefly for Middle Dutch.[4]

The first convincing motivation given by Stockwell for exbraciation is the following: 83% of the sentences in the part of the Anglo-Saxon Chronicle that he analyzes have simple verbs and consequently all objects and adverbial material appear in those sentences after the main verb. This led to the abducing of a rule that nominal and adverbial complements followed their head verb (Stockwell 1977: 302-305). My data for Middle Dutch are presented in Table VII. It appears that complex unit verbs occurred in all clause types more frequently than in Old English. This might have had a restraining effect on exbraciation (cf. Gerritsen forthcoming).

	simple unit verbs		complex unit verbs	
relative clauses	206	65%	112	35%
subordinate clauses	220	50%	224	50%
declarative main clauses	724	70%	304	30%
Total Middle Dutch	1150	64%	640	36%
Total Old English	186	83%	37	17%

Number of clauses with simple unit verbs and with complex unit verbs in *Het Limburgse leven van Jezus* (caput 1-100) compared with Stockwell's (1977:302) counts for the Anglo-Saxon Chronicle (892-900)
TABLE VII

Stockwell's second motivation for exbraciation is the occasional occurrence of certain rightward movement rules, which lifted constituents out of the sentence brace and destroyed the verb final appearance of surface clauses: extraposition of relative clauses, conjuncts and appositives (1977:305-308). Although all these extrapositions occur in Middle Dutch and are sometimes mentioned in the literature on Middle Dutch syntax (Weijnen 1971:16, 20, Stoett 1921:143) they are anything but frequent. At any rate, it seems to me that these extrapositions were too rare to destroy the verb final appearance of Middle Dutch surface clauses.

It is true that Stockwell's third motivation for exbraciation, postdeposition of adverbs and afterthoughts

(1977:308-309), does occur in Middle Dutch, but it is questionable whether it occurred with the same force as in Old English (Van Ginneken 1938:157). Stockwell's last motivation for exbraciation, the rightward movement of sentential subjects and objects, is roughly true for Middle Dutch too, except that sentential subjects also take a preverbal position.

(2) Dat ik van katten houd, is duidelijk.
    That I   cats like, is obvious.

In short, it is clear that Stockwell's motivations for exbraciation are of less force in Middle Dutch than in English. This may account for the fact that Dutch did not become an SVO language (perhaps this holds too for Frisian and German). Nevertheless this is only a shifting of the problem, for now the question is why did English exbraciate to a larger extent than Dutch (and perhaps German and Frisian)? I hope to deal with this problem at another time.

NOTES

*This paper reports on research in progress on the change in word order in the Germanic languages. I am grateful to Paul Hopper, Frank Jansen, Jan Kooij, Jaap de Rooij, Sture Ureland and A. Weijnen for comments on earlier drafts of this paper. I thank Jeanne Winner for polishing my English.

[1] These counts are based on the raw unpublished data of Van Ginneken (1938).

[2] The stronger SVO character of Middle Dutch is also displayed by the irregular use of inversion in main clauses. The verb second constraint was not as closely followed in Middle Dutch as it is in Current Dutch. Examples of XSVO main clauses did not occur in the Middle Dutch text analyzed in Table II. They are however cited in a number of studies on Middle Dutch syntax (see for example Van den Berg 1971, Weijnen 1971, Ornée 1955).

[3] Perhaps this theory is not as general as has been claimed (cf. Stockwell 1977:296).

[4] Time has not permitted a full study. Motivations for exbraciation would be more convincing if for each motivation figures were given for how often it occurred, or still better, how often it could have occurred. Further investigation in this matter is in progress.

REFERENCES

Albering, L.A.H. 1934. *Vergelijkend-syntactische studie van den Renout en het volksboek der Heemskinderen.* Groningen: J.B. Wolters.
Allard, E. 1937. *Een grammatikaal onderzoek naar het proza van Hadewych.* Amsterdam: Succes.
Behaghel, Otto. 1932. *Deutsche Syntax.* Vol. 4. Heidelberg: Carl Winter.
Canale, M. 1976. "Implicational hierarchies of word order relationships". In *Current progress in historical linguistics,* 36-39. Ed. by William M. Christie, Jr. Amsterdam: North Holland.
Christie, William M. Jr. (ed.). 1976. *Current progress in historical linguistics.* Amsterdam: North Holland.
Ebert, Robert Peter. 1978. *Historische Syntax des Deutschen.* Stuttgart: J.B. Metzlerische Verlagsbuchhandlung.
Fokkema, K. 1948. *Beknopte Friese Spraakkunst.* Groningen: J.B. Wolters.
Givón, Talmy. 1977. "The drift from VSO to SVO in Biblical Hebrew. The pragmatics of Tense-Aspect". In *Mechanisms of syntactic change,* 181-255. Ed. by Charles N. Li. Austin: University of Texas Press.
Haugen, Einar. 1976. *The Scandinavian Languages.* London: Faber & Faber Ltd.
Hammarström, Emil. 1923. *Zur Stellung des Verbums in der deutschen Sprache.* Lund: Gleerupska Universitetsbokhandeln.
Jansen, F. 1978. "Hoe krijgt een spreker zijn woorden op en rijtje? Taalgebruiksaspekten van de 'PP over V' konstruktie". In *Aspekten van woordvolgorde in het Nederlands,* 70-104. Ed. by J.G. Kooij. Leiden: Vakgroep Nederlandse Taal- & Letterkunde.
Li, Charles N. (ed.). 1977. *Mechanisms of syntactic change.* Austin: University of Texas Press.
Lightfoot, David. 1976. "The base component as a locus of syntactic change". In *Current progress in historical linguistics,* 17-37. Ed. by William M. Christie Jr. Amsterdam: North Holland.
Maurer, F. 1926. *Untersuchungen über die deutsche Verbstellung in ihrer geschichtlichen Entwicklung.* Heidelberg: Carl Winter's Universitätsbuchhandlung.
Ornée, W.A. 1955. *De zin in het Nederlands proza en de poëzie van Philips van Marnix.* Groningen: Rijksuniversiteit.
Pulles, J.A.M. 1950. *Structuurschema's van de zin in Middelnederlands geestelijk proza.* Nijmegen: Centrale Drukkerij N.V.
Schweistal, K.G. (ed.). 1971. *Grammatik, Kybernetik, Kommunikation. Festschrift für Alfred Hoppe.* Bonn: Ferd. Dümmlers Verlag.
Stellinga, G. 1954. *Zinsvormen en zinsfuncties in de abele spelen.* Groningen: J.B. Wolters.
Stockwell, Robert P. 1977. "Motivations for exbraciation in Old English". In *Mechanisms of syntactic change,* 291-317. Ed. by Charles N. Li. Austin: University of Texas Press.
Stoett, F.A. 1923. *Middelnederlandse Spraakkunst.* 3rd ed. The Hague: Nijhoff.
Traugott, Elizabeth Closs. 1972. *A history of English syntax.* New York: Holt, Rinehart and Winston.

Ureland, P.S. 1976. "Typological, diachronic and areal linguistic perspectives of North Germanic Syntax". In *The Nordic languages and modern linguistics 3*. Ed. by John Weinstock. Austin: University of Texas Press.

Van den Berg, B. 1971. *Inleiding tot de Middelnederlandse Syntaksis*. Groningen: Wolters-Noordhoff.

Van der Kallen, Maria. 1938. *Een grammaticaal en rythmisch onderzoek van Hadewijchs poëzie*. The Hague: Cedo.

Van Ginneken, Jac. 1938. *De taalschat van het Limburgse leven van Jezus*. Maastricht-Vroenhoven: Gebr. van Aelst.

Van Kersbergen, G.C. 1936. *Het Luiksche Diatessaron in het Nieuw-Nederlandsch vertaald met een inleiding over de herkomst van den Middelnederlandschen tekst*. Rijswijk: Drukkerij Nieuwvoorde.

Venneman, Theo. 1974a. "Analogy in generative grammar; the origin of word order". In *Proceedings of the Eleventh International Congress of Linguists*, 79-83. Ed. by Luigi Heilmann. Bologna: Il Mulino.

──────. 1974b. "Theoretical word order studies. Results and problems". *Papiere zur Linguistik* 7.5-25.

Weijnen, A.A. 1971. *Schets van de geschiedenis van de Nederlandse Syntaxis*. Assen: Van Gorcum & Comp. N.V.

Wessén, Elias. 1970. *Schwedische Sprachgeschichte*. Vol. 3. Berlin: Walter de Gruyter & Co.

DEVELOPMENTS IN THE DUTCH LEFT-DISLOCATION
STRUCTURES AND THE VERB-SECOND CONSTRAINT

FRANK JANSEN
Moller Instituut
Tilburg, The Netherlands

0. *Introduction.* This paper deals with three types of
Left-Dislocation structures (henceforth: LD's) in Middle
Dutch (1200-1500). Only one of these LD's survived the
seventeenth century, and we have to ask why. I propose an
explanation which is grounded on the changing of Dutch from
a language in which verb-second word order is common into
a strict verb-second language.

In section (1) I will give the characteristics of the
LD's in Middle Dutch. In (2) I will go into the features
of the only LD existing in Modern Dutch. Section (3) is
devoted to my (tentative) explanation of the changes and
the section (4) to conclusions regarding the theory of syntactic change, and of changing LD's in particular.*

1. *Three types of LD in Middle Dutch.*

1.1. *Dem-LD.* The following structure has been proposed
(by, among others, Chomsky 1977 and Gundel 1977) for the
description of LD sentences in English:

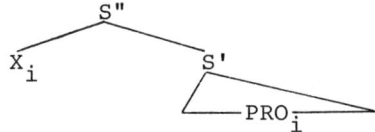

FIGURE I

In other words, a constituent is followed by a sentence
with a proform in it, which is coreferential with that constituent. This description seems to be apt for Middle
Dutch LD's also. In the case of the first type of LD, the
proform takes the form of a demonstrative pronoun, *die*

'this', 'that', 'these' or *dat* 'that'. Therefore I shall call this type Dem-LD's. Relevant properties of this type of LD are:

(i) The proform has to undergo an obligatory fronting transformation, irrespective of its syntactic function in the sentence (for example subject, direct object). After the operation of this fronting transformation, the proform precedes all other elements in the sentence, except the LD-constituent to which it is coreferential. An example of a typical Dem-LD in a Middle Dutch text is:[1]

(1) Ferguut die kwam daer sciere

   'Ferguut that-one came there rapidly'

   (*Ferguut*, 1.2495 (ed. E. Verwijs)).

(ii) The demonstrative pronoun is congruent with its antecedent (the LD-element) for number, gender and case. I give no examples because of lack of space.

(iii) The presence of Dem-LD is not conditioned by a special pragmatic function of this constituent. It is not the case that the use of Dem-LD is restricted to sentences where the possible LD-elements refer to someone or something totally new or unexpected. On the contrary, only 5 of the 31 examples of Dem-LD which I studied involved fronting totally new or unexpected information.[2]

(iv) Besides the obligatory operation of the fronting rule which moves the demonstrative pronoun, other, optional, fronting rules can operate. Operation of these rules always results in a sentence with the following order of constituents: LD-element - proform - fronted constituent (for example an adverb) - finite verb. An example is:

(2) Maer die poortren die vroomelike bescudden die ridder coene

   'But these burghers those-ones bravely protected the knight gallant'

   (*Heinric en Margriete van Limborgh* II, 1. 1170)

There are no examples of Dem-LD's with a constituent between the LD-element and the demonstrative pronoun: **die poortren vroomelike die bescudden.*

1.2. *So-LD*. The second type of LD in Middle Dutch has the deictic adverb *so* 'so' as the proform in the sentence which is coreferential with the LD-element. A typical example of this LD-construction, henceforth *so*-LD, is:

(3) den coninc so verhinghen si
    'the-(acc.) king so hanged they'.
                        (Van Maerlant, *Rijmbijbel* l. 6721)

Relevant properties of this type of LD are:

(i) The proform *so* undergoes an obligatory fronting rule, which moves it into a position before the finite verb, see for example (3).

(ii) The proform *so* is never congruent with its antecedent. It is invariant, as is characteristic for deictic adverbs of manner.[3]

(iii) The pragmatic function of the LD-element depends on its form. If the LD-element is an NP, PP or dependent clause, it refers in all cases to someone or something new or unexpected, or to something that has to be resumed; this is the case in (3), where the king is mentioned 20 verses earlier. If the LD-element is a pronominal form itself, it is in almost all cases (36 out of 38) used anaphorically, for example:

(4) Hi so maecte gheeste twee
    'He (God, mentioned in previous verse) so made two minds'.
                        (Van Boendale, *Der Leken Spieghel*,I,1, l. 27)

(iv) Besides the obligatory fronting of *so*, another optional fronting rule may operate, which always results in the following order of constituents: LD-element - *so* - fronted constituent (for example the subject) - finite verb:

(5) want boven alle leden so dit let vanghet den mensche meest
    'for above all organs so this organ (sc. the mouth of a wife) entraps the people in most cases'.
                        (*Spieghel der Sonden*, l. 798)

The optional fronting rule never moves a constituent into the position between the LD-element and *so*.

(v) There existed what I call a 'double LD-construction'. In that case, the LD-element is followed by a coreferential demonstrative pronoun and *so*, in that order.

(6) Want Lodewijc die coninc die so was haer naeste bloet
    'For Lodewijc the king, that-one so was her nearest relation'
                        (*Die Borchgravinne van Couchi* II, l. 131)

There are no attestations of a double LD with the other order of proforms: *die coninc so die.

1.3. *Pers-LD.* The third and last type of LD in Middle Dutch has one of the personal pronouns as its proform in the sentence. An example of this type, henceforth Pers-LD, is:

(7) die patriarke hi deede all bescrive cleen ende groet

'the patriarch he did everything describe small and big'

(*Roman der Lorreinen*, nieuwe fragmenten 1. 81)

Relevant properties of Pers-LD are:

(i) The proform (the personal pronoun) may be fronted by an optional fronting rule. If it is not fronted, it has a position directly after the finite verb (see (10) below).

(ii) The pronoun is congruent with the LD-element in number, gender and case.

(iii) Pers-LD is clearly conditioned by the pragmatic function of the LD-element. Only 7 of the 29 examples of Pers-LD have an LD-element which refers to old or expected information. Thus, Pers-LD is specifically used for new and important LD-elements (see also Stellinga 1954:10 for stylistic comments on Pers-LD).

(iv) Besides the optional fronting transformation which moves the personal pronoun to a position before the finite verb, another optional fronting rule can operate. This rule can move a constituent towards the position between the LD element and the proform, which results in the following order of constituents: LD-element - fronted constituent (for example the direct object) - proform - verb:

(8) Christus twee blinden hi sien dede

'Christ two blind men he did see'

(Stoett, *Middelnederlandse syntaxis*, 31)

(v) Pers-LD can be combined with *so*-LD. There are two possibilities in that case. The first is the structural analogue of the combination of Dem-LD and *so*-LD.

(9) Centurio hi so bat ons heere over sijnen kind

'Centurio he so prayed (to) our Lord for his child'

(*Spieghel der Sonden*, 1.5427)

The other possible combination is that *so* is fronted to its position before the finite verb, and the personal pronoun is not moved. This construction is only possible if both types of LD have a different LD-element, for example (10):

(10) So wien so van iemants doet ghedeel ghevalt altehant
na sinen doet wilhi so sal hi gaen te sinen huus

'So (the one to whom belongs a part of an inheritance)$_i$
(if he wants to)$_j$ (so)$_j$ will he$_i$ go to their house'

(*Gentse Keuren* (ed. Koch), 51,12-14)

2. *Left-Dislocations in present day spoken Dutch.* In this section, I will give some results of an inquiry into LD's in Modern spoken Dutch. The data are taken from a corpus of spoken Dutch, which has been designed and assembled for a sociolinguistic survey of syntactic constructions in speech.[4]

The first result is that *so*-LD has completely vanished. It is highly improbable that this must be attributed to differences in dialects (the Middle Dutch texts being written mainly in Flemish dialects, while the spoken language corpus is based on Hollandic speech), for two reasons. In the first place, all three types of LD also show up in Middle Dutch texts which are written in a Northern dialect. Second, *so*-LD is not reported in any of the dictionaries of the Southern dialects of today.

The second result concerns Pers-LD. I did not find any example of it in the corpus. This is an embarrassing result, because Pers-LD has recently been amply described by Van Riemsdijk and Zwarts 1974. Moreover, Pers-LD does not sound ungrammatical, provided that it is pronounced with a 'comma intonation', for example:

(11) Pi$^{\text{e}\,t\,(?)}$ / hij komt straks nog even langs

'Pete (rising intonation - pause) he will come along in a few minutes'.

This Pers-LD has all the features of the so-called 'hanging topic' construction (Cinque 1977). It is possible that the characteristics of our corpus, especially the predominance of monologues, strongly disfavored the use of hanging topics, and that this has to be the reason for its absence. I think however that the corpus is extensive enough (ca. 19,000 sentences) for us to conclude that Pers-LD is very scarce in present day spoken Dutch.

The remaining type of LD, Dem-LD, is found frequently in the corpus. Relevant properties of Modern Dem-LD are:

(i) The proform is obligatorily fronted to a position before the finite verb.

(ii) The pronoun is congruent with the LD-element in number and gender.

(iii) The presence of Dem-LD is conditioned by the length and complexity of the LD-element. This is demonstrated in Figure II:

type of LD-element*	Complex NP	Dependent Clause	NP	PP	Adverb	Pronoun
non-left-dislocated	65	155	682	440	666	10,000>
left-dislocated	55	84	140	83	18	1
% of LD	46%	35%	20%	16%	3%	0%

FIGURE II

I have also investigated whether or not LD is conditioned by a special pragmatic function of the LD element. The results of this investigation are given in Figure III.

Pragmatic function	topical	new
non-left-dislocated NP's	55 (68%)	26 (32%)
left-dislocated NP's	117 (56%)	94 (44%)

The difference between the percentages of LD of new and topical NP's is not statistically significant when tested with a χ^2 test

FIGURE III

As Figure III makes clear, there are no statistically significant differences between LD-elements and sentence-initial constituents, as far as their pragmatic function is concerned.

(iv) The most important feature of Modern Dem-LD is its intonation. The actual intonation found contrasts with descriptions of LD based on intuitions (Van Riemsdijk and Zwarts 1974; Koster 1978). Such descriptions invariably give a comma intonation between the LD-element and the sentence; however, I found this intonation in only 15% of the LD-sentences. Thus, there is no reason to assume that the LD-element is set off from the remainder of the sentence by comma intonation. A typical example of Modern Dem-LD is:

(12) een boer die heeft altijd werk

'a farmer that-one has always work'

Finally, I must mention another intonation, which is by no means scarce in my corpus. In this type of LD-sentence, the pause is between the proform and the finite verb. For example:

(13) de derde die / zal nu de derde klas atheneum gaan doen
  'the third that-one (referring to a daughter) / will now take a course on the third level'

This sort of intonation pattern indicates that the LD-element has become part of the syntactic structure of S' in spoken Dutch. Our description of Dem-LD will probably be even more accurate, if we assume that the LD-element and the proform have become one constituent.

(v) An investigation of the sociolinguistic properties of LD made clear that the use of LD is not conditioned by the class or sex of the speaker, nor by the formality of the speech situation. Thus, the LD-construction is an option in the syntax of all members of the Dutch speech community.

My conclusion is, that Modern Dem-LD has been grammaticalized almost completely. Its underlying structure is something like Figure IV.

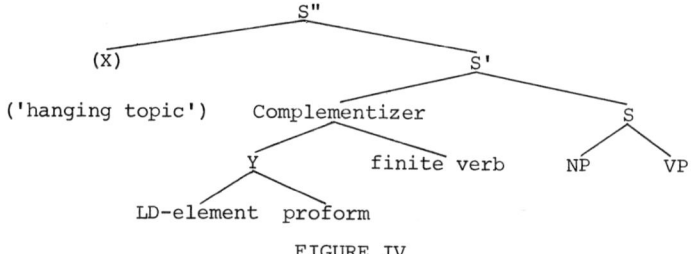

FIGURE IV

The next section is devoted to the problem of why Pers-LD and *so*-LD disappeared, and why Dem-LD changed as it did. My explanation is based on the different properties of the three LD's in Middle Dutch. These properties are summarized in the following figure:

	So-LD	Dem-LD	Mod. Dem-LD	Pers-LD
Proform congruent with LD-element?	no	yes	yes	yes
Proform directly follows LD?	no	yes	yes	no
LD-element has a marked pragmatic function?	yes, for non-pronominal LD's	no	no	yes

FIGURE V

3. *A tentative explanation of the changes.*

3.1. *The verb-second restriction.* Dutch has always been a verb-second language. The order of constituents in declarative main clauses is: one and only one constituent, and then the finite verb (see also Gerritsen, this volume). However, it is necessary to make a distinction between strict verb-second languages and moderate verb-second languages. In the first type, (14) is an obligatory rule:

(14) No declarative main clause may have more than one constituent before the finite verb.

In the second type, the moderate verb-second language, (14) is only a norm. A sentence with a structure which does not follow (14) is not ungrammatical, only marked. Dutch has evolved from a moderate verb-second language (up to the seventeenth century) to a strict verb-second language (Debrabandere 1976, Koelmans 1975).

I will illustrate this change by citing two sentences from Middle Dutch prose with the finite verb in third (15) and fourth (16) position. These are completely ungrammatical in modern Dutch because it is a strict verb-second language.

(15) ende darnar alleene bi sine ede ende sonder bevanc sal hi sin quite

'and after that by his oath alone and without reservation will he be without debts'

(*Gentse Keuren* (ed. Koch) 1960, 51, 4-5)

(16) Mar Judas nochtan onwaerdich bleef

'But Judas still angry remained'

(*Dat lyden ende die passie ons heeren Jesus*, 5, 32-33)

Structures like the ones in (15) and (16) are not common. However, they are frequent enough, and occur in so many different kinds of literature, that they cannot be considered ungrammatical (Koelmans 1975).

3.2. *Why are there no longer any so-LD's?* Before we can look for a successful explanation of the disappearance of *so*-LD, we have to ask why Dem-LD did not disappear. The Dem-LD-sentences in Modern spoken Dutch do not follow restriction (14), and should therefore be as ungrammatical as (15) or (16). The reason why this is not so is, in my opinion, that the LD-element and its proform were reinterpreted as one constituent. This could happen because the demonstrative pronoun always followed its antecedent immediately. The original proform in the sentence became a kind of an appositive to its antecedent (see Figure IV).

Now we have to ask why *so*-LD did not persist. Dem-LD and *so*-LD have much in common; in particular they share the property that the proform has to be fronted before the finite verb. In my opinion, the reason for their divergent development must be sought in the morphological properties of *so* and the demonstrative pronouns. The invariant form of *so* made it different from the other words with pronominal functions, which are always in concord with their antecedents. Furthermore, *so* could function as a pronoun, not only in LD-constructions, but also independently (17):

(17) numer en moeten sy ooc sien dat sy seer van ons begheren *so* en sullen sy ooc (sc. sien) moghen wij t verweren

'furthermore, they are not allowed to see the things which they want so ('that') won't they see, if we can prevent it'

(Van Maerlant, *History van Troijen* II, 1. 147888)

However, *so* was used much more frequently as a deictic adverb of manner. These adverbial characteristics of *so* made it difficult for a learner of Dutch to reinterpret *so* together with its LD-element as one part of speech. When Dutch became a strict verb-second language, the LD-element and the proform *so* could not constitute one sentence initial element, and the construction became obsolete.

This explanation predicts that *so*-LD would have remained if the LD-element was of the same word class as *so*. In those cases the learner of the language could reinterpret the two elements as one constituent. This prediction is borne out by the facts. Deictic adverbs, such as *daar* 'there' and *hier* 'here' have two other variants in Modern colloquial Dutch, viz. *daarzo*, *hierzo* and *daaro*, *hiero*. Both variants are direct descendants of the *so*-dislocated adverbs in Middle Dutch (Simons 1912), for example:

(18) Al blies se God den mensche in, daar so was haer eerste begin

'All blew it (the spirit) God in men, there (sc. in God) so was their first beginning'

(Van Boendale, *der Leken Spiegel*, I,1, 62)

In these cases we have a completed grammaticalization of the original LD-element and proform, as one constituent.

3.3. *Why are there no longer Pers-LD's?* The main difference between Pers-LD and Dem-LD is the fixed position of the demonstrative pronoun directly after its antecedent, while the personal pronoun could have several positions in the sentence. This is the reason why the LD-element together with the proform could not be reinterpreted as one constituent. If both constituents were placed before the finite verb, they were felt to violate the verb-second restriction. Therefore, Pers-LD disappeared as a normal LD-construction. The only LD-type that could remain was the one exemplified in (11). The LD-element, which functions as a 'hanging topic', is separated maximally from the sentence. The sentence starts with a new intonation pattern after the LD-element, and this is the reason that this type LD is not felt to be a violation of the verb-second constraint, but more as two distinct sentences.

Another possible factor may have been the resemblance of the unmarked pragmatic function of Dem-LD to the unmarked pragmatic function of fronting. There are two types of fronting in Dutch: a) the fronting of constituents referring to old or expected information (topic-fronting); and b) the fronting of constituents referring to new or unexpected information (comment-fronting). The b)-type of fronting is marked: it is very scarce in spoken Dutch (Jansen, 1978), and only acceptable with an additional stress on the fronted constituent. Thus, Dem-LD and the unmarked a)-type of fronting both result in a topical sentence initial constituent. Perhaps this fact facilitated the reinterpretation.

The pragmatic function of Pers-LD, on the other hand, corresponds to the marked comment-fronting. It does not seem unreasonable that the reinterpretation of the LD-element and the personal pronoun as one constituent was difficult here, because the target of this reinterpretation, comment-fronting, is highly marked.

4. *Concluding remarks.* In this last section, I shall make a few more general remarks, first about changes in LD-sentences in other languages, and second about the place of the Dutch changes in LD's in the general pattern of changes in Dutch.

As far as I know, only one type of development of LD-sentences has been described. Keenan 1972 and Givón 1976 mention the incorporation of the proform of an LD-sentence in the verb. The end result of this development is that the original LD-element is the subject of the sentence, and the original proform has become a suffixed subject marker on the verb.

If I am right, there are two other possible developments. The first one is exemplified by Pers-LD: from a normal LD-construction to an obligatory 'hanging topic' reading, in which the LD-element has very loose (if any) syntactic and intonational ties with the following sentence. The second development is the incorporation of the proform into its LD-element. This has happened in Dutch with the *daarzo* subtype of *so*-LD, and, less completely, with Dem-LD.

Both new types of development are conditioned by the strict verb-second constraint; the first one, because one of the two constituents before the finite verb has been 'thrown out' of the intonational unity of the sentence, and the second one, because the LD-element and the proform had to become one constituent in order to keep their position before the finite verb. It goes without saying that this explanation has to be tested by looking for the developments of LD-structures in other languages with a strict or moderate verb-second constraint.

Finally, a short remark is in order concerning the extent to which the changes in the Dutch LD's, and the development of a more strict verb-second order, fit into the general pattern of changes in Dutch. In my opinion, both changes, and the ones described by Gerritsen (this volume), point in one direction: Dutch has changed from a language in which the word order, at least before the finite verb and after the non-finite verb, was determined by the pragmatic function of the elements, towards a language with a word order which is determined by the syntactic function of the elements. This change is only partially related to the typology put forward by Li and Thompson 1976 of subject-prominent and topic-prominent languages: Dutch is, and has always been, a subject-prominent language. However, it had various devices (fronting transformations, LD's), for the indication of the topical elements and the unexpected elements. Now only one of those devices is left: movement towards the first position. In other words, the power of pragmatic factors as determinants of the order of constituents has diminished.

Needless to say, we are only at the beginning of research into the changes which have occurred, and are occurring, in the Dutch language.

NOTES

*This paper is a revised version of a paper originally written in Dutch. I am very grateful to all those who criticized that paper, in particular E. van den Berg, S.C. Dik and P.C. Muysken. Section 2 of this paper is based on the results of an investigation of syntactic constructions in spoken Dutch, which would not have been possible without a subsidiary grant from the Netherlands Organization for the advancement of Pure Research (Z.W.O.).

[1] The sources of my Middle Dutch examples are indicated within brackets. However, I did not do any philological work for this investigation. All examples are taken from the *Middelnederlands Woordenboek* 'Middle Dutch Dictionary' by Verdam, or one of the two Middle Dutch grammars, Stoett 1923 and Van den Berg 1971. All sentences (except one, (8)) were checked in the Middle Dutch texts, together with their context, see fn. 2.

[2] In order to explore the pragmatic function of the different types of LD, I investigated the LD-sentences in context. I distinguished three pragmatic functions of the LD-element: (i) comment, if there was no linguistic element in the 20 sentences before the LD-sentence, which referred to the same person or thing, (ii) resuming, if there was at least one linguistic element in one of the sentences between the fourth and the 20th previous sentences which referred to the same thing, and (iii) topical, if the LD-element referred to something which (or someone who) was referred to in one of the four preceding sentences.

[3] Middle Dutch *so* had more or less the same range of syntactic possibilities as Modern English *so*, for example in: *I hope so*.

[4] The material on the basis of which the frequencies have been computed, is a corpus of about 17 hours of Spoken Dutch. This corpus consists of interviews of 40 inhabitants (aged 50 years or older) of Leiden, a town of 100,000 people in the Western part of the Netherlands. Both sexes are equally well represented, as are the lowest and highest socioeconomic classes. The interviewer asked all the informants the same questions, and none of them were aware of the linguistic purpose of the interview.

REFERENCES

Berg, Berend van den. 1971. *Inleiding tot de Middelnederlandse syntaxis*. Groningen: Wolters.
Chomsky, Noam. 1977. "On *Wh*-movement". In *Formal syntax*, 7-132. Ed. by Peter Culicover, Thomas Wasow, and Adrian Akmajian. New York: Academic Press.
Cinque, G. 1977. "The movement nature of Left Dislocation". *Linguistic Inquiry* 8.397-412.

Debrabandere, I. 1976. "De SVf-woordorde in zinnen met aanloop". *Handelingen Koninklijke Commissie voor Toponymie en Dialectologie* 50.87-97.
Gerritsen, Marinel. This volume. "An analysis of the rise of SOV patterns in Dutch".
Givón, Talmy. 1976. "Topic, pronoun and grammatical agreement". In *Subject and topic*, 151-88. Ed. by Charles N. Li. New York: Academic Press.
Gundel, Janet K. 1977. "The role of topic and comment in linguistic theory". Indiana University Linguistics Club, mimeo.
Jansen, Frank. 1978. "Sentence initial elements in spoken Dutch". In *Linguistics in the Netherlands* 2.101-114. Ed. by W. Zonneveld. Lisse: Peter de Ridder Press.
Keenan, Edward. 1972. "On semantically based grammar". *Linguistic Inquiry* 3.413-462.
Koelmans, L. 1975. "Zeventiende eeuws en Modern Nederlands: overeenstemming en verschil in de syntaxis". *Nieuwe Taalgids* 68. 125-32.
Koster, J. 1978. "Why subject sentences don't exist". In *Recent transformational studies in European languages*. Ed. by S. Jay Keyser. Cambridge, Mass.: MIT Press.
Li, Charles N. and Sandra A. Thompson. 1976. "Subject and topic: a new typology of language". In *Subject and topic*, 457-89. Ed. by Charles N. Li. New York: Academic Press.
Riemsdijk, H. van, & F. Zwarts. 1974. "Left dislocation in Dutch and the status of copying rules". Ms. MIT.
Simons, P.J. 1912. "Langs en op de rand van zelfstandigheid". *Nieuwe Taalgids* 6.173-182.
Stellinga, G. 1954. *Zinsvormen en zinsfuncties in de abele spelen*. Groningen: Wolters.
Stoett, Frederik A. 1923. *Middelnederlandse spraakkunst*. The Hague: Nijhoff. 3rd ed.

FROM PASSIVE TO ACTIVE IN KURDISH
VIA THE ERGATIVE CONSTRUCTION

THEODORA BYNON
School of Oriental and African Studies
University of London

In his introductory remarks to the chapter in *Mechanisms of Syntactic Change* dealing with syntactic change and ergativity, Li (1977:xv) poses two questions:

(1) 'How does an accusative language become ergative?'
and
(2) 'How does an ergative language become accusative?'

and goes on to say:

> While the passive-to-ergative reanalysis appears to be an important mechanism for the development of ergative languages ..., we have not yet come to grips with question (2).

The following discussion is primarily concerned with the second of Li's questions.* Since, however, it deals with an Iranian language, and as the most recent account of the rise of ergativity in Iranian (Anderson 1977) would appear to be unnecessarily at variance with Li's hypothesis, we will also touch briefly upon the first of Li's questions.

In the case of the Indo-Iranian languages we are in the fortunate position of having a fair amount of documentary evidence not only for the development of ergativity but also for its subsequent loss, since certain of the languages which in the past acquired the feature have subsequently ceased to be ergative. We are on the other hand dealing in Indo-Iranian with only one specific variety of ergativity, that characterized as being 'morphological' and 'split' (Anderson 1976, Tegey 1978, Comrie 1978). The first epithet refers to the fact that the ergativity is confined to case marking and verb agreement, the syntactic relations seemingly remaining those of an accusative language, the second to the fact that it is further restricted to certain tenses or aspects, in our case to the past tenses of transitive verbs (that is, historically speaking, to verb forms derived from the Indo-Iranian perfect participle). Bearing these limitations in mind, we shall first discuss the development of ergativity in Western Iranian and then, using dialect comparison to supplement the documentary evidence, attempt to account for its subsequent loss in one of the Kurdish dialects.

Ergative constructions developed in both Middle Indic and Middle Iranian from Old Indic and Old Iranian syntagms containing the periphrastic past tense of a transitive verb, the source construction consisting of two noun phrases and the perfect participle together with the appropriate present tense form of the verb 'to be' (this latter being absent under certain conditions). In both cases one of the two noun phrases, representing what was at the same time the grammatical subject and logical object of the sentence, was in the nominative. As regards the other noun phrase, the situation differed somewhat in the two branches of the family. In Old Indic it was in the instrumental case, which was that normally employed to indicate the agent of a passive, whereas in the Old Iranian branch things were more complex. In Old Persian it was in the genitive, which was a syncretistic case incorporating also the old dative, while in Avestan it was in either the genitive or the dative, apparently with some subtle semantic distinction (Reichelt 1909, §§461, 501; cf. however Cardona 1970:10). In his attempt to account for this situation, Anderson (1977:329ff) correlates the formal difference between Old Indic and Old Iranian in the choice of case with a presumed difference in function, claiming that the Indic construction was passive whereas the Iranian one was possessive. That is to say, following Benveniste, he interprets the genitive of the Old Persian construction as the reflex of a former dative with possessive function and analyzes Old Persian *tya manā kartam* (literally 'what of-me [was] done') as meaning 'what I have done'. He thus compares it not only with the Latin verbal construction *mihi factum est* ('to-me done is') 'I have done' but also with the formally parallel nominal one *mihi filius est* ('to-me son is') 'I have a son', assuming this latter pattern to have been the model for the former one (Benveniste 1952:54ff.). Since in synthetic passive constructions the agent, when present, was normally represented in Avestan by the instrumental case and in Old Persian by a specific prepositional phrase, this leads Anderson to conclude that the Old Persian periphrastic perfect could not have had passive value and must therefore be separated from the Old Indic construction, which clearly did have passive value, so that the ergative constructions of Indic and Iranian could not have had a common origin.

The traditional position on the other hand held that the Old Persian construction was in fact a passive, and this interpretation has been revived recently by Cardona (1970), who points to the existence of exact formal counterparts not only in Middle Indic but also elsewhere in Indo-European. His main argument is that a perfect participle, being a nominal, may perfectly well be accompanied by nominal rather than verbal syntax and that in such co-occurrence with a participle, a noun phrase in the genitive (or even in the dative) could therefore in no way be precluded from having agentive function. Especially in view of two examples where the agent of even a synthetic passive construction is in the genitive,[1] he holds that the genitive in the periphrastic passive construction could equally well have fulfilled agentive function. Most recently, Statha-Halikas (1979) has carried the argument a step further by showing that it is impossible to determine whether a periphrastic construction is passive or not merely from the cases taken by the accompanying noun.phrases and that in a number of Indo-European languages agentive function may be only one among several performed by the same oblique case. With regard to the Old Persian construction, she supports Cardona's analysis of this as a passive by pointing to the fact that it is characterized not only by the cases of its noun phrases but also, as is true of passives in general, by the topicalization of the logical object, by the presence of the stative-existential verb 'to be' (unless deleted by rule), and by the possibility of omitting the agent. A return to the traditional interpretation of the Old Persian construction as a passive would thus seem well justified.

Sound changes apart, the developments between Old and Middle Persian, while leaving the construction formally unaffected, fundamentally changed its syntactic distribution. This change was the result of the total loss by the language of the synthetic active past tense forms of the verb, so that once the construction could no longer contrast with a corresponding active it ceased to be marked for voice and was reanalyzed as an active. Thus, while Old Persian *(tya) manā kartam* '(what) was done by me' contrasted with *(tya) adam akunavam* '(what) I did' (Kent 1950:88), its Middle Persian reflex *man kird* 'I did [it]' lacked any corresponding counterpart. The only opposition that remained was one of tense, *man kird* 'I did [it]' contrasting with *az kun-am* 'I do [it]'. It can, however, be seen that despite its active status the Middle Persian construction retained two formal features resulting from its passive ancestry. The first was that the verb continued to agree with the logical object. Thus in *man kird* the verb 'to be' (which in the third person singular was represented by zero) agreed with the covert logical object 'it' and not with the agent 'I'.[2] The second, which separates it from the corresponding present tense construction as well as from that employed by intransitive verbs, is the use of the oblique rather than the direct case in order to denote the agent. Thus, again comparing *man kird* 'I did [it]' with *az kun-am* 'I do [it]', the oblique form *man* of the first person singular pronoun continues the old genitive (cf. Old Persian *manā*) whereas the direct case form *az* of the same pronoun continues the old nominative (cf. Old Persian *adam*, Latin *ego*, etc.). In short, the Middle Persian construction had become ergative, since morphologically it resembled a passive while distributionally it belonged within the paradigm of the active verb.

The Old Persian case system was reduced in Middle Persian to two members, namely the direct case and the oblique case, their distribution being partly dependent upon the tense and transitive or intransitive nature of the verb. Thus, a noun phrase in the direct case acted as agent with intransitive verbs in all tenses and with transitive verbs in the present tense, but as direct object with transitive verbs in the past tenses. A noun phrase in the oblique case had exactly the reverse distribution. In point of fact the case system rested entirely on the pronouns; for, while in nouns the formal opposition had become lost, at least certain pronouns still inflected for case, and there existed in addition a set of pronominal clitics (inherited from Old Iranian) which, although invariable formally, had the syntactic distribution of an oblique. Being enclitic, these forms had limited positional freedom and were as a rule attached to the first constituent of the sentence; and, like oblique noun phrases in general, they represented the logical object in the present but the agent in the transitive past.

It is the survival or loss of these inherited clitics which today constitutes one of the major isoglosses dividing the Kurdish dialects of Iraq into a northern and a southern group. Of the various syntactic functions which they fulfilled, it is their agentive role in transitive past tense sentences which has had the most interesting repercussions on the syntax of Modern Kurdish (MacKenzie 1961:222, 106-19, 193-5). The development in the northern dialects was straightforward. With the total loss of the clitics from the grammar the sentence type with the clitic as agent was also lost, so that transitive past tense sentences now consist of a nominal or pronominal noun phrase in the oblique case (the marked form) in the role of agent, followed by a nominal or pronominal noun phrase in the direct case (the unmarked form) in the role of direct object, and finally by a verb with ergative concord. Thus, in northern Kurmanji (Bedir Khan and Lescot 1970:94, 176ff.):

(1) &ivēn hesp dīt
  shepherd [obl.] horse [dir.] saw [3.sg.]
  'The shepherd saw the horse'.

(2) &ivēn hesp dītin
  shepherd [obl.] horses [dir.] saw [3.pl.]
  'The shepherd saw the horses'.

(3) min mirov dīt
  I [obl.] man [dir.] saw [3.sg.]
  'I saw the man'.

(4) we ez dītim
  you [obl.] I [dir.] saw [1.sg.]
  'You saw me'.

The ergative morphology of these past tense sentences can be readily seen when they are compared with corresponding sentences in the present tense, where the agent is in the direct case, the object is in the oblique, and the verb agrees with the agent:

(5) hesp mirovī dibīne
  horse [dir.] man [obl.] sees [3.sg.]
  'The horse sees the man'.

(6) hesp mirovan dibīne
  horse [dir.] men [obl.] sees [3.sg.]
  'The horse sees the men'.

(7) ez mirovī dibīnim
  I [dir.] man [obl.] see [1.sg.]
  'I see the man'.

(8) ez we dibīnim
  I [dir.] you [obl.] see [1.sg.]
  'I see you'.

The southern dialects on the other hand, despite certain differences of detail, have all retained the clitics. The agent of a transitive past tense sentence may therefore simply be a clitic. This, being by nature a suffix, cannot of course occur in sentence-initial position despite the otherwise strict subject-object-verb order. In the following sentences from the Mukri dialect the clitic (underlined in the examples) is attached to the first constituent, that is to say to the direct object, and the verb shows agreement through its zero marker with the third person singular object (Mann 1906:lxxxiff.):

(9)   *diz*   +   *im*   *girt*
       thief [dir.]+   I [clit.]   caught [3.sig.]
       'I caught the thief'.

(10)   *ci*   +   *t*   *kušt*
       what [dir.] +   you [clit.]   killed [3.sg.]
       'What did you kill?'

What is of particular significance, however, is that if the agent is nominal or pronominal its syntactic features must still be resumed within the sentence by the appropriate clitic. There is, in other words, no counterpart[3] of the construction in the northern dialects without the clitic and every transitive past tense sentence has to contain a clitic agent. Thus, in Suleimaniye, the order is subject, object+clitic, verb (MacKenzie 1961:108ff.):

(11) *pyāwaka   sagaka*   +   *y*   *kušt*
      man-the   dog-the   +   he [clit.] killed
      'The man killed the dog'.

(12) *min   pyāwaka*   +   *m*   *kušt*
      I   man-the   +   I [clit.]   killed
      'I killed the man'.

and similarly in Mukri (Mann 1906:lxxxviff.):

(13) *kurākä*   *añgustīläkä*   +   *i*   *hatgirt*
      son-the [dir.]   ring-the [dir.] +   he [clit.]took[3.sg.]
      'The son took the ring'.

(14) *amin*   *girt*   +   *im*   -   *in*
      I [dir.] seized +   I [clit.]   -   [3.pl.]
      'I seized them'.[4]

Two points are noteworthy in these last examples, and we shall see that they are interdependent. The first concerns the position of the clitic, which is not attached to the first noun phrase, the agent, but to the constituent immediately following it. In sentences (11) to (13) this is the nominal object whereas in sentence (14), in which the direct object is represented by the ergative agreement marker *-in*, it is the past stem of the verb. We have then, here, a direct violation of the rule stated above whereby the clitic attaches itself to the first constituent of the sentence. It would seem, therefore, that the nominal and pronominal agents have to be excluded from this rule.

Such a conclusion receives support from the second noteworthy point, which concerns the case used to mark the agent. From the situation obtaining in the northern dialects, we would expect this to be the oblique case. This however is not so, or at least is so only in part. For all the southern dialects which have retained case as a grammatical category can use the direct case to denote the agent. In the Sorani group the direct case is in free variation with the oblique case in this function, but in Mukri its use is obligatory and this provides the key to the problem as a whole. As we shall see, the simplest hypothesis is that Mukri has retained the earlier state of affairs, the situation in Sorani then being readily explainable as the result of levelling, be this internal (between the transitive past and all the other sentence types) or be it external (between the northern and the southern dialects). The selection of the direct case in order to indicate the nominal or pronominal agent can on the other hand be readily justified if it is assumed that this was originally a topic rather than a syntactic subject. This assumption simultaneously explains both the selection of the unmarked form of the noun or pronoun and the obligatory presence of the clitic. For if we accept that the present nominal or pronominal agent was originally a preposed topic and not a constituent of the sentence proper, the clitic would then have been the original agent and as such a necessary constituent of the sentence.

This hypothesis is fully supported by the historical evidence, a fact which Mann (1906:lxxxvf.) had already seen. In the transitive past both nominal or pronominal noun phrases are in the direct case because they are both reflexes of old nominatives, albeit for quite different reasons. The first is in the nominative because as a topic it would naturally have the unmarked or citation form, the second because it continues the surface subject of the Old Iranian periphrastic passive. A sentence such as (13) is thus to be interpreted historically as deriving from a passive with topicalized agent, 'The son, the ring was taken by him'. Such a derivation fully explains both verb agreement and case marking.

The formal possibility of resuming by means of a clitic a noun phrase positioned near the beginning of a sentence certainly existed in Middle Persian, although there is no evidence that the construction was employed as a device for topicalizing the noun phrase.[5] It is on the other hand well attested in this function in Modern Kurdish. In present-day Suleimaniye, for instance, it is possible to

topicalize any nominal constituent in this way except the
agent. Thus, while we find such pairs of sentences as:[6]

(15) *min xwardinakān* + *im* *xwārd*
    I foodstuffs-the + I [clit.] ate
    'I ate the food'.

(16) *xwardinakān* *min xwārd* + *im* - *in*
    foodstuffs-the I ate + I [clit.]- [3.pl.]
    'the food, I ate it'.

where (15) is unmarked and (16) is marked (the object being
topicalized), the agent can not be topicalized in this way
and is the only nominal constituent which is *obligatorily*
resumed by a clitic (see (11), (12) above). From this we
must deduce that a syntactic reanalysis has taken place in
the south consisting in the integration of the topic into
the sentence proper as the grammatical subject and the
functional demotion of the clitic which formerly performed
this role to the status of an apparently redundant echo of
the subject. This reanalysis was not, however, accompanied
by any formal restructuring so that the rules of clitic
placement still accord exceptional treatment to the agent-
subject.

    To resume the syntactic developments which must have
taken place between Middle Iranian and Modern Kurdish we
may say that, whereas in Middle Persian a clitic and a
nominal or pronominal agent were in complementary distribution, in southern Kurdish the clitic has been generalized
to all transitive past tense sentences and in northern
Kurdish the possibility of a clitic having the syntactic
function of an oblique noun phrase has been altogether lost
so that all noun phrases are now either nominal or pronominal. Despite certain superficial similarities, transitive past tense sentences with nominal or pronominal agent
are thus structurally quite different in the north and in
the south. Whatever may have been the reason for this
polarization, it seems likely that the conflict resulting
from the inability of a clitic to occupy sentence-initial
position and the otherwise strict subject-object-verb order of the sentence must have been an important factor.
Looked at in this light, both the obligatory preposing of
the agent in the south and the loss of the clitic in the
north may be seen as mechanisms for generalizing the 'canonical' word order.

    We should on the other hand be careful not to project
the strict word order pattern of Modern Kurdish too far
back in its history. For, in Middle Persian at least, the

word order was free to the point of creating syntactic
ambiguity, and only transitive past tense sentences with
nominal agent and nominal object (not differentiated by
case) required the strict sequence agent-object-verb
(Henning 1933:243). If it is accepted that in an accusative language the difference between active and passive
sentences resides essentially in their thematic structure,
the agent in active sentences being simultaneously topic
and grammatical subject whereas both these roles fall to
the logical object in passive ones, and that ergative sentences have an active rather than passive type thematic
structure,[7] then we must assume that both dialect groups
have undergone topicalization of the agent. And since as
a general principle topic precedes comment, simple transitive sentences in (early) Middle Iranian might ideally
have looked as follows:

    Present: agent + object + verb
    Past: object + agent + verb

both types having the structure NP [dir.] + NP [obl.] +
verb, except that in the present the verb agreed with the
agent and in the past with the object. Since, however, the
transitive past had by this time ceased to be passive,
there was no need for it to retain a different thematic
structure from that of the corresponding present and its
restructuring on the model of the present would seem perfectly reasonable. According to this interpretation, the
two dialect groups would simply have adopted different
strategies to rectify this anomaly, topicalizing the agent
in the transitive past by different means, namely by a
simple word order change in the north and by an agent preposing rule in the south. Presumably initially both these
devices must have been optional, the new sentence types
thus created being marked, but have subsequently by becoming obligatory lost their markedness. In the present-day
dialects at any rate, the resulting structures are just as
unmarked as those of the present tense.

    If ergativity is a characteristic feature of Kurdish,
it has however been totally lost in one dialect, that of
Suleimaniye in the south-eastern corner of Iraq. In this,
as can be seen from the following sentences, the transitive
past tense verb is uninflected for either person or number,
as if the zero suffix marking agreement with a third person
singular logical object had been extended to all persons
and numbers:

(17) šwānaka   aspaka   + y   bīnī
     shepherd-the horse-the + he [clit.] saw
     'The shepherd saw the horse'.

(18) šwānaka   aspakān   + i   bīnī
    shepherd-the horses-the + he [clit.]   saw
    'The shepherd saw the horses'.
(19) min ēwa + m   bīnī
     I   you + I [clit.]   saw
     'I saw you'.
(20) ēwa min + tān   bīnī
     you I   + you [clit.]   saw
     'You saw me'.

Given the loss of ergative agreement marking in the verb, the clitic must, it would seem, now definitely be analyzed as a marker of agreement with the agent-subject despite its anomalous position in the sentence. For only when, in the absence of any nominal constituent to act as host, the clitic attaches itself to the first constituent of the verb-form does it give the impression of being a proper traditional personal ending:

(21) bīnī + m   - in   [= min ēwa-m bīnī]
     saw + I [clit.]   -[2.pl.]
     'I saw you'.
(22) bīnī + tān   - im   [= ēwa min-tān bīnī]
     saw + you [clit.]   - [1.sg.]
     'You saw me'.

The possibility exists, of course, that this construction may at some time in the future act as a model and also attract the clitic to the verb in sentences with nominal object,[8] thus eventually effecting a simplification of the morphology. At present the morphological anomalies are numerous but, in spite of its various no longer functional traces of ergativity, Suleimaniye must be considered to have ceased to be ergative.

This final step from ergative to accusative morphology appears on the face of it rather undramatic.[9] Our comparison of the situation in the various Kurdish dialects suggests that it could only be taken in a dialect which had already undergone obligatory agent preposing and had thus lost the syntactic pattern without clitic. This would seem to imply that the presence of the clitic, and perhaps the indeterminacy of its synchronic status, was instrumental in the reanalysis. Be this as it may, both the passive-to-ergative and the ergative-to-accusative reanalyses may be seen as the integration of a newly created marked sentence type, after its unmarked partner had been lost, into the basic syntax.

The postulated steps may be summarized as follows:

OLD IRANIAN: (1) Periphrastic perfect of transitive verbs with passive meaning.

MIDDLE IRANIAN: (2) Loss of the corresponding active construction; passive reanalyzed as active with ergative morphology.

MODERN KURDISH: (3) Obligatory topicalization of agent by:

(a) in the northern dialects, loss of clitic and change of word order,

(b) in the southern dialects, generalization of clitic and preposing of agent.

(4) Loss of ergative morphology and reanalysis of the clitic as marker of agreement with the subject, in Suleimaniye.

NOTES

*I am grateful to my colleague N. Sims-Williams for help with the Middle Persian and for a number of valuable comments on an earlier draft of this paper. He is not, of course, responsible for any remaining oversimplifications and inaccuracies.

[1] For example: *utāšām auramazdā naiy ayadiya auramazdām ayadaiy* (and-of-them Auramazda [nom.] not revered-was Auramazda [acc.] I-revered) 'and by them Auramazda was not revered. I revered Auramazda' (Cardona 1970:2); cf., for Avestan, Reichelt 1909, § 501, Note 1.

[2] Compare, with an overt 3.sg. object: *man ēn bōxtagīh ... ō ašmā nizist* me [obl.] this salvation ... to you [was] taught [3.sg.] 'I have taught you this salvation' Boyce 1975:183.

[3] For vestiges of the construction without the clitic, see Mann 1906:lxxxviii and MacKenzie 1961:110.

[4] An alternative order of the suffixes is possible, see Mann 1906: lxxxviii.

[5] N. Sims-Williams has convinced me that the cases in Brunner (1970:104, 111) must not be interpreted as instances of topicalization. The same applies to the following example which he kindly provided to illustrate the syntactic pattern of an initial agent noun phrase resumed by a clitic:

tahm ud nēw pus-ī -dōšist vizišt+ iš če -m -iš strong and brave son-most-beloved taught+he [clit.] what-me-him

pursīd [was] asked [3.sg.]

'the strong and brave most beloved son, he taught what I asked him' (Boyce 1975:102).

Here the logical object, being sentential, follows the verb.

[6] I am grateful to W.O. Amin, a native speaker of Suleimaniye, for drawing my attention to this syntactic device and for providing this and the following Suleimaniye examples.

[7] For discussion see Tegey 1978:24.

[8] 'Object' in fact stands for the top item in a hierarchy of potential hosts; for details see MacKenzie 1961:78.

[9] Schmidt 1973:115 has shown that corresponding cases of levelling in the morphology of the *noun* have led to the loss of ergativity in various Caucasian languages.

REFERENCES

Anderson, Stephen R. 1976. "On the notion of subject in ergative languages". In *Subject and topic*, 3-25. Ed. by Charles N. Li. New York: Academic Press.

———. 1977. "On mechanisms by which languages become ergative." In Li 1977:317-63.

Bedir Khan, Emir Djeladet and Roger Lescot. 1970. *Grammaire kurde (dialecte kurmandji)*. Paris: Adrien Maisonneuve.

Benveniste, Émile. 1952. "La construction passive du parfait transitif". *BSLP* 48. 52-62.

Boyce, Mary. 1975. *A reader in Manichaean Middle Persian and Parthian*. Téhéran-Liège: Bibliothèque Pahlavi.

Brunner, C.J. 1977. *A syntax of Western Middle Iranian*. Delmar, N.Y.: Caravan Books.

Bynon, Theodora. 1979. "The ergative construction in Kurdish". *BSOAS* 42. 211-24.

Cardona, George. 1979. "The Indo-Iranian construction *manā (mamā) kr̥tam*". *Lg.* 46.1-12.

Comrie, Bernard. 1978. "Ergativity". In *Syntactic typology*. Ed. by Winfred P. Lehmann. Sussex: Harvester Press.

Henning, Walter. 1933. "Das Verbum des Mittelpersischen der Turfanfragmente". *Zeitschrift für Indologie und Iranistik* 9.158-253.

Kent, Roland G. 1950. *Old Persian*. New Haven, Conn.: American Oriental Society.

Li, Charles N. (ed.). 1976. *Subject and topic*. New York: Academic Press.

———. (ed.). 1977. *Mechanisms of syntactic change*. Austin: University of Texas Press.

MacKenzie, David N. 1961. *Kurdish dialect studies, I*. London: Oxford University Press.

Mann, Oskar. 1906. *Die Mundart der Mukri-Kurden*. Berlin: Georg Reimer.

Reichelt, Hans. 1909. *Awestisches Elementarbuch*. Heidelberg: Winter.
Schmidt, Karl H. 1973. "Transitiv und Intransitiv". In *Indogermanische und allgemeine Sprachwissenschaft: Akten der IV. Fachtagung der Indogermanischen Gesellschaft*, 107-24. Ed. by G. Redard. Wiesbaden: Dr. Ludwig Reichert Verlag.
Statha-Halikas, Hariklia. 1979. "How *not* to tell a passive: the case of Old Persian *manā kr̥tam* reconsidered". *Proceedings of the Fifth Annual Meeting of the Berkeley Linguistics Society*.
Tegey, Habibullah. 1978. "Ergativity in Pashto". *Paṣto Quarterly* 1.3-88.

POSTSCRIPT

Professor D. N. MacKenzie has pointed out that the correct Middle Persian form for 'I' is *an* in the direct case and not *az*, which latter form is restricted to Parthian. (See p.3ff.)

ON THE LOSS OF A RULE OF SYNTAX

ALICE C. HARRIS
Harvard University

0. *Introduction.* The purpose of this paper is to investigate one aspect of syntactic change by comparing details of rule loss in two languages.* The approach is to focus on a single syntactic rule, Inversion; this rule has also been called 'Flip' and 'Psych Movement'. In Section 1, I will briefly discuss the nature of the rule. In Sections 2 and 3 I will describe the loss of this rule in English and in Udi, a language of the Northeast Caucasian family. Finally, in Section 4, I will compare the loss of the rule in the two languages.

1. *Inversion.* Sentence (1) illustrates the inversion construction in English.

(1) þam   wife   þa   word   wel   licodon.
    the-DAT woman-DAT these-NOM words-NOM well liked-PL

   'The woman liked these words well'.   (*Beowulf* 640)

The analysis assumed here is that Inversion demotes the initial subject--here *þam wife*--to indirect object. A second rule, Unaccusative, which is obligatory, advances the initial direct object--here *þa word*--to subject. The correctness of this analysis in universal grammar is argued in Perlmutter (to appear a, b) and in Harris (to appear b). It is argued in Harris (1973) and Harris (to appear a) that a rule of this nature applies in these two languages in particular. The analysis is summarized below.

	wife	*word*
Initial Relations	Subject	Dir.Obj.
Relations after Inversion	Ind.Obj.	Dir.Obj.
Relations after Unaccusative	Ind.Obj.	Subject

Since Unaccusative applies in other environments as well, this study focuses on Inversion alone, that is, the demotion of the initial subject to indirect object.

2. *Description of the loss of Inversion in English.* In Old English, Inversion applies as an optional rule triggered by a set of affective predicates. By the Middle English period it is being lost. Some verbs lost the rule sooner than others. Thus, in a given manuscript, one verb may still govern Inversion, while another no longer does. The rule was also lost in different dialects at somewhat different times. Abstracting from the different verbs and from the different dialects, the process of loss can be described in terms of the interaction of Inversion with the three coding rules of English: Word Order, Case Marking and Subject Agreement.

The establishment of word order as a means of indicating grammatical relations might be considered the first step in the loss of Inversion. The SVO word order identifies the initial subject, not the final subject, of the inversion construction with other subjects in the language. Example (1) is thus typical of the unmarked word order for this construction, having the initial subject, *þam wife*, in sentence-initial position.

But while Word Order was stated with respect to the grammatical relations of the input to Inversion, the other coding rules were stated on the output of the rule. In (1), for example, *þam wife* does not have the case marking of its initial grammatical relation, subject. Rather, it is marked with the dative case, appropriate to its final relation, indirect object. Similarly, Subject Agreement in the verb is triggered, not by the initial subject, which is singular, but by the final subject, *þa word*, which is plural. Thus, both Case Marking and Subject Agreement apply to the output of Inversion.

The second step in the loss of Inversion is characterized by the fact that Subject Agreement begins to apply to the input of Inversion, rather than to its output, as formerly. Interestingly, Case Marking continues to apply to the output grammatical relations. Thus, in example (2), the verb *eilen* agrees with the initial subject *hem*. This nominal, however, is case marked for its final grammatical relation, indirect object.

(2) Sum men þat han suche likynge wondren what hem eilen.
    'Some men who have such a desire wonder what ails them'.
                               (*The Chastising of God's Children* 103, 15)

Eilen is plural to agree with *hem* 'them', which is dative plural. Thus, in (2) both Word Order and Subject Agreement are stated on the input grammatical relations of Inversion, while Case Marking is stated on the output relations.

Butler (1977), however, has pointed out that there are three examples of a different kind from about the same period.

(3) Do as ye   seems   best.
    you-PL-NOM seem-3.SG
    'Do as seems best to you'.   (*Generydes* 6007)

Here the interaction of Inversion with the coding rules is different. In particular, Case Marking applies to the input relations, marking the initial subject, *ye*, with the nominative case, rather than with the dative appropriate to its final grammatical relation. It is clear, however, that Inversion has applied in (3), since Subject Agreement in these examples is stated on the output grammatical relations of Inversion. The verb is third person singular to agree with the unspecified final subject. Thus, in (3), Word Order and Case Marking apply to the input relations, while Subject Agreement alone applies to the output relations.

As a final step in the loss of the rule, all three coding rules apply to the input relations, and none to the output. This is illustrated in (4).

(4) thou   shalt   like it for ever.
    you-SG-NOM shall-2.SG
    'You will like it for ever'.   (*Gesta Romanorum* p.281)

The changes are summarized in (5).

(5)

Example	(1)	(2)	(3)	(4)
Rules Applying to Input	WO	WO Agreement	WO Case	WO Case Agreement
Rules Applying to Output	Case Agreement	Case	Agreement	

In the loss of this rule in English, two facts stand out. First, because of the discrepancy between examples like (2) and (3), discrete stages cannot be isolated, not even with respect to a single verb. Second, since Inversion was an optional rule with most of the predicates that conditioned it, even in Old English, it is remarkable that in the process of loss the rule did not simply cease to apply.

3. *Description of the loss of Inversion in Udi.* The first full linguistic description of Udi was published in 1863 by Schiefner; his description and the texts that support it represent the first attested stage in the history of Inversion in Udi. Today there are two dialects. One of these, spoken in the village of Niji, represents the final stage of the loss of Inversion. An intermediate stage is represented by the dialect spoken today in the villages of Vartashni and Oktomberi. These dialects are described and illustrated in Panchvidze (1942, 1974) and elsewhere.

In Udi, Inversion is obligatory with the verbs that trigger it; these are listed in Panchvidze (1942, 1974) and in Harris (to appear a). The loss of Inversion can be described in terms of its interaction with Udi's three coding rules, Agreement Trigger Selection (ATS), Case Marking, and Agreement Marker Selection (AMS). The first- and last-named are parts of the phenomenon of subject-verb agreement (cf. Harris (to appear a) for a complete analysis of agreement and case marking in Udi).

In noninversion constructions, the verb agrees with the subject, regardless of its case. At the earliest attested stage of Udi, ATS already applied to the input grammatical relations in the inversion construction. Thus, the initial subject triggers agreement, as in (6), where *za* 'I' is the initial subject.

(6) Za   wa-ķe   ayel   te-za-ake.
    I-OBJ you-like child-ABSL NEG-1.SG-see
    'I have never seen a child like you'.   (Schiefner VI)

Udi has ergative Case Marking; the subject of transitive verbs is in the ergative case, and the subject of intransitives in the absolutive case. (7) illustrates a noninversion construction, showing the subject in the ergative case.

(7) Eṭu-xol   zu   š'ŭm   uk-al-zu.
    what-COMIT I-ERG bread-ABSL eat-FUT-1.SG
    'With what shall I eat my bread?'   (Schiefner VI)

At the earliest attested stage of the language, Case Marking, unlike ATS, applied to the output grammatical relations in the inversion construction. In (6) the initial subject, *za* 'I', is not marked with a subject case, but with the case of the indirect object, its final grammatical relation.

In the earliest texts, the third coding rule, AMS, was also sensitive to the output grammatical relations of Inversion. In Udi there are two complete sets of agreement markers, partially given below.

	Set I	Set II
1st person singular	zu	za(x)
2nd person singular	nu	va(x)
3rd person singular	ne	ṭu(x)

Set II indicates agreement with subjects that are demoted to indirect object by Inversion; Set I marks agreement with other subjects. The former is illustrated in (6), the latter in (7). Since the agreement marker is determined by the final grammatical relation of the agreement trigger, it is clear that AMS is sensitive to the output of Inversion.

The first attested step in the loss of Inversion in Udi involves the fact that Case Marking begins to apply to the input relations in the inversion construction, as in (8).

(8) ...te, zu bak-al-te-zax.
    no I-ERG can-FUT-NEG-1.SG
    '...No, I cannot'.   (Panchvidze 1974:141)

Here the initial subject is marked with the ergative case, not with the objective, as in (6). It is important, however, that the agreement marker in (8) is the same as that used in (6), where Inversion applies; it is not the same as that used in (7), where Inversion does not apply. Thus, in (8) Case Marking applies to the input grammatical relations, while AMS alone applies to the output relations of Inversion.

The final change involves the AMS rule and is illustrated by (9). (9) differs from (8) in that the marker of agreement is from Set I, not from Set II, which was originally used with the inversion construction.

(9) Šoṭin ak̆-e-ne k̆ož.
    he-ERG see-AOR-3.SG house-ABSL
    'He saw the house'.   (Panchvidze 1974:142)

In (9) the selection of the agreement marker is based on the initial relations, just as ATS and Case Marking are. These changes are summarized in (10).

(10)   Example   (6)   (8)   (9)
     Rules Applying   ATS   ATS   ATS
         to Input   Case   Case
                                    AMS
     Rules Applying   Case   AMS
         to Output   AMS

It is important that sentences like (8) do not exist alone in any dialect. They occur in the modern Vartashni dialect, but coexist with sentences of type (6) in that system.

4. *On the nature of syntactic rule loss.* Superficially, the systems of English and Udi are quite different. They differ in ergativity, in coding rules used to mark grammatical relations, in optionality of Inversion, and in other ways. But with respect to the loss of Inversion, the differences between the two are trivial; there is a degree of correspondence between these two processes of loss that is much more significant than the differences.

One observed similarity is the fact that an intermediate stage in rule loss may be considered as unstable. In English this is reflected both in the fact that there are few examples like (2) and very few like (3), and in the fact that types (2) and (3) coexist with examples of type (1). In Udi the sign of instability is the fact that type (8) has no independent existence; it exists synchronically only in a system that also tolerates type (6).

The most striking resemblance between the losses in English and Udi is that in both the initial subject ceases to be treated as indirect object gradually, with respect to one coding rule at a time (cf. (5) and (10)). Since Inversion was already optional in English, here especially, it would have been simpler just to cease applying the rule.

There is no doubt that change in language can be discrete or abrupt; there is some question as to whether it can be gradual. The present paper illustrates two senses in which one type of change--syntactic rule loss--may be gradual. First, loss may be gradual in the sense that an intermediate construction is not an independently viable system, but exists only concurrently with another construction. Second, the rule may be lost with respect to one rule of the grammar at a time, rather than by abruptly ceasing to apply. The data presented here establish that rule loss may be gradual, at least in these two restricted senses.

NOTE

*The research reported here was supported in part by a National Needs Postdoctoral Fellowship from the National Science Foundation.

REFERENCES

Butler, Milton Chadwick. 1977. "Reanalysis of object as subject in Middle English impersonal constructions". *Glossa* 11:155-70.
Harris, Alice C. 1973. "Psychological predicates in Middle English". Paper read at the LSA Annual Meeting.
_____. To appear a. "Case marking, verb agreement, and inversion in Udi". In *Studies in relational grammar* I. Ed. by David M. Perlmutter.
_____. To appear b. "Inversion as a rule in universal grammar: Georgian evidence". In *Studies in relational grammar* I. Ed. by David M. Perlmutter.
Panchvidze, Vl. 1942. "Micemit-subiekṭiani zmnebi udur enaši". *Enemkis moambe* 12.51-72.
_____. 1974. *Uduris gramṭikuli analizi*. Tbilisi: Gamomcemloba 'Mecniereba'.
Perlmutter, David M. To appear a. "Evidence for inversion in Russian and Kannada". In *Studies in relational grammar* I. Ed. by David M. Perlmutter.
_____. To appear b. "Working 1s and inversion in Italian, Japanese, and and Quechua". *Proceedings of the Fifth Annual Meeting of the Berkeley Linguistics Society 1979*.
Schiefner, A. 1863. "Versuch über die Sprache der Uden". *Mémoire de l'Academie Imperiale des Sciences de St. Petersbourg*. Series 7, vol. 6, no. 8.

* Pages 173 and 174 omitted in numbering

THE DEVELOPMENT OF
ACCUSATIVE-INFINITIVE CONSTRUCTIONS

W.J. PEPICELLO
Temple University

Of the factors involved in characterizing syntactic change, one of the most important is correct synchronic analysis. That is, the endpoints of syntactic change are synchronic states, and statements of relationships between two states are dependent on the analyses of the individual states. This paper addresses the importance of a theoretical model in analyzing synchronic states, and so in characterizing the nature of change between two states.

The historical development of the accusative-infinitive construction (AIC) in Greek and Latin has long occupied scholars.[1] From the many works concerning AIC, two approaches emerge. The first is that of the traditional grammarians, who begin from examples like (1)-(3) in Latin and (4)-(6) in Greek.[2]

(1) Lat.   Dicit feminam paenitere
                 acc   inf
          'He says the woman is sorry'

(2) Lat.   Admonet feminam paenitere
                   acc   inf
          'He warns the woman to be sorry'

(3) Lat.   Feminam paenitere apparet
            acc   inf
          'It appears that the woman is sorry'

(4) Gk.   Ephē anera ienai
               acc   inf
          'He said that the man is going'

(5) Gk.   Keleuei anera ienai
                  acc   inf
          'He orders the man to go'

(6) Gk. Anera ienai prosēkei
         acc   inf
    'It behooves the man to go'

They propose that such AIC originate as monoclausal constructions where the infinitive is complementary in function. Then a syntactic realignment occurs whereby the direct object of the main verb (the accusative noun in the above examples) is disassociated from that verb and associated with the infinitive, becoming its subject. This new construction, i.e. the AIC, is then treated as a full subordinate clause, so that the monoclausal construction yields a biclausal one. This AIC becomes established as a grammatical unit (viz. as a type of complement clause) and spreads in that use from object to subject position, e.g. with impersonal verbs as in (3) and (6), and in impersonal passive constructions, as in (7) and (8).

(7) Lat. Dicitur feminam paenitere
                  acc   inf
    'It is said that the woman is sorry'

(8) Gk. Legetai anera ienai
                 acc   inf
    'It is said that the man is going'

A more recent treatment of AIC is found in Miller 1974. Utilizing generative-transformational theory, Miller claims two basic sources for AIC. The first is Equi NP Deletion. Equi deletes the subject of a subordinate clause under identity with some NP in the main clause. Deletion of this subject causes the verb of the subordinate clause to become nonfinite (see Kiparsky and Kiparsky 1970). Thus Miller claims that sentences like (2) have an underlying structure like (9):

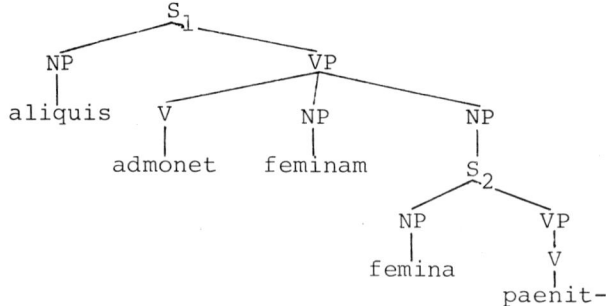

Here Equi deletes the subject of S_2 under identity with the direct object of S_1. The subordinate verb in such constructions becomes nonfinite, giving rise to a type of Infinitive Complementation. This complementation applies in other cases in combination with an Accusativization rule which marks the subject of the infinitive as accusative, e.g. in *Scio feminam paenitere* 'I know the woman is sorry'. Infinitive Complementation, plus the Accusativization rule, together become interpreted as a new type of complementation, and so spread to the uses outlined above.

These two proposals contain a common flaw, in that they fail to delimit exactly what is meant by an 'accusative-infinitive construction'. As pointed out in Pepicello (1978), there are a variety of AI sequences which exhibit a variety of syntactic behaviors. Failure to identify the types of AIC prevents explanations of AIC, either synchronically or diachronically. Let us now consider a third analysis of AIC.

Based on syntactic behavior, we can identify three types of AIC synchronically. The first type is simply that in which the accusative and infinitive are morphological markings indicating complementation, as in (3), (6), (7), and (8) above. Here the AIC is a single constituent and is treated as a single grammatical unit. The second type of AIC results from Equi, as just described, yielding sentences like (2) and (5).

However, there is a major difference between these two types of AIC. For in (2) the AIC is not a constituent, as was the case, e.g., in (7) and (8). This is shown by the impossibility of treating the AIC in (2) as a unit, e.g. in passivization. Thus, the direct object *feminam* in (2) will passivize to give *Femina admonetur paenitere* 'The woman is warned to be sorry', but the entire AIC does not passivize, so that **Admonetur feminam paenitere* 'It is warned for the woman to be sorry' is ungrammatical. The proposed analysis accounts for this difference, since it predicts that *feminam* and *paenitere* are not constituents of the same clause, and so should not act as a unit. The same analysis holds for Greek with verbs like *anagkazdo* 'I force', which take AIC, as in (10), or a personal passive like (11), but not the impersonal passive in (12).

(10) Gk. Enagkase tous Persas poieisthai sunthēkas
                     acc   inf
       'He forced the Persians to make pacts'

(11) Gk. Hoi Persai ēnagkazdonto poieisthai sunthēkas
       'The Persians were forced to make pacts'

(12) Gk. *Ēnagkazdeto tous Persas poieisthai sunthēkas
       'It was forced for the Persians to make pacts'

A final source for AIC is the Raising (to object) transformation. It is this source which allows us to relate sentences like (1) and (4), which contain AIC, to their corresponding personal passives in (13) and (14).

(13) Lat. Femina dicitur paenitere

            'The woman is said to be sorry'

(14) Gk. Aner legetai ienai

            'The man is said to be going'

The derivation of such sentences, i.e. (1), (4), (13) and (14), begins from a structure like that on the left in (15):

(15)
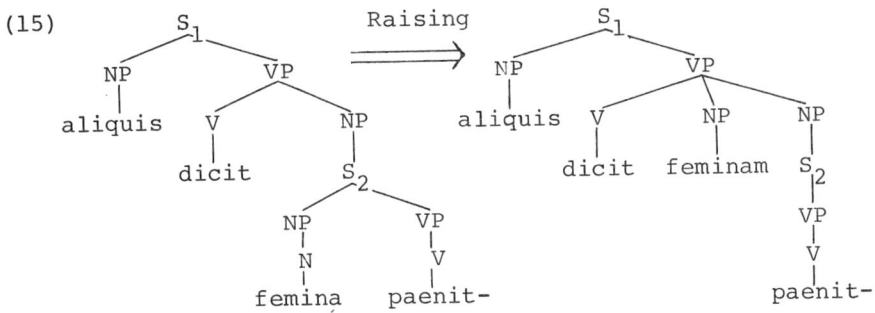

In such cases, the AIC of (1) may be derived in two ways. First, AI Complementation may apply in the subordinate clause, as outlined above. That this is true is shown by the possibility of impersonal passives where the AIC is treated as a unit, as in (7) and (8). However, this AIC may also result from Raising, which promotes the subject of the subordinate clause to direct object position in the main clause. This process is shown in (15). Here the accusative marking on *feminam* comes about as the natural marking for a direct object, and the infinitive results from the subject of the subordinate clause having been extracted from that clause, preventing subject-verb agreement. That this Raising occurs is supported by the fact that the Raised NP may then be passivized within the main clause, giving personal passives like (13) and (14).[3]

Let us now consider the relative merits of the three proposals in accounting for AIC. The proposal of the traditional grammarians raises several problems. First, it assumes that subordinate clauses may be created from the constituents of main clauses. This clause creation, in addition to being an unprecedented type of change, raises problems in accounting for personal passives. For if the

accusative noun shifts away from the main verb to become
the subject of the infinitive, it should not then act like
a direct object of the main verb, as it does in personal
passives. Finally, the infinitive in this analysis is a
given, and its source remains a mystery.

The three-source theory proposed in this paper reme-
dies all of these problems. We see, first, that we need
not try to create a biclausal construction from a monoclausal one, since all AIC are biclausal in underlying structure. Secondly, the associational shift of the traditional
grammarians is unnecessary, since the noun in question:

(a) remains as the direct object of the main verb, in Equi-
derived AIC;

(b) is never the direct object of the main verb, as in AI
Complementation; or

(c) becomes the direct object of the main verb via Raising.

This latter source then allows us to explain personal passives. Finally, we see that the infinitive arises from
cases where the subject of a subordinate clause is either
deleted (Equi) or promoted (Raising). The sources of the
infinitive and the accusative noun in AI Complementation
will be considered later in this paper.

Miller correctly identifies the role of Equi in AIC.
However, his Infinitive Complementation and Accusativization rules turn out to be labels rather than explanations.
For example, the spread of Infinitive Complementation to
verbs like *scio* 'I know', is simply assumed, and his Accusativization rule is a given. He thus fails to address
fully the questions of how individual sequences of accusative nouns and infinitives arise in the first place, and
how these sequences then come to be reinterpreted as a type
of complementation.

This last point is crucial, since previous analyses of
AIC are focussed on explaining its spread as a type of complementation. Failure to characterize the synchronic sources, however, frustrates these efforts. The three-source
theory, in defining the synchronic sources, reveals the
link which explains the development of AIC as a complementizer. Thus, in the case of Equi, we have two identical
NPs, one the direct object of the main verb, and one the
subject of the subordinate clause. Equi deletes the subject of the lower clause, yielding sentences like *Admonet
feminam paenitere*. Here *feminam* is syntactically a constituent of the main clause, although an exact copy of it
served as subject of the lower clause. Thus it is also

felt to belong to the infinitive. This intuition is borne out by examples like *Admonet feminam ut paenitat* 'He warns the woman to be sorry', where both coreferential NPs appear in the surface syntax, viz. *feminam* and the subject of the finite subordinate verb *paenitat*, *femina*, which here has been pronominalized and subsequently deleted after triggering subject-verb agreement.

While it supports the intuitions of the traditional grammarians, the development outlined above is insufficient to explain the spread of AIC as a complementizer. Consider, however, the instances of AIC derived via Raising. In these cases, the derivation of sentences like *Dicit feminam paenitere* involves promoting the subject of the subordinate clause into direct object position in the main clause. Thus the constituency of the accusative noun (here *feminam*) is ambiguous, for the noun which originates in the subordinate clause actually becomes a constituent of the higher clause. It is thus at once the object of the main verb and the subject of the subordinate verb (the infinitive).

This 'double constituency' of the accusative noun leaves unclear whether it should be treated as the direct object of the main verb or as part of the subordinate clause. Thus the AIC which result from Raising, as well as those which result from Equi, point toward a stage for Latin in which the constituency of the accusative noun is ambiguous. This situation represents the point at which AIC may be reinterpreted as a marker of complementation.

It must first be assumed that AIC are at first derived only via Equi and Raising. As shown, this stage admits of two parsings for the AIC in question, both of which are supported either by syntactic behavior of the construction or by alternate constructions containing a finite subordinate clause. It is this stage, then, which allows the AIC to be reinterpreted as a complement clause in object position. From here, once the construction was firmly entrenched as an object complementizer, it could spread to the subject position in the uses which have been described. The same development can be reconstructed for AIC in Greek, where we also find Equi- and Raising-derived AIC being ambiguous and finally giving rise to a type of complementation through a reinterpretation of the AIC in object position.

So it is that a systematic synchronic analysis of AIC in Greek and Latin allows us to employ the methodology of internal reconstruction to trace the development of AIC in these languages. In this way the theories of previous analyses are both clarified and corrected to reveal some of the major factors involved in the rise and spread of AIC.

NOTES

[1] Based on theoretical orientation, previous scholarship is divided into two schools in this paper. The first, to which I refer throughout as the traditional grammarians, includes Brugmann and Delbrück (1916), Meillet and Vendryes (1924, Schwyzer (1950), Ernout and Thomas (1951), Woodcock (1959), Kuryłowicz (1964), and Leumann, Hofmann and Szantyr (1965), among others. The second school, which is best represented by Miller (1974), is discussed briefly also in Lightfoot (1974).

[2] For clarity, all examples in this paper are artificial. However, every construction represented exists in actual Greek and Latin texts, so that none of the arguments herein is based on nonoccurring sentence types.

[3] A counterproposal to this Raising analysis is put forth in Chomsky (1973). There it is proposed that personal passives like (13) and (14) are derived by a rule of NP Preposing which promotes the subject of a subordinate clause directly to subject position in the main clause, without Raising or passivization. This rule has been the subject of much debate (see Bach 1977 for discussion and presentation of the literature). Since the Latin data favor neither proposal, this theoretical issue will not be addressed in this paper.

REFERENCES

Bach, Emmon. 1977. "Review of Paul Postal 1974. *On raising*, Cambridge, Mass.: MIT Press". *Lg.* 53.621-654.
Brugmann, Karl and B. Delbrück. 1916. *Grundriss der vergleichenden Grammatik der indogermanischen Sprachen, Vol. 2.* Strassburg: Karl J. Trübner.
Chomsky, Noam. 1973. "Conditions on Transformations". In *A Festschrift for Morris Halle*. Ed. by Stephen R. Anderson and Paul Kiparsky. New York: Holt, Rinehart and Winston.
Ernout, Alfred and F. Thomas. 1951. *Syntaxe Latine*. Paris: Klincksieck.
Kiparsky, Paul and Carol Kiparsky. 1970. "Fact". In *Progress in linguistics*, 143-73. Ed. by Manfred Bierwisch and K. Heidolph. The Hague: Mouton.
Kuryłowicz, Jerzy. 1964. *The inflectional categories of Indo-European*. Heidelberg: Carl Winter.
Leumann, Manu, J. B. Hofmann, and A. Szantyr. 1965. *Lateinische Grammatik, Vol. 2.* Munich: Beck'sche.

Lightfoot, David. 1974. *Natural logic and the Greek moods.* The Hague: Mouton.

Meillet, Antoine and J. Vendryès. 1924. *Traité de grammaire comparée des langues classiques.* Paris: Champion.

Miller, D. Gary. 1974. "On the history of infinitive complementation in Latin and Greek". *Journal of Indo-European Studies* 2.223-46.

Pepicello, W. J. 1978. "Pseudo-syntactic change". To appear in the Proceedings of the University of Michigan Conference on Syntactic Change.

Schwyzer, Eduard. 1950. *Griechische Grammatik, Zweiter Band.* Munich: Beck'sche.

Woodcock, E. C. 1959. *A new Latin syntax.* Cambridge, Mass.: Harvard University Press.

SYNTACTIC DIFFUSION

MARIO SALTARELLI
University of Illinois

0. *Introduction*. Chen and Wang (1975) present evidence that a sound change implements itself through 'lexical' diffusion. Observations of morphological change in progress (Calvano and Saltarelli 1979) indicate that 'paradigmatic' diffusion is another mechanism necessary for defining the gradual schedule of evolving inflectional patterns. This paper lends further support to the diffusionist hypothesis by showing that syntactic change spreads gradually through the range of possible structures. A particular syntactic change may reach only partial implementation or may be overtaken by another syntactic change and as a consequence be stopped or even reversed. The gradient continuum, I claim, is not defined by discrete mutations in the grammar in the form of addition, deletion, or reordering of whole rules. Rather the chronological sequence is viewed as a bundle of competing patterns defined by subgrammatical increments on configurational, relational, and semantic planes. It is the intersection on these three planes of evolution that forms the basis for a more precise characterization of syntactic change.

Syntactic diffusion, as presented in this paper, finds empirical support in the development of causative complementation from early Latin to present day Romance. From a simple sentential complement today's reflexes of Latin *facere* have acquired two competing types of infinitival complements defined in transformational grammar by the syntactic processes known as Subject to Object Raising and Verb Raising or Clause Union (Aissen 1974, Postal and Perlmutter 1974). It will be assumed that the Subject to Object Raising (SOR) causative patterns are accounted for as an implementation through lexical diffusion of an already existing rule evidenced by the accusativus cum infinitivo constructions (Saltarelli 1976; cf. also Pepicello, this volume). Clause Union (CU) patterns arise, on the other hand, from a reanalysis of passive SOR complements and represent Romance innovations in a gradient state of evolution. It will be argued that the intricate distributional patterns of CU constructions observed in a snapshot view of the Romance languages today is best explained by an evolutionary hypothesis according to which a syntactic process such as CU is propagated by syntactic increments defined in part by a semantically augmented relational hierarchy (Gary and Keenan 1977). The analysis proposed here differs in significant ways from previous accounts of the origin of Romance causatives (Muller 1912, Gougenheim 1929, Norberg 1945, Radford 1976, van Tiel-Di Maio 1976, to mention a few), but relies crucially on their reading of the Latin texts.

1. *Complement types in Latin.* The types of complement clauses which describe Classical Latin include the following:

(1.a)   *rogo ut veniat*   'I pray that he comes'

(1.b.i) *dicit se latine scire*   'he$_i$ says that he$_i$ knows Latin'

(1.b.ii) *dicit me latine scire* 'he says that I know Latin'

(1.c)   *exire volo*   'I want to go out'

(1.a) has a sentential complement introduced by *ut* governing the subjunctive. (1.b) illustrates two types of accusative with infinitive defined by SOR. (1.b.i) is typical of Classical Latin (Ronconi 1946:162) and has no reflex in Romance. Its peculiarity is in that coreferent subjects are involved, a structural description sensitive to Equivalent Noun Phrase Deletion yielding the infinitival type (1.c). Before the classical period the infinitive construction with *facere* was rarely found (Muller 1912, III). The sentential complement was found, however, before Cicero, as in Plautus and in the popular language of the inscriptions (cf. items (2) through (4)). In the popular language we find also an incipient case of SOR (cf. items (5) and (6)).

(2)   *Dolabellae procuratores fac admoneantur*
      (Cic., *Famil.*, 16, 24)

(3)   *me meus herus fecit ut vigilarem, hic pugnis faciet hodie ut dormiam*   (Plaut., *Amphi.*, 141)

(4)   *fecit tamen ut me amares*
      (*C.I.L.*, 13, I, 1188)

(5) *fac Sextilium ... ne somnum contingat*
    (*Def. Tabel.*, 270)

(6) *fac eos ne currere possint*
    (*Ibid.*, 289)

The subject of the lower clause appears as the object of the higher verb, but the lower verb remains tensed. This case testifies to the gradual nature of SOR. It represents also the derivational link between the sentential complement pattern and the competing accusative with infinitive as in the following:

(7) *quem Plato ... in Phaedro laudari ab Socrate facit*   (Cic., *Opt. gen. or.*, 17)

(8) *Poetae impendere apud inferos saxum Tantalo faciunt*   (*Id., Tusc.*, 4, 5)

(9) *flumina abundare ut facerent (nebula) camposque natare*   (Lucr., *De r.n.*, 511)

(10) *Commeatus a senatu peti solitos beneficii sui fecit*   (Suet., *Claud.*, 23)

(11) *quatuor arietes occidi fecit et parari epulas omnibus vicinis suis*   (Vulg., *Tob.*)

(12) *ut pervenire facerent ad eum clamorem egeni*
     (Vulg., *Job*, 34, 28)

(13) *haec properare facit*
     (Cl. Claudian. *Carm.*, 8, 12)

(14) *si pro pessimis servis filium bonum facisset occidi*   (Salv. *de gub.Dei*, 9, 44)

(15) *causas enim non fecit dicere*
     (Cass. *Var.* 10, 4, 4)

It was typical of these infinitive complements to appear either in the active or in the passive form. That is, SOR complements could undergo passive in the lower clause. We find both active and passive types in Cicero, as in (7) and (8). Both cases are found in Lucretius (9), the historians (10), the Vulgate (11), and the Christian poets down to Cassiodorus (11) in the sixth century. In sum, *facere* complements underwent a gradual change in configuration (cf. (16) below), rather than a clear cut addition of the SOR rule.

(16.a) Sentential with *ut*

(16.b) Sentential without *ut*

(16.c) SOR with tensed complement

(16.d) SOR with active and passive infinitive

According to Muller (1912:24) the use of the SOR constructions of (16.d) was more frequent with intransitive than with transitive and ditransitive complements. This indicates diffusion on the relational plane, an evolutionary feature not characterized by the simple addition of the SOR rule to the grammar.

2. *Reanalysis of passive infinitives*. Between the fifth and the eighth century the passive infinitive in SOR patterns disappears. We find an active infinitive in sentences where we would have expected the passive, as exemplified in (17) through (24).

(17) *filium suum ... tonsorare facit*
(Fred., 3, 4)

(18) *ampliare facimus ipsum sanctum Vincentium*
(*Cod. Lon.*, t.III, 406, 208, an. 715)

(19) *cartas ... conscribi fecerunt*
(*Ep. Mer. et Kar.*, t.I, 411, 12, an. 552)

(20) *archas de saxis ... fecit excidi*
(*V. Caesarii*, I)

(21) *prima omnium fecimus legere ipsam offertionem*
(*C.I.L.*, t.IV, 703)

(22) *dicere feceret*
(*Esp. Sagrad.*, t.XLIII, 439, an. 816)

(23) *hoc testamentum fieri iussimus et legere audivimus* (*Esp. Sagr.*, t.XXXVII)

(24) *qui hac pagina ... ficere rogavit*
(*C.I.L.*, t.IV, 717, 657, an. 757)

Muller (1912, Chap. V) attributes this phenomenon to the sound change that by the sixth century merged final [i] with [e]. As a consequence, the passive conjugation was no longer distinguished from the active conjugation. A period of confusion persisted until the eighth century, accounting for the gradually decreasing number of passive examples found in the texts. There is evidence that the phonetic sound change promoted a morphological reanalysis which involved the first, second, and fourth conjugation verbs, subsequently the third conjugation verbs, and finally the irregular passive verbs, as outlined in (28.b), below. There is also evidence that a syntactic reanalysis occurred as well (cf. (28.c)), which, I propose, is the source of Romance CU patterns. Contrary to Muller's claim that the active (formerly passive) infinitive maintained passive meaning, the replacement of *a* plus ablative case by dative case constructions indicates that the derivational history

of reanalyzed SOR passive infinitives no longer involved
the passive transformation applying on the lower clause
(cf. examples (25) through (27)). The syntactic reanalysis
which I propose for the passive infinitive constructions
is illustrated in (28.c).

(25) *nullo modo a nostris irrationabiliter patimur
detinere* (*C.I.L.*, t.I, 238, 501, an. 600)

(26) *it fecisse vobis ex more conscripse(i)*
(*Form. And. C.*, 24, p. 5)

(27) *aperire fecit filiis matris viscera*
(*V. Caes.*, I, 33)

(28.a) Phonetic Vowel Lowering

(28.b) Morphological reanalysis

(28.b.i) *-ari, -eri, -iri > -are, -ere, -ire*
ex. *tonsorari > tonsorare*

(28.b.ii) *-i > -ere*, ex. *legi > legere*

(28.b.iii) irregular passives, ex. *fieri > facere*

(28.c) Syntactic Reanalysis

(28.c.i) [*facit* [(*aliquis*) *domum aedificare*]]
(28.c.ii) ↳[*facit* [*domus aedificari* (*ab aliquo*)]]
Passive
(28.c.iii) ↳[*facit domum* [*aedificari* (*ab aliquo*)]]
Subject to Object Raising
(28.c.iv) ↳[*facit domum aedificare*]
Active Reanalysis (CU)

(28.c.i) is one source for the passive (28.c.ii) and the
SOR pattern in (28.c.iii). The syntactic reanalysis consists in deriving the reduced active complement (28.c.iv)
directly from the sentential structure (28.c.i) without the
application of the passive transformation in the lower
clause.

3. *Competing causative complements in Romance.* In
Romance the etymological reflexes of Latin *facere* exhibit
sentential, SOR, and CU complements. CU appears to be
overtaking the other two complement patterns. CU is at
present in a gradient state on the relational plane, propagating in a geographically western direction. In Italian
and French CU complements are the only possibility with
fare and *faire* respectively, whereas in other western Romance languages SOR is still a competitor, although a weaker one. In Spanish CU is the only possibility with intransitive constructions, but with ditransitive complements the

language reverts to its pristine sentential complementation. The significant fact which emerges from an overall view of the Romance languages except Rumanian is that CU is general with intransitive complements (as in (29) through (34), in competition with SOR with transitive complements (as in (35)), but grammatically impossible in Spanish and Catalan with ditransitives (as in (36)).

'Mary makes Johnny write'
(29.a) *Maria fa che Gianni scriva   (Italian)
(29.b) *Maria fa Gianni scrivere
(29.c) Maria fa scrivere Gianni

(30.a) *Marie fait que Jean écrive   (French)
(30.b) *Marie fait Jean écrire
(30.c) Marie fait écrire Jean

(31.a) la Maria fa que en Joan escrigui   (Catalan)
(31.b) *la Maria fa en Joan escriure
(31.c) la Maria fa escriure en Joan

(32.a) ?María hace que Juan escriba   (Spanish)
(32.b) *María hace Juan escribir
(32.c) María hace escribir a Juan

(33.a) ?Maria faz que João escreva   (Portuguese)
(33.b) Maria faz João escrever
(33.c) Maria faz escrever João

(34.a) Maria face ca Ion să scrie   (Rumanian
(34.b) Maria îl face pe Ion să scrie
(34.c) *Maria îl face (să) scrie pe Ion

'Mary makes Johnny write the letter'
(35.c) Maria fa scrivere la lettera a Gianni   (Italian)
        Marie fait écrire la lettre à Jean   (French)
        la Maria fa escriure la lletra a en Pere (Catalan)
        María le hace escribir la carta a Pedro (Spanish)
        Maria faz escrever a carta a João   (Portuguese)

'Mary makes Johnny write the letter to Peter'
(36.c) Maria fa scrivere la lettera a Piero   (Italian)
        da Gianni
        Marie fait écrire la lettre à Pierre   (French)
        par Jean

*la María fa escriure la lletra al Pere   (Catalan)
per en Joan

*María le hace escribir la carta a   (Spanish)
Pedro por Juan

Maria faz escrever a carta a Pedro por   (Portuguese)
João (Lisboa)

The propagation on the relational plane is characterized by an extended version of the Keenan-Comrie demotion hierarchy, as in (37):

(37.a) Subject to Object Raising: Rumanian and Portuguese

(37.b) Clause Union: Catalan, French, Italian, Portuguese and Spanish

(37.b.i)   Subject is DO   Cat, Fr, It, Port, Sp

(37.b.ii) Subject is IO/DO   Cat, Fr, It, Port, Sp

(37.b.iii) Subject is IO/DO IO   Cat, Fr, Port

(37.b.iv) Subject is AG/DO IO   Fr, It, Port

4. *The synchrony and diachrony of raising.* I have discussed an account of raising with the matrix verb *facere* from a text-based diachronic view and from a synchronic/typological perspective. I also have suggested that the Latin texts, as analyzed in previous studies, give some indication of a syntactic reanalysis of SOR constructions into CU constructions occurring between the fifth and the eighth century. By way of conclusion I would like to point out that the significant distributional characteristics of *facere* constructions in Romance follow not from a discrete-grammar view of diachronic syntax but from a diffusionist hypothesis based on the intersection of configurational, relational, and semantic planes.

Consider first the non-occurrence of CU in Rumanian. This typological feature correlates with the absence of infinitive formation in SOR complements (34.b), a present day syntactic situation which we observe in the Latin texts of the popular language (cf.(5) and (6)). It appears reasonable to infer that if Rumanian did not develop an infinitive, the reanalysis of (28) would have not occurred in this language, and hence the absence of CU. This speculation can only follow from a diachronic view in which SOR has at least two stages: SOR and Infinitive Formation. Moreover, the reduction processes need not be fully implemented.

Second, the agreement among the rest of the Romance languages as to CU intransitive complements follows from the observations made by Muller regarding the relative frequency of SOR patterns in Latin with intransitive as opposed to transitive and ditransitive complementation. A diachronic explanation of this typological phenomenon follows from a diffusionist view of raising on the relational plane, and is not implied in a discrete-rule conception of syntactic change.

The third, and most significant, typological variation concerns the distribution of the indirect object versus the agent phrase, technically the possibility for the complement subject to be 'demoted' to indirect object or Agent as a consequence of CU (cf. (37.b.iii-iv). We have seen that the syntactic reanalysis of the eighth century posited in (28.c) precludes the application of the passive rule in the lower clause. This hypothesis finds support in the texts (cf. (25) through (27)). The indirect object/agent phrase syntactic distinction was only reintroduced in French and Italian around the seventeenth century. This distinction with transitive infinitives, I claim (cf. Saltarelli 1977), is a surface syntactic specification of the semantic distinction between Experiencer and Agent constructions. The degree of variation in speakers' judgements attested in modern French and Italian finds a direct explanation in the diffusionist hypothesis.

REFERENCES

Aissen, Judith. 1974. *The syntax of causative constructions*. Unpublished dissertation. Harvard University.
Calvano, William and Mario Saltarelli. 1979. "The morphological measure of phonological rules". *Lingua* 48.1-14.
Chen, Matthew and William S.-Y. Wang. 1975. "Sound change: actuation and implementation". *Lg*. 51.255-81.
Gary, Judy and Edward Keenan. 1977. "On collapsing grammatical rules in universal grammar". In *Syntax and Semantics VIII: Grammatical relations*, 83-120. Ed. by Peter Cole and Jerry Sadock. New York: Academic Press.
Gougenheim, Georges. 1929. *Étude sur les périphrases verbales de la langue française*. Paris: Les Belles Lettres.
Muller, Henri-François. 1912. *Origine et histoire de la preposition 'à' dans les locutions du type 'faire faire quelque chose à quelqu'un'*. Poitiers: Masson.
Norberg, Dag. 1945. "'Faire faire quelque chose à quelqu'un'; recherches sur l'origine latine de la construction romane". *Uppsala Universitets Årsskrift* 12.65-106.

Postal, Paul and David Perlmutter. 1974. "Unauthorized notes on relational grammar from the summer linguistic institute". Xerox.
Radford, Andrew. 1976. "On the non-transformational nature of syntax: synchronic and diachronic evidence from Romance causatives". In *Romance Syntax*, 69-95. Ed. by Martin Harris. University of Salford.
Ronconi, Alessandro. 1946. *Il verbo latino*. Bologna: Zanichelli.
Saltarelli, Mario. 1976. "Accusativus cum infinitivo". In *Current Studies in Romance Linguistics*, 88-99. Ed. by Marta Luján and Fritz Hensey. Washington, D.C.: Georgetown University Press.
──────. 1977. "Where do agent phrases come from?" Paper read at the winter meeting of the Linguistic Society of America, Chicago.
van Tiel-Di Maio, Francesca. 1976. "Du latin vulgaire aux langues romanes: sur l'origine des constructions causatives". Mimeo.

TEXTS AND ABBREVIATIONS

Audollent, Defixionum Tabellae, Paris 1904	*Def. Tabel.*
Cassiodori Variarum (M.G.H., t.X)	*Cassi. Var.*
Cicero, Epistolae ad Familiares	*Cic. Fam.*
──────, De Optimo Genere Oratorum	*Cic. Opt. Gen. Or.*
──────, Tusculanae	*Cic. Tusc.*
Claudii Claudiani Carmina (M.G.H., t.X)	*Claud. Carm.*
Corpus Inscriptionum Latinarum	*C.I.L.*
Epistolae Merovingicae et Karolovingicae (M.G.H.)	*Ep. Mer. et Karol.*
España Sagrada	*Esp. Sag.*
Formulae Merovingicae et Karolovingicae (M.G.H,5)	*Form. And. C.*
Fredegarius, Chronicae (M.G.H.S.R.M., t.I)	*Fred.*
Lucretius, De Rerum Natura	*Lucr., De r.n.*
Monumenta Germaniae Historicae, Scriptores Rerorum Merovingicarum, 1877	*M.G.H.S.R.M.*
Plautus, Amphitryo	*Plaut., Amphi.*
Salviani, De Gubernatione Dei (M.G.H., t.V)	*Salv., de Gub. dei*
Suetonius, Caesar	*Sue., Caes.*
Troya, Codice Longobardo	*Cod. Lon.*
Vita Caesari (M.G.H., t.III)	*V. Caes.*
Vulgate, édition canonique, Tobias/Job	*Vulg. Tob./Job*

INFINITIVAL COMPLEMENTS TO VERBS OF MOTION IN ONTARIAN AND QUEBEC FRENCH

MICHAEL CANALE, RAYMOND MOUGEON,
AND EDOUARD BENIAK
The Ontario Institute for Studies in Education

0. *Introduction.* Traditional French grammarians (e.g. Grevisse 1975) generally recognize two types of infinitival complements to verbs of motion such as *aller* 'go' and *venir* 'come' in Modern French.* One is the infinitive not introduced by a preposition, which we will refer to as the bare infinitive; the other is the infinitive introduced by the preposition *pour* 'for', or the *pour* infinitive in this study. These constructions are illustrated in examples (1) and (2) respectively.

(1) le plombier est venu réparer le robinet

   'the plumber came and repaired the faucet'

(2) le plombier est venu pour réparer le robinet

   'the plumber came to repair the faucet'

The present paper examines a tendency in the French of young Franco-Ontarians to generalize the *pour* infinitive at the expense of the bare infinitive and discusses several possible causes of this tendency. We will conclude with several reasons why we think this to be an instructive case study for historical linguists.

1. *Standard usage.* One aspect of the infinitival complement to verbs of motion in Standard French is worth noting. As revealed in examples (1) and (2), the bare infinitive and *pour* infinitive are not semantically equivalent. Whereas the bare infinitive signals a result, or an action whose realization is presupposed, the *pour* infinitive signals only purpose, or an action whose realization is not presupposed. Thus (3) is ungrammatical and (4) grammatical in Standard French.

(3) *le plombier est venu réparer le robinet, mais il ne
l'a pas réparé

'the plumber came and fixed the faucet, but he didn't
fix it'

(4) le plombier est venu pour réparer le robinet, mais il
ne l'a pas réparé

'the plumber came to fix the faucet, but he didn't fix
it'

2. *Ontarian French and Quebec French*. We examined the use
of the infinitival complement to verbs of motion in the
spoken French of 90 bilingual (French and English) Franco-
Ontarian students at the elementary and secondary levels.
For purposes of comparison we also examined the spoken
French of 28 monolingual students from Quebec City at the
same grade levels. Both groups were fairly equally represented in terms of sex and socioeconomic background. All
the data were gathered in taped semi-directed interviews of
approximately 30 minutes duration designed to elicit informal speech on several specific topics (see Canale, Mougeon,
and Bélanger (1978) for further discussion of the research
methodology used here).

Our findings are that the Franco-Ontarian students but
not the Quebec City students are using the *pour* infinitive
with verbs of motion in two ways: on the one hand as a
signal of the purpose reading of the infinitival complement
(conforming to its usage in Standard French), and on the
other hand as a semantically equivalent variant of the bare
infinitive (not conforming to its usage in Standard
French). It is as if these students are generalizing the
structure but not the function of the *pour* infinitive by
using a semantically empty (or nonpurposive) *pour* to introduce the bare infinitive. Thus as a result of this structural generalization, the *pour* infinitive is often semantically ambiguous in our data between its purpose and nonpurpose readings. For more detailed discussion of these
data, see Canale, Mougeon, and Beniak (1979).

3. *Causes of this generalization*. Assuming the correctness of the analysis just presented, it remains to be established why the bare infinitive might be giving way to
the *pour* infinitive. For the reasons given below, we maintain that this generalization is a simplification of the
syntax of infinitival complements to verbs of motion in
French and that it is due to the *combined* influence of
intrasystemic factors (i.e. internal properties of French),
intersystemic factors (i.e. structural borrowing from

English), and extralinguistic factors (i.e. the low level of exposure to Standard French in Ontario and the high level of exposure to English).

The bare infinitive complement is highly restricted in its usage in Standard French. It is found only after a small set of verbs, namely the verbs of motion, perception (e.g. *penser* 'think'), causatives (e.g. *faire* 'make'), and the modals (e.g. *vouloir* 'want')-- cf. Grevisse (1975:748). The majority of verbs taking infinitival complements require the preposition *à* or *de* before the infinitival phrase, where these prepositions are semantically empty. It is thus possible that the use of the *pour* infinitive in contexts requiring the bare infinitive represents a tendency to regularize the predominant infinitival complement pattern of verb + preposition + infinitival phrase. Although it is not clear to us why bare infinitive complements to verbs of motion should be affected earlier than infinitive complements to perception verbs, causatives, and modals, the fact that *pour* rather than another preposition is being used in Ontarian French to introduce the nonpurpose or resultative infinitival complement to verbs of motion seems to be related to several internal factors. First, the constructions *aller* + *pour* + infinitival phrase and *venir* + *pour* + infinitival phrase are frequently used in Canadian and Standard French in a nonpurposive sense, viz. to express the notion 'to be about to'. Second, in earlier studies of these students' spoken French we isolated several innovative uses of *pour*, among them its substitution for *à* and *de* before an infinitival complement to verbs such as *demander* 'ask' and *inviter* 'invite', where these latter two prepositions are semantically null. Third, Aub-Buscher (1976) presents data that suggest a similar extension in the use of *pour* in the French-based creoles spoken in the Caribbean. In particular, she notes that *pour* is used frequently to introduce a nonpurpose infinitival complement while maintaining its purpose function in other contexts.

It is thus possible that a number of internal properties of French have played a role in the extension of the use of *pour* before nonpurpose infinitival complements in Ontarian French. However, there is no reason to believe that the generalization of the *pour* infinitive in our data is due to intrasystemic factors alone. Certain of these factors are, we assume, relevant in Quebec French and Standard French as well, yet we know of no evidence suggesting a similar generalization in these varieties. We are thus led to believe that still other factors, more or less unique to the Franco-Ontarian sociolinguistic setting, have contributed to the observed generalization. Two such factors seem to be (a) borrowing influence due to contact with English, along with (b) the low degree of exposure to Standard French in Ontario.

Consider the first factor. In English the preposition *to* serves as a sandhi form to introduce the infinitival complement of the majority of verbs. This infinitival complement may have a purpose or nonpurpose function when used with a verb of motion, as in (5).

(5) a. I went there to study, not to eat. (purpose)
    b. I went to eat at a Mexican restaurant last night and enjoyed the food. (nonpurpose)

Thus one might expect to find a higher occurrence of the nonstandard use of *pour* to introduce a nonpurpose infinitive among French speakers having a good command of English (e.g. Franco-Ontarians) than among those having a poorer command of English (e.g. Quebeckers).

As concerns the second factor, Mougeon, Canale, and Bélanger (1978) have reported that Standard French is in general little used or valued by Franco-Ontarians. Thus the low level of exposure to Standard French may contribute to the weakening of the bare infinitive and to the generalizing of the *pour* infinitive that we have detected among young Franco-Ontarians.

4. *Conclusion.* We think that the data and findings we have reported in this study are of interest to historical linguists for several reasons.

First, the generalization that we have observed seems to be motivated by structural or syntactic factors alone; it is not at all obvious that there is any semantic or phonetic motivation involved. This is thus an important case study given the view among many historical linguists that such 'pure' syntactic change is not possible (cf. Lightfoot 1979 for documentation and discussion of such views).

Second, it has been claimed by certain historical linguists (e.g. Anttila 1972) that one of the major principles of language change is that of 'one meaning, one form': i.e. language learners strive to avoid polysemous linguistic forms. However, the structural generalization that we have examined here seems to be taking place *in spite of* the fact that it gives rise to semantic ambiguity of the *pour* infinitive between its purpose and nonpurpose readings.[1]
Thus, to the extent that this generalization represents an

innovation in Ontarian French (a point suggested, but not confirmed, by data from earlier French dialects discussed in Brunot 1966), our findings are inconsistent with those predicted by the principle 'one meaning, one form'. This principle would appear, therefore, to be inadequate in accounting for some linguistic changes.[2]

Finally, much recent work in historical linguistics and second language learning has claimed to isolate single causes for various innovative linguistic developments, rather than examining the possible interaction of different causal factors (cf. Canale 1978 and Lightfoot 1979 for discussion). In our own work on Ontarian French (cf. Canale, Mougeon, and Bélanger 1978, for example) we have found that those nonstandard usages that are systematic and persistent tend to be attributable to an interaction of intrasystemic, intersystemic, and extralinguistic factors. In the context of the present study, it is certainly reasonable to propose (a) that the tendency to phase out the bare infinitive complement to verbs of motion was latent in Ontarian French and (b) that the existence of related infinitival constructions in French, the borrowing influence of English, and the low level of exposure to Standard French have reinforced this latent tendency, and have set into motion and directed the observed generalization. Evidence that there is at least a latent tendency in all French dialects to discard productive rules for forming the bare infinitive complement to verbs of motion is suggested by the history of this construction in the Romance languages. For example, Italian, Portuguese, and Spanish have all generalized the pattern of verb of motion + preposition + infinitival phrase with a cognate of French *à* introducing a nonpurpose infinitive and one of French *pour* introducing a purpose infinitive.

NOTES

*The research reported here was funded in part by grants from the Ontario Ministry of Education and the Ontario Institute for Studies in Education. We gratefully acknowledge this support.

[1]It should be pointed out that although the observed generalization of the *pour* infinitive results in a loss of the distinction between purpose and resultative infinitival complements at the surface syntactic level, this distinction may be signaled at a broader discourse/pragmatic level. However, this must not be taken to mean that this generalization is motivated by discourse/pragmatic factors; we find no evidence that such factors disambiguate the purpose and resultative readings any more (or less) effectively in the Franco-Ontarian

data than in the Quebec data. The only relevant differences observed between these two dialects is in the extent to which the bare infinitive is used at all.

[2] To counter our argument, one might adopt the position that the change in question is an 'unnatural' one since it is not in keeping with the principle 'one form, one meaning' (and seems to be a candidate for 'pure' syntactic change). One might then attribute this 'unnaturalness' to the influence of the extralinguistic factors we have discussed. As Sarah G. Thomason (personal communication) has pointed out, there are some obvious difficulties with such a position, one being that there is no way as yet to characterize which set of extralinguistic factors will give rise to 'natural' change and which to 'unnatural' change.

REFERENCES

Anttila, Raimo. 1972. *An introduction to historical and comparative linguistics*. New York: The Macmillan Co.

Aub-Buscher, G. 1976. "A propos de quelques rapports prépositionnels en créole". In *Actes du XIIIème congrès international de linguistique et de philologie romanes*. Ed. by M. Boudreault and F. Möhren. Quebec: Laval University Press.

Brunot, Ferdinand. 1966. *Histoire de la langue française des origines à nos jours*. Paris: Librairie Armand Colin.

Canale, Michael. 1978. *Word order change in Old English: base reanalysis in generative grammar*. Unpublished Ph.D. thesis, McGill University, Montreal, Canada.

_____, Raymond Mougeon, and M. Bélanger. 1978. "Analogical leveling of the auxiliary *être* in Ontarian French". In *Contemporary studies in Romance linguistics*. Ed. by M. Suñer. Washington, D.C.: Georgetown University Press.

_____, _____, and Edouard Beniak. 1979. "Generalization of *pour* after verbs of motion in Ontarian French". In *The fifth LACUS forum*. Ed. by A. Makkai. Columbia, S.C.: Hornbeam.

Grevisse, Maurice. 1975. *Le bon usage*. Gembloux, Belgium: Duculot, 10th Ed.

Lightfoot, David. 1979. *Principles of diachronic syntax*. Cambridge: Cambridge University Press.

Mougeon, Raymond, Michael Canale, and M. Bélanger. 1978. "Rôle de la société dans l'acquisition et le maintien du français par les élèves franco-ontariens". *Canadian Modern Language Review* 34.3:381-94.

VERB COMPOUNDS IN GREEK:
THE ELIMINATION OF A TRANSFORMATIONAL RULE

GEOFFREY C. HORROCKS
*School of Oriental and African Studies,
University of London*

The early Greek of the Homeric poems[1] has eighteen spatio-temporal adverbial particles which exhibit a wide range of syntactic behavior. These occasionally appear as locative adjuncts:

(1) kteinon d' *epi* me:lobote:ras

'they killed and (there)upon the shepherds'

(Iliad 18:529)

But this is a residual usage, and more usually in this function we find newer forms, often derivatives of the original particles. Kuryłowicz (1964:171ff.) suggests that the renewal of the old forms in their adverbial function was concomitant with the development of their hitherto secondary uses as preverbs and prepositions--what were originally independent adverbs that could optionally stand preverbally or prenominally eventually lose their independent status and become fixed in these positions. In Homer this process is by no means complete. For example, a common use of these particles is as complements to locative or directional verbs. Though other positions are possible, preverbal position is usually taken to be the most neutral (cf. Watkins 1964):

(2) all' age nun *ei*selthe

'but come now in(to)-go'   (Il. 6:354)

In most texts particle (Prt) and verb (V) are written as a single word (in comformity with later practice), but it is clear that in Homer this type of particle-verb combination (henceforth PVC) is still simply a collocation of discrete elements. First, there are many connectives in Greek which occupy second position in a clause, and these regularly separate an initial Prt from its V:

(3) *es* d' agage Priamon
   'in(to) and he led Priam'   (Il. 24:447)

The type where both Prt and V precede such a connective also occurs, but is rather rare:[2]

(4) *apo*ptuei d' halos akhne:n
   'forth-he spits and of the sea the spray' (Il. 4:426)

Nevertheless, the existence of such cases confirms that Prt and V may form a single constituent, even if they do not yet form a compound. Secondly, the Prts in this complement function are freely separable from their V, and may stand either before the direct object or clause initially, both of which are marked positions (cf. Watkins 1964):

(5) hoi *kata* bous Huperionos...e:sthion
   'who down the cattle of the Sun...ate' (Odyssey 1:8)

(6) *hupo* de xula kankana keitai
   'below and wood dry lies'   (Il. 21:364)

I assume that both these types are derived by movement rules from a structure in which Prt immediately precedes V (see Figure 1 below). The basic character of this structure is confirmed by the existence of idiomatic PVCs in which the Prt has a resultative force. Here the choice of Prt is not free, but is a more or less unpredictable property of individual verbs. Since, as a consequence, many PVCs must be listed in the lexicon, the entries will clearly have to be of the form: Prt V. Examples of such resultative PVCs are very common:

(7) *apa*ltheo: 'heal off', i.e. 'remove (e.g. a wound) by healing'

   *kata*sbennumi: 'quench down', i.e. 'reduce (to nil) by quenching'

These also allow Prt to be moved to either of the marked positions.

   In Homer nominal case endings can express spatial relations:

(8) Argeioi de *neo:n*...ekho:re:san
   'the Argives and from the ships (genitive)...retreated'
                                                        (Il. 16:655)

A very common use of the Prts is to specify the value of such case inflections:

(9) Peisandron *aph' hippo:n* o:se

'Peisander off from the chariot (genitive) he pushed'

(Il. 11:143)

The use of supported case inflections is already more common in Homer, but the Prts are not yet true prepositions since the use of the cases alone proves that these still have independent semantic content. The case ending is the crucial morpheme, the Prt merely modifies it (cf. Kuryłowicz 1964:176). Such Prt + NP combinations occur both as verbal complements (as in (9)), and as optional adjuncts:

(10) ho:s hoi...ta penonto *kata straton*

'thus they...these things toiled at up and down via the army (acc.)' (Il. 1:318)

Both possibilities are illustrated in Figure I:[3]

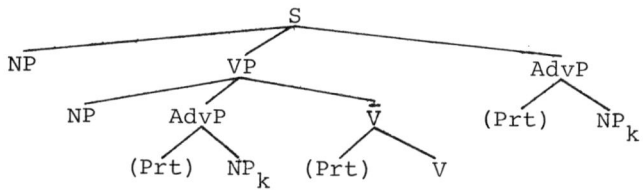

FIGURE I

Clearly Prt and inflected NP (henceforth NP_k) form a single constituent since they may appear together before a connective in second position:

(11) *peri tripodos* gar emellon theusesthai.

'for a tripod for they were about to run'

(Il. 11:699-70)

An interesting relationship exists between structures of the form (12a) and structures of the form (12b):

(12a) ...Prt NP_k...V

(12b) ...NP_k...Prt V (which allows Prt fronting)

Examples of pairs of this kind are easily found:

(13a) païs ek Pulou e:lthen

'the child out from Pylos went' (Od. 16:377)

(13b) exe:lthe domo:n

'out-he went from the house' (Od. 20:371)

Since both structures can be base generated (cf. Fig. I), and since the restrictions on the case of NP are predictable one from the other (no change), it is possible to capture the relationship lexically as in (14) or transformationally (cf. Wasow 1977:328), as in (15).

(14) Lexical redundancy rule:

$$+ \text{Prt}, +[\text{---NP}_k] \longrightarrow + \text{Prt}, +[\text{---V}]$$

(i.e. a 'prepositional' Prt)   (i.e. an 'adverbial' Prt)

(15) Transformational rule; two possible formulations:

(a)   X - Prt - NP_k - V - X

       1   2   3   4   5 $\Longrightarrow$ (Opt.)

       1   0   3   2+4   5

(b)   X - NP_k - Prt - V - X

       1   2   3   4   5 $\Longrightarrow$ (Opt.)

       1   3+2   0   4   5

In choosing between these a number of criteria suggest themselves:

(a) The lexical rule claims that there are two subcategories of Prt, 'prepositional' (i.e. pre-NP_k) and 'adverbial' (i.e. pre-V).[4] We would expect therefore a shift in the relationship of NP_k to Prt when the latter stands pre-V; in this case the rule predicts that this relation is terminated and that a new relation is established between Prt and V. If there were no shift of relation, Prt would still have two contexts of insertion, but *without* any subcategory shift; i.e. it would be the same item in the same function merely occupying two different positions. There would be little point in writing a lexical rule to relate the two items in such circumstances, and a transformational account would clearly be preferable, especially if one type is more marked than the other.

(b) Lexical rules may refer only to material in the frames determining an item's context(s) of insertion, and this material must include only those features of the item's deep structure environment that crucially condition its appearance. If the relationship cannot be stated locally in this way, we must opt for the transformational analysis, since transformations can refer to properties of whole phrase markers (cf. Wasow 1977:330).

(c) We would expect lexical rules relating sets of items to have exceptions reflecting accidental gaps in the lexicon. If the relationship is exceptionless, we should adopt the transformational analysis, since transformations, as structure-dependent operations, should not be subject to lexical exceptions (cf. Wasow 1977: 330-1).

Taking (a)-(c) in turn, we have the following results:
(a) There are a number of apparent exceptions to the relationship (12):
(16a) *edu ana polie:s halos
   'he came up from the grey sea (gen.)'
(16b) anedu polie:s halos
   'up- he came from...'   (Il. 1:359)

But 'prepositional' Prts must be subcategorized according to the cases that they can co-occur with:[5]

(17a) ana: Prt, $+[---NP_{acc}]$
              $+[---NP_{dat}]$

(17b) ek: Prt, $+[---NP_{gen}]$ (cf. (13))

These restrictions are always carried over from type (12a) to type (12b), so the only explanation for the facts in (16) is that the pre-V Prt is here independent of the NP_k. But when this is the case there is no corresponding structure of the form (12a), as (16a) makes clear. This is bad for the lexical analysis since it predicts the existence of just this prohibited relationship. Furthermore, when the relationship goes through as expected, the Prt is clearly *not* independent of NP_k, even in pre-V position. The co-occurrence restrictions on case are carried over and the Prt remains 'prepositional' despite its position. We therefore have two instances of the same item in the same function in examples such as (13a) and (13b); they differ only in terms of their position and so the transformational account is to be preferred. In choosing between (15a) and (15b) it is important to notice that we need the following subcategorization features for Prts in any case:

(18a) $+[---V]$ (for 'adverbial' Prts, cf. (2) and (16b))

(18b) $+[---NP_k]$ (for 'prepositional' Prts in AdvP outside VP, cf. (10))

(18b) is necessary because where AdvP is outside VP we do *not* find analogues with Prt in Pre-V position; contrast (10) with (19):

(19) *ho:s hoi...katapenonto straton

When we turn to AdvP inside VP, without any further addition to (18), the correct case for NP_k follows automatically if the T-rule takes the form (15a). If we adopt (15b), we need conditions on the movement of Prt which simply duplicate the restrictions expressed by (18b). Therefore (15a) is the correct account of the relationship (12).

(b) Because of the localness requirement on lexical rules there is no means of specifying the distinction between AdvP inside VP and AdvP outside. This is important because only the former have analogues with Prt in pre-V position (cf. (10) and (19)). Any further items used to make this distinction are illegitimate, since the frames in (14) *already* contain all the items which crucially condition the appearance of Prts, and any additional items would thus lack independent justification. If we accept this, (14) will wrongly relate pairs like (10) and (19). The only way in which the use of additional items could be justified is if there were evidence of a subcategory difference between Prts inserted in contexts containing such an item and Prts inserted in otherwise identical contexts that do not. But clearly the fact that some 'prepositional' Prts can stand before V or NP_k, while others can stand only before NP_k, is determined exclusively by structural facts (the position of the AdvP containing Prt in the phrase marker) and not by any subcategory difference. Therefore the T-rule analysis is confirmed.

(c) Given a structure of the form (12a) the corresponding structure of the form (12b) can always be derived; the T-rule analysis is again confirmed.

In summary: PVCs in the structure (12b) are always transformationally derived, provided that there is a corresponding structure of the form (12a). Examples such as those in (2) and (16b) are, of course, base generated.

There are, however, other types of PVC in Homer. Many pre-V Prts seem to have a completive or intensive force - 'completely', 'greatly', etc.

(20a) *ap*ekhthairo: 'detest utterly'

(20b) *ex*ophello: 'greatly augment'

The choice of Prt in this function is fairly unpredictable on the whole, though *apo*-verbs seem to be quite freely coined. Some Prts also have a number of rather specialized senses:

(21a) *apo*tino: 'pay back'

(21b) *aph*andano: 'displease'

The productivity of the rules forming these PVCs varies according to the choice of Prt and its particular function, but in no case are they fully productive, a fact which suggests that lexical rules of word formation are involved.[6] What is interesting about all these cases is the absence of examples in which Prt is separated from V. This fact would follow automatically if we adopted a lexical account of these PVCs, since we would then be dealing with true *compounds* which by definition would not be subject to separation of their elements by transformation. The development of this type of PVC may perhaps be the result of the fossilization and subsequent (idiosyncratic) semantic development of certain high frequency PVCs which then provided a model for new formations; (examples like (23b) might constitute such a model--see below).

There are a number of complex transitive verbs (taking both a direct object and an AdvP complement) which fall into a partially regular relationship with completive compounds; the NP_k within AdvP corresponds to the direct object of the compound, and the Prt of AdvP corresponds to the prefix of the compound:

(22a) NP_x - Prt NP_y - V
(22b) NP_y - $[_V \text{Prt V}]$

For example:

(23a) Aias d' amphi Menoitiade:i sakos...kalupsas

'Ajax and around Patroclus his shield...having wrapped' (Il. 17:132)

(23b) nephele: de min amphekalupse

'the cloud and him around-wrapped (i.e. encircled completely)' (Il. 20:417)

The relationship (22) is far from fully productive, and seems to be confined to verbs of 'washing', 'wiping', 'wrapping', etc. Since the rule is lexically governed and subject to exceptions, we must set up a lexical rule to capture the relationship:

(24) $[_V V]$, $+[NP_x \text{ Prt } NP_y \underline{\quad}] \longrightarrow [_V \text{Prt V}]$, $+[NP_y \underline{\quad}]$

In summary: many PVCs in Homer must be analyzed as compounds derived by word formation rules. These are quite distinct from both the transformationally derived and base generated PVCs already discussed.

When we turn to Classical Greek (5th-4th centuries B.C.), we find a very different situation. Following the analysis of Kuryłowicz (1964:176) it seems that the case endings of NPs in local constructions now merely discriminate between various senses of a single preposition; e.g.

epi + dat. 'on', + acc. 'onto' or 'over'. The case endings function as determinants of prepositions and NP_ks can no longer occur freely without support. Their appearance is rather conditioned by the appearance of a preposition, and so the preposition is always positionally bound to NP_k. This contrasts sharply with the situation in Homer, and it seems that we are dealing with a case of category split contingent upon the shift of the status of case endings from free to bound morphemes. In Homer there is a single category Prt whose members can be inserted pre-NP_k or pre-V. The lack of a true category distinction is demonstrated by the fact that, because Prts inside VP simultaneously modify a case ending and complement the verb, a pre-NP_k Prt may be moved to pre-V position without a change of function --the freedom of positioning reflects the double function. But in Classical Greek the subcategory distinction between 'adverbial' and 'prepositional' Prt has become a true category distinction between Preverb and Preposition, the latter now always appearing pre-NP_k because of the dependency of the case ending. PreVs never govern a case and Preps are never verb complements.[7] Some examples will make this clear:

(25) *ap*edrasan *eis* Klazdomenas

'away-they fled into Clazomenae'

(Xenophon Hellenica I.1.10)

(26) *ek* Rhodou *eis* Helle:sponton *eis*eplei

'out of Rhodes into the Hellespont in-he sailed'

(Xen. Hell. I.1.2)

The appearance of prepositions in local constructions is obligatory. Verbs may have preverb complements, but this is never the result of movement from pre-NP_k position, as (26) makes clear. Whereas in Homer a single occurrence of *eis* in one or other position would have been the norm, in Classical Greek we find both a preverb and a preposition, even where these are formally identical--i.e. each has one function only. The loss of the T-rule (15a) is an automatic consequence of the category split affecting Prt. Once items in pre-NP_k position are reclassified as true Preps (i.e. Prts bound to NP_k) the rule is deprived of its domain of application and becomes redundant. The loss would presumably be a gradual process, since the rule would remain functional until such time as the reclassification of pre-NP_k Prts was complete.

Another interesting fact about Classical Greek is the complete absence, except in archaizing poetry influenced by the Homeric model, of examples where PreV is separated from V, even in those cases where it is a local or resultative complement. The order Prt V is the only order:

(27) Athe:naioi de *ap*epleusan
  'the Athenians and away-sailed' (Xen. Hell. I.1.7)

Any explanation of this must be tentative, but one possibility is that *all* PVCs have been reanalyzed as compounds by the existing rules of word formation (cf. Aronoff 1976: ch. 2), thus rendering PreVs immune to separation; i.e. PreVs become bound to V as Preps to NP_k. Such a process would be aided by two factors. First, the disappearance of Prts used as independent adverbs (cf. the first paragraph) would tend to encourage the fixing of PreVs in the 'bound' pre-V position. Secondly, there developed in Greek a tendency to restrict or eliminate leftwards operations (concomitant with a shift towards SVO word order), and this too would tend to fix PreVs in immediately pre-V position (cf. Aitchison 1977). In such circumstances there would be increasingly little evidence for the discreteness of PreV and V, and eventually all PVCs would be assimilated to the existing compound paradigm.

If all PVCs in Classical Greek are in fact compounds, we have a simplification process in which three types of PVC in Homer (transformational, base-generated, and compound) are reduced to one (compound). The direction of the simplification runs counter to that suggested for English passives by Wasow (1977:355-56), who argues that English is now in the process of eliminating lexical passives in favor of transformational passives. By constrast, Greek, or rather its IE ancestor, began with just transformationally derived PVCs--with independent complement Advs optionally moved to pre-V position. These gradually became increasingly bound to the V, and PVCs were eventually analyzed as compounds. The transformational PVCs of Homer represent something of an aberration in this process, the rule (15a) being simply a device to permit pre-V positioning for 'prepositional' Prts functioning simultaneously as verb complements. Once such pre-NP_k Prts are reclassified as Preps the rule disappears and the class of transformational PVCs disappears with it.

NOTES

[1] In their present form the Iliad and Odyssey probably date from the sixth century B.C., but because they are the product of an oral tradition, they contain many features of greater antiquity.

[2] By contrast this type is absolutely regular in Classical Greek of the fifth and fourth centuries B.C. because by that time all particle-verb constructions are compounds; see below.

[3] The word order represented here is somewhat arbitrary (cf. e.g. Friedrich 1975), but some support for basic SOV order may be found in Dover 1960:25, Frisk 1933:39ff.

[4] Such lexical rules have generally been proposed to capture a relationship between *distinct* but related lexical items, for example: active V : passive V (Bresnan 1978:14ff.) causative V : intransitive V (Wasow 1977:331ff.).

[5] This is evidence of the growing dependence between Prt and certain case endings even though both are still to some extent free morphemes.

[6] For the more or less productive types, the rules would presumably have the form: [Prt (X)] + [V] = [$_V$[Prt (X)][V]].

[7] There are an number of apparent counter-examples such as:

*ep*eisbaino:n *to:i hippo:i* eis te:n thalattan

'upon-into-going his horse into the sea (i.e. riding (in) upon his horse into the sea.)'   (Xenophon Hellenica I.1.6)

But these are all 'prepositional' verbs which are logically transitive, (cf. English *rely on*, etc.); the correct translation of the above example is 'riding his horse into the sea'. The Prep and V form a compound with a special sense and the combination is presumably due to a word formation rule and not a T-rule as in Homeric examples such as (13b).

REFERENCES

Aitchison, Jean. 1977. "The order of word order change". Unpublished manuscript.
Aronoff, Mark. 1976. *Word formation in generative grammar*. Linguistic Inquiry monograph 1. Cambridge, Mass.: MIT Press.
Bresnan, Joan. 1978. "A realistic tranformational grammar". In *Linguistic theory and psychological reality*, 1-59. Ed. by Morris Halle, Joan Bresnan, and George A. Miller. Cambridge, Mass.: MIT Press.
Dover, K.J. 1960. *Greek word order*. Cambridge: Cambridge University Press.
Friedrich, Paul. 1975. *Proto-Indo-European syntax*. Journal of Indo-European Studies, Monograph 1. Butte, Montana.
Frisk, Hjalmar. 1933. *Studien zur griechischen Wortstellung*. Göteberg.
Kuryłowicz, Jerzy. 1964. *The inflectional categories of Indo-European*. Heidelberg: Winter.
Wasow, Thomas. 1977. "Transformations and the lexicon". In *Formal*

syntax, 327-60. Ed. by Peter W. Culicover, Thomas Wasow, and Adrian Akmajian. New York: Academic Press.

Watkins, Calvert. 1964. "Preliminaries to the reconstruction of Indo-European sentence structure". In *Proceedings of the Ninth International Congress of Linguists*, 1035-42. The Hague: Mouton.

THE ROLE OF PERCEPTION
IN RESTRUCTURING AND RELEXICALIZATION:
TWO CASE HISTORIES

ROBERT K. HERBERT
State University of New York, Binghamton

0. *Introduction.* In this brief paper, I would like to discuss one aspect of the role of perception in a theory of language change.[1] Certainly the notion is now commonplace that a theory of change must be not only descriptive, but at some level of analysis explanatory. The interest in perception stems in part from the question of where change originates -- in competence or performance. The position of early generative grammarians favored origin in competence, but this view was expressly challenged by Weinreich et al. (1968), and many others, who argue that change originates in performance. However, the examples they cite really concern *spread* rather than initiation of change. In the long run, we will probably need to recognize that a complete explanation of the different types of change will involve aspects of origin in both competence and performance.

The paper considers two cases of change involving a restructuring and relexicalization of forms, which have their origins, it is claimed, in misperceptions of morphemic boundary placement. In both cases, the change involves the loss of no phonetic material. As Jeffers (1977:18) has pointed out, such a change is necessarily arbitrary unless we can provide some perceptual basis for reanalysis. The two examples, taken from Bantu and Austronesian, will be discussed separately and then set within the above framework.

1. *Bantu.* One of the two principle criteria generally used for identifying a language as Bantu is a system of grammatical genders or noun classes, which do not correspond to sex reference or, in many cases, to any clearly defined idea. The sign of Bantu gender is a prefix, and

there is a regular association of pairs of classes to indicate the singular and plural of the various genders. Among the prefixes traditionally reconstructed for Proto-Bantu are the following singular/plural pairs:

(1) Singular   Plural
     1. *mu-*   2. *ba-*
     3. *mu̧-* (*mu-*)   4. *mi-* (*mi̧-*)
     5. *li̧-*   6. *ma-*
     7. *ki-*   8. *bi-* (*bi̧-*)
     9. *ni-*   10. *li̧-ni-* (pl. to 9 and 11)
    11. *lu-*

The so-called 'nasal class' (Cl. 9/10) is interesting for a number of reasons. Morphologically, this is the only class in which singular and plural are identical in many, if not most, Bantu languages. The prefix for *both* sg. and plural is (V)N-, (V)N-, although historically and in some languages synchronically they are differentiated by the presence of an 'extra' prefix in the plural (Cole 1967). This identity raises the interesting theoretical question of how nonalternating singular/plural forms are represented in the lexicon of the native speaker. That is, there is a great deal of evidence which suggests that the underlying representations for the Luganda pairs in (2) are identical to their surface forms, e.g., /Ø + mbaata/, /Ø + nte/, etc.[2]

(2) *embaata*   *embaata*   'duck(s)'
     ente   *ente*   'cow(s)'
     ensuwa   *ensuwa*   'water pot(s)'
     enjovu   *enjovu*   'elephants(s)'
     eŋgo   *eŋgo*   'leopard(s)'

There are several different types of evidence which bear on such a determination,[3] which are considered in detail in Herbert (1978).

Among the relevant evidence cited is the behavior of Class 11/10 nouns, in which the plural is identical with the plural of Cl. 9, but the singular shows a non-nasal prefix (< */lu-/). Examples of this alternation are found in (3) below. (Hereafter the plural of Cl. 9 will be referred to as Cl. 10a and the plural of Cl. 11 as 10b in order to distinguish them in discussion.)

(3) *olulimi*   *endimi*   'tongue(s)'
     oluviiri   *eɱviiri*   '(a) hair'
     olgalo   *eŋgalo*   'finger(s)'
     olusozi   *ensozi*   'hill(s)'

The demonstrable presence of a separable nasal prefix in Cl. 10b is frequently used to argue for the existence of a prefix in Cl. 9/10a nouns. This analysis is based on

THE ROLE OF PERCEPTION   213

the often cited, though never defended principle of generative grammar: if some occurrences of X are derived from remote representations distinct from X, then all occurrences should be so derived (cf. Zwicky 1975). Despite its questionable soundness, Latta (1978) has recently proposed that this same principle is one of the operating methodological principles of internal reconstruction. However, it should be pointed out that the fact that this principle is borne out on some occasions provides no justification for its essential methodological validity.

If, however, it is possible for a language to restructure nonalternating 9/10a forms so that underlying representation is identical with surface facts, we might expect that Cl. 10a and 10b would develop differently in some languages. The Makonde data in (4) and (5) suggest that such a restructuring has occurred:

(4a) 9/10a   *imbau* (/i+N+*bau*/)   *dimbau* (/di+N+*bau*/)   'board(s)'
                 imbidi   *dimbidi*   'boa(s)'
N + C̥ → NC   *indila*   *dindila*   'road(s); path(s)'
                 iŋguo   *diŋguo*   'cloth(s)'

(4b)   *imepo* (/i+N+*pepo*/) *dimepo* (/di+N+*pepo*/) 'wind(s)'
                 inembo   *dinembo*   'elephant(s)'
N + C̥ → N   (Makua: *thepo*)
                 imaka   *dimaka*   'cat(s)' '(*paka*)
                 iŋuku   *diŋuku*   'fowl(s)' '(*kuku*)

(5a) 11/10b   *lumbau*   *dimbau*   'rib(s)'
                 lumbuhu   *dimbuhu*   'thread(s)'
                 lundomo   *dindomo*   'lip(s); beak(s)'
                 lunduyu   *dinduyu*   'feather(s)'
                 luŋgayo   *diŋgayo*   'foot/feet;
                                                                        track(s)'

(5b)   *lupembe*   *dimembe*   'horn(s)'
                     (/*lu*+*pembe*/)   (/di+N+*pembe*/)
N + C̥ → N   *lupapa*   *dimapa*   'wing(s)'
                 lutavi   *dinavi*   'branch(es)'
                 lukoni   *diŋuni*   'firewood'
                 lukombe   *diŋombe*   'fingernail(s)'

Thus, Makonde has a rule, which it shares with a number of neighboring languages, which deletes a voiceless stop after a nasal: NC̥ → N. The operation of this rule is observed in (4b) and (5b) and also in historical forms, e.g., **muntu* > *munu* 'person'. Sequences of nasal plus voiced stop, however, remain and are realized as unit prenasalized stops [^{n}C]. The forms of interest at present are Cl. 11/10b nouns in (5a), which show stem-initial prenasalized stops.

The presence of a nasal as part of the prefix or stem is historically unjustified and unexplained in the Cl. 11 singular forms; cf. Maβiha *luβawo/dimbawo* 'rib(s)'.

Our analysis of the Makonde data is as follows. After the NC → N rule was established, a restructuring occurred in 9/10a forms whereby the nasal was analyzed as part of the noun stem. Thus, the 9/10a prefixes became /i-, di-/.[4] No Cl. 9/10a stem now begins with a voiced stop, the voiced stops having been replaced by prenasalized stops. This generalization was extended to Cl. 10b forms so that the prenasalized stops of the plural were interpreted as stem-initial consonants. This resulted in the extension of the prenasalized stop into Cl. 11 singulars, which is unexpected otherwise. However, the rule NÇ → N continues to be a productive rule in Cl. 11/10b as the forms in (5b) demonstrate. Since this rule no longer functions in Cl. 9/10a forms, the Makonde data provide some evidence that Cl. 10a and 10b may be formally distinct in certain languages. The question of why the reanalysis of voiced stops as prenasalized stops was extended in Cl. 11/10b, but not the reanalysis of voiceless stops as simple nasals, will be discussed in Section 3.

2. *Western Austronesian.* There is an interesting morphophonological process operative in Western Austronesian languages whereby a limited series of nasal-final morphemes elicit various changes in stem-initial consonants. The most commonly occurring of these prefixes are *maŋ-, *paŋ-. Some examples from Indonesian demonstrate the effects of prefixation:

(6) (a) *damar*   'resin'   *mendamar*   'to gather resin'
        darat   'terra firma'   *mendarat*   'to go ashore'
        gergaji   'saw'   *meŋgergaji*   'to saw'
        (*buka*)   ('open')   *membuka*   'to open'

    (b) *uak*   'lowing'   *meŋuak*   'to low'

    (c) *tari*   'a dance'   *menari*   'dance'
        pekik   'a scream'   *memekik*   'scream'
        kapur   'chalk'   *meŋapur*   'whitewash'
        keluh   'sigh, complaint' *meñeluh*   'sigh, complain'
        sayur   'vegetables'   *meñayur*   'to make vegetable soup'

    (d) *merah*   'red'   *memerah*   'to turn red'

The forms in (c) demonstrate the process known as Nasal Substitution, whereby the sequence nasal plus voiceless consonant is replaced by a simple nasal homorganic to the

original consonant. The development of this rule is one
of the major criteria used for subgrouping Western languages as a whole (Dahl 1973). The traditional analysis
of these forms is that they involve position assimilation
of the nasal consonant (N → [αposition]/___[αposition]^C),
and then the complete assimilation of the oral consonant
(Ç → N/N___) and cluster simplification as exemplified in
(d) (Dahl 1973:127). I have argued against this position
and in favor of a perceptually conditioned deletion elsewhere (Herbert 1977). The arguments for this analysis are
complex, involving a consideration of cross-language phonetic variation of NÇ sequences and implicational universals
such as that proposed by Hutcheson (1973) that the complete
assimilation of unlike segments implies the complete assimilation of more like segments, which situation does not
obtain in Western Austronesian, as the forms in (6a) demonstrate. This analysis ascribes variation in realization to
both derived and internal NÇ sequences, and claims that the
variation [NŇÇ, NÇ̌Ç], etc., would be first eliminated when
morphological marking is involved. Thus, the rule of Nasal
Substitution applies only to derived clusters, but medial
clusters are unaffected by it. This distinction has traditionally been a puzzle in Austronesian phonology. However, recent phonetic work has shown that medial·/mp/ in
Malagasy, for example, may be [m m̥ hp mh mɦ ʔp mm̥p] as a
result of phonetic variation due to the inherent difficulty of articulating the NÇ sequence.

The behavior of Nasal Substitution stems in reduplication has been the subject of considerable discussion in
the recent literature. For example, in Indonesian there
is a pattern of derivation in which the entire base is
reduplicated according to the formula: meŋ + base + dup$_2$,
where dup$_2$ refers to the entire lexical base. This pattern
of formation is generally associated with an iterative or
durative function (Kähler 1965:138):

(7) (a) *masak*   'ripe; cook'   *memasak-masak*
        balik   'back, turn over'   *membalik-balik*
        jadi   'become'   *menjadi-jadi*
        gigit   'bite'   *meŋgigit-gigit*

    (b) *pikir*   'idea; think'   *memikir-mikir*
        tari   'dance'   *menari-nari*
        takut   'afraid'   *menakut-nakut*
        kira   'guess'   *meŋira-ŋira*

    (c) *injak*   'set foot on'   *meŋinjak-injak*

Forms such as those in (c) demonstrate that reduplication does not refer to surface syllables as some analysts have proposed, since we should then expect *meŋinjak-ŋinjak. Reduplication necessarily refers to a reduplication of the base form, yet we then expect forms such as *menari-tari, etc. The only way to explain these forms in (b) is to posit a second lexicalized base form, following the proposal put forward by Hudson (1974), who argues specifically against the use of exception or diacritic features in phonological description. He suggests that certain types of alternation are most satisfactorily represented in terms of phonological alternation within the lexical entry itself:

> The lexical representation of an alternation means that the segments in alternation ... are both entered as parts of the lexical or underlying phonological form of an alternating item. (Nothing is gained in rules of alternation by insisting that one or the other of the alternates is bound to be taken as the segment to the left of the arrow (the underlying segment), and the other(s) on the right (the derived segment(s)) (1974:217).

Thus, the segmental representation of the lexical entries for the Indonesian forms in (7) might be as shown in (8), with the appropriate form selected by morphological selection rules.

(8) $\begin{bmatrix}\{t \atop n\} & ari\end{bmatrix}$ 'dance' $\begin{bmatrix}\{k \atop \eta\} & ira\end{bmatrix}$ 'guess'

This proposal obviously has broad theoretical implications which cannot be discussed adequately in the present context.

The same problems are also evident in a more widespread pattern of reduplication, e.g., Tagalog: maŋ + dup$_1$ + base, where dup$_1$ refers to a reduplication of the first stem syllable. This pattern derives nominals expressing persons associated with the activity designated by the base (Schachter and Otanes 1972:103-4):

(9) (a) basa   'read'   mambabasa   'reader'
        dambon   'armed robbery'   mandarambon   'bandit'

    (b) tahi   'sew'   mananahi   'dressmaker'
        tangol   'defend'   mananangol   'lawyer'
        kalakal 'business'   maŋaŋalakal   'businessman'

    (c) halal   'vote'   maŋhahalal   'voter'
        awit   'sing'   maŋaawit   'singer'

Were Nasal Substitution a phonological rule, we would expect forms such as *manatahi (</maŋ+ta+tahi/), *maŋakalakal (</maŋ+ka+kalaka/), etc. It has been proposed that ordering Nasal Substitution before Reduplication will generate the correct surface forms:[5] /maŋ + tahi/ → man<u>ahi</u> → man<u>anahi</u>. However, the derivation of forms from vowel-initial stems is problematic here since reference to syllables in reduplication should give *maŋaŋawit, i.e., /maŋ + awit/ → maŋ<u>awit</u> → *maŋaŋawit. Thus, only the relexicalization hypothesis allows for the generation of all correct surface forms. Reduplication in both of the above cases, Indonesian and Tagalog, refers to a reduplication of all or part of the *appropriate base form*. Reanalyses resulting in representations such as the alternating base forms in (8) are arbitrary unless some perceptual motivation for the reanalysis can be established. This issue is discussed below.

3. *Motivation for reanalysis*. In the case of Western Austronesian Nasal Substitution, it is claimed that reanalysis, resulting in lexical representations such as those in (8), is due to a misperception of morphemic boundaries, which may in part be attributed to the not-fully segmental status of morphological information, i.e., the morpheme boundary falls within a single surface segment in forms such as /meŋ + tari/ [menari]. On the other hand, the same morphological information with segmental status is not incorporated into the stem, e.g., *membalik*, and the nasal does not function in reduplications. This issue obviously has wider theoretical significance, but accepting this analysis predicts the correct reduplicative formations in all cases.

The same type of motivation is proposed for the reanalysis of Makonde prefixes discussed in Section 1. The nasal of $_n$Cl. 9/10a prefixes is realized only as prenasalization [^{n}C] of initial consonants or, in many languages, merely effects the voicing, aspiration, hardening, etc. of initial consonants. There might be, then, a tendency to perceive the nasal of the prefix or its effect as part of the stem and therefore to restructure these forms. This would explain the apparent incorporation of the nasal even in reduplicative formations, e.g., Bolia (Mamet 1960):

(10) $e^m pu^m pulu$ 'poor little bird'   (cf. $e^m pulu$ 'bird')
     $e^n ta^n taba$ 'miserable goat'   (cf. $e^n taba$ 'goat')

Thus, this reanalysis, without the loss of phonetic material, is due to a misperception of the placement of morphemic boundaries as a result of the not-fully segmental status of morphological information. In the case of the prenasalized consonants of Makonde, the morpheme boundary falls within a single surface unit.

It should be mentioned that the analysis given here may explain the anomalous shape of the reconstructed Bantu Cl. 10 composite prefix *$li̧$-ni. It appears that *$li̧$- was the original plural prefix, superimposed on the Cl. 9 singular prefix *ni-, which had become *n- by the time of Proto-Bantu. The tendency to incorporate nonsegmental prefixal elements into the stem may account for this anomaly within the reconstructed prefix system.[6]

NOTES

[1]This paper is for Robert J. Jeffers, on the occasion of his academic retirement. It is a token of my appreciation for his encouragement, able instruction, and friendship during my tenure as a graduate student at Ohio State University. A longer version of this paper was presented at the University of North Carolina, and I wish to acknowledge here the constructive comments given by Maria Tsiapera.

[2]The presence of the optional initial vowel (I.V.) in the Luganda forms cited is determined by the syntax; its shape is predictable by a general phonological rule.

[3]Identity in Cl. 9/10 forms does not carry over into the corresponding concords since the plural reflects the 'extra' prefix, e.g.:

(11) *Ente erwadde eri wa? Sigiraba.* 'Where is the sick cow? I don't see it.'

Ente ezirwadde ziri wa? Siziraba. 'Where are the sick cows? I don't see them.'

/ e + n te {e, ezi} + rwadde {e, zi} + li wa
I.V. + cow(s) CONC + sick SUBJ + be where?
                              PREF

si + {gi, zi} + laba /
I + OBJ   + see
NEG   PREF

[4]That these are indeed the synchronic prefix forms is demonstrated by the treatment of loanwords in Cl. 9/10a:

igalapa	*digalapa*	'bottle(s)'	(<Port. *garrafa*)
itinda	*ditinda*	'ink(s)'	(<Port. *tinta*)
iboina	*diboina*	'cap(s)'	(<Port. *boina*)
ikamiyola	*dikamiyola*	'vest(s)'	(<Port. *camisola*)

[5]Wilbur (1973) has argued that the reduplication of the nasal in Nasal Substitution forms is explained by a universal tendency for there to be identity between reduplicated and original material. This identity would be lost in forms such as *manatahi. However, this explanation is not particularly satisfying since its fundamental claim, asserted to be universal, is easily falsified by scores of languages, including many Austronesian languages.

[6]Meinhof (1932) believed that the plural in Ur-Bantu was regularly formed by the addition of a plural prefix to the appropriate singular prefix. There is little evidence to support this belief.

REFERENCES

Cole, Desmond T. 1967. "The prefix of Bantu noun class 10". *African Studies* 26.119-37.
Dahl, Otto Chr. 1973. *Proto-Austronesian*. Lund: Scandinavian Institute of Asian Studies, Monograph 15.
Guerreiro, M. Viegas. 1963. *Rudimentos de Língua Makonde*. Lourenço Marques: Institute de Investigação Científica de Moçambique.
Herbert, Robert K. 1977. "Reconstructing phonetic process in Austronesian". Paper presented at the Symposium on Austronesian Linguistics, University of Hawaii.
_____. 1978. "Morphological reanalysis in the Bantu nasal class". *African Studies* 37.125-37.
Hudson, Grover. 1974. "The representation of non-productive alternation". In *Historical Linguistics* II, 2.203-29. Ed. by J.M. Anderson and Charles Jones. Amsterdam: North-Holland Publishing Co.
Hutcheson, James. 1973. "Remarks on the nature of complete consonantal assimilations". *CLS* 9.215-22.
Jeffers, Robert J. 1977. "Morphological reanalysis and analogy: two case histories from Latin and Greek". *Lingua* 41.13-24.
Kähler, Hans. 1965. *Grammatik der Bahasa-Indonésia*. Wiesbaden: Otto Harrassowitz.
Latta, F. Christian. 1978. "Paradigmatic allomorphy and internal reconstruction". Paper presented at the LSA Annual Meeting, Boston.
Mamet, M. 1960. *Le langage des Bolia*. Tervuren: Annales du Musée Royal du Congo Belge.
Meinhof, Carl. 1932. *Introduction to the phonology of the Bantu languages*. Transl. by N.J. van Warmelo. Berlin: Dietrich Reimer/Ernst Vohsen.
Schachter, Paul and Fe T. Otanes. 1972. *Tagalog Reference Grammar*. Berkeley: University of California Press.
Weinreich, Uriel, William Labov and Marvin Herzog. 1968. "Empirical foundations for a theory of language change". In *Directions for Historical Linguistics*, 95-195. Ed. by Winfred Lehmann and Yakov Malkiel. Austin: University of Texas Press.

Wilbur, R.B. 1973. "The phonology of reduplication". Bloomington: Indiana University Linguistics Club.
Zwicky, Arnold M. 1975. "The strategy of generative phonology". In *Phonologica 1972*, 152-68. Ed. by Wolfgang Dressler and F. Mareš. Munich: Wilhelm Fink Verlag.

THE EVOLUTION OF CLITICS

ROBERT J. JEFFERS
and
ARNOLD M. ZWICKY
The Ohio State University

0. *Introduction.* In the recent literature on synchronic structure and diachronic change the class of *clitic* elements has assumed considerable importance, undoubtedly in part because of the intermediate (or mixed) status of these elements with respect to the division between morphology and syntax, but also because of the complex interrelationships manifested in them with regard to phonology, morphology, syntax, semantics, pragmatics, style, and discourse structure. In the growing literature on the historical development of clitics (exemplified by the contributions by Chafe, Haas, and Steele to Li 1977 and by several unpublished papers by Wanner), there are a number of standard assumptions and suppressed premises about the synchronic and diachronic properties of these elements, assumptions that in many cases seem to us to be dubious or significantly short of the full story. We propose to enumerate these assumptions, in the hope that stating them forthrightly and challenging them will lead to fruitful debate, the framing of new hypotheses, and the search for fresh relevant data.

We begin by recalling the distinction made in Zwicky 1977 between *simple clitics* and *special clitics*. The paradigm case of a simple clitic is the ordinary unaccented form of a word that attaches phonologically to an adjacent word; such forms include proclitics, like the English indefinite article in *a pear* and *an apple*, and enclitics, like the English complementizer *to* in *I should go, but I don't want to.* The paradigm case of a special clitic is not so regularly associated phonologically with a full form (in a related type of clitic, the *bound word*, there is no associated full form at all; the Latin enclitic *-que* 'and' is a typical bound word), and rather than attaching itself to a word that happens to be next to it, a special clitic is located within sentences by genuinely syntactic principles. In brief, special clitics attach either to the head of a phrase or to one of its margins. The Romance 'weak' or 'conjunct' pronouns are clearly special clitics, and again these include both proclitics, as in Spanish *lo vi* 'I saw it', and enclitics, as in Spanish *ver lo* 'to see it'.

1. *Pronouns and particles*. One widely held assumption about clitics is that the prototypical clitic is pronominal, like the Romance clitics. Indeed, although we have not seen this position stated or defended in print, we believe that many scholars would subscribe to the view that if a language has any clitics at all, it has pronominal clitics. On this view there would be two types of languages with respect to the items that appear as clitics in them: pronoun-only languages, like Spanish, and languages with other types of clitics besides pronouns, as in the many Slavic languages with clitic forms of the copula and in Tagalog, which has a very rich collection of nonpronominal clitic particles (marking questions, imperatives, honorifics, emphasis, various adverbials, etc.).

But systems with *only* particle special clitics are not unknown; indeed, they seem to be fairly widespread in Southeast Asia. Hmong (also known as Miao or Meo), for instance, has two classes of particles, each occurring in one of the canonical locations for clitics (in 'second position', which for Hmong is between subject and verb; or in final position) and each subject to rigid ordering constraints. The interrogative and negative particles are in the 'second position' class, while tense and modal particles are distributed between the two classes. Pronouns, however, have the same privileges of occurrence as full noun phrases, and do not act like clitics at all (Indochinese Refugee Education Guide 15).

Our intention here is not to claim that particle clitics imply pronominal clitics, or the reverse. Rather, we want to emphasize that pronominal clitics do not have a special status, and in particular that their historical development does not necessarily precede the development of particle clitics.

2. *The morphological cycle and semantic weakness*. It is a widely held hypothesis for the prehistories of many languages that a system of inflectional affixes and perhaps derivational affixes as well reflects one stage in a cycle that proceeds from free morpheme to clitic to affix. The assumption is that free morphemes initially come to occur in unaccented positions in a clause, being associated with

adjacent accented words as clitic particles. Phonological reduction results in a gradual disintegration of lexical autonomy for these morphemes. Such an hypothesis has, for example, been put forward for the prehistory of Proto-Indo-European (Lehmann 1975).

If we give any credence to such theories concerning a diachronic cycle in morphological systems, we must include in any investigation of the evolution of clitics not only morphemes referring to person, number and gender, but also morphemes referring to such notions as agency, location, instrumentality, modality, tense, aspect, and so on. It would be difficult to argue that morphemes of this type are semantically weak, or that languages show any tendency to mark redundantly the notions to which such morphemes refer, although such reasons have been given for the demotion from free to clitic to affixal morpheme for pronominals and other commonly discussed participants in the morphological cycle, as when Janson (1976:242) supposes that Latin -*que* and *enim* 'for' become clitic because they are 'semantically so weak that they are not allowed to carry a main accent'.

3. *Decliticization*. Although many of the developments that have been discussed in the literature--as in Givón 1971 and in Kahr's 1976 treatment of the development of inflectional suffixes from postpositions--illustrate the morphological cycle, there is nevertheless no empirical basis for the assumption of many linguists that clitics do not emerge, or re-emerge, as independent words. On the contrary, many Indo-Europeanists concerned with the morphological and syntactic prehistory of IE pronouns and pronominal constructions make just such an assumption. It is widely held that the particles *k^we/k^wo and *$\underset{\sim}{i}e/\underset{\sim}{i}o$ occurred as clitic particles in PIE. There is ample comparative evidence in languages like Latin (-*que*), Sanskrit (-*ca*), and Greek (-*te*) that the clitic particle *k^we/k^wo occurred after the first word of a clause and that it was either a simple prosecutive or that it marked some aspect of interclausal relationship. The particles -*ia* and -*a* (*-$\underset{\sim}{i}e/o$) of the Anatolian languages correspond in position and in function to the reflexes of *k^we/o.

These two PIE particles are almost universally identified with the roots of relative/indefinite/interrogative words in the descendent Indo-European languages, such as Latin *quis*, *quod* (*k^wo), Greek *hos* (*$\underset{\sim}{i}o$), Sanskrit *yas* (*$\underset{\sim}{i}o$), and Hittite *ku-is*, *ku-it* (*k^wo). Moreover, in a series of articles and monographs appearing in the past 15 years (most notably Watkins 1963, 1964, Gonda 1971, Jeffers and Pepicello 1979), many of the details by which the ac-

cented pronouns probably come to be historically derived
from the cognate particles have been explicitly presented.
In brief, the reconstruction of these developments proceeds
as follows.

First, we have the evidence already cited that a
series of enclitic particles could follow the first accen-
ted word in a clause in PIE. The particles *$k^u\!_\wedge o$ and *$i_\wedge o$
may be followed by clitic pronouns, which in turn may be
followed by other categories of clitics. We might then
reconstruct patterns like

$$*X \begin{Bmatrix} -i_\wedge o \\ -k^u\!_\wedge o \end{Bmatrix} -(o)s \quad (\text{nom.}).$$

With the shift away from the use of cliticization toward a
greater dependence on isolated words, a development which
we see in virtually all the extant dialects outside Anatolian, several such sequences might well be interpreted as
monolexical inflected words (Hitt. *ia-ăs*, Skt. *yas*). Such
a reinterpretation probably established a pattern for the
spontaneous generation of full pronominal paradigms--the
origin of relative pronouns/adjectives.

We conclude that the tacit assumption that clisis is
invariably one stage in an inexorable development toward
the status of an affix, or toward ultimate oblivion, is
simply false. In particular, the evolutionary trends which
affect a language must be taken into consideration, as in
our example above, where the IE drift towards analytic
rather than synthetic constructions plays a critical role.
A further example can be seen in the development of the
finite verb in Indo-European: in the early IE dialects the
finite verb could occur in unaccented clitic position in a
clause; but every modern IE language which is verb-medial
inherits an *accented* finite verb system which is, at least
in part, derivative of the ancient system whose members so
commonly occurred in clisis.

4. *Deaccentuation*. A more specific assumption about the
development from independent word to inflectional affix is
that it proceeds through a stage in which the independent
word loses its accent (for whatever reasons), to a stage at
which this unaccented morpheme becomes a simple clitic, to
a stage at which the simple clitic becomes a special clitic, to the incorporation of the special clitic as an affix.

Cases where simple clitics have become special clitics
are not hard to find. These include the rather common phenomenon called *freezing* in Zwicky 1972:sec. 5.5, in which

simple clitic combinations become fixed phonologically and specialized semantically, as in the English hortatory *let's* and the Welsh emphatic negative *mo'r*. They also include more subtle developments, as in the recent history of the English negative particle *n't*, which is no longer merely a variant of unstressed *not*, since it occurs in a variety of environments in which unstressed *not* is barred (for instance, in tags like *Can't they?* vs. **Cannot they?* and in imperatives like *Don't you touch me!* vs. **Do not you touch me!*). The classic example of the Romance special clitics has now been treated in detail by Wanner (1978), who argues for a series of developments contingent upon lack of stress, which leads to simple cliticization.

No convincing examples of special cliticization following historically on deaccentuation *without* an intervening stage of simple cliticization are known to us. There is, on the other hand, rather a large number of apparent examples of the opposite sort, in which morphemes customarily described as bearing accent (like Latin *enim* cited above) are positioned like special clitics. We would suppose that in such cases it can be argued (on independent grounds) that the morphemes in question bear only a weak accent. However, the issue is still open.

5. *Derivational affixes.* We have been talking about the passage from independent word to clitic to affix as if an inflectional affix were always its goal. But derivational affixes can arise in this way, too. This is undoubtedly the mechanism that has given rise to the modern English derivational suffixes *-ful*, *-less*, *-ly* (and their modern German counterparts *-voll*, *-los*, *-lich*), cognate with the independent adjectives *full*, *less*, *like* (German *voll*, *los*, *gleich*).

Whether the end product is an inflectional or derivational affix seems to depend heavily on the meanings expressed, in particular on whether a change of word class is involved or not; but this topic requires further study.

6. *Portmanteau forms.* Even when clitics are moving towards becoming inflectional affixes, this development does not necessarily involve clitics 'melting into' stems one by one. Instead, we may see sequences of clitics contracting into portmanteau forms, which are then eligible to be reinterpreted as affixes.

The beginning of such a development can be observed in many Romance dialects. One route has been taken by Romagnol (Gregor 1972:83-7), where nearly all the clitic pro-

nouns have been reduced to single segments--a vowel, as in
the clitic subject *a* (1 sg., 1 pl., 2 pl.) and the dative
or adverbial clitic *i* (3 sg. or pl.); or a consonant, as in
the object (acc. or dat.) clitics *m* (1 sg.), *t* (2 sg.), *s*
(1 pl.), and *v* (2 pl.). Note also that there is considerable syncretism in this system. The result is that *ai*
stands for a 1 sg./1 pl./2 pl. subject in combination with
any third person dative object or with a place adverbial,
while *at* stands for a 1 sg./1 pl./2 pl. subject in combination with any sort of 2 sg. object, and so on. The analysis of these forms into meaningful subparts has clearly
become difficult, and the system is ripe for reinterpretation as a set of inflectional endings.

Another route has been taken by Gascon (Kelly 1973:
199-201) where many combinations of clitics are contracted:
nun for *nus ne* 'nous en', *bun* for *bus ne* 'vous en', *lazi*
for *la luzi* 'la leur' or *las luzi* 'les leur'. These contractions are irregular, a fact that again makes the combinations difficult to analyze and opens the way for reinterpretation.

A similar diachronic process resulting in a clear example of morphological reinterpretation is seen in the history of certain infixed pronouns in Old Irish. In Irish, a
sequence of two clitics, only the second of which is etymologically pronominal, comes to be reinterpreted as a mono-
morphemic monolexical infixed pronoun. The so-called Class
C singular pronouns of OIr are: *dom/dam* (1); *dot* (2);
de/da (3 fem.). These forms are derived from a sequence of
clitics which in each case includes as a first element the
correlative clause particle *-de* (cf. Greek -δε). The
sources of the Irish forms, then, are *-de-me* (1), *-de-te*
(2), *de-*C (3). As a result of regular sound change, the
vowels of the pronominal clitics are lost, as is the final
C in the third person form. That the first and second person forms were originally vowel-final, while the third person form was not, is demonstrated by the fact that an initial consonant of the following word--always a verb--under-
goes a mutation termed lenition. Lenition results in the
spirantization of stops, among other things, in intervocalic position: *-crocha* 'crucifies', but *nudam-chrocha*
'(which) crucifies me' < *no-de-me-kroke*.

Apparently, as a consequence of the demise of clause
particles as functioning morphemes of the language, in conjunction with the phonological reduction of the pronominal
elements attached to such particles, a sequence of clitics
has been contracted and has come to be reinterpreted as a
single morpheme. Such contraction accounts for the first

and second person pronouns. In the case of the third person, the etymological source of the person marker has itself been lost, leaving the first clitic of the sequence--a clause particle--to be reinterpreted as a personal pronoun.

7. *Metathesis*. On occasion clitics may move inside stems. Two large classes of metathesis may be distinguished: the relatively familiar *infixing* type, in which a clitic moves over a consonant cluster or a syllable (the motivation for the shift being primarily phonological, involving an alteration in the direction of a more favored syllable structure); and the somewhat more exotic *endoclitic* type, in which a clitic moves over a morphological constituent, either a single morpheme or a larger subpart of a word (the motivation for the shift being a morphological reanalysis).

Infixing metathesis can be illustrated by the well-known Austronesian cases in which historically original prefixes of the shape VC have been moved over the initial C of stems, to yield forms like Tagalog *sumulat* 'wrote' and *ʔumibig* 'loved', from the stems *sulat* and *ʔibig*, respectively.

Endoclitic metatheses in Madurese, Estonian, Turkish, and Hua are described briefly in Zwicky (1977:sec. 3); these examples include some in which proclitics have moved over a following morpheme and some in which enclitics have moved over a preceding morpheme. Movement over larger morphological constituents can be illustrated by Portugese forms like *descreve-lo-íamos* 'we would describe him', obtained from the enclitic *o* 'him' attached to *descreveríamos* 'we would describe'; *-íamos* 'we would' is a trimorphemic subpart of *descreveríamos*.

Reanalysis as the motivation for endoclitic metathesis has been argued at some length by Haiman (1977) for the Hua case, and similar arguments can undoubtedly be adduced for the other examples we have referred to, as well as to cases from Ewe, Pashto, and Sundanese, though the details need working out.

One lesson we should wish to draw from this brief survey of the facts is that the extent of clitic metathesis -- especially of the endoclitic variety -- as an historical process seems to have been seriously underestimated until recently.

8. *Other sources for word-internal clitics*. Metathesis is not the only way word-internal clitics can develop. They may also arise because of morphological changes by which

certain morphemes come to be interpreted as infixed elements. We return to the example of OIr Class C pronouns.

To elucidate this development, we must present a few facts about Celtic languages and about general IE. The Celtic languages in general are distinguished from other IE languages in being verb-first (VSO). Most of the ancient IE dialects are verb-last (SOV) languages, although all of these SOV languages provide the marked order VSO as an alternative. Consequently, the hypothesis that certain verb-first patterns of OIr are indeed archaic, and that they have undergone a status change from marked to unmarked, is widely held (Watkins 1963).

All ancient IE languages reflect an inherited system of preverbal particles (P). They occur in one of two positions in a clause: directly before the verb or clause-initially. The following patterns result: #...PV#, #P....V#. The comparative evidence also demands the reconstruction for PIE of a series of enclitics (E), which are suffixes to the first accented element in a clause; recall that the OIr Class C pronouns like -*dom* are derived from a sequence of such particles. IE can then be assumed to show the patterns #VE... and #PE..., in verb-first clauses and in clauses with initial preverbal particles, respectively. V́E and ṔE comprise accent groups, and would function as phonological words.

In certain OIr clauses which do not include P and which begin with a simple verb, suffixed pronominal clitics occur; compare *berid* 'he carries' with *beirthi* < *bhéret-i* 'he carries it'. OIr sequences of verb plus suffixed pronoun apparently derive straightforwardly from the assumed PIE pattern #VE....#.

In clauses that begin with P, clitic pronouns will occur in second position, again a reflection of an IE pattern, namely #PE...#. The situation in OIr becomes more complex. All ancient IE dialects show a drift towards univerbation, that is, towards the treatment of PV as a unit, with a meaning assigned to the complex rather than to its parts. This tendency toward univerbation, coupled with the Celtic typological shift to VSO structure, results in the movement forward in a clause of finite verbs in OIr. Where P was once separated from its associated verb (#P....V#), we have instead clause-initial PV units (#PV...#). However, in clauses with initial PE, the forward movement within the clause of the finite verb results in the replacement of *PE...V# by #PEV... Recall that the sequence PE is a phonological word, and that the process of univerbation reflects a trend toward establishing the lexical unity of the sequence PV (as in *do-beir* < **to-b^{h}erti* 'he takes'). Consequently, the construction PEV comes to be reinterpreted as a lexical unit, incorporating infixed pronominal objects, as in *dom-beir* < **to-me-b^{h}erti* 'he takes me'.

Note that the clause position of E remains stable throughout history, and that it is as a result of changes in clause position for other forms and of morphosyntactic reinterpretations that infixation develops as a productive process in OIr.

9. *Morphology as frozen syntax.* Synchronic studies of clitics have concentrated largely on two issues--where the string of clitics is located within the sentence and how the clitics coöccur and are ordered with respect to one another. The range of facts to be described can be exemplified by the following observations on French clitic object pronouns: these are proclitic to the verb, except in affirmative imperative sentences, when they are enclitic; a nonthird person or reflexive may occur with a third person (in that order) if the former is dative and the latter is accusative, while if two third persons are combined the accusative precedes the dative (the reverse for enclitics) --and no other combination of object pronoun clitics is possible.

The most natural assumption about the historical source for these phenomena is that they represent survivals of earlier syntactic orders, and indeed such an assumption is explicitly made by several scholars: this is the position of Givón 1971, for instance, on the development of a number of clitic systems, including the Romance pronominals. Yet when this attractive hypothesis is pursued in detail, many difficulties and anomalies arise. Thus, Green 1976 points out with respect to the Romance developments that in Classical Latin, Vulgar Latin, and Old Spanish, neither pronoun object *nor* full NP objects were fixed in position with respect to the verb, so that the modern procliticization of object pronouns to the verb can scarcely be explained as the simple survival of earlier syntactic orders.

10. *Second position.* In reaction to simple persistence theories of clitic syntax, other writers have described the historical developments as if they arose from forces impelling clitics towards certain positions in the sentence and arranging them in certain favored orders. Steele 1977, for instance, examines a Uto-Aztecan version of Wackernagel's

Law by which clitics move into second position, though for mysterious reasons. As things stand, such an account explains nothing (as Steele herself realizes) and can only function as a spur to further analysis.

An additional complexity is that even though second position is greatly favored as a location for clitics, the definition of 'second position' differs from language to language. Walbiri, Serbo-Croatian, Tagalog, and Pashto differ in detail on this point (Zwicky 1977:18-20), and the historical linguist is entitled to wonder if there are any reasons for these differences.

11. *Clisis and typology.* One largely unexplored area in which answers to the questions we have raised might be sought concerns the relationships between (syntactic) typological classification and clitic syntax. To what degree is the occurrence of clitics correlated with language type? Do certain typological shifts result in the development of clitics, or in specifiable alterations in existing clitic systems?

A correlation between syntactic typology and the nature (or even presence) of clitic systems cannot be a simple one. Consider, for example, that ancient IE languages of all three syntactic types make use of clitic particles of one kind or another, and that they all share certain specific kinds of clitics, such as proclitic preverbal particles.

A further source for explanation in clitic diachrony is the relationship between accentual systems (at the word and at the sentence level), and clitic syntax. To what degree is the occurrence of clitics correlated with accent type? To what extent can the placement or ordering of clitics be predicted from accent type? Do certain accent shifts result in the development of clitics, or in specifiable alterations in existing systems?

Finally, areal relationships might also be considered. To what extent can contact situations promote the development of clitics or alterations in existing clitic systems?

REFERENCES

Chafe, Wallace L. 1977. "The evolution of third person verb agreement in the Iroquoian languages". In Li 1977, 493-524.
Givón, Talmy. 1971. "Historical syntax and synchronic morphology: an archaeologist's field trip". *Chicago Linguistic Society* 7.394-415.
Gonda, Jan. 1971. *Old Indian*. Leiden: Brill.
Green, John. 1976. "How free is word order in Spanish?" In Harris 1976.
Gregor, D.B. 1972. *Romagnol: language and literature*. Stoughton, Wisc. and Harrow, Middlesex: Oleander Press.
Haas, Mary R. 1977. "From auxiliary verb phrase to inflectional suffix". In Li 1977, 525-37.
Haiman, John. 1977. "Reinterpretation". *Lg.* 53.312-28.
Harris, Martin (ed.). 1976. *Romance syntax: synchronic and diachronic perspectives*. University of Salford.
Indochinese Refugee Education Guide 15. n.d. "The Hmong language: sentences, phrases and words". National Indochinese Clearinghouse, Center for Applied Linguistics, Washington, D.C.
Janson, Tore. 1976. "Placement of enclitics in Latin and the relation between syntax and phonology". In Karlsson 1976, 237-44.
Jeffers, Robert and William Pepicello. 1978. "The expression of purpose in IE". IF 82.
Kahr, Joan Casper. 1976. "The renewal of case morphology: sources and constraints". *Working Papers in Language Universals* 20.107-51, Stanford.
Karlsson, Fred (ed.). 1976. *Papers from the Third Scandinavian Conference of Linguistics*. Text Linguistics Research Group. Turku: Academy of Finland.
Kelly, Reine Cardaillac. 1973. *A descriptive analysis of Gascon*. The Hague: Mouton.
Lehmann, Winfred. 1974. *Proto-Indo-European Syntax*. Austin: University of Texas Press.
Li, Charles N. (ed.). 1977. *Mechanisms of syntactic change*. Austin: University of Texas Press.
Steele, Susan. 1977. "Clisis and diachrony". In Li 1977, 539-79.
Wanner, Dieter. 1978. "The development of clitics". MS.
Watkins, Calvert. 1963. "Preliminaries to a historical and comparative analysis of the Old Irish verb". *Celtica* 6.1-49.
_____. 1964. "Preliminaries to the reconstruction of Indo-European sentence structure". In *Proceedings of the Ninth International Congress of Linguists*, 1035-45. The Hague: Mouton.
Zwicky, Arnold M. 1972. "On casual speech". *Chicago Linguistic Society* 8.607-15.
_____. 1977. "On clitics". Indiana University Linguistics Club, Bloomington, Indiana.

CIRCUMFIXES AND TYPOLOGICAL CHANGE

JOSEPH H. GREENBERG
Stanford University

Agreement among even a very few languages in regard to a typologically rare phenomenon in historically independent instances, especially when accompanied by other typological resemblances in related linguistic properties, is generally worth investigating as a putative symptom of a parallel change of type.

An example of this sort is the agreement between Amharic, a Semitic language of Ethiopia, and Pashto, an Iranian language of Afghanistan in a possessive construction consisting of a sequence preposition-possessor-possessed, as illustrated by Amharic *yä-saw bet* and Pashto *da sari kor*, both of which can be literally translated 'of-man house'. What is unusual here is that both show genitive-noun (GN) order which on a worldwide basis is strongly correlated with postpositions, while the possessive itself is expressed by a preposition. This construction together with its mirror image in NG languages may be called an asymmetrical genitive construction.

Given that in adpositional constructions, the adposition is itself often a noun construed as the possessor in a genitive construction, e.g. Hausa *kâ-n gídá·* 'upon the house', literally 'head of the house', we might expect that in languages with an asymmetrical genitive construction, we will find correspondingly expressions like 'of-house upon', in other words, expressions with a circumfix corresponding to the preposed or postposed markers of other languages. Both Amharic and Pashto have such expressions in abundance although the prepositions need not be the same as in the genitive construction. Thus Amharic *bä-bet wəst* parallels Pashto *pa kor kše*, both being glossed as 'in-house interior', for 'inside the house'. Further agreements include the following. In both languages the prepositions can usually occur without the postpositions, but not vice versa. The postpositions are often analyzably nouns and much more specific in meaning than the prepositions in such combinations. Both languages are adjective-noun (AN) and SOV. In both, contrasting with nominal possessors, pronominal possessors have two alternative constructions. One involves a suffixed possessor, e.g. Amharic *bet-e*, Pashto *kor mu* 'house-my'. The other parallels the nominal construction employing an independent pronoun in place of the possessor nouns, e.g. Amharic *yäna bet*, Pashto *dzma kor* 'of me house'.

The intragenetic synchronic comparison of the cluster of constructions just considered in both the Ethiopian Semitic and Iranian languages will show that only certain types occur and these facts can be restated in terms of similar implicational chains. For example, in both families there are no postpositional-NG languages while there are instances of prepositional-NG and postpositional-GN languages. Thus we may say that postpositions imply GN for these languages. However, such synchronic facts are compatible with the two opposite courses of diachronic development. We might in the present case posit either that the GN-postpositional type is earlier, that then the postpositions changed to prepositions and subsequently GN changed to NG. On the other interpretation, the starting point is NG-prepositional and first the genitive order changes, followed by the replacement of prepositions by postpositions.

In fact, general typological theory, internal linguistic facts, and comparative and direct historical evidence all point at least in the case of Ethiopian Semitic to the latter interpretation. This interpretation is of course not novel. Among others, Leslau (1949) in the context of suggested Cushitic influence and Ferguson (1971) in schematic outline have proposed for the Ethiopian Semitic a comprehensive movement from a VSO, NG, Prepositional, NA type of language to an SOV, GN, Postpositional, AN structure. However, this course of events has not, so far as I know, been discussed in any detail, while the Iranian case has apparently not been considered as a whole anywhere in the existing literature.

Given the limitation of space and the very large number of Iranian languages, the bulk of this paper will be devoted to Ethiopian languages. The results will then be applied in broad outline to the Iranian language. In closing, the mirror image situation involved in a change from postpositional to prepositional structures will be considered.

Instead of presenting the Ethiopian Semitic material in strict typological terms with correlated intragenetic implicational statements, the material will be presented rather as a scenario, with the languages retaining the largest measure of VSO structure, hypothesized as the earliest type of structure, being discussed first. Among contemporary Ethiopian Semitic languages, this starting point is represented by Tigre, a North Ethiopian Semitic, while the language with the closest approximation to SOV structures is Harari, a South Ethiopian language.

However, rather than Tigre, we will start with Ge'ez, or classical Ethiopic, for which the earliest manuscripts date from the fourteenth century but probably represent a form of speech current perhaps a millenium earlier. Ge'ez word order in regard to S, O and V constituents is very free but as noted by Dillmann, in ordinary unimpassioned discourse, 'the predicate stands at the beginning of the sentence, the subject follows and then the object follows' (p. 503). In other words, the unmarked order is VSO. The same source notes that in spite of variation between AN and NA 'in uniform and level discourse the adjective [is] placed oftener after the noun' (p. 479). Ge'ez only has prepositions, and the usual genitive order is NG. There is also a construction with *zä*, a relative of demonstrative origin preceding the possessor. This phrase normally follows the noun, e.g. *ʔäklil zä wärq* 'crown of gold', but it less often precedes, *zä wärq ʔäklil* 'of gold crown'. This last is of course like the usual Amharic construction; here also the marker *yä* functions as a relative.

Among contemporary Ethiopian Semitic languages, Tigre is closest typologically to Ge'ez. However, SOV is the usual order, although, according to Leslau's description of the dialect of Mensa, verb initial constructions occur 'for emphasis' while adverbial modifiers often follow the verb. There is variation between AN and NA orders and I have no data on their relative frequency. Only prepositions are found. As in Ge'ez, there are three genitive constructions, the marker *nay*, derived from a word meaning 'property, possession', playing the role of Ge'ez *zä*. Here also, in the construction with a marker, the postposed order is normal, i.e. N + *nay* + G. The Semitic suffixed pronouns are used for pronominal possessions and, as generally in Semitic, a similar but not identical set is suffixed to the verb to express the verb pronominal object.

In Tigrinya, the other major Semitic North Ethiopian language, we find that verb final is the normal order and AN the rule with rare exceptions. This is the contemporary situation, but in Praetorius' grammar of 1871, NA still occurs, although it is less frequent than AN. For the genitive in Tigrinya, the same three alternatives exist as in Tigre with the identical marker *nay*. However, the preposed structure is relatively frequent and, according to Leslau (1941), is normal when the noun in the genitive has an adjective modifier, e.g. *nay subbuq tämähari mäṣḥaf* 'of good pupil, book'. Further, although the inherited suffixes provide the usual method of expressing personal pronominal possession, there is an alternative method based on *nay* with pronominal suffixes in the form *natäy* 'my possession', etc., which may precede the noun, e.g. *natki qʷalʕa* translated by Leslau as *ton fils (à toi)*. It may be noted that such forms in these languages are invariably also used as and probably arise from possessive pronouns, e.g. Tigrinya *əzu biet natay ʔəyu* 'this house mine is'. Such fuller forms fulfill these and other functions not conveniently expressed by bound forms. Tigrinya has prepositions almost exclusively, but in a few expressions they are supplemented by elements postposed to the noun. In most of the examples cited the framed element is however a relative clause rather than a noun, e.g. *bə-----məknəyat* 'because', so that the complex is translated as a conjunction rather than an adposition.

We next encounter a group of South Ethiopian languages which exemplify approximately the same stage of further advance toward SOV structures, Amharic, Gafat, and the so-called Gurage languages; the latter are not a single genetic grouping within South Ethiopic.[1] The chief differences between this group and Tigrinya is that the sole genitive construction is GN with the same preposed marker *yä-* in all the languages, a marker which also functions as a relative pronoun and is of demonstrative origin like Ge'ez *zä*. Furthermore, prepositions are frequently supplemented by simultaneous postpositions which provide further specificity of meaning. In colloquial *Amharic*, as noted by Klingenheben (1966) and Ferguson (1971) among others, the common prefixes *bä-* and *lä-* are frequently reduced to *ʔə-*, or even omitted entirely, resulting in pure postpositions. Further, in all these languages, although the suffixed pronominal possessives are in use, it is equally possible to use independent pronouns in the same construction as that used with nouns. For example, in Amharic one can say either *bet-e* 'house-my' or *yäna bet* 'of-me house'.

We have some early documents in Amharic, notably the Royal Songs which date from the fourteenth century. In these it is interesting to note, along with other deviations from present day word order usage, the use of the *yä* genitive following the noun as is usual with *nay* in Tigre and Tigrinya.

Finally, with Harari we reach the most extreme SOV structures to be found in any Semitic Ethiopian languages. In the genitive construction we have GN without any marker, although the possessed noun may have a suffixed possessive in cross-reference, e.g. 'man house-his'. With a few exceptions, only postpositions occur. There is one circumfix *ta---bah* 'with' in which *ta* can never occur without the postposition and two prepositions, *takil* 'together with' and *miša* 'according to'. The only other remnant of VSO structure is that possessive suffixes are still used with nouns, but these are normally strengthened by preposed independent pronouns, e.g. *azzo gar-zo* 'he house-his', thus resulting in a circumferential construction. In a similar fashion, but less frequently, the verb object pronoun suffixes can be supplemented by an independent pronoun preceding the verb.

For Harari there is historical evidence. A Harari translation in Arabic script of the *Kitabu l-Farā'id* was discovered by Paulitschke in 1885. Its date is not known. Cerulli's edition of it is accompanied by a grammatical sketch of the language which he calls Old Harari. In regard to matters relevant in the present context, it differs from the contemporary language in two important respects. Along with postpositions, in contrast to the present-day language, which has only one circumfix *ta-bah*, as noted above, Old Harari has numerous circumfixes. As contrasted with the present language, which has no prefixes, there are two, *ti-* 'with' and *li-* 'to, for', the latter of which may also be suffixed. Even more interesting is the fact that in place of the contemporary direct GN construction without marker, which is unique among Ethiopian Semitic languages, we find *zi + G + N*, in which *zi* is an element which still functions as a relative pronoun in the present-day language. It is of demonstrative origin and thus completely parallels Ge'ez *zä-* and Amharic *yä-*.

In summary, we find in the Ethiopian Semitic word order shift a very consistent sequence of events. First VSO order changes and then NA. The genitive construction with nominal possessor follows. It employs a mechanism in which a marker, either relative-demonstrative in origin or a noun meaning possession used first in predicative and other independent and contrastive uses, follows the possessed in construction with the possessor, but ultimately precedes. That is, from expressions like 'the house is that-of-the-man/the-possession-of-the-man', we move to 'house possession-of man' and finally 'possession-of-man house'. This marker ultimately disappears as in modern Harari, leaving a direct GN construction. After the first stages of the genitive shift, earlier prepositions, while still appearing as pure prepositions, are supplemented by postpositions mainly of nominal origin and incorporating the new genitive order, e.g. 'in house-interior', thus producing circumfixes. Finally, the prepositions mainly disappear, leaving a strong predominance of postpositions. A further regularity is that the pronominal possessor suffixes change more slowly than the nominal possessor construction, and still survive even in the most advanced SOV languages, although alongside of preposed marker + independent pronouns which are representative of the new SOV structures. Further, these elements suffixed to verbs as objects are even more tenacious.

Turning now to the Iranian languages, space will allow only a brief and much more schematic treatment than was possible for Ethiopian Semitic. Confining ourselves for the moment to purely synchronic data, the Iranian languages can be arranged in a sequence much like that of the Ethiopian Semitic from Standard Persian and its close congeners, which constitute the Southwestern group, to Ossetic in the Caucasus, genetically a Northeastern group which exhibits full SOV characteristics even more extreme than that of Harari in Ethiopia.

All of these languages have basic SOV order, with the extent to which verb final constructions are required differing from language to language. This is not in itself surprising, inasmuch as among the Ethiopian languages even Tigre has normal SOV order. With regard to adjective-noun order, all the contemporary languages except Kurdish and languages of the Persian group have AN order. Even among the latter, however, Tat in the Caucasus, which is under strong Azerbaijani Turkish influence, has AN order and the Tadjik-derived language of the Afghan Khazara, who are ethnically of Mongol origin, have both the Persian *izafet* N-i A and AN constructions. Thus the relation 'AN implies SOV but not necessarily vice versa', holds here as in Ethiopian Semitic.

The relation NA implies NG holds, but almost all Iranian languages are both GN and AN anyway and a few, like Persian and Kurdish, NA and NG. What we are looking for are languages with NG and AN to show that the change in the genitive construction is later than that in adjective-noun order. Although no language with NG only and AN is found synchronically, there are some straws in the wind. One is

Tat, which as was noted earlier is AN. It has two types
of constructions, NG and a GN construction of the form
'father his-house', evidently more recent and the result of
Azerbaijani influence, and which is said to be replacing
the NG construction. Another case is Minjan, a northeastern language, also AN, which has both a GN construction
without marker and, reminiscent of Ethiopian Semitic, an
NG construction with žə 'from' preceding the genitive.
More rarely, the genitive phrase precedes, thus resulting
in an asymmetrical genitive construction. Most cogent of
all is some historical evidence from Pashto which, as was
noted in the initial portion of the paper, has an asymmetrical genitive construction. In Trumpp's grammar, published in 1873, it is noted that the genitival phrase may
follow as well as precede, while contemporary grammars mention only the latter possibility.

Paralleling the situation in the Ethiopian languages,
most Iranian GN languages have suffixes expressing pronominal possession, sometimes along with the opposite order
modeled after nominal constructions, as in Pashto. A major
difference between Ethiopian Semitic and Iranian is the
relative rarity of the asymmetrical genitive construction
in the latter. It is found only in Pashto, Minjan, and
Ormuri, and in Talysh only in pronominal possession. The
explanation here is possibly the widespread existence in
Iranian of genitive case markers which sufficiently distinguish the members of the genitive construction regardless of order.

Again, as in the Ethiopian languages, most Iranian GN
languages have suffixes expressing pronominal possession
sometimes along with the opposite order modeled after the
nominal construction, as in Pashto. As in Semitic, these
suffixes may also express the verb pronominal object and
here too they tend to survive the nominal shift to SOV even
longer than the pronominal possessives.

Finally, the change to postpositions is clearly later
than the shift in the genitive construction. Except for
Ossetic, all Iranian languages, whether NG or GN, have prepositions often, as in Pashto, specified by more recent
postpositions, mostly of nominal origin and more specific
in meaning, thus resulting in circumfixes. Besides Pashto,
languages of this sort include in the Eastern group most of
the Pamir languages as well as Wakhi and Yaghnobi. Minjan,
which we have seen is conservative in its genitive construction, only has prepositions. Among Northwestern languages, Ormuri has GN with both prepositions and circumfix-

es as do Talysh and the Caspian languages. A few languages have prepositions and postpositions without circumfixes, e.g., Balochi. In general, it is clear that the postpositions are innovations and that circumfixes are a frequent transition phenomenon by which postpositions are introduced.

The historical Iranian evidence cannot be considered in any detail here. In general it is corroborative, but there is one major discrepancy. In the Persian subgroup which has the strongest VO structures, SOV order should be the latest to appear, but it is already normal in Old Persian which is generally reckoned as ancestral to it. Early Modern Persian had circumfixes of the expected type but contemporary Persian has developed into a typologically deviant language with basically VO characteristics in spite of being verb final.

What is clear is that all the contemporary languages start from an SOV situation but that other VO structures have been shifted to a greater or lesser extent to OV structures. Unfortunately, there has been little study of Avestan word order. I have made use of Friedrich's data (1975) and examined these texts myself. My very tentative conclusions are these. Starting from a Proto-Iranian SOV phase (*pace* Friedrich) marked by the additions in some cases of postpositions to existing case forms, by the time we get to Avestan main sentence constituent order is very free but, as noted by Nyberg (1974, II, 284) in his manual of Pahlavi, while normal Middle Iranian order is SOV, "another type, placing the verb first in the sentence . . . is directly taken over from Avestan and is only met with in Avestan texts." Corresponding with this VSO order, we have from the Gathas to Young Avestan an increase in prepositions and NG order as noted by Friedrich. This was the situation when a wave of SOV spread over Iranian territory during the middle Iranian period and produced the situation which underlies the present one.

The following points may be noted in conclusion. Further studies parallel to the present one are needed to test the typicality of the sequence of events noted here. The mirror image situation of change from postpositions to prepositions and the role of circumfixes in such change needs to be investigated. In addition to the rise of prepositions in Indo-European in general, a further interesting case is that of Chukotian which makes extensive use of circumfixes and which is the only group in northern Asia without basic SOV order. It should be carefully noted that no claim is made that *all* discontinuous elements of this kind in languages are evidence of change of word order type. Only affixes and particles governing nouns have been considered. Thus a discontinuous element such as third plural *ya---ūna* in the imperfective of the Classical Arabic verb is not relevant to the present study.

NOTE

[1] For a detailed discussion of subgrouping within Ethiopian Semitic, see Hetzron (1975).

REFERENCES

Cerulli, Enrico. 1936. *La lingua e la storia di Harar*. Rome: Instituto Per l'Oriente.
Dillmann, August. 1907 (1889). *Ethiopic grammar*. Transl. by James A. Crichton. London: Drugulin.
Ferguson, Charles A. 1971. "A sample research strategy in language universals". WPLU:6:1-22.
Friedrich, Paul. 1975. *Proto-Indo-European syntax*. Butte, Montana: Journal of Indo-European Studies, Monograph 1.
Hetzron, Robert. 1975. "Genetic classification and Ethiopian". In *Hamito-Semitica*. Ed. by James and Theodora Bynon. The Hague: Mouton.
Klingenheben, August. 1966. *Deutsch-Amharischer Sprachführer*. Wiesbaden: O. Harrassowitz.
Leslau, Wolf. 1941. *Documents Tigrigna*. Paris: C. Klincksieck.
_____. 1945. "Grammatical sketches in Tigre (North Ethiopic)". JAOS 65:164-203.
_____. 1949. "The influence of Cushitic on the Semitic languages of Ethiopia: a problem of substratum". *Word* 1:59-82.
Nyberg, Henric S. 1964-1974. *A manual of Pahlavi*. 2 vols. Wiesbaden: O. Harrassowitz.
Praetorius, Franz. 1871. *Grammatik der Tigriñasprache in Abessinien*. Halle: Waisenhaus.
Trumpp, Ernst. 1873. *Grammar of the Pašto or language of the Afghans*. London: W.H. Allen.

ON THE DECLINE OF DECLENSIONAL SYSTEMS:
THE OVERALL LOSS OF OE NOMINAL CASE INFLECTIONS AND
THE ME REANALYSIS OF -*ES* AS *HIS*

RICHARD D. JANDA
University of California, Los Angeles

  In his article 'Gedanken über die slovakische Deklination', Trubetzkoy (1966:98) spoke of a 'heartland of declension' in the Old World--comprising essentially Russia and both the Slavic and non-Slavic language areas on its periphery--in which the 'sense' or 'feel' for case was still alive, but to the west and south of which 'declension [was] either unknown or in the process of disappearing'. In the present paper, I will discuss a particular instance of what Trubetzkoy, in the same article, called the *Verfall der Deklination*, the 'decline (or decay) of declension'; namely, the loss of *all nominal case inflections* that took place in the historical development of English, a language far to the west of the 'declensional heartland'. In so doing, I will draw on the work of Trubetzkoy and his fellow Praguian Jakobson (cf. 1966a, 1966b), with special reference to their notion of morphological markedness. I will also draw on Greenberg's (1966) typological extension of this notion. It will be shown that--given what is known beyond any doubt about the Old English (henceforth OE) case system--both synchronic language typology and the diachronic aspect of markedness theory lead one to have serious doubts about the quite commonly accepted two-inflection analysis of Modern English (henceforth NE) cases. These doubts can then be substantiated on the basis of purely synchronic, language-particular evidence: NE (full) nouns have no case inflections at all, for the -'*s* (~ -*s*' ~ -') of the genitive is a phrase-final enclitic particle. But this means that English nouns have lost, not just some, but in fact *all* of their case inflections, and that OE -*es* has been 'liberated', as it were, from morphology into syntax. The specific mechanism of this change in status of the former inflection -*es* can be shown to have been its *reanalysis* as an invariant reduced form of the possessive adjective *his*.

It has been known for hundreds of years that OE had a
four-case inflectional system for nouns, with what are usually labeled as nominative, accusative, dative, and genitive cases. No single OE noun had a different inflection for each of the four cases, but examination of a combination of nouns (or of nouns in conjunction with demonstratives) shows there to have been four formally distinguished nominal case inflections; cf. the singular paradigms in (1):

(1) OE Nominal case inflections:

```
         MASC.                          FEM.
Nom.   (sē)    ⎫                  (sēo)      tal-u
Acc.   (þone)  ⎬  stān(-∅)        (þā)    ⎫
Dat.   (þǣm)      stān-e                  ⎬  tal-e
Gen.   (þæs)      stān-es          (þǣre) ⎭
       '(that)   stone'            '(that)   tale'
```

Now, it is commonly claimed that '[one] of the most important events in the history of the English language [was] the decay of the OE inflectional system' (Mustanoja (M) 1960:67), and that 'English has come to depend upon particles--mainly prepositions and conjunctions--and word order to express grammatical relations which had previously been expressed by inflection' (Pyles (P) 1971:169). Just as commonly, however, a major exception to this general trend is claimed to exist: '...genitive case has continued to be distinctly marked right up to the present day. All other case-markings have been lost for nouns.... Only the genitive has remained fully functional as an inflection' (Traugott (T) 1972:121-23). That is, although traditional grammar's absurd postulation of six cases for English on the basis of Latin inflections has been firmly rejected, many linguists still propose to analyze NE as having *two* case inflections; cf. the singular paradigms in (2):

(2) NE nominal case inflections--

   (a) The accepted analysis:

       GENERAL   *stone*
       GENITIVE *stone's*

   (b) According to traditional grammar (cf. Hall 1964: 152):

       Nom. *a table*
       Gen. *of a table*
       Dat. *to a table*
       Acc. *a table*
       Abl. *from a table*
       Voc. *o table!*

But notice what this claim entails: that the genitive
--what was, according to the criteria of Greenberg (1966),
precisely the most marked case inflection in OE--has been
retained, while all of the less marked case inflections
have been lost, that is, syncretized as ∅. Furthermore,
there do not appear to be any (other) languages of the
world in which a genitive case inflection is opposed to a
general case, as is claimed for English. The analysis in
question is thus not only typologically unheard-of, but
also flies in the face of what markedness predicts for historical change: that (more) unmarked cases should never be
lost without (more) marked cases also being lost.

Indeed, it is not at all difficult to show that the NE
-'s genitive marker is *not* a case inflection, where inflections are defined as elements 'which serve to indicate a
grammatical relationship between the form to which [they
are] attached and other parts of the sentence' (Hall 1964:
148). For so-called 'group genitives' show that genitive
-'s does not occur *attached to* the form whose grammatical
relationship to the rest of the sentence it shows. That is,
rather than occurring as a suffix on the head of the noun-
phrase with which it occurs, as does the homophonous, bona-
fide -s inflection of the plural, -'s appears at the end of
the entire NP, and so is found suffixed to whatever lexical
category and item is last in that NP; contrast (3) and (4):

(3) Plural:

    (a) [two [crook]s from Philadelphia]
        *[two [crook] from Philadelphia]s
    (b) [several [book]s that I've read]
        *[several [book] that I've read]s

(4) Genitive:

    (a) [the [newspaper] in the window]'s headlines
        *[the [newspaper]'s in the window] headlines
    (b) [the [guy] that I mentioned to you]'s address
        *[the [guy]'s that I mentioned to you] address

Such constructions provide exactly the kind of evidence
needed to decide the question of whether NE -'s is an inflection or some kind of phrase-final particle, and they
show it clearly to be the latter. This conclusion, it
should be mentioned, has also been reached by a number of
previous scholars, from Hockett (1958) to Zwicky (1975),
but it does not seem to have had much resonance. In any
case, what is important for our purposes here is that, if
-'s is not an inflection, then NE indeed has no case inflections whatsoever, and so must have lost them *all* in the
course of its development from OE and Middle English
(henceforth ME).

This fact, however, has far greater significance than merely being the correct synchronic and diachronic analysis of the English case inflectional system. If NE -'s is historically derived from OE -es--which, prima facie, it certainly seems to be--then this historical development represents a change whereby a *morphological* element (one below the word-level) became a *syntactic* element (one bound only at the phrasal level, as a clitic). This innovation thus demonstrates that, however overwhelmingly more common it may be for syntactic elements to become morphological ones (e.g. for clitics to become inflections) than vice-versa, the opposite directionality of change is nevertheless possible; cf. (5):

(5) (a) Usual continuum of change for linguistic elements:

(full) $\begin{Bmatrix} \text{noun} \\ \text{verb} \end{Bmatrix}$ → $\begin{Bmatrix} \text{preposition} \\ \text{classifier} \\ \text{auxiliary verb} \\ \text{pronoun, etc.} \end{Bmatrix}$ → clitic →

inflection → ∅

(b) Change of OE -es to NE -'s: clitic ← inflection

In order to substantiate this rather egregious exception to the usual course of diachronic change for linguistic elements, one must establish that NE -'s is, in some sense, a *continuation* of OE -es; that is, that -'s was a *reinterpretation* of -es. It is to this task that I now turn; crucial to my argument will be the role that the ME reanalysis of -es as *his* plays.

As is well known, OE -es was, itself, the result of a generalization of only one out of a large number of genitive inflections. A significant fact about OE genitives, both before and at the time (extending into ME) when -es was generalized--from the singular of one type of noun, first to almost all singular nouns, and then to all plurals --was that group genitives were not permitted. Rather than saying something equivalent to, say, *the king of this country's sister*, one had obligatorily to extrapose, in transformational terms, any material in the possessor NP that would have separated the case inflection on the head of that NP from the possessed NP, cf. (6):

(6) [þæs [kyning]-es] sweostor [þisses londes] (hypothetical)

But, once agreement had been lost between nouns, adjectives, and what were becoming articles, this rule of obligatory extraposition of posthead complements from possessor NP's had the effect of destroying precisely the evidence that would have shown unambiguously whether the OE and ME genitive marker -*es* was an inflection or a phrase-final enclitic, since the extraposition in question would leave both corresponding underlying structures identical on the surface; cf. (7):

(7) (a) [þe [*king*]-*es*⏞] *suster*⟶[*of France*] (1140; from T:124)
    (b) [þe [*king*]⏟]-*es suster* ⟶[*of France*] 'the king of France's sister'

This ambiguity may have contributed to the reanalysis of -*es* from a morphological element into a syntactic one, a clitic, but it does not seem to have been the sole reason for that change, since, if it was, one has no explanation for why -(*e*)*s* genitives were lost *postnominally*. That is, OE constructions like *þæm mægene Hālges Gāstes* 'to the power of (the) Holy Ghost', where the possessor NP followed its head, the possessed NP, became impossible in ME (and have remained so, of course), but, if OE -*es* was reanalyzed directly as an NP-final particle, then that reanalysis should also have been possible for such constructions as this, and one has no account for why they should have been lost. To cite the data proving that the reanalysis had taken place--namely, the emergence of group-genitives, which started with late, Chaucerian ME and had become dominant by Shakespeare's time--is merely to describe the change, not to explain it. For this, one must consider the so-called *his* genitive of ME and later.

'In late ME, a construction...came to be popular: genitive expressed by an uninflected...noun and third person pronoun marked for the genitive, as in ...*the child is gwnys* (='[the child his] gowns, clothes')' (T:124-25). This method of indicating the genitive was 'fairly general in [the] writing' of the period (Krapp/Marckwardt 1909/ 1969:74). Traces of the construction can be seen as early as c. 1250, in *Genesis* and *Exodus*, 'where the suffix is already separated, though joined to the noun by a hyphen-- adame-is sune' ['Adam's son'] (Wyld (W) 1953:315). In the fourteenth century, this construction is common in the southwest of England, e.g. in Lawman's *Brut* and Trevisa'a (c. 1387) *Polychronicon* (ibid.). Though 'very rare in the North and infrequent in the rest of the country, [it] gains ground considerably in the 15th century and remains a popular means of expression right down to the 17th' (M:161). 'The use of *his*...as a sign of the genitive...had its widest currency in the sixteenth and seventeenth centuries' (P:196). Use of the construction declined gradually thereafter, so that it was virtually lost by the mid-eighteenth century. It has been conjectured that '[t]he pronoun form dropped out partly perhaps because of the antipathy of most stylists from the sixteenth century on to "pleonastic" or repetitive pronouns' (T:125)--and, in general, to any analyticity (periphrasis) in English where it diverged from Latin syntheticity. The following are examples of the *his*-genitive spanning three centuries (from W: 315); these could be multiplied almost indefinitely.

(8) (1420) *Seynt Dunstone his lore*
    (1467) *Harlesdone ys name*
    (1493) *therle of Ormond is deppute* [='the earl ... deputy']
    (1526) *the Busshoppe of Rome his laws*
    (1583) *the daulphin of France his power*
    (1639) *Dr. Read his treatise on wounds*
    (1693) *Mr. Careless his letter*

Certain peculiarities of the *his* genitive, taken in conjunction with the phonological facts of late OE and of ME, make it clear that the construction arose via a reanalysis of OE *-es*. The crucial factor in this development was the homophony of *-es* and *his*. According to Wyld:

> During the fifteenth century, the suffix *-es* tends to be written more and more as *-ys*, *-is*, both in private letters and official and literary documents.... The *-ys* forms are very common everywhere in the fifteenth century.... From the moment that on the one hand the pronoun *his* had lost its aspirate in unstressed positions, and on the other the Possess. suffix had become *-is*, *-ys*, there could be no distinction in pronunciation between a Noun inflected with the latter suffix and the same noun followed by a weakened form of *his*. Thus confusion arose, and is revealed by the detachment of the suffix *-ys* from the Noun to which it belongs, and then by the spelling of the latter *hys* or *his*. (W:314-15).

The *his* of the *his* genitive, then, was not pronounced with an initial aspirate, as far as can be determined, but was syllabic (as *-es* had been), at least in late ME.

If the *his* genitive arose from a reinterpretation of *-es*--if it was what 'became of' *-es*--then we have an explanation for the loss of postnominal *-es* genitives in ME, for it was precisely where the *-es* inflection was not followed by a noun (phrase) that it could not be reanalyzed as *his*. The most conclusive proof that the *his* genitive arose from a reanalysis of homophonous *-es* is provided by the fact *his* was used invariantly, occurring with feminine and neuter nouns as well as masculine ones; cf. (9):

(9) *my moder ys sake* (1469) (T:125) [= '...mother...']
   the quene ys modyr (1467) (W:315)
   Margaret ys doughter (1488) (W:315)
   her Grace is requeste (P:197)
   Gwenayfer his love (M:161)
   at þare ditch his grunde (M:161) ['...that ditch...
                                         bottom']
   Winchestre his toun (M:81)

Attempts to mark gender were made only in the Early NE period, cf. *Juno hir bedde* (W:316). This is also true of the plural: *Canterbury and Chillingworth their books* (ibid.). Furthermore, the *his* genitive spread *last* precisely to those nouns which were last to acquire the generalized genitive marker *-es* (replacing *-Ø*): *father*, *uncle*, etc. Although occasional uses of a periphrastic possessive adjective can be found in OE, these occur mostly with uninflected foreign nouns, and they occur in all numbers and genders. Given this, it seems clear that the invariant *his* genitive of ME arose via reanalysis of *-es*, since no other explanation that has yet been forwarded for the rise of the former construction--including reinterpretation of dative constructions like *to save someone his life* = *to save someone's life*, or massive anacoluthon, or a general trend toward analyticity in ME--can account for this invariance and the peculiar delay in the spread of the *his* genitive to certain nouns.

Thus, although ME speakers could have reinterpreted the case inflection *-es* as a phrase-final enclitic (which later became *-'s*, etc.) solely on the basis of the potentially ambiguous constituent structure of genitive constructions with extraposed posthead complements, as in (6) and (7), the evidence just mentioned strongly suggests that it was the reanalysis of *-es* as its homophone, the reduced form of *his*, that was responsible for the preservation of the morpheme /-ɨz/ by its liberation (back) into syntax. It should be mentioned that *-es* genitives were also common during the period of the *his* genitive, so that the reanalysis in question may have been made only by some speakers; on the other hand, it is entirely possible that the spelling *-es* represented the fact that *his* in the *his* genitive occurred as a reduced or contracted form. In fact, given the general lag of orthography behind pronunciation and grammatical change, the reanalysis of *-es* as *his* may well have taken place some time before it can be directly documented in texts. In support of the contention that the rise of the *his* genitive played a crucial role in the history of the English (non-*of*) genitive and that it was due to the reinterpretation of *-es* as *his*, one may mention two crucial facts: (1) that the spread of the *group* genitive exactly parallels the spread of the *his* genitive, and (2) that, in the north of England, where the *his* genitive was last to show up in written texts, Wright (1905:265) reports that, in *spoken* dialects, the genitive is generally marked by -∅, as in *the lad father stick* 'the lad's father's stick'. It is as if the genitive inflection *-es* had been lost everywhere except where it could be reanalyzed as *his*.

It is extremely doubtful, of course, whether any speakers today conceive of the (non-*of*) genitive as involving a reduced form of *his*. This suggests that the *his* genitive as such has been lost. However, the demise of the *his* genitive need not concern us much here, since that event is actually orthogonal to our present purposes. Though the *his* genitive remained common and, indeed, reached the peak of its popularity in Early NE, the *his* in this construction--as well as *-es*, which was, again, also common--increasingly became *non-syllabic* in its pronunciation (except after sibilants), though a syllabic pronunciation appears to have been optional as late as in Shakespeare's time. With this nonsyllabicity (which may or may not have resulted in the spelling -'*s*, for the apostrophe here may just as well represent an elided *-e-* as *-hi-*; the evidence is unclear, on this point), the connection of this type of genitive with the possessive adjective *his* became increasingly difficult to maintain. In combination with the stylists' attack on the non-Latinate *his* genitive, the phonological development just mentioned led to the establishment of the spelling -'*s* as the norm, and, thus, to both the orthographic and the grammatical loss of the *his* construction. For further details on these and other matters discussed here, see Janda (1978) and references therein.

In summary, then: the existence of group genitives in the language shows NE to have no genitive inflection and, hence, no case inflections at all. The reason for this is that, in the development from OE to late ME, English case inflections were all lost. Most were lost by outright phonological and/or morphological loss, but genitive *-es* was lost through reanalysis as unstressed *his*, due to the homophony of the two forms. Thus, on the one hand, the English case inflectional system actually turns out to be quite unexceptional and to follow the predictions that are made by synchronic typology and the diachronic aspects of the theory of markedness, since it has lost its most marked case inflection along with all of its historically less marked cases. On the other hand, however, the mechanism of this loss contradicts another very well established principle:

that syntactic elements reduce to morphological ones, but not vice versa. It was a belief in this principle that prompted Givón to sloganize: 'Today's morphology is yesterday's syntax' (1971:413). Nevertheless, the ME reanalysis of the case inflection -*es* as the phrase-final enclitic *his* demonstrates that change along the diachronic continuum of development for linguistic elements given in (5) potentially may proceed in either direction. Thus, one may also say that, sometimes: 'Today's morphology is *tomorrow's* syntax'.

REFERENCES

Cohen, David and Jessica R. Wirth (eds.). 1975. *Testing linguistic hypotheses*. Washington: Hemisphere.
Givón, Talmy. 1971. "Historical syntax and diachronic morphology: an archaeologist's field trip". CLS 7.394-415.
Greenberg, Joseph H. 1966. *Language universals. With special reference to feature hierarchies*. Janua linguarum, 59. The Hague: Mouton.
Hall, Robert A., Jr. 1964. *Introductory linguistics*. Philadelphia: Chilton Books.
Hamp, Eric P., Fred W. Householder, and Robert Austerlitz (eds.). 1966. *Readings in Linguistics II*. Chicago: University of Chicago Press.
Hockett, Charles F. 1958. *A course in modern linguistics*. New York: Macmillan.
Jakobson, Roman. 1966a. "Zur Struktur des russischen Verbums". In Hamp et al. (eds.), 22-30. (First published in 1932 in *Charisteria Guilelmo Mathesio quinquagenario...oblata*, 74-83.)
_____. 1966b. "Beitrag zur allgemeinen Kasuslehre. Gesamtbedeutungen der russischen Kasus". In Hamp et al. (eds.), 51-87. (First published in 1936 in *Travaux du Cercle Linguistique de Prague* 6.240-88).
Janda, Richard D. 1978. "A case of liberation from morphology into syntax: the fate of the English genitive-marker -(e)s". Paper presented in summary-form at the Conference on Syntactic Change; University of Michigan, Ann Arbor; April 21-22.
Krapp, George P./revised by Albert H. Marckwardt. 1909/1969. *Modern English: its growth and present use*. New York: Charles Scribner's Sons.
Mustanoja, Tauno F. 1960. *A Middle English syntax. Part I. Parts of speech*. Mémoires de la Société Néophilologique de Helsinki, 23. Helsinki: Société Néophilologique.
Pyles, Thomas. 1971. *The origins and development of the English language*. New York: Harcourt Brace Jovanovich. Second edition.
Traugott, Elizabeth C. 1972. *A history of English syntax. A transformational approach to the history of English sentence structure*. New York: Holt, Rinehart and Winston.
Trubetzkoy, Nicolai S. 1966. "Gedanken über die slovakische Deklination". In Hamp et al. (eds.), 96-103. (First published in 1937 in

Sbornik Matice slovenské 15.39-47.)
Wright, Joseph. 1905. *The English dialect grammar.* Oxford: Clarendon Press.
Wyld, H.C. 1953. *A history of Modern Colloquial English.* Oxford: Basil Blackwell. (Reprinting of third edition with additions; first edition 1920.)
Zwicky, Arnold M. 1975. "Settling on an underlying form: the English inflectional endings". In Cohen and Wirth (eds.), 129-85.

CONDITIONS ON OBJECT MARKING: STAGES IN
THE HISTORY OF THE EAST SLAVIC GENITIVE-ACCUSATIVE

EMILY KLENIN
Harvard University

The present paper is concerned with the problem of describing stages in the implementation of a single long-term change, namely the extension of genitive-accusative syncretism in some East Slavic case paradigms. I will be concerned with how the different stages are related to one another, and, in particular, with the role of discourse functionality in motivating the extension of the genitive-accusative. It has often been suggested that functional motivation may historically precede grammaticalization on the levels of syntax and morphology (for current work in this area, see e.g. Givón 1978); and the genitive-accusative has often been said to have had such a discourse functional historic basis (Thomson 1908, Comrie 1978). I will show that the genitive-accusative in East Slavic proceeded as a succession of innovations characterized by common discourse functional preconditions and by outputs analogous to one another; this conclusion differs from the widely accepted view, that the change in question represented a single very gradual development. I will also show that, although detailed analysis tends to support a functionalist approach in some respects, nevertheless the extension of the genitive-accusative in East Slavic was historically always mediated through available grammatical categories, and was at no stage a direct response to surface-level ambiguities. Moreover, even though the only preconditions on the extension of the genitive-accusative common to all its stages were indeed discourse functional, still, these preconditions can also be described by rules without any reference to discourse functionality. My results thus tend to limit rather severely the sense in which the innovation of the genitive-accusative can be considered to have been remedial, as this term is defined by Andersen (1978); and my results tend to support his treatment of the nominal (animate) genitive-accusative as an example of spontaneous morphological innovation of a grammatical category (ibid.).

In the modern East Slavic languages, as in all other Slavic languages of every attested period, there are some declensional paradigms in which accusative case forms are identical with the corresponding genitives. This is illustrated in the following Russian sentences:

(1) Vot novyj student.

'Here (is the) new (nom.) student (nom.)'.

(2) Vot ideja novogo studenta.

'Here (is the) idea (of the) new (gen.) student (gen.)'.

(3) Professor smotrel na novogo studenta.

'(The) professor looked at (the) new (acc.) student (acc.)'.

Genitive-accusative syncretism in East Slavic affects nouns, adjectives, and pronouns. The three standard languages (Russian, Ukrainian, and Belorussian), as well as most of their dialects, share, for the most part, a common pattern for the pronouns; but there are significant differences in the noun patterns. Modern Russian (stable since the seventeenth century) has genitive-accusative syncretism only for animate nouns in both singular and plural; in the singular, syncretism is further restricted to masculine nouns with nominative null-form endings. In Ukrainian, genitive-accusative syncretism is less highly correlated with animacy. In the singular, some masculine inanimates also permit the genitive-accusative; for example

(4) *lyst* (nom.) 'letter'

lysta (gen.)

permits both *lyst* and *lysta* in the accusative singular. In the plural, only nouns referring to persons regularly require the genitive-accusative; it also occurs with animals, and cannot occur with inanimates. The Ukrainian data show considerable dialectal variation. Belorussian data coincide partly with Russian and partly with Ukrainian. For further information, see Carlton (1971:32-36) and *Hramatyka* (1962:26-28).

Thomson (1908) proposed that nominal genitive-accusative syncretism in East Slavic was discourse functional, and served to disambiguate subjects (or agents) of transitive personal verbs from their direct objects. Thomson provided detailed documentation of conditions on the genitive-accusative in early East Slavic; and he claimed that these otherwise heterogeneous conditions could be reason-

ably explained only on the basis of discourse function.
One of the conditions on nominal genitive-accusative is
that they arose only in declensions with pre-existing nominative-accusative syncretism; in these declensions, the
grammatical and semantic distinction between the subject or
agent of a verb and its direct object lacked any morphological correlate. This situation was remedied by innovating
the genitive-accusative. As I have pointed out elsewhere
(Klenin, to appear), nominative-accusative syncretism seems
to have been relevant also to the development of pronoun
genitive-accusatives in East Slavic, since the pronouns to
generalize the genitive-accusative first were precisely
those that had nominative-accusative syncretism.

It is well known that nominative-accusative syncretism
in itself was never sufficient to trigger the genitive-accusative. For example, feminine plural nouns had nominative-accusative syncretism in early East Slavic, but acquired genitive-accusative syncretism only after the modern
languages in general had lost plural gender distinctions.
(Some Ukrainian dialects have still not generalized genitive-accusative syncretism in the feminine plural, even of
nouns with human referents.) Note also that the gradual
acquisition by masculine nouns of nominative-accusative
plural syncretism did not have as its consequence the
equally gradual acquisition of plural genitive-accusative
syncretism, as a kind of antidote. As pointed out by
Istrina (1923:147ff.), the early-14th-century *First Novgorod Chronicle* (Synod Copy), for example, shows widespread
nominative-accusative syncretism for certain morphological
classes of masculine plural nouns; but genitive-accusative
syncretism was restricted to one or two examples. Instead,
after all masculine plural nouns had generalized nominative-accusative syncretism, masculine plural genitive-accusative syncretism was quickly generalized for all masculines referring to persons. From these facts it can be
concluded that, although nominative-accusative syncretism
was a prerequisite for genitive-accusative syncretism in
the noun paradigms, and although the relation between the
two types of accusative syncretism can be viewed as discourse functional, nevertheless, genitive-accusative syncretism cannot be regarded as a discourse-level response
to individual instances of surface-level ambiguities. Even
when genitive-accusative syncretism was in the process of
being implemented and was not yet a stable rule of grammar,
genitive-accusative syncretism was always mediated through
grammatical, in this case morphological, categories. These
findings tend to limit the sense in which genitive-accusative syncretism can be said to have a functional explana-

tion, and also tend to militate against treating genitive-accusative syncretism as an example of gradual change, since it seems to have progressed more in a series of rapid morphologically defined quantum leaps. (On this point, see also Klenin, to appear.)

Other than nominative-accusative syncretism, there is only one other historical condition characterizing the implementation of both pronoun and noun genitive-accusatives. At each stage of the implementation of the genitive-accusative, direct objects generalized the genitive-accusative first, and accusative objects of prepositions acquired the genitive-accusative later. This syntactic condition, like the morphological one described above, is readily characterized as discourse functional: since prepositional government ipso facto excluded the possibility of a form being a nominative subject, only direct objects needed to be marked as genitive-accusatives, and, hence, nonsubjects. The fact that the only two conditions common to all types of East Slavic genitive-accusative syncretism are so easily functionally explained (and the fact that these conditions are diffcult to explain or relate to each other on any other basis) tends to substantiate a functionalist analysis of the origins of genitive-accusative syncretism.

On comparing the two general conditions of the East Slavic genitive-accusative, we see that the syncretism condition can be viewed as a general condition on the rule(s) throughout their/its history, until such time as grammaticalization occurred and functional motivation was lost. However, the direct object condition recurred and was lost at each separate stage of genitive-accusative innovation. Thus, for example, the rise and loss of this condition is described by Thomson and others with respect to the singular of masculine nouns, and by Thomson (1908) and Unbegaun (1935:225ff.) for the plurals of these nouns, where the genitive-accusative was innovated after the singular genitive-accusative had been generalized. The pronoun development, documented in Klenin (to appear), shows the same phenomenon, as does the history of the genitive-accusative in nouns referring to animals. The direct object condition is thus not chronologically continuous, but characterizes the early period of innovation at each morphological stage. There is no doubt, given the order in which different form classes generalized the genitive-accusative, that the newer classes of genitive-accusative syncretism represent an extension of a pre-existing phenomenon, not rule innovation a novo; for this reason, it is noteworthy that new classes of syncretic forms did not simply take over the fully grammaticalized genitive-accusative, but recapitulated the whole process of rule innovation and grammaticalization. If the direct object condition is regarded as discourse functional, then we observe a recurrent correlation between rule innovation and functional motivation, on the one hand, and grammaticalization and loss of functional motivation on the other. In the history of the East Slavic genitive-accusative, we can also observe that rule innovation and stabilization occurred not as a single process, but in morphologically defined stages. The East Slavic genitive-accusative thus provides an interesting illustration of how a discourse functional condition can help to articulate stages in a long-term historical language change.

REFERENCES

Andersen, Henning. 1978. "Morphological change: towards a typology". To appear in *Recent developments in historical morphology*. Ed. by Jacek Fisiak. The Hague: Mouton-De Gruyter.
Carlton, T.R. 1971. *The declension of nouns in Ukrainian*. Edmonton, Alberta: Department of Slavic Languages, University of Alberta.
Comrie, Bernard S. 1978. "Genitive-accusatives in Slavic: the rules and their motivation". *International Review of Slavic Linguistics* 3.27-42.
Givón, Talmy. 1978. "The rise of syntax". Paper presented at the Symposium on Synchrony and Diachrony in Linguistics, SUNY at Buffalo, 9 August 1978.
Hramatyka Belaruskaj movy, I: Marfalohija. 1962. Minsk: Akad. navuk BSSR.
Istrina, E.S. 1923. "Sintaksičeskie javlenija Sinodal'nogo spiska I Novgorodskoj letopisi". *Izvestija otdelenija russkogo jazyka i slovesnosti Rossijskoj Akademii nauk 1919* g., t. 24, kn. 2, 1-172.
Klenin, Emily. To appear. "On the genitive-accusative of anaphoric pronouns in the Laurentian manuscript of 1377". *Slavic and East European Journal* 24 (1980).
Thomson, A.I. 1908. "Roditel'nyj-vinitel'nyj padež pri nazvanijax živyx suščestv v slavjanskix jazykax". *Izvestija otdelenija russkogo jazyka i slovesnosti*, t. 13, kn. 2, 232-264.
Unbegaun, Boris O. 1935. *La langue russe au XVIe siècle (1500-1550): la flexion des noms*. Paris: Champion.

REDUCTION OF CASE MARKERS IN LITHUANIAN: DATA FOR DISCUSSION

JANINE K. REKLAITIS
University of Illinois at Chicago Circle

Interest in language change has continued to grow, but, as has been noted by Labov (1974) and King (1976), long range studies which would provide the data and documentation of ongoing change in languages remain scarce. This study presents selected results from the first stage of an investigation of changes in the nominal paradigms of Lithuanian, principally as spoken in the United States, and thereby contributes organized data which bear on certain major issues in the theory of language change. Three topics have been isolated for discussion in the present paper. These are:

1. the relationship between changes in word order and changes in inflectional morphology;

2. the significance of the position of stress for the reduction of inflectional morphology; and

3. the roles of ambiguity avoidance and perceptual simplicity as determinants in language change.

The first question investigated has been formulated as follows: Does a diachronic sampling of Lithuanian texts reveal a direct relationship between stabilization of word order and the reduction of inflections? The usual method was applied here: a tally of frequencies of verb order patterns in Old and Modern Lithuanian,[1] and a similar count and comparison of nominal inflectional forms were undertaken. Before proceeding to a summary of results, one essential point should be noted: word order is not stable in Lithuanian. There does exist an unmarked order of verbs, which is VO. However, all permutations of verb position, namely, initial, medial and final, are possible and do occur. These, of course, are contingent on the stylistic or topicalizing effect intended. The situation is further complicated by patterns indicative both of a VO and an OV language type. In other words, Lithuanian is clearly in a state of transition and it is imperative to record the specifics of ongoing changes now, even if a more consistent picture will not emerge for several centuries. The same is true regarding reduction of inflectional endings - very little has been lost thus far. But what is normally a slow, internally motivated eroding of morphology has been accelerated within the last few decades by external social factors as a result of prolonged and intimate contact with English in the United States and Russian in Lithuania.

The frequency counts of verbal position performed on three texts representative of the 16th century and three from the present decade[2] exhibit a development which is consistent with a decrease in inflectional morphology. As expected, they reveal an increase in the occurrence of verb medial positions. However, the results unexpectedly document a very rapid and very clear preference for the unmarked verb order. Also unexpected is the statistical regularity obtained from what was essentially a random sampling.[3]

As can be seen from the data presented in Table I, already in Old Lith. the incidence of verbs preceding direct objects is on the average twice the number of verbs following their objects. The two to one proportion favoring verb non-final (VO) over verb final (OV) position for the verb itself increases to a dramatic five to one proportion in Mod. Lith. Lithuanian has been characterized by Friedrich (1975) as an OV type language. In view of the figures obtained here, this applies only to the order typical of other relevant nominal and verbal phrases, particularly those in Old Lith., such as preposed adjectival and adverbial modifiers, retention of OV order in compounds and comparative constructions, and so forth (these have all been investigated in Reklaitis 1977). Although the two to one preference for non-final verb position which is seen in Old Lith. may appear inconsistent in view of these many other OV patterns, such differences in rates of retention have been frequently noted. Patterns involving the verb are typically found to have innovated first (Lehmann 1978:9,41).

With these results, it becomes possible to address the more specific question: can the increase in verb medial position be related to a decrease in inflectional morphology in Lithuanian? While this question is answered in

	OLD LITHUANIAN			RATIO $\frac{VO}{OV}$		MODERN LITHUANIAN			RATIO $\frac{VO}{OV}$
	SVO	9	SOV	16		SVO	28	SOV	2
1591	SV	38	OVS	2	1969	SV	11	OVS	2
Bretkūnas	VO	14	OSV	4	Novel	VO	34	OSV	1
			OV	14				OV	10
		61:		36	1.7		73:		15	4.8
	SVO	0	SOV	2		SVO	22	SOV	1
1599	SV	11	OVS	0	1972	SV	28	OVS	5
Daukša	VO	0	OSV	0	Literature	VO	2	OSV	5
			OV	3	Textbook			OV	0
		11:		5	2.2		52:		11	4.7
	SVO	12	SOV	8		SVO	28	SOV	1
1629	SV	22	OVS	4	1976	SV	9	OVS	3
Širvydas	VO	11	OSV	0	Biography	VO	18	OSV	0
			OV	9				OV	5
		45:		21	2.2		55:		9	6.1

Change in word order preference
TABLE I

the affirmative, evidence for it remains sparse because, as previously noted, the inflectional apparatus of noun paradigms has retained its synthetic complexity: five noun classes are differentiated in both Old and Mod. Lith.; seven cases (nom., gen., dat., acc., instr., loc., and voc.) are also differentiated in both Old and Mod. Lith. The major developments in morphological simplification which have taken place are summarized in Table II. (See next page.)

Of significance is the fact that most of the changes consolidated in Mod. Lith. are incipient in Old Lith.[5]

OLD LITHUANIAN	MODERN LITHUANIAN
Category A: Declensional Class Markers	
1. some loss of distinct 5th class (consonantal) nouns	1. substantial loss of 5th class to 3rd; and 3rd class to 1st
2. good retention of distinct 4th class iu-stem nouns in plural	2. complete loss of these to 1st class ia-stem plurals
3. retention of distinct 2nd class adjectival patterns	3. partial loss of these to 1st class ia-stem pattern
Category B: Case Markers	
1. retention of full dative plural ending -*mus*	1. loss of final syllable: *mus* > *ms* > *m*
2. full pronoun dative singular ending *mui*	2. loss of final syllable: *jamui* > *jam* 'to him'
3. full instrumental plural in 3rd and 4th class	3. frequent reduction: *mis* > *ms* ~ *m*
4. full locative (inessive) ending	4. frequent reduction in class 2, 3, 4, 5 of singular and class 1 and 2 of plural nouns
5. presence of postpositional locatives: allat. -*pi*; illat. -*na*, adess. -*pi*[4]	4. loss of all, with the exception of occasional stylistic usage of illative

Major changes in surface inflections
TABLE II

Hence, there is a great discrepancy between the rapid progression in the preference for verb medial order from Old to Mod. Lith. and the slow pace at which morphology declines from Old to Mod. Lith. Clearly, Lithuanian has pushed ahead with changes in word order, drastically reducing its preference for all other options in sentential verb position, but has not exercised the option to reduce its inflectional morphology at a remotely comparable rate. It can be seen very conclusively that word order change has preceded any major erosion in synthetic morphology. Yet this does not imply that it causes the latter. The developments in Lithuanian do not contradict the traditional view that *stabilization* of word order, or a fixed verb medial position, will ensue as a compensatory effect in the syntax after the central subject and object case markers are no longer differentiated in the surface morphology. That point is still remote for Lithuanian.

If word order change can at best be seen only as a facilitator of inflectional reduction, what is its cause? The phonetic reduction of unstressed syllables is probably the most commonly cited mechanism in the process of morphological erosion. Although it would be too simplistic to accept this as the single direct cause of such change, its consequences in the history of many languages have been such as to definitely establish it as a major prerequisite to inflectional loss.[6] For this reason it is of interest to ascertain how significant a factor it has been in the simplification of Lithuanian nominal paradigms.

Bear in mind that stress is mobile in Lithuanian. It may fall on any syllable of a noun. Secondly, it may shift its position through the course of a declensional paradigm, within the constraints, however, of four basic patterns and at least an equal number of subtypes (for details of this system, see Laigonaitė 1978). The position of stress is fixed in just one accent class, the first, where it remains on the initial syllable of the noun stem throughout. The situation in spoken Lithuanian is in a state of flux. Even in the standard variety, a definite tendency to retract stress, especially from final short vowel syllables, has been in effect for some time (Laigonaitė 1978:29). However, as is obvious from Table II, this trend has not yet resulted in any substantial restructuring of the morphological component for one good reason.[7] A careful analysis of those instances where stress retraction followed by syllable reduction has occurred shows that at least at the present period it is a selective and self-limiting process. It is generated by formal pressures; at the same time it is held in check by functional pressures. The formal motivation for stress retraction is not some external surface criterion such as length of syllable (viz. a word like *siěnoj* 'in the wall' has been reduced from three to two syllables, whereas *bitininke* 'in the bee-keeper' has retained its four syllables). The motivation is system-internal pressure for paradigmatic uniformity. Stress is retracted primarily in those forms which deviate from the dominant stress pattern. For example, final stress in *mokyklà* 'school' and *mokyklàs* (acc.pl.) has been shifted to the penultimate syllable, rendering *mokỹkla*, *mokỹklas* in conformity with the accent position of every other form in this paradigm.[8] Hence this stress pattern is no longer mobile and irregular, but fixed and regular.

(For discussion of this phenomenon in dialects, see Grinaveckis 1973.) Furthermore, if and when syllable reduction follows, it takes place only in certain cases, namely, the oblique cases: dative, instrumental, and locative. Use of these shortened forms is very common, indeed is the rule in spoken standard Lithuanian. Thus, the synchronic primacy of terms in respect to nonterms[9] is reflected in their privileged diachronic status. Only the markers of cases which are in a semantic relationship to the verb have been affected by natural simplificatory phonological processes, leaving untouched the pure or syntactically related cases. As for the oblique cases, even here, the erosion has had only superficial results. For in Lithuanian, these case inflections are lost only in those declensional classes in which case meaning is not lost. In other words, ambiguity has been forestalled. The simplification of forms that has taken place has not involved simplification of semantic content. Because the process of inflectional reduction is in its early stages, ambiguity is circumvented in ways other than the typically cited rise of analytic markers and rigid word order. The specific means and manner by which this is accomplished are the subject of the next section.

Examples of instances of change in Lithuanian in which the expected outcome is ambiguity in case distinction can be classified into three groups, depending on whether phonological, morphological or semantic-syntactic elements have been harnessed to neutralize potentially ambiguous situations.

A) Prevention of case merger via phonology:

a) The suffixless loc. sing. of a 3rd cl. noun such as *pilyjè* 'in the castle' > *pilỹ* [pɪlĩ] is still readily differentiated from the acc. sing. form *pìlį* [pɪ̀li] by final versus initial stress position.

b) In the truncated 1st cl. pl. loc. form *laukuose* 'in the fields'>*laukuõs* the diphthongal theme serves to set this form apart from others in this class such as acc. pl. *laukùs*.

c) Both difference in stress and thematic vowel prevent the merger of reduced 2nd cl. loc. sing. *gėlėjè* 'in the flower' > *gėlėj* [gelěj] with dat. sing. *gėlei* [gělɛj].

As illustrated, differentiation of case distinctions has been retained via previously redundant differences in a) stress, b) thematic vowel, or c) both. Loss of final vowel does *not* occur in 3rd class loc. *pilysè*, since the resultant form would merge with nom. pl. *pilys*; nor does it occur in the 1st cl. sing. for similar ambiguous results, e.g., merger with imperative *laũk* 'leave'.

B) Prevention of case merger via morphology: As a result of two natural phonological processes, namely, loss of final short vowel and simplification of consonant clusters, the originally distinct dat. and instr. cases of cl. 2, 3, 4, and 5 have become identical. Yet the potential ambiguity in meaning has been countervened by competing changes in morphology. The merger of meaning-carrying cases has been circumvented by merger of purely formally differentiated classes. First class forms with very distinct endings in both these cases are replacing the original masc. noun forms:

	Original	Potentially Ambiguous		Resolution
Dat.	*vagims* 'to thieves' > *vagims ~ vagim*	>	*vagim ~ vagiam*
Instr.	*vagimis*	> *vagims ~ vagim*	>	*vagiais*

An alternate means of resolution -- the only one possible for cl. 2 nouns -- is the firmly entrenched preference for expressing the instr. function by the analytic construction: prep. *su* 'with' plus either reduced or full instr. noun form.

C) Prevention of merger via semantics-syntax: Even if actual identity of case forms results, differences in their meaning may be retained through the inherent semantic or syntactic features of verbs to which the noun is related.

    a) Loss of the loc. sing. ending leaves the form *suñkvežimy* 'in the truck' phonetically indistinguishable from the acc. sing. *suñkvežimį* 'truck', both [suŋkvεʒιmi]. Nonetheless only the locative case relationship would be understood by a native Lithuanian in the following two sentences.

        1) *Jìs stovéjo suñkvežimy*   'He was standing in the truck'

        2) *Jìs láukè suñkvežimy*   'He was waiting in the truck'

The verb in 1) is intransitive in its forms, opposed to the causative-transitive form *stãtè* which would allow the meaning 'He stood up his truck' with the acc. object form. The verb in 2) always requires a genitive case object; therefore, it too is incompatible with an acc. object form.

b) Two time concepts are ordinarily distinguished with two different cases in Lithuanian. The concept 'extended duration of time' is marked by the acc., whereas 'intended period of time' is marked by the dative.

3) *Jìs padìrbo dvì dienàs* (acc.) 'He worked <u>for two days</u>'

4) *Jìs atvỹko padìrbti dvíem dienóm* (dat.) 'He <u>arrived</u> to work for two days'

More and more frequently the second concept is also rendered by the accusative. And, just as in English, the differing semantic properties of the two verbs serve to keep the two time concepts distinct. In cases where the verb is insufficient to prevent ambiguity in these related time meanings, an analytic construction may be used: *Jis pasiliko dẽl dviejų dienų* 'He remained <u>for two days</u>'.

This last example, although not ascribable to phonetic reduction, is equally symptomatic of inflectional breakdown. An unmarked case, the acc., takes over an ever increasing number of the functions previously expressed by the oblique cases. However, communication has not been impeded. Several strategies have been adopted. Previous redundancy has been sacrificed for a more efficient signalling of case. Or, the switch has been made to an unambiguous signal of case from another noun class. Analytic constructions have been substituted. Even when a distinction previously specifically marked by an oblique case has been absorbed into a neutral case, ambiguity is prevented by inherent syntactic or semantic properties of related constituents. Finally, although this is too broad an area to exemplify here, in Lithuanian, as in every language, any potentially ambiguous interpretation may be clarified within the hyper-syntactic scope (Patel 1977: 39), by the many extra-linguistic devices available within the total context of discourse.

Since overt signals have not as yet been discarded in every case in Lithuanian, the opportunity exists for assessing the efficacy of a complex synthetic system in conveying internal relations by way of surface inflections. The intent here is to examine the Bever and Langendoen (1972) hypothesis that such a language structure, although difficult to learn, promotes ease of perception.

Consider that even with the maximum number of cases

recorded for PIE (eight, as in Skt.) very little transparency between oblique surface case and actual meaning existed. The number of functions differentiated has always been disproportionate to the number of differentiating elements. For instance, approximately ten functions are typically listed for the genitive case in the classical languages, and at least that many are recognized in Mod. Lith. But despite the minimally six separate gen. case endings that occur in these languages (five for each sing. class and at least one for pl.), there is only one genitive case morpheme. The others are meaningless declensional variants, once gender and number categories have been abstracted as separate morphemes. Superficial familiarity with this structure suffices to point out the basic fallacy in a theory which holds that it was the resultant benefits of perceptual simplicity in PIE inflectional languages which served to counterbalance the difficulties entailed in learning this type of system. Inflectional complexity as such cannot in fact be equated with perceptual simplicity at any attested stage for PIE languages. The oblique cases have always been ambiguously opaque since each marked a large number of relationships. Therefore it is essentially not the inherent difficulty in mastering all the separate inflections (e.g., in Lithuanian totalling at least 5 classes x 7 cases x 2 numbers), but as coping with the inherent imbalance in the system, which is the stimulant in its breakdown. If each of these case forms corresponded to specific functions, even if their number were far greater, the effort in learning would be directly purposeful. However, this was never the case. Table III illustrates the efficiency in facilitating perception of functions that both analytic and synthetic systems are capable of. At the same time, it demonstrates the perceptual ambiguity prevailing in each. Note in particular the six functions listed for the sing. instr. inflection in Lithuanian.

It becomes very evident that it is the balance between one unique form per function which is responsible for ease in perception. Neither the presence of inflections nor analytic constructions per se promote this. Still, the distribution of functions being equal, analytic markers are generally considered superior for perceptual processing. It may be that within the history of individual languages, the maximally efficient structure is the very one which has commonly been adjudged a transitional stage. This is one which does not make use of overwhelmingly synthetic or analytic means, but has a judicious mixture of both types to express grammatical relationships. It is precisely this

Column A			Column B			Column C	
Ambiguity of Instr. inflection in Lith.	Unambiguous signals in Eng.		Ambiguity of Prep. *by* in Eng.	Unambiguous signals in Lith.		Ambiguous in both English	Ambiguous in both Lithuanian
1. *šautuvu* (instr. of means)	by means of a gun		by the father	*tėvo* (father, gen. of agent)		for Mary	*Marijai* (dat. I.O. 'to')
2. *lauku* (instr. of place)	along the field		by the train	*traukiniu* (train, instr. of means)		for the country	*šaliai* (dat. of benefit 'on behalf of'
3. *baisiu balsu* (instr. of manner)	with a horrid		by herself	*pati* (nom. sg. emphatic pro.)		for the summer	*vasarai* (dat. of time, i.e., come when)
4. *tuo laiku* (instr. of time)	at that time		by the river	*prie upės* (near river)			
5. *baisiu skausmu* (instr. of cause)	on account of horrid pain		by the hand	*už rankos* (ahold-of hand)			
6. *(virto) baisiu paukščiu* (pred. instr.)	(turned) into a horrid bird		by mistake	*per klaidą* (through mistake)			

Assessment of transparency in perception by analytic vs. synthetic markers

TABLE III

type of system with fewer inflectional cases and greater reliance on analytic elements such as particles and adverbials which is now reconstructed as pre-PIE, and towards which Mod. Lith. is drifting.

The situation in Lithuanian has served to focus attention again on the long-recognized importance of balance between form and function in language, and to reaffirm its primacy as a factor in language change. The interesting question of whether one can determine the saturation point for imbalance has not been broached. Obviously that point has been reached in Lithuanian. It would be useful to check the early stages of IE languages to compare the maximum covert categories that were distinguished via a single overt case marker before a breakdown of the established system and shift towards optimal marking set in. Even in respect to the earlier issues discussed in this paper, no final conclusions can be advanced until the process of inflectional simplification advances. On the other hand, the end products of inflectional change are already evident in many other languages. It is the transitional types of processes that have been lost to history, but which can be investigated in Lithuanian today.

NOTES

[1] The data presented in Table I are limited to sentential verbal position and exclude tabulation of verb initial position. Other relevant patterns and constructions are reported in detail in Reklaitis (1977).

[2] The material for Old Lith. was taken from three of the earliest, contemporary writers: Daukša (1527-1613), Bretkūnas (1536-1602), and Širvydas (1580-1631), as reprinted in Korsakas 1957. These were selected first because their writings are relatively free of influence from either Latin or Polish. Daukša's *Postilla* alone is not an original work, but a free translation of a Polish text. Nevertheless it is regarded as largely true to the structure of the Lithuanian language. Daukša himself is considered a cornerstone figure in the development of standard Lithuanian. Second, the three texts are fairly similar in content -- all being exegesic homilies -- and in style, which can be characterized as informally didactic. The choice of modern texts is intended to be representative of the language as written and published in Lithuania today. These were taken from Sluckis (1969), Riškus et al. (1972), and Matuzevičius (1976).

[3] Length of the Old Lith. samples was predetermined by my source, the most recent reprinting of major Old Lith. texts (Korsakas 1957). Everything therein was tabulated. Unfortunately that consisted of only one passage from Daukša's *Postilla*. I originally strove for 100 consecutive instances of verbal positions from the modern texts, but fell far short of this number.

[4] The allative suffix is added to the gen. case (*manęspi* 'towards me'), whereas the adessive suffix is added to the archaic loc. (in-essive) case (*staliepi* 'at the table'). The illative marker is suffixed to the acc. case (*miškan(a)* 'into the forest').

[5] For additional examples and loss of entire categories such as dual, see Palionis (1967).

[6] Recently Fairbanks (1977) has unwarrantedly disregarded the first component of this process (115: 'position of stress seem(s) negligible'), completely overlooking the significance absence of stress has as a conditioning environment for the total process. His conclusion that the role of stress is negligible is at variance with his earlier statement in the same article that 'What is common to the languages that have lost inflections is that they have through phonetic change ... lost final *unstressed* syllables ...' (1977:112; emphasis mine).

[7] The relatively stable situation in standard Lith. is in sharp contrast to the widespread loss of final short vowels with resultant loss of morphological distinctions which has taken place in dialects, particularly in those of Žemaitija.

[8] Lith. is said to have preserved the IE pitch-stress or word intonation system. Every *stressed* long vowel and diphthong in Lith. is pronounced in one of two ways: either with a falling or acute intonation marked by ´ or with a rising or circumflex intonation marked by tilde ˜. The latter should not be confused with nasality which is marked as a hook below the vowel. The symbol ˋ (grave mark) indicates stress alone and occurs only on short vowels. In certain stress classes, e.g., the fourth (see example below), all three types will occur throughout the course of the noun paradigm. Depending on the noun's accent class and case, the final grave stress will appear as acute or circumflex stress/intonation when retracted.

Class 4 stress pattern: plural paradigm

N.	*vaikaĩ*	*šãkos*	_ _ ˜	_ _ ˜
G.	*vaikų̃*	*šakų̃*	_ _ ˜	_ _ ˜
D.	*vaikáms*	*šakóms*	_ _ ´	_ _ ´
A.	*vaikùs*	*šakàs*	_ _ ˋ	_ _ ˋ
I.	*vaikaĩs*	*šakomìs*	_ _ ˜	_ _ ˜
L.	*vaikuosè*	*šakosè*	_ _ _ ˋ	_ _ _ ˋ
V.	*vaikaĩ!*	*šãkos!*	_ _ ˜	_ _ ˜

        'children'   'branches'

[9] Current appreciation of grammatical relations (Gary and Keenan, Johnson, Pullum in Cole and Sadock 1977) unfortunately has failed to take into account the central role such issues have had in traditional diachronic schools, e.g. in Praguean functionalism. New terminology has thus been coined replacing earlier labels such as central vs. peripheral.

REFERENCES

Bever, T. and D.T. Langendoen. 1972. "The interaction of speech perception and grammatical structure in the evolution of language". In *Language change and generative theory*. Ed. by Robert P. Stockwell and Ronald K.S. Macaulay. Bloomington: Indiana University Press.

Cole, Peter M. and J.M. Sadock, eds. 1977. *Syntax and semantics. Vol. 8: grammatical relations*. New York: Academic Press.

Fairbanks, Gordon H. 1977. "Case inflection in IndoEuropean". *Journal of IE Studies* 5.2,3.101-31.

Friedrich, Paul. 1975. *Proto-Indo-European syntax*. Journal of Indo-European Studies, Monograph No. 1. Butte, Montana.

Grinaveckis, V. 1973. "Kirčiavimo sistemos reikšmė kirčio atitraukimui" ("The importance of the stress paradigm for the retraction of stress"). *Baltistica* 9.151-60.

King, Robert D. 1976. "Competing generalizations and linguistic change". Bloomington: Indiana University Linguistics Club.

Korsakas, K. 1957. *Lietuvių literatūros istorijos chrestomatija*. Vilnius: Valstybinė grožinės literatūros leidykla.

Labov, William. 1974. "On the use of the present to explain the past". In *Proceedings of XIth Congress of Linguists*. Ed. by Luigi Heilmann. Bologna: Il Mulino.

Laigonaitė, A. 1978. *Lietuvių kalbos akcentologija*. Vilnius: Mokslas.

Lehmann, Winfred P. 1978. *Syntactic typology*. Austin: University of Texas Press.

Matuzevičius, E. 1976. *Mane Jūs jausite darbe, kovoj*.220-222. Vilnius: Vaga.

Palionis, Jonas. 1967. *Lietuvių literaturine kalba*. Vilnius: Mintis. 1977.

Patel, P.G. 1977. "Psycholinguistic remarks on disambiguation: some implications for grammatical theory". *Linguistics* 186.33-50.

Reklaitis, Janine. 1977. "The Baltic data for word order typology". AATSEEL Conference, Dec, 28, 1977.

Riškus, J. Šalčiūtė, A., Umbrasas, K., eds. 1972. *Lietuvių literaturos vadovėlis*.215-223. Kaunas: Šviesa.

Sluckis, M. 1969. *Adomo obuolys*, 240-242. Vilnius: Vaga. 2nd ed. 1978.

ANALOGY AND INFLECTIONAL AFFIX REPLACEMENT

MAX W. WHEELER
University of Liverpool, England

In the last few years, those who have been working on analogy in morphological change have been moving away from the view that analogical changes can be interpreted as 'grammar simplification'. In the case of the evolution of inflectional paradigms, it is plausible to suggest that at least one of the reasons why such changes may not, in fact, result in simplified grammars is that the different principles involved naturally conflict in their operation. It may be this factor of essential conflict in the operation of general principles which has meant that the outcomes of analogical forces can appear to be unpredictable or arbitrary. Some psychological and functional principles, such as those proposed by Kiparsky (1974), Koefoed (1974), and others, provide a framework in which conflicting analogical developments may be explained. The basic tendencies proposed are in the direction of 'ease of production', 'ease of perception', and 'ease of acquisition' or 'learnability of the system'. In the search for explanations of the kinds of changes to be observed in morphological systems with arbitrary classes (cf. Thomason 1976), known conventionally as 'declensions' and 'conjugations' in Indo-European languages, we can relate these psychological principles to the oft invoked 'Humboldt's Universal' (cf. Vincent 1974:433, Anttila 1977:55), which I paraphrase as 'One form tends to correspond to one meaning; that is, avoid synonymy; avoid ambiguity'.[1]

From these four principles we can derive three tendencies which we can expect to observe in the development of morphological class inflection systems. Tendencies A and B represent two aspects of Humboldt's Universal.

> A. Each meaning is expressed by only one form. This favors ease of production. It works *against* synonymy (allomorphy), but permits ambiguity (syncretism).

> B. Each form expresses only one meaning. This favors ease of perception. It *allows* synonymy (allomorphy) but works against ambiguity (syncretism). In a system already displaying syncretism, Tendency B may lead to the loss of semantic distinctions.

When it is split into these two parts, A and B, we can see more clearly how Humboldt's Universal can work in opposite directions. When it is applied to a morphological class system, we tend to find that a compromise results, whereby the one meaning ↔ one form relation is (nearly) obtained in the context of each class. For example: "In Class I, at least, meaning 'X' is expressed uniquely by form p, and form p uniquely expresses meaning 'X'". The result of such a compromise, however, is a system that is difficult to learn. That is, abstract and arbitrary morphological class features must be induced (or abduced, cf. Andersen 1973, Anttila 1977) from surface forms plus meanings. So Tendency C results:

> C(i). Each intersection of form and meaning identifies the morphological class of the lexeme concerned. The system becomes (relatively) easy to acquire.
>
> C(ii) (stronger version). Each morphological class is overtly and uniquely expressed, e.g., by extending a distinct 'thematic' element throughout the paradigm. This, even more than C(i), makes the inflectional system easy to learn; but since 'morphological class' has no semantic content, the conflict with Humboldt's Universal is most evident. 'Empty morphs' which identify morphological class can equally be interpreted by the learner as combining with 'full morphs' of e.g., person, number, or case, so as to create arbitrary allomorphs of these morphemes.

Let us consider a simplified model of analogical change in a system which corresponds ideally to Tendency C(i). We might have:

(1)

Morphological Class	I	II	III
meaning 'X'	p	q	r
meaning 'Y'	r	p	q

Then suppose that a change, by 'analogical extension', takes place:

(2) $r > p \ / \ \left[\overline{\ I\ } \right]$

The following developmental tendencies can be observed operating here: Tendency A, in that meaning 'Y' comes to be expressed by two forms (p, q) rather than three (r, p, q); and Tendency B in that form r comes to express only one meaning. But Tendency B is contradicted in that form p comes to be ambiguous not only in the language as a whole, but also within the context of Class I (syncretism). As for Tendency C(i), the intersection "meaning 'Y' - form p" no longer uniquely identifies Class II, and signals only not-III. On the other hand, form r now identifies Class III without regard to meaning. It should be clear from this model how the three psychological principles relating to ease of production, ease of perception, and ease of acquisition can conflict in the process of one analogical extension, which does not significantly simplify the grammar either.

The Appendix cites inflectional paradigms of some Catalan verb forms at three periods. The 'tenses' illustrated are those which have been most subject to inflectional affix replacement. The Conjugation Classes I, IIa, IIb, IIIa, and IIIb are synchronically arbitrary, except that the distinction between IIa and IIb is based on the final consonant of the stem.[2] The changes after 1300 A.D. in the past indicative perfective are of the kind quite easily dealt with in terms of standard proportional analogy, contamination and semantic change. The remaining developments offer several intriguing problems. I concentrate here on the development of the present tenses between 1500 A.D. and the modern standard language.[3] What we observe is a paradoxical development, in which a distinct, overt, and unique morph ($-i-$), contrasting 'subjunctive' with 'indicative', has been introduced and extended throughout the singular and 3rd plural of all verbs, while the distinction between 'subjunctive' and 'indicative', previously present in the 1st and 2nd plural of all verbs, has been largely obliterated there, that is, in all but Class IIb verbs, where the distinction is maintained by stem alternants.

It is likely (following Mourin 1969:369) that it is the place of the imperative forms in the system which has provoked this divergence, together with the fact that in the present tenses the 1st and 2nd plurals alone are stressed on the endings rather than the stem. I am proceeding on the basis that 'imperative' is a distinct function necessarily restricted to those persons which can include reference to the addressee (i.e., 2nd person, and 1st persons (inclusive)). We should note, too, that throughout the history of the language negative imperatives have been expressed with the subjunctive forms, and that from the beginning the 1st plural imperative form was always identical with the subjunctive. One of the earliest changes was to replace the distinct forms of the 2nd plural imperative (in -t) with forms identical to the indicative. This change was in progress already by 1300, having arisen, perhaps, through adstratum influence, or for phonological reasons at a stage when the 2nd plural indicative (like other tenses and moods) ended in a voiced dental fricative /ð/, and the imperative (uniquely in the finite system) in a voiced dental plosive /d/. (Subsequently the realizations of these phonemes diverged.) As a result, by 1500, in the 1st and 2nd plural indicative, imperative, and subjunctive in each Conjugation Class only two forms express the three meanings, and the forms exhibit a rather unbalanced distribution:

(3)   Indicative   Imperative   Subjunctive

I	1	*pregam*	*no pregam*	*preguem*	*no preguem*	*preguem*	*no preguem*
	2	*pregau*	*no pregau*	*pregau*	*no pregueu*	*pregueu*	*no pregueu*
II	1	*batem*	*no batem*	*batam*	*no batam*	*batam*	*no batam*
	2	*bateu*	*no bateu*	*bateu*	*no batau*	*batau*	*no batau*
III	1	*dormim*	*no dormim*	*dormam*	*no dormam*	*dormam*	*no dormam*
	2	*dormiu*	*no dormiu*	*dormiu*	*no dormau*	*dormau*	*no dormau*

The box contains the forms with an -a- morph.

Such a system would appear to be difficult to learn (and not easy to produce or perceive either). In fact, the endings -am, -au, -em, -eu do not unambiguously denote any of the three meanings, or identify any of the three Conjugation Classes. The state of this part of the system is nearly pathological. What happens next is an aspect of a broader tendency to reduce the distinction between Classes I and II, while strengthening the distinctiveness of Class III. The assimilation of Classes I and II was partly provoked, even before 1500, by a phonological development - the introduction of a Vowel Reduction rule (cf. Wheeler 1979:55-8), which converts to schwa unstressed vowels which are neither high nor rounded. A consequence is that future and conditional suffixes of Class I become phonetically identical to some (but not all) of those of Class II, and that the endings of the singular and 3rd plural present subjunctive become phonetically the same for all classes, and identical to the indicative, i.e., schwa, in Class I, cf. Appendix, 1500 paradigms (the standard orthography is used in this appendix, and therefore does not reflect all the phonetic changes discussed here).

What is especially interesting about the verb system at this stage of the language is that it is not so much the forms themselves, or their 'proportions', which provide the key to subsequent analogical extensions, but rather, more abstract models of similarity and contrast, which motivate divergent developments. In the surface phonetic forms of the subjunctive singular and 3rd plural endings we have a model for subjunctive morphs which do not distinguish Conjugation Class and in Class I singular and 3rd plural we have a model for syncretism between indicative and subjunctive. If we add to this the model we have already noted in the 1st and 2nd plural for syncretism between indicative and imperative, and between imperative and subjunctive, it becomes easier to conceive of the changes that take place, particularly if we concentrate on the models rather than the forms themselves. A considerable amount of ambiguity has been introduced into the system, which is easy enough to produce (Tendency A), but which has become rather harder to perceive and to learn. The change which takes place, in the 1st and 2nd plural of Classes I and II, is that the endings *-em*, *-eu* are extended at the expense of thsoe in *-am*, *-au*, whatever the meaning involved. Such spread reflects Tendency A, reducing the degree of arbitrary allomorphy involved in the Conjugation Classes, but increasing the ambiguity. The syncretic model in the 1st and 2nd plural spreads to Class III, where it is the indicative forms *-im*, *-iu* which are extended; these have the virtue of indicating the Conjugation Class unambiguously, reflecting Tendency C (ii).

The singular and 3rd plural forms in *-i-* (earlier *-ia-*), which were original only in very few verbs of Class II, spread first to the subjunctive of Class I where they were most needed for functional distinctiveness. The new set of subjunctive endings *-i*, *-is*, *-i*, *-in* is notably easy to produce, to perceive, and to learn. The extension reflects Tendency A especially, but also Tendency B, in that the previous endings *-a*, *-es*, *-en* are ambiguous: indicative in Class I, subjunctive elsewhere. But here too the model for extension of these forms to the other Conjugation Classes seems to have been not so much the forms and functions themselves, as the change which affected them, the replacement of schwa by /+i+/. Only if we take this approach can we account for the spread of the *-i-* subjunctive morph into the Past Subjunctive paradigm. If the extension had been proportional, we should have expected *-i-* to be found in the singular and throughout the plural, a coincidence in only two places out of the six. But this makes sense if the model is the original change itself: replace schwa by /+i+/ in subjunctive endings.

In summary, I have tried to show how:

1) Three general tendencies for inflectional change in morphological class systems can be derived from Kiparsky's psychological principles plus Humboldt's Universal.

2) These tendencies will inevitably conflict in the direction of the changes they promote, preventing grammar simplification from appearing as a general trend.

3) Abstract models of paradigmatic contrast, or models of change themselves, may be important in explaining the direction and scope of affix replacement.

NOTES

[1] Anttila (1977:57-8) makes it clear that in his view Humboldt's Universal cannot be the only principle operating: 'the creativity of language depends on this breaking up of one-to-one relations'.

[2] Cf. Wheeler (1979:87-93), but the phonetic context is not a very natural one, and it is ignored by traditional grammarians.

[3] The philological histories of the development of 1st singular present indicative -o, and of the singular and 3rd plural present subjunctive affix -i- are adequately dealt with by Coromines (1971:204-7) and Gulsoy (1976) respectively.

REFERENCES

Andersen, Henning. 1973. "Abductive and deductive change". *Lg.* 49.765-93.
Anderson, John M. & Charles Jones. 1974. *Historical linguistics, II*. Amsterdam: North-Holland.
Anttila, Raimo. 1977. *Analogy*. The Hague: Mouton.
Coromines, Joan. 1971. *Lleures i converses d'un filòleg*. Barcelona: Club Editor.
Gulsoy, Joseph. 1976. "El desenvolupament de les formes del subjuntiu present en català". *Actes del Tercer Col·loqui Internacional de Llengua i Literatura Catalanes*, 27-59. Oxford: Dolphin.
Kiparsky, Paul. 1974. "Remarks on analogical change". In Anderson & Jones, 257-275.
Koefoed, Geert. 1974. 'On formal and functional explanation: some notes on Kiparsky's "Explanation in phonology"'. In Anderson & Jones, 276-293.
Mourin, Louis. 1969. "Le présent du subjonctif en catalan, et la morphologie comparée". *Mélanges offerts à Rita Lejeune, I*, 367-377. Gembloux: Duculot.
Thomason, Sarah G. 1976. "Analogic change as grammar complication". In *Current progress in historical linguistics*, 401-409. Ed. by William M. Christie, Jr. Amsterdam: North-Holland.

Vincent, Nigel. 1974. "Analogy reconsidered". In Anderson & Jones, 427-445.
Wheeler, Max W. 1979. *Phonology of Catalan*. Publications of the Philological Society, 28. Oxford: Blackwell.

APPENDIX

Catalan Verb Paradigms (partial)
(Given in Standard Orthography)

Key:

PrI = Present Indicative

Imp = Imperative

PrS = Present Subjunctive

PsI = Past Indicative Perfective (Preterite)

PsS = Past Subjunctive

\+ = a form now obsolete in all dialects

^ = analogical innovation

Conjugation			I	IIa	IIb	IIIa	IIIb
c. 1300			'ask'	'strike'	'move'	'sleep'	'serve'
PrI	sg	1	prec	bat	moc	dorm	+servesc
		2	pregues	bats	mous	dorms	+serveis
		3	prega	bat	mou	dorm	serveix
	pl	1	pregam	+batem	movem	dormim	servim
		2	+pregats	+batets	+movets	+dormits	+servits
		3	preguen	baten	moven	dormen	serveixen
Imp	sg	2	prega	bat	mou	dorm	serveix
	pl	1	preguem	batam	mogam	+dormam	+sirvam
		2	+pregat	+batet	+movet	+dormit	+servit
PrS	sg	1	prec	bata	moga	dorma	servesca
		2	precs	bates	mogues	dormes	servesques
		3	prec	bata	moga	dorma	servesca
	pl	1	preguem	batam	mogam	+dormam	+sirvam
		2	+preguets	+batats	+mogats	+dormats	+sirvats
		3	preguen	baten	moguen	dormen	servesquen
PsI	sg	1	+pregué	+batí	+moc	+dormí	serví
		2	+preguest	+batest/-ist	+moguest/-ist	+dormist	+servist
		3	+pregà	+baté	+moc	+dormí	serví
	pl	1	+pregam	+batem	+moguem	+dormim	+servim
		2	+pregàs	+batés	+mogués	+dormís	+servís
		3	pregaren	bateren	+mogren	dormiren	serviren
PsS	sg	1	pregàs	batés	mogués	dormís	servís
		2	pregasses	batésses	moguesses	dormísses	servísses
		3	pregàs	batés	mogués	dormís	servís
	pl	1	+pregàssem	batéssem	moguéssem	dormíssem	+servíssem
		2	+pregàssets	+batéssets	+moguéssets	+dormíssets	+servíssets
		3	pregassen	batessen	moguessen	dormissen	servissen

282 MAX W. WHEELER

Conjugation I

c. 1500		'ask'	IIa 'strike'	IIb 'move'	IIIa 'sleep'	IIIb 'serve'
PrI sg	1	^pregue	bat	moc	dorm	servesc
	2	pregues	bats	mous	dorms	serveixes
	3	prega	bat	mou	dorm	serveix
pl	1	pregam	batem	movem	dormim	servim
	2	pregau	bateu	moveu	dormiu	serviu
	3	preguen	baten	^mouen	dormen	serveixen
Imp sg	2	prega	bat	mou	dorm	+serveix
pl	1	preguem	batam	mogam	dormam	sirvam
	2	^pregau	^bateu	^moveu	^dormiu	^serviu
PrS sg	1	^pregue	bata	moga	dorma	servesca
	2	^pregues	bates	mogues	dormes	servesques
	3	^pregue	bata	moga	dorma	+servesca
pl	1	preguem	batam	mogam	dormam	+sirvam
	2	pregueu	batau	mogau	dormau	+sirvau
	3	preguen	baten	moguen	dormen	servesquen
PsI sg	1	^preguí	batí	^moguí	dormí	serví
	2	^pregares	^bateres	^mogueres	^dormires	^servires
	3	pregà	baté	^mogué	dormí	serví
pl	1	^pregàrem	^batérem	^moguérem	^dormírem	^servírem
	2	^pregàreu	^batéreu	^moguéreu	^dormíreu	^servíreu
	3	pregaren	bateren	mogueren	dormiren	serviren
PsS sg	1	pregàs	batés	mogués	dormís	servís
	2	pregasses	batesses	moguesses	dormisses	servisses
	3	pregàs	batés	mogués	dormís	servís
pl	1	pregàssem	batéssem	moguéssem	dormíssem	servíssem
	2	pregàsseu	batésseu	moguésseu	dormísseu	servísseu
	3	pregassen	batessen	moguessen	dormissen	servissen

INFLECTIONAL AFFIX REPLACEMENT 283

NOW							
PrI	sg 1	ˆprego	ˆbato	moc	ˆdormo	ˆserveixo
	2	pregues	bats	mous	dorms	serveixes
	3	prega	bat	mou	dorm	serveix
	pl 1	ˆpreguem	batem	movem	dormim	servim
	2	ˆpregueu	bateu	moveu	dormiu	serviu
	3	preguen	baten	mouen	dormen	serveixen
Imp	sg 2	prega	bat	mou	dorm	serveix
	pl 1	preguem	ˆbatem	ˆmoguem	ˆdormim	ˆservim
	2	ˆpregueu	bateu	moveu	dormiu	serviu
PrS	sg 1	ˆpregui	ˆbati	ˆmogui	ˆdormi	ˆserveixi
	2	ˆpreguis	ˆbatis	ˆmoguis	ˆdormis	ˆserveixis
	3	ˆpregui	ˆbati	ˆmogui	ˆdormi	ˆserveixi
	pl 1	preguem	ˆbatem	ˆmoguem	ˆdormim	ˆservim
	2	pregueu	ˆbateu	ˆmogueu	ˆdormiu	ˆserviu
	3	ˆpreguin	ˆbatin	ˆmoguin	ˆdormin	ˆserveixin
PsI	sg 1	vaig pregar	vaig batre	vaig moure	vaig dormir	vaig servir
	2	vas/vares pregar	vas/vares batre	vas/vares moure	vas/vares dormir	vas/vares servir
	3	va pregar	va batre	va moure	va dormir	va servir
	pl 1	vam/vàrem pregar	vam/vàrem batre	vam/vàrem moure	vam/vàrem dormir	vam/vàrem servir
	2	vau/vàreu pregar	vau/vàreu batre	vau/vàreu moure	vau/vàreu dormir	vau/vàreu servir
	3	van/varen pregar	van/varen batre	van/varen moure	van/varen dormir	van/varen servir
PsS	sg 1	ˆpregués	batés	mogués	dormís	servís
	2	ˆpreguessis	ˆbatessis	ˆmoguessis	ˆdormissis	ˆservissis
	3	ˆpregués	batés	mogués	ˆdormís	servís
	pl 1	ˆpreguéssim	ˆbatéssim	ˆmoguéssim	ˆdormíssim	ˆservíssim
	2	ˆpreguéssiu	ˆbatéssiu	ˆmoguéssiu	ˆdormíssiu	ˆservíssiu
	3	ˆpreguessin	ˆbatessin	ˆmoguessin	ˆdormissin	ˆservissin

RUSSIAN CONJUGATION:
ACQUISITION AND EVOLUTIVE CHANGE

HENNING ANDERSEN
University of Copenhagen

0.0. In this paper I wish to examine a problem in the description of Russian conjugation in the light of two kinds of data, from the history of the language and from the acquisition of Russian as a first language. I have two aims. First, I would like to determine how in reality speakers of Russian account for a certain morphophonemic alternation in their internalized grammars, and I hope to show that data of the kinds I will examine here have a bearing on this question. Second, I would like to contribute to the clarification of the respects in which language acquisition data can be correlated with diachronic data.

0.1. I assume that a speaker's internalized grammar can be understood as a composite system in which one can distinguish -- for each level of linguistic structure -- between a structured core system and an additive system of rules accounting for the norms of usage in all respects in which these are not directly derivable from the relations that constitute the core system. This is a conception of grammar which has fairly close parallels in various European structuralist schools and which most recently has been elaborated by Coseriu (e.g., 1952, 1969).

0.2. On this assumption, one can view the task any language learner sets for himself as consisting (a) in the formation of a system of relations that forms the core of his linguistic competence, and which embodies what is motivated and productive in his language, and (b) in the formulation of special rules (adaptive rules, in the sense of Andersen 1973) which permit him to adjust his speech to what he perceives to be the norms of his speech community. It should be mentioned that while language learners perhaps form the structured parts of their linguistic competence exclusively during their preadolescent years, the business of elaborating and revising the systems of adaptive devices to make these account for the perceived usage of the community goes on throughout a speaker's life, regardless of whether he actively takes others as his models or not. The crude distinction between 'children' and 'adults' customarily made in discussions of language acquisition and language change is of no value in principle. In some contexts it should be replaced by the distinction between learners acquiring language structure and learners acquiring adaptive devices; in other contexts it seems preferable to speak simply of learners and their models.

Against this background, deviating forms occurring in child speech can be evaluated as evidence for (a) the hypotheses the learner formulates regarding the structured core system, or any revisions of these, or for (b) inadequately conceived adaptive rules. The gradual disappearance of deviating forms, on the other hand, may be taken as evidence either for (a) an appropriate revision of the core system or for (b) the formulation of adequate adaptive devices.

0.3. As for diachronic data -- provided these reflect the transmission of a language from generation to generation without interference from significantly different systems -- they can be interpreted as evidence for structural innovations or innovations in the effects or domains of adaptive rules. Since speakers rely on their conception of the structure of the language in all respects where they do not know the norms, innovations which deviate from the established norms can often be taken as evidence for the structured core system at the time in question, and long term trends in the development of a language can often be understood as a gradual modification of the norms, by which -- in some specific respect -- these are brought into greater conformity with the structure of the language.

1.0. The question I want to examine in this paper is the chief point in Jakobson's (1948) description of Russian conjugation, the morphophonemic process of truncation.

Almost all Russian verbs have two stem alternants, one ending in a consonant, occurring before desinences beginning with a vowel (or Ø alternating with a vowel) -- for short, the prevocalic stem; and one alternant ending in a vowel, occurring before desinences beginning with a consonant -- the preconsonantal stem. In some verbs, the prevocalic stem is the longer of the two (cf. (1a)), which suggests the generalization in (1b). In other verbs, the

preconsonantal alternant is the longer (cf. (2a)), which
suggests the generalization in (2b).

(1a) Verb types with longer prevocalic stem alternant.

	I-1	I-2	I-3	I-4	I-5
Infinitive	zná --t,	stá --t,	ží --t,	m,os--t,í	v,os--t,í
Past masc.	zná --l	stá --l	ží --l	m,ó --l	v,ó --l
Pres. 3 pl.	znáj--ut	stán--ut	živ--út	m,ot--út	v,od--út
Imperative	znáj--∅	stán,--∅	živ,--í	m,ot,--í	v,od,--í

(1b) Generalization: C → ∅ / __ --C

(2a) Verb types with longer preconsonantal stem alternant.

	II-1	II-2	II-3	II-4	II-5
Infinitive	stáv,i--t,	s,id,é--t,	p,isá--t,	koló--t,	tonú--t,
Past masc.	stáv,i--l	s,id,é--l	p,isá--l	koló--l	tonú--l
Pres. 3 pl.	stáv, --at	s,id, --át	p,iš --ut	kól,--ut	tón --ut
Imperative	stáv, --∅	s,id, --í	p,iš --í	kol,--í	ton,--í

(2b) Generalization: V → ∅ / __ --$\begin{Bmatrix} V \\ \emptyset \end{Bmatrix}$

Jakobson combined these generalizations into a single
phonologically conditioned morphophonemic process, truncation, and postulated for each Russian verb as its basic
stem (or 'full-stem', as he termed it) the alternant from
which the other could be derived by this and other morphophonemic processes. See, for example:

(3) 'Full stems' of the verbs in (1a) and (2a):

| znáj-- | stán-- | živ-- | m,ot-- | v,od-- |
| stáv,i-- | s,id,é-- | p,isa-- | kolo-- | tonu-- |

Thus, Jakobson cut through the century old controversy over
whether the infinitive stem or the present tense stem should
be taken as primary in a classification of Russian verbs,
citing as the motto for his article Bloomfield's well known
argument in favor of the principle of simplicity:

> We have seen that when forms are partially similar, there may
> be a question as to which one we had better take as the un-
> derlying form, and that the structure of the language may
> decide this question for us, since, taking it one way, we
> get an unduly complicated description, and, taking it the
> other way, a relatively simple one (Bloomfield 1933:218).

In 1951, Halle showed that this model of description can be applied to Old Russian as well.[1]

After it has been established that truncation is the simplest way of accounting for the segment/zero alternations according to 'the structure of the language' itself, i.e., in a description of a corpus of verb forms, the God's truth linguist will wonder if such a description corresponds to the speakers' conception of these alternations. To answer this question one can take the given description as a hypothesis and try to confirm it or disconfirm it by confronting it with further data from the language.

As it happens, there are data available on three dynamic dimensions of this language which are relevant to this hypothesis: (1) differences in the conjugation of a number of verbs between Old Russian and modern Russian and its dialects, specifically concerning the stem final segment/zero alternations; (2) deviating forms in child speech which can be interpreted as diagnostic for the rules a language learner formulates as he acquires the morphophonemic system of the Russian verb; and (3) stylistic variation between alternative forms of a number of verbs in contemporary standard Russian which reflect a change in progress. We will look at these in turn.

2.0. From a historical point of view, the hypothesis that stem alternants were produced by truncation in Old Russian as in modern Russian -- and this hypothesis must evidently be extended to cover all intervening stages of the language -- is somewhat problematic. There have been innovations in stem final segment/zero alternations in a number of verbs both in the standard language and in Russian dialects, but contrary to what one might expect from the truncation hypothesis, most of these innovations have consisted in the addition either of a vowel, to form a new preconsonantal stem, or of a consonant, to form a new prevocalic stem. See (4).[2]

(4) Innovations in stem final segment/zero alternations in CSR and Russian dialects.

Historically expected forms	New preconsonantal stem by V-addition	by C-deletion	New prevocalic stem by C-addition	by V-deletion	
$ví$ --t, $vój$--ut	$vója$--t, $vój$ --ut				'twist'
$krí$ --t, $krój$--ut		$kró$ --t, $krój$--ut			'cover'

RUSSIAN CONJUGATION   289

br,í --t,		br,é --t,	br,í--t,	'shave'
br,éj--ut		br,éj--ut	br, --át	
p,é--t,	p,éja--t,	p,é --t,		'sing'
poj--út	p,ej --út	p,éj--ut		
čú --t,	čúja--t,			'feel'
čúj--ut	čúj --ut			
r,ú --t,	r,ev,é--t,			'roar'
r,ev--út	r,ev --út			
žd--t,	žmd--t,			'press'
žm--út	žm --út			
m,d́--t,	mnd--t,			'crumple'
mn --út	mn --út			
dú--t,	dmd--t,	dm,í--t,	dú --t,	'blow'
dm--út	dm --út	dm, --át	dúj--ut	
p,er,é--t,	prd--t,			'force one's way'
pr --út	pr --út			
t,er,é--t,	trá--t,			'rub'
tr --út	tr --út			
gn,es--t,í	gn,et,í--t,			'oppress'
gn,et--út	gn,et, --át			
žé--č	žgd--t,	žgá --t,		'burn'
žg--út	žg --út	žgáj--ut		
gnd--t,		gná --t,		'drive'
žen--út		gnáj--ut		
sosd--t,	sós,i--t,			'suck'
sos--út	sós, --at			
jéxa--t,		jéxa --t,		'ride'
jéd --ut		jéxaj--ut		
davd--t,		davá --t,		'give'
daj --út		daváj--ut		
sm,ejd--t,-sa	sm,é --t,-sa			'laugh'
sm,ej --út-sa	sm,ej--út-sa			
ugor,é--t,		ugor,é --t,		'suffocate'
ugor, --át		ugor,éj--ut		
smotr,é--t,	smotr,í--t,			'look'
smótr, --at	smótr, --at			

Some verbs, e.g., dú--t,/dm--út appear to have developed
reflexes in different Russian dialects exemplifying both
alternatives, contrast dú--t,/dúj--ut (thus Contemporary
Standard Russian) and dmd--t,/dm--út. Some have apparently

developed longer stems first by vowel addition and subsequently by consonant addition, cf. the historically expected žē--č/žj--át with the dialectal žgá--t,/žg--át and žgá--t,/žgáj--ut. Innovations involving segment deletion are few, surprisingly few if one assumes that a truncation rule has been productive through the entire historical development of the language.

The historical data evidently do not confirm the truncation hypothesis. On the other hand, they do not clearly disconfirm it, for one may suppose that learners who have a truncation rule as part of their morphophonemic system would be used to interpreting the stems of unfamiliar verbs as produced by truncation and would complement their truncation rule with a strategy to posit longer underlying stems than the ones actually encountered. If innovated forms of all the types represented in (4) have to be accounted for, it seems that one must hypothesize for the grammars of the speakers of this language either both segment deletion and segment addition rules or one or the other type of rule and a learner's strategy with the opposite effect.

With these various possibilities in mind we can approach the language acquisition data.

3.0. In Gvozdev's well known longitudinal study (1949) verb forms deviating from the norms of the standard language are recorded between the ages of 2.0 and 7.7, the majority occurring during the child's third year. Tables (5) and (6), which are intended as exhaustive lists of forms deviating with respect to preconsonantal and prevocalic stems, show at a glance that segment addition is used much more than segment deletion.[4]

3.1. Preconsonantal stems are formed by the addition of *i* (24 infinitives, 11 preterites), *a* (3 infinitives, 3 preterites), *e* (1 infinitive, 1 preterite), and *u* (1 preterite).

(5a) Infinitive formed from prevocalic stem by vowel addition.

Age recorded	Deviating forms	Normal forms	Prevocalic stems	
2;0.13	doxn,ít,	doxnú--t,	doxn--át	'breathe'
2;0.22	p,ít,	spá--t,	sp, --át	'sleep'
2;0.24	tučít,	stučá--t,	stuč--át	'knock'

2;0.27	rost,ít,	ro--st,í	rost--út	'grow'
2;1.4	dad,ít,	dá--t,	dad--út	'give'
2;1.8	páxn,it,	páxnu--t,	páxn--ut	'smell'
2;1.9	motr,ít,	smotr,é--t,	smótr,--at	'look'
2;2.8	klad,ít,	klá--st,	klad--út	'put'
2;2.22	sor,ít,	sorvá--t,	sorv--út	'pluck'
2;2.25	amn,ít,	vz,á--t,	voz,m--út	'take'
2;2.25	gon,ít	gná--t,	gón,--at	'chase'
2;3.9	b,er,ít,	brá--t,	b,er--út	'take'
2;3.9	sún,it,	súnu--t,	sún--ut	'stick'
2;4.26	iščít,	iská--t,	išč--ut	'look for'
2;5.7	upad,ít,	upá--st,	upad--út	'fall'
2;5.26	raspor,ít,	rozporó--t,	rozpór,--ut	'unstitch'
2;6.7	vík,in,it,	vík,inu--t,	vík,in--ut	'throw out'
2;7.5	razv,edát,	rozv,o--st,í	rozv,od--út	'mix'
2;8.18	tópčit,	toptá--t,	tópč--ut	'trample'
2;8.27	kol,ít,	koló--t,	kól,--ut	'pierce'
2;9.16	pliv,ít,	plí--t,	pliv--út	'sail'
2;9.25	zapr,ít,	zap,er,é--t,	zapr--út	'lock'
2;9.21	pr,igotóvl,it,	-gotóv,i--t,	-gotóvl,--u	'make'
2.10.23	pozov,ít,	pozvá--t,	pozov--út	'call'
2;11.7	mn,át,	m,á--t,	mn--út	'crumple'
3;0.8	rójit,	rí--t,	rój--ut	'dig'
2;0.8	soskr,ebát,	soskr,o--st,í	soskr,ob--út	'scrape off'
5;7.14	tr,ét,	t,er,é--t,	tr--út	'rub'

(5b) Preterite formed from prevocalic stem by vowel addition.

2;1.1	d,énula	d,é--l-a	d,én--ut	'put'
2;1.1	b,egála	b,ežá--l-a	b,eg--út	'run'
2;2.22	gon,íl,i	gná--l,-i	gón,--at	'chase'
2;2.25	pl,ún,il,i	pl,únu--l,-i	pl,ún--ut	'spit'
2;2.25	gon,íl	gná--l	gón,--at	'chase'
2;2.28	sor,íl	sorvá--l	sorv--út	'pluck'

2;2.29	zaprál	záp,or	zapr--út	'lock'
2;4.25	búxn,il	búxnu--l	búxn--ut	'go bang'
2;4.25	glóxn,il	glóxnu--l	glóxn--ut	'go deaf'
2;6.1	otkol,íl	otkoló--l	otkól,--ut	'break off'
2;7.17	dogon,íl	dogná--l	dogón,--at	'catch'
2;9.8	zaprála	zap,or--l-á	zapr--út	'lock'
3;0.1	grábl,ila	gráb,i--l-a	grábl,--u	'grab'
3;2.11	vím,et,il,i	vím,o--l,-i	vím,ot--ut	'sweep'
3;4.27	zamn,íla	zam,á--l-a	zamn--út	'crumple up'
3;6.20	tr,él,is,	t,ór--l,-i-s,	tr--út-sa	'rub'

(5c) Infinitive formed from prevocalic stem by consonant deletion.

2;3.8	celút,	celová--t,	celúj--ut	'kiss'
2;2.29	r,isút,	r,isová--t,	r,isúj--ut	'draw'

(5d) Preterite formed from prevocalic stem by consonant deletion.

3;3.22	kl,ul,í	kl,ová--l,-i	kl,uj--út	'bite'
3;6.9	pl,úl	pl,ová--l	pl,uj--út	'spit'

A few of these forms can be interpreted as incorrectly acquired normal forms, e.g., *rost,it,* (2;0.27) for *ro--st,i,*, *mn,át,* (2;11.7) for *m,á--t,*, *tr,ét,* (5;7.14) for *t,er,é--t,*, but most of them are unmistakably original formations with no support in normal forms and clearly derived from actual prevocalic stems. In two instances stem alternants specific to the 1st sg. of the present tense are involved, *pr,igotóvl,it,* (2;9.21) and *grábl,ila* (3;0.1).

The predominance of *i* as the vowel added to form preconsonantal stems may be due to the high frequency of verbs with infinitive and preterite stems in *i* in the standard language, but it may -- alternatively or additionally -- be conditioned by the fact that the imperative of all verbs with unstressed stems or stems ending in a consonant cluster ends in --*i*, e.g., *motr,it,* (2;1.9) for *smotr,é--t,*, imperative *smotr,--i*, *iščít,* (2;4.26) for *iská--t,*, imperative *išč--i*.

The corpus contains only four examples of preconsonantal stems formed by truncation (cf. (5c) and (5d)), all belonging to the same verb type, in which a preconsonantal *-ova-* alternates with a prevocalic *-uj-*.

RUSSIAN CONJUGATION   293

3.2 Prevocalic stems are formed by the addition of
j to actual preconsonantal stems ending in a (25 present
tense forms, 5 imperatives), i ($kónčiju$ (2;5.9)), e ($p,éj$
(2;8.14), and o ($porój$(2;10.27)).

(6a) Present tense formed from preconsonantal stem by j-addition.

Age Recorded	Deviating form	Normal form	Preconsonantal stems	
2;0.13	p,isáju	p,iš--ú	p,isá--t,	'write'
2;1.2	tajájet	vstaj--ót	vstavá--t,	'get up'
2;1.2	p,isájet	p,iš--ot	p,isá--t,	'write'
2;2.10	m,áju	mn--ú	m,á--t,	'crumple'
2;2.4	poloskáju	pološč--ú	poloská--t,	'rinse'
2;2.8	p,jatáju	spr,áč--u	spr,áta--t,	'hide'
2;2.13	sosájet	sos,--ót	sosá--t,	'suck'
2;2.14	sosájut	sos--út	sosá--t	'suck'
2;3.16	amn,ú	voz,m--ú	vz,á--t,	'take'
2;4.17	vz,áju	voz,m--ú	vz,á--t,	'take'
2;4.25	az,mú	voz,m--ú	vz,á--t,	'take'
2;4.19	poloskáju	pološč--ú	poloská--t,	'rinse'
2;4.30	vz,ájem	voz,m,--óm	vz,á--t,	'take'
2;5.9	kónčiju	kónč--u	kónči--t,	'finish'
2;5.9	pr,ičesájus,	pr,ičeš--ú-s,	pr,ičesá--t,-sa	'comb'
2;6.17	iskáju	išč--ú	iská--t,	'look for'
2;9.21	daváju	daj--ú	davá--t,	'give'
2;9.1	celováješ	celúj--oš	celová--t,	'kiss'
2;9.28	daváješ	daj--óš	davá--t,	'give'
2;9.28	davájet	daj--ót	davá--t,	'give'
2;10.26	plákajut	pláč--ut	pláka--t,	'cry'
2;11.8	ub,ežáju	ub,eg--ú	ub,ežá--t,	'run away'
2;11.28	daváju	daj--ú	davá--t,	'give'
3;0.23	ščeb,etájet	ščeb,éč--ot	ščeb,etá--t,	'chirp'
3;4.28	zvájut	zov--út	zvá--t,	'call'
3;3.29 4;10.1	zav,ájut	zav,án--ut	zav,á--l	'wither'
6;6.1	vijexajet	vijed,--ot	vijexa--t,	'drive out'

(6b) Imperative formed from preconsonantal stem by j-addition.

2;0.25	kas,áj	skaž--í	skazá--t,	'tell'
2;0.13	p,isáj	p,iš--í	p,isá--t,	'write'
2;4.24	poiskáj	poišč--í	poiská--t,	'look for'
2;8.14	p,éj	pój--∅	p,é--t,	'sing'
2;9.13	nar,isováj	nar,isúj--∅	nar,isová--t,	'draw'
2;10.27	porój	por,--í	poró--t,	'unstitch'
6;6.3	sošíj	sšéj--∅	sší--t,	'sew'
6;6.10	jéxaj	pojezžáj--∅	jéxa--t,	'ride'

(6c) Present tense formed from preconsonantal stem by vowel deletion.

3;0.15	nabr,ú	nabr,éj--u	nabr,í--t,	'shave'
3;4.19	nan,ím	najm,--óm	nan,á--t,	'hire'
3;6.27	torgajú	torgúju	torgová--t,	'trade'
4;8.21	obodrú	obd,er--ú	obodrá--t,	'skin'
6;6.18	st,er,ótsa	sotr,--ót-sa	st,er,é--t,-sa	'erase'
7;7.8	st,erú	sotr--ú	st,er,é--t,	'erase'

(6d) Imperative formed from preconsonantal stem by vowel deletion.

2;3.9	tróg	trógaj--∅	tróga--t,	'touch'
2;10.27	pór,	por,--í	poró--t,	'unstitch'
3;0.13	otodr,í	otd,er,--í	otodrá--t,	'peel off'
7;6.5	zap,er,í	zapr,--í	zap,er,é--t,	'lock'

The predominance of formations with j added to a preconsonantal a correlates nicely with the most productive and most frequent verb type in the language, type I-1 in (1a).

But there are also prevocalic stems formed by vowel deletion. The present tense forms in (6c) are clearly original formations presupposing a vowel deletion procedure. torgajú (3;6.27) is particularly interesting as an indication that the conjugation of verbs of the type davat, has been mastered (cf. (6a) 2;1.2, 2;9.21, 2;9.28, 2;11.28), and as evidence that the child can derive the present tense of these verbs from the preconsonantal stem by deleting -va- and adding j without recourse to the imperative, which in Jakobson's description contains the 'full-stem'; cf. (7).

(7) Infinitive   davá--t,   torgová--t,
    Past masc.   davá--l   torgová--l
    Pres. 1 sg. daj --ú   torgajú   torgúj --u
    Imperative   daváj--∅   torgúj --∅

Among the imperative forms, the early *trog* (2;3.9) -- a bare verb root -- does not conform to any pattern in the language. The form *pór*, (2;10.27) is recorded the same day as the alternative *porój* (cf. (6b)); it is the earliest form indicating that the learner has discovered that prevocalic stems can be derived by vowel deletion.

The forms in (6c) and (6d) exemplify deletion of *i*, *e*, *a*, and *o*.

3.3. The child speech data suggest conclusions of two kinds.

First, segment addition is by far the most frequently used procedure for deriving new stems. It is used throughout the period in which deviating forms occur.

Secondly, of the two ways of forming preconsonantal stems, vowel addition is well represented, but ceases to be used by about age 3;0 with the exception of two forms of the verb *t,er,é--t,*, which may be based on a misremembered normal infinitive stem; the examples of consonant deletion are few and sporadic. By contrast, both the ways of forming prevocalic stems have the appearance of established patterns. Yod addition is established early; it is productive from age 2;0 on, the last deviating form being recorded at 6;6.10. Vowel deletion seems to be acquired later; it is in evidence from age 2;10 on, with the last deviating form recorded at 7;7.8.

Since it goes without saying that conclusions based on a single child's speech cannot simply be assumed to be relevant for all speakers, let it be emphasized instead that

(a) this analysis demonstrates that child speech data can be brought to bear on questions like the one under consideration, and that even data from a single learner can yield definite indications as to the validity of descriptive hypotheses.

(b) These data in particular offer no support for the general truncation hypothesis derived from Jakobson's description.

(c) They show the historically attested innovations discussed in sec. 2 can arise as the result of a learner's procedure to derive new stems by segment addition.

(d) They suggest that a learner may master the stem final segment/zero alternation by a combination of two rules, *j*-addition and vowel deletion.

It is hard to say how much more complicated this solution is than Jakobson's wholesale truncation rule. But one thing is clear: it allows for qualitatively different basic stems. While Jakobson's 'full-stems' are purely morphophonemic constructs with no grammatical identity -- some of them, being purely artificial forms, lack phonological identity as well -- the combination of *j*-addition and vowel deletion makes it possible to derive all conjugational forms of the vast majority of Russian verbs from the stem of the infinitive, a phonologically real form whose grammatical content makes it particularly fit to represent the verb and to serve as its natural citation form (cf. Jakobson 1932).

4.0. In sec. 3.3 it was noted that *j*-addition is attested in the child speech data from the earliest deviating forms recorded, whereas vowel deletion is in evidence only from age 2;10 on. One cannot make much of this difference on the basis of this small corpus, but it so happens that this apparent difference between a primary and a secondary procedure for forming prevocalic stems correlates with a well documented stylistic variation in modern Russian, to which we now turn.

4.1. In standard Russian, a number of verbs with preconsonantal stem in *a* (see (8a)) occur more or less freely with alternative prevocalic stems, a shorter one -- apparently formed by vowel deletion (and with a concomitant consonant alternation), and a longer one -- apparently formed by *j*-addition; see the sample paradigms in (8b).

(8a) *alkát*, 'crave', *brízgat*, 'splash', *glodát*, 'gnaw', *dvígat*, 'move', *kápat*, drip', *kl,epát*, 'malign', *kl,íkat*, 'call', *kolixát*, 'rock', *krápat*, 'spit (of rain)*, kudáxtat*, 'cackle', *maxát*, 'wave', *m,etát*, 'throw', *murlíkat*, 'purr', *míkat*, 'suffer', *m,aúkat*, 'meow', *pl,eskát*, 'splash', *poloskát*, 'rinse', *prískat*, 'sprinkle', *rískat*, 'rove', *tíkat*, 'poke', *xníkat*, 'whimper', *ščepát*, 'splinter',*ščipát*, 'pinch' (Vinogradov 1953: 554).

(8b) Sample paradigms (cf. II-3 in (2a) and I-1 in (1a)).

Infinitive	dv,íga--t,		maxá--t,	
Past masc.	dv,íga--l		maxá--l	
Pres. 3 pl.	dv,íž--ut	dv,ígaj-ut	máš--ut	maxáj--ut
Imperative	---------	dv,ígaj--∅	maš--í	maxáj--∅
Gerund	---------	dv,ígaj--a	maš--á	maxáj--a
Pres.act.ptc.	dv,íž--ušč-ij	dv,ígaj--ušč-ij	máš--ušč-ij	maxáj--ušč-ij

In some verbs, the alternative stems are associated with different contextual meanings; the shorter stem is in such verbs used in more abstract or figurative senses, while the longer stem is used in concrete, literal senses. In some verbs, such a semantic distinction is possible only in colloquial usage, whereas in formal style the shorter stems are used also in concrete, literal senses. In some verbs, the two stems are associated only with a stylistic difference, the shorter stem being appropriate in more formal, the longer in less formal styles (cf. Vinogradov 1953:554-5). In a number of verbs, the use of the alternative stems is ceteris paribus correlated with the sociolinguistic variables of age and level of education, the shorter stems being used more by older than by younger speakers, more by better educated than by less well educated speakers (Krysin 1974:199-205). For a synchronic description it is particularly important to note that shorter and longer alternative stems may have different stylistic values in different grammatical forms of the same verb; cf. the entries for *alkát,, kolixát,, maxát,, murlíkat,, pl,eskát,, poloskát,, rískat,* in Avanesov & Ožegov 1960. It must also be noted that in some verbs not all grammatical forms can be made with the shorter stem (cf. (8b)). This is due to the fact that the shorter stems tend to occur in relatively fixed collocations and hence to be limited to certain grammatical forms (especially the 3rd sg.); cf. Vinogradov (1953:556). The longer stems are subject to no morphological restrictions.

The synchronic situation of these verbs has all the earmarks of a change in progress. Synchronic grammars mention that the current variation in the 1700's-1800's embraced a number of verbs which now only have prevocalic stems ending in *j* (Vinogradov 1953:554). In fact, a change of verbs from type II-3 (cf. (2a)) to type I-1 (cf. (1a)) has been in progress throughout the attested history of Russian (cf. Kiparsky 1967:208ff.), and one can safely assume that at all times during the last thousand years a number of verbs have exhibited the kinds of variation outlined above.

4.2. The state of affairs sketched in sec. 4.1 is incompatible with a descriptive hypothesis which posits one 'full-stem' for each verb and accounts for stem final segment/zero alternations uniformly with a rule of truncation.

To preserve the truncation hypothesis one could postulate two 'full-stems' for each of the verbs in (8a). This would produce a static description of a patently dynamic situation at the cost of abandoning the notion of a basic stem.

Alternatively one can take the infinitive stem of all verbs as basic and admit two processes for deriving prevocalic stems, vowel deletion -- productive for stems in i, u (types II-1 and II-5), and $-ova-$, but unproductive (i.e., depending for its application on lexical markings) for other stems in a; and j-addition -- productive for stems in a other than those in $-ova-$.[5] This descriptive hypothesis agrees well with the attested tendency for verbs of type II-3 (and also of other types, cf. sec. 2) to acquire new prevocalic stems in j, and obviously it agrees with the available evidence for the order in which j-addition and vowel deletion are acquired by the Russian child.

5.1. In this paper I have tried to do two things.

I have adduced some language acquisition data and some evidence from the history of Russian, including evidence for a change in progress, reflected in synchronic variation, which shed light on the stem final segment/zero alternations which are central to the morphophonemics of the Russian verb. Although these alternations can be described uniformly as the result of deletion rules, the two kinds of evidence indicate that the speakers of this language account for them by a combination of segment addition and segment deletion rules.

At the same time, the data that have been examined show how an on-going change, by which an unproductive morphophonemic pattern is replaced by a productive one, can be found reflected in child speech. The ages at which the child produces deviating forms of one and the other kind show that the productive pattern for stems in a is acquired early, whereas the unproductive pattern, which is dependent on adaptive devices, comes in later.

A number of questions that the material examined in the preceding sections raises cannot be discussed here. But it has been shown that acquisition data can be correlated with historical evidence and can be of value in determining the validity of descriptive hypotheses.

5.2. On a more general level, this study may, together with others, contribute to an understanding of how language acquisition strategies determine evolutive change in morphophonemics.

It was pointed out in sec. 2.3 that the eventual combination of addition and deletion rules evidenced by the child speech data indicates that the learner's choice of basic stems may be motivated by grammatical meaning. This conclusion is in accord with the programmatic statement of Vennemann (1972:237) and with recent findings of several studies of the acquisition of morphophonemics synthesized in Bybee Hooper (1978). These findings provide an explanation for several of the general tendencies of morphophonemic change formulated by Mańczak (1963).

As for the rules operating on the basic stems, it is remarkable that the acquisition of vowel deletion is preceded by a period in which both preconsonantal and prevocalic stems are derived by segment addition. The historical evidence surveyed in sec. 1 shows that this preference for segment addition is not idiosyncratic with this one learner. It can perhaps be understood as a corollary of a learner's strategy to retain as much of the phonological material of known stems as possible in the derivation of new stems. If there is such a strategy, which seems reasonable, it will have a bearing on the general viability of addition and deletion rules in diachrony. It would lead one to expect that deletion rules will be more subject to curtailment and loss than addition rules and will more often be reinterpreted as addition rules than vice versa. These predictions we will leave for future investigations to confirm or disconfirm.

NOTES

[1] An evaluation of the impact of this influential article is offered by Matejka (1975:17-20). Thelin (1975) cites most of the literature on Russian conjugation which directly or indirectly is inspired by Jakobson (1948). For more recent treatments with selective bibliographies, see Flier (1978) and Shapiro (MS).

[2] The data are from Bromlej & Bulatova (1972).

[3] There is clear evidence from many Russian dialects that the truncation rule has been curtailed in the formation of infinitives from obstruent stems. Cf. Flier (1978).

[4] The deviating forms from Gvozdev (1949) are cited following Gvozdev's phonetic transcription. The normal forms, as well as all other forms cited in this paper, are given in a phonemic transcription.

[5] The productive verb types of Russian are types I-1, II-1, II-5, and the type in -*ova*-. It is remarkable that the unproductive, lexically infrequent types I-2, I-3, I-4, and I-5, which count heavily in favor of consonant deletion (the generalization in (1b)) are hardly represented among the deviating forms of the acquisition data. The high text frequency of these types might make it possible for learners to acquire their segment/zero alternations prior to the formulation of the *j*-addition and vowel deletion rules. When they change, however, they usually provide evidence that in these verbs, the infinitive stem is derived from a prevocalic stem. Cf. Flier (1978).

REFERENCES

Andersen, Henning. 1973. "Abductive and deductive change". *Lg*.49.567-95.

Avanesov, R.I. and S.I. Ožegov. 1960. *Russkoe literaturnoe proiznošenie i udarenie. Slovar'-spravočnik*. Moscow: Gos. izd. in. i nac. slovarej.

Bloomfield, Leonard. 1933. *Language*. New York: Holt.

Bromlej, S.V. and L.N. Bulatova. 1972. *Očerki morfologii russkix govorov*. Moskow: Nauka.

Bybee Hooper, Joan. 1978. "Child morphology and morphophonemic change". *Buffalo papers in linguistics*, 1(2).38-84. To appear in *Recent developments in historical morphology*. Ed. by Jacek Fisiak. Paris and the Hague: Mouton-DeGruyter.

Coseriu, Eugenio. 1952."Sistema, norma y habla".*Revista de la Facultad de Humanidades y Sciencias* 9.113-77, Montevideo. Reprinted in his *Teoria del lenguaje y lingüistica general*, 11-113. Madrid: Editorial Gredos, 1961. Trans. as "System, Norm und Rede", *Sprachtheorie und allgemeine Sprachwissenschaft*, 11-101. Munich: Fink, 1975.

―――. 1969. "Sistema, norma e 'parola'". *Studi linguistici in onore di Vittorio Pisani*, I, 235-53. Brescia. Trans. as "System, Norm und 'Rede'" in his *Sprache. Strukturen und Funktionen*, 53-72. Ed. by Uwe Petersen, Tübingen: T.B.L., 1971.

Flier, Michael S. 1978."Is *Kljast'* iconoclastic?" *Studia linguistica... A.V. Issatschenko ... oblata*, 111-27. Ed. by L'ubomír Ďurovič et al. Lisse: De Ridder.

Gvozdev, A.N. 1949. *Formirovanie u rebenka grammatičeskogo stroja russkogo jazyka*, I-II. Moscow: Izd. Ak. Ped. Nauk RSFSR.

Halle, Morris. 1951. "The Old Church Slavonic conjugation (with an appendix on the Old Russian conjugation)". *Word* 7.155-67.

Jakobson, Roman. 1932. "Zur Struktur des russischen Verbums". *Charisteria Guilelmo Mathesio quinquagenario .. oblata*, 74-84. Prague. Reprinted in Jakobson 1971:3-15.
―――. 1948. "Russian conjugation". *Word* 4.155-67. Reprinted in Jakobson 1971:119-29.
―――. 1971. *Selected Writings, II. Word and language.* The Hague: Mouton.
Kiparsky, Valentin. 1967. *Russische historische Grammatik, II, Die Entwicklung des Formensystems.* Heidelberg: Winter.
Krysin, L.P. 1974. *Russkij jazyk po dannym massovogo obsledovanija. Opyt social'no-lingvističeskogo izučenija.* Moscow: Nauka.
Mańczak, Witold. 1963. "Tendances générales du développement morphologique". *Lingua* 12.19-38.
Matejka, Ladislav. 1975. *Crossroads of sound and meaning.* Lisse: De Ridder.
Shapiro, Michael. MS. "Russian conjugation: theory and hermeneutic".
Thelin, Nils B. 1975. *Towards a theory of verb stem formation and conjugation in Modern Russian* (=Acta Universitatis Upsaliensis, Studia Slavica Upsaliensia, 17). Uppsala: Almquist & Wiksell.
Vennemann, Theo. 1972. "Rule inversion". *Lingua* 20.209-42.
Vinogradov, V.V. 1953. *Grammatika russkogo jazyka, I. Fonetika i morfologija.* Moscow: Izd. AN SSSR.

SOUND CHANGE AND CHILD LANGUAGE

MARILYN MAY VIHMAN
Stanford University

0. *Introduction.* A time-honored tradition in linguistic theory holds that the sources of language change must ultimately be traced to the child.* Thus, Hermann Paul wrote in 1886:

> It is quite clear that the processes in the course of learning language are of the highest importance for the explanation of the variations in the usages of language--that they afford the weightiest reason for these variations (Paul 1886, tr. 1888: 15)

while Grammont (1902), without insisting on a cause-and-effect relationship, was rather more explicit as to the alleged parallelism:

> Toutes les modifications fonétiques, morphologiques, ou sintaxiques qui caractérisent la vie des langues apparaissent dans le parler des enfants.... En réunissant les particularités de langage d'un très grand nombre d'enfants, on pourrait constituer une sorte de grammaire de toutes les transformations qui se sont produites et peuvent se produire dans toutes les langues umaines (Grammont 1902:60: spelling as in the original)

(Cf. also Sturtevant 1917). De Saussure was skeptical of children's errors as 'the starting point of all changes', on the grounds that it is unclear

> what prompts a generation to retain certain mistakes to the exclusion of others that are just as natural.... Besides, why did the phenomenon break through at one time rather than another? (1959:149)

Bloomfield, similarly, argued

> against the theory that sound change arises from imperfections in children's learning of language...[since] no permanent factor...can account for specific changes which occur at one time and place and not at another (1933:386).

The implication that children everywhere and at all times make the same errors received no more documentation in the course of this debate than did the basic thesis it was intended to counter.[1]

In recent years generative theory has adopted the view that children's mislearning is at the root of language change. Thus, Halle (1962) conjectures that 'changes in later life are restricted to the addition of a few rules in the grammar'. The child, on the other hand, 'constructs his own optimal grammar by induction from the utterances to which he has been exposed', and thus need not finally arrive at a grammar identical to that of the adults, since 'a given set of utterances can be generated by more than one grammar' (1962:344f.). Kiparsky (1965, 1968) takes up this line of thought, emphasizing discontinuity between the generations, restructuring, simplification, and imperfect learning by the child as sources of historical change. Kiparsky's arguments are based almost entirely on data reflecting the form and distribution of phonological rules in adult language. He does not indicate how actual child language data could be used to support or refute his thesis.[2] In a later article Kiparsky cautions that

> the extent to which the process of simplification can cause change presumably depends on the degree of pressure towards linguistic conformity that prevails in the community (1970: 313).

In his more recent article written with Lise Menn (1977) Kiparsky does adduce child language data, but he and Menn do not refer to the Halle/Kiparsky conception of language change, confining themselves to a critical review of the theories of Jakobson and Stampe (and presentation and extension of a convincing model of phonology acquisition prefigured by Menn's earlier work).

It is in Stampe's writings (1969, 1973) that we find more specific claims regarding the relationship between child language and change. According to Stampe,

> a phonetic change occurs when the child fails to suppress some innate process which does not apply in the standard language... The conservative influence of the standard exerts itself by rejecting most of the innovations of children (1969:448).

But some innovations are gradually admitted, if only optionally at first, and in casual speech only:

> The account of phonetic acquisition presented here appears to explain fully all the currently known mechanisms of phonetic change (Ibid. 449).

Clearly basing his theory on the Halle/Kiparsky views
sketched out above, Stampe concludes in the same sweeping
vein:

> The apparent addition, generalization, and unordering of processes arise in the child's failure, respectively, to suppress, limit, or order processes of the innate system to the extent required by the standard language. (1969:449)

It is apparent that for Stampe's claims to be true or even plausible, there must be very extensive parallels between the phonological processes used by children and sound change. It will be the burden of this paper to suggest that though many disparate parallels may be found, some of the most common or typical child language processes are either virtually non-existent or totally different in detail in adult synchronic processes and in sound change. In pursuing this point we will consider three types of process, in increasing order of significance as determined by average frequency of use across several children: consonant harmony, long word reduction, and consonant cluster reduction. Rather than draw on words and processes from scattered children and languages, as has been the custom of both Stampe and his loyal opposition (Dressler 1974, Drachman 1978), I shall restrict myself to an exhaustive analysis of the data recorded for eleven children learning to speak five languages: English, Spanish, Czech, Slovenian, and Estonian. (Note that this small sample does include one non-Indo-European language and three separate sub-families within Indo-European.) The reasons for using this particular sample are detailed in Vihman 1978. Briefly,

> in order to make a meaningful evaluation of the relative importance of any particular type of phonological process in a given child's speech, I required access to a complete set of data for the child for a given time period (1978:283).

The thirteen children included in that study were the only ones I could find for whom such complete data were available. In the present study the three Chinese-speaking children are not included, as I no longer have access to those data; one Estonian-speaking child--my son, Raivo, who was not yet speaking at the time of the earlier study--has been added.[3]

1. *Consonant harmony*. The process of consonant harmony, or the assimilation of consonants at a distance, which was dealt with in detail in Vihman (1978), may be reviewed here. In the language of the thirteen children I studied, it affected an average of 14% of the words in their vocabularies, with over half the children showing 12% or more con-

sonant harmony words (once words with adult models lacking dissimilar consonants have been eliminated). The range for individual children was from 2% to 38%. Consonant harmony, then, is a significant process in child language. What parallels can we find in the domain of sound change?

In brief, I am familiar with no documented instances of change in this direction, although it must have occurred to have produced the very few cases of synchronic assimilation of consonants at a distance I am aware of. Through a retrieval run on the computer-based Stanford Phonology Archive I found three such instances, out of 88 languages for which a full phonological description, including morphophonemic rules, had been coded. The cases involved sibilant place harmony in Moroccan Arabic, sibilant harmony in Navaho, and a case of place harmony in Alawa. Drachman (1978) cites Sanskrit retroflex and Arabic emphatic harmony, both of which I would be inclined to view as word or syllable prosodies, operating, like nasalization in Guarani, through the vowel by contact-assimilation, rather than at a distance, as must be the case with the place and manner harmony typical of children's speech. He also notes cases of sibilant harmony in Sanskrit and in Chumash, r-harmony in Javanese, and palatal harmony in Paiute. I would not be surprised to hear of a few more examples. Under any reckoning, however, the process is rare in adult language and may safely be said not to occur at all in the phonological system of the vast majority of the world's languages.

2. *Long word reduction*. Omission of syllables--apheresis, syncope, and apocope--is another common phenomenon in child speech, and one that certainly has its counterpart in sound change as well. I would like, first, to explore just how great a role it plays for the eleven children in this study, and then to examine the nature of the process in some detail, restricting myself in both cases to words which have more than three syllables in the adult model. I will then turn to some data on language change to see how far the parallel extends.

Table I presents the frequency of use data on what I am calling 'long words' for the eleven children. A serendipitous result in the ranking of children by percent of long words in their productive lexicon is the finding that there is a strict language-based order. The Spanish-speaking children come first, with 27% and 24% three- or four-syllable words, then the Slovenian and Czech speakers, then Estonian, and finally English, with one of the oldest of the children studied, an English-speaker aged 26 months, coming next-to-last with only 3% long words.

a. % long words			b. % reduction		
1.	Jesus (Sp)	27%	1.	Hildegard	90%
2.	Sofia (Sp)	24%	2.	Raivo	89%
3.5	Maja (Sl)	22%	3.	Tomaž	82%
3.5	Tomaž (Sl)	22%	4.	Jacob	75%
5.	Jiři (C)	19%	5.	Jesus	72%
6.	Virve (Es)	11%	6.	Maja	61%
7.	Linda (Es)	9%	7.	Linda	53%
8.	Raivo (Es)	7%	8.	Sofia	49%
9.	Hildegard (En)	5%	9.	Virve	37%
10.	Amahl (En)	3%	10.	Amahl	29%
11.	Jacob (En)	2%	11.	Jiři	26%
	mean	12%		mean	56%

(Language key: Sp = Spanish, Sl = Slovenian, C = Czech, Es = Estonian, En = English)

Long word ranking: Frequency of use
TABLE I

In part (b) of Table I the children are ranked according to their relative ability to handle the long words without omitting syllables. Here the language being acquired is no longer relevant. Notice that seven out of eleven children reduce more than half the long words in their vocabulary, all reduce over a quarter, and the child at the top of the list, Hildegard Leopold, reduces fully 90% of the long words she attempts.

Turning to Table II, we see the pattern of syllable loss as it relates to the position of stress in three-syllable words across the eleven children. The language being learned will obviously affect the task facing the child, since Czech offers only stress-initial words, and last-syllable stress is rare in English and Estonian, while Spanish and Slovenian show all three possibilities. By comparing percentages of syllables omitted relative to the position of stress, however, we equalize the languages, so to speak, though the actual figures underlying those percentages are very small in some cases. From these data a few facts emerge quite clearly. First, the stressed syllable is very rarely omitted, though one child, Pačesová's son Jiři, omitted the initial stressed syllable in nine out of thirteen long words. Drachman cites Pačesová's data to show that '"recency" is more important than "primacy" in young children's auditory memory' (1978:4), where 'recency' refers to the tendency of subjects to recall the last word in list-learning tasks, while 'primacy' refers to a novel

Initial syllable stress

Total words reduced: 72

		Omit			
Estonian	36		first syllable	9	12%
Slovenian	14		second syllable	30	42%
English	10		third syllable	24	33%
Czech	9		first and second	3	4%
Spanish	3		second and third	6	8%

Medial syllable stress

Total words reduced: 81

		Omit			
Slovenian	50		first syllable	72	89%
Spanish	20		second syllable	2	2%
English	6		third syllable	5	6%
Estonian	5		first and third	2	2%

Final syllable stress

Total words reduced: 10

		Omit			
Spanish	7		first syllable	5	50%
Slovenian	2		second syllable	4	40%
English	1		first and second	1	10%

Three-syllable words: pattern of syllable omissions across eleven children
TABLE II

stimulus — here, the stressed syllable. My data from Estonian, which, like Czech, is a primarily initial-stress language, do not seem to corroborate this. Here we find that out of 49 long words which the three Estonian-speaking children attempted and reduced, only 6 (or 11%) show omission of the stressed syllable. However, the data on initial-stressed three-syllable words across all five languages do show that the second syllable is rather more likely to be omitted than the last. While this might relate to the 'recency' effect cited by Drachman, it could also be due to a quite different phenomenon, namely, the tendency (familiar from the history of Spanish, for example) for syllables adjacent to the stressed syllable to be lost, or conversely, for syllables at two removes from the stress to be retained. To determine which of these is most likely, we can look at the four-syllable words attempted by the children.

The numbers are very small here, since there are only 33 four-syllable words in the five combined data sets for which it is clear which syllable was omitted. And while the phenomenon of loss of stress-adjacent syllables makes sense in a language like Spanish, or Estonian, with regularly alternating stresses, it is not so clearly relevant to a child's treatment of a word like *automobile*, say. The complete figures are in any case presented as Table III.

First syllable stress

Total words reduced:	13	Omit first syllable	2
Estonian	8	first and second	2
Czech	4	second syllable	2
English	1	second and fourth	1
		third syllable	2
		third and fourth	3
		fourth syllable	1

Second syllable stress

Total words reduced:	2		
Estonian	1	Omit first syllable	2
Spanish	1		

Third syllable stress

Total words reduced:	18	Omit first syllable	1
Spanish	11	first and second	11
Slovenian	6	second syllable	5
Estonian	1	fourth syllable	1

Fourth syllable stress: No instances

Four syllable words: pattern of omissions
TABLE III

We see that a syllable adjacent to the stress is omitted in 22 cases (or 66% of the time), while a non-adjacent stress is omitted 21% of the time.[4] What seems more striking, however, is that the final syllable, which is in no case stressed, is retained in all but six words (or 82% of the time), while the first syllable, stressed or not, is omitted 55% of the time.

To return to Table II, when stress is medial, we find a similar preference for omitting the first syllable, across all the children: the figure is 89% first syllable omissions vs. only 6% last syllable (also unstressed), 2% both first and last syllables, and 2% omission of the stressed syllable. The data on the small number of final-stressed syllables again reveal a tendency to omit the first syllable and fail to lend support to the sound-change-like distance-from-stress hypothesis. Combining all relevant data from both three- and four-syllable words, we find that the final unstressed syllable is preserved 78% of the time, which does seem to suggest that in processing phonological patterns, as in processing syntactic units,

Slobin's operating principle--'Pay attention to the ends of words' (1973:191)--holds for children.

One last point deserves attention in our review of the children's handling of long words. We have spoken of the process involved as syllable omission or loss, rather than vowel loss: How well does this description correspond to the facts? In Appendix I I present a selection of data from each of the children. I have tried to offer a range of examples illustrating the relations between stress and syllable loss that I have been discussing, but the data will serve to make a different point as well. In almost every instance one or more consonants, preceding or following the nuclear vowel of the syllable deleted by the child, are lost along with the vowel. Thus, in the derivation of Hildegard's [babu] from *pocket-book* the entire medial syllable -*ket*- is lost; in deriving [mu·si] from Estonian *muusika* my subject Linda omitted the full final syllable -*ka*.

Let us now quickly inspect some data on sound change. Just as I preferred to look at complete data sets for a few children rather than pick examples here and there from a larger number, I chose to review the range of sound changes affecting a given language or language family to the fullest extent possible, given limitations of time and access to sources. I will thus base my remarks on the data I was able to locate in just four sources, three standard historical grammars--Prokosch 1939 on Germanic, Shevelov 1964 on Slavic, and Menéndez-Pidal 1949 on Spanish--and my own collection of over 1000 cognate sets from the Western Finnic languages.

The data on the treatment of unstressed vowels in these sources can be consulted with regard to the two major findings I reported with respect to children. First, to refer to the last point made in that connection, in virtually every case it is not a full syllable which is lost in sound change but only the vowel, though often with subsequent readjustments of the resulting cluster in the case of syncope (as in Spanish *semana* from Latin *septimana*, via Old Spanish *sedmana*). Some Western Finnic examples are given in Appendix II.

Second, there is a strong tendency for final vowels to be lost, at least in initial-stress languages like the Germanic languages and Estonian. (Of course the history of French would have provided ample examples as well.) At the same time, Menéndez-Pidal explicitly notes with regard to Spanish that word-initial position is the most stable, the one that gives the most resistance to vowels, the one that most resembles the accented position [in which vowels are never lost] (1949:67).

Finally, two different factors affect the loss or retention of vowels, aside from position relative to stress and word-boundary. In some languages syllable weight is relevant, that is, whether or not the unstressed vowel immediately follows a long or a closed syllable. In other languages, the vowel -a- stands apart from the rest as the most resistant to loss. (Estonian and Germanic provide examples of the first type, Livonian and Spanish, of the second. Some Western Finnic instances are included in Appendix II.) Neither of these factors plays any notable role in our child language data, despite the fact that -a- is well known to be among the first vowels acquired by children.

3. *Consonant cluster reduction.* The last type of process I would like to examine is cluster reduction, a still more far-reaching phenomenon that plays a considerable role both in child language and in sound change. Table IV gives the frequency of use data for the children in absolute and percentual terms, with further indication of the percent of clusters reduced by each child (the range is from a low of 52% to a high of 100%), the percent deleted altogether, and the percent of three-consonant clusters attempted. I should note that the percent of words containing clusters attempted by the child is again, at least in part, a func-

Key: A = no. of words with clusters, B = percent cluster-words in lexicon, C = percent clusters reduced, D = percent clusters deleted, E = percent three-consonant clusters

		A	B	C	D	E
English	Amahl	69	31%	100%	--	7%
	Hildegard	96	30%	98%	11%	5%
	Jacob	36	23%	98%	29%	3%
Estonian	Linda	103	28%	59%	--	8%
	Virve	87	23%	72%	4%	5%
	Raivo	122	23%	83%	3%	6%
Spanish	Jesus	39	27%	87%	5%	2%
	Sofia	39	25%	90%	3%	--
Czech	Jiři	122	41%	79%	--	5%
Slovenian	Tomaž	104	32%	52%	3%	16%
	Maja	54	40%	68%	--	16%
			mean 29%	mean 80%		

Consonant clusters: frequency of use and reduction
TABLE IV

tion of the language being learned, with an average of 38% for the three Slavic language learners vs. 26% for the other children.

The question for us here, however, is not whether children tend to reduce clusters, as they obviously do, but what principles, if any, underlie these reductions. The answer to this question is displayed in Table V. We can assert with confidence that in any stop + liquid combina-

	stop + liquid (203)	liquid + stop (85)	288
stop preserved	176	54	
liquid preserved	3	3	
cluster preserved	5	21	
cluster deleted	4	5	
epenthesis	4 (Czech)		
other treatment	11	2	
	stop + fricative (82)	fricative + stop (130)	212
stop preserved	26	73	
fricative preserved	21	10	
cluster preserved	31	34	
cluster deleted	2	6	
epenthesis	1 (Czech)		
metathesis		4 (Estonian)	
other treatment	1	3	
	nasal + stop (146)	stop + nasal (14)	160
nasal preserved	30	4	
stop preserved	30	4	
cluster preserved	75	1	
cluster deleted	8	1	
epenthesis		1 (Czech)	
metathesis	1 (Spanish)		
other treatment	2	3	
	fricative + liquid (45)	liquid + fricative (27)	72
fricative preserved	19	15	
liquid preserved	7	5	
cluster preserved	3		
cluster deleted	1	1	
other treatment	15	5	
	nasal + liquid (4)	liquid + nasal (21)	25
nasal preserved	4	16	
liquid preserved		1	

TABLE V. (Continued on the next page)

	nasal + liquid	liquid + nasal	
cluster preserved		1	
cluster deleted		2	
other treatment		1	
	nasal + fricative (8)	fricative + nasal (12)	20
nasal preserved	2	7	
fricative preserved	3	3	
cluster preserved		2	
cluster deleted	1		
other treatment	2		

Types of consonant retained in two-consonant cluster reduction
TABLE V

tion (in either order) the liquid is overwhelmingly more likely to be deleted. The case is roughly the same for the smaller number of fricative + liquid clusters and the rare instances of nasal + liquid. In stop + fricative combinations, the stop is slightly more likely to be retained in the order stop-fricative (in a ratio of 1.24:1) and considerably more likely in the opposite order (with a ratio of better than 7:1). The type fricative + nasal is minimally represented in these data, with no obvious preference for either segment. Lastly, the nasal + stop clusters are the only ones more likely to be preserved as a whole than reduced. When they are reduced, neither segment type is preferred over the other, though closer examination of the data will show that the voicing of the stop is a crucial factor: voiceless obstruents are more likely to be retained when the cluster is reduced, whereas the nasal is more likely to be the segment retained when a voiced obstruent follows. We may infer a strength hierarchy from these data which ranks stops and nasals together at the top, followed by fricatives, and ending with liquids.

For cluster reduction the clearest sound change data I was able to find came from Slavic. The trend exhibited there is as follows: (1) consonant + liquid clusters tend to be preserved in Common Slavic, though dental stop + l was later reduced to l in several Slavic languages; (2) stop + fricative and stop + nasal are reduced by loss of the stop in Common Slavic.

In the history of Spanish, Latin stop + r clusters tended to be preserved word-initially, while voiceless stop + l was palatalized in the central dialects and reduced to palatal l; the cluster bl- was preserved, while gl- was reduced to l. Medially, liquid + stop was preserved, while voiced stop + liquid clusters sometimes show loss of the stop, as do *-mb-* and sometimes *-ng-* in Castilian, and also *-gn-*, which yields a palatal *n*.

In my own Western Finnic data there are only a few cases of cluster reduction, all medial (see Appendix II). We find loss of *n* before *s* (with compensatory lengthening of the vowel) in both Estonian and Livonian (see the word *maasikas* 'strawberry'; the same change occurs in some Germanic branches and, without lengthening, in Spanish as well) and vocalization of *k* before a liquid in Estonian and Finnish (see *naeris* 'turnip'). In addition, we can note that older loan words into Estonian from Baltic, Slavic, or Germanic characteristically show reduction of any word-initial clusters such that only the last consonantal segment is retained (and that segment is often a liquid), as in these examples:

   peegel 'mirror': cf. Germ. Spiegel
   raamat 'book':   cf. Russ. грамота 'reading and writing'
   rand   'shore': cf. Germ. Strand
   rist   'cross': cf. Russ. крест
   tumm   'mute':   cf. Germ. stumm
   vaba   'free':   cf. Russ. свобода

In Germanic, finally, the few instances of cluster reduction show retention of the liquid in fricative + liquid and liquid + nasal clusters, and loss of the nasal in nasal + fricative or stop + nasal clusters.

In summary, then, liquids seem to be highly favored in the historical data, fricatives are favored over nasals and stops, and position in the cluster is sometimes relevant, especially word-initially. As each of these tendencies contradicts the corresponding child language data, there is little motive here to look to child language for the source of phonological change. In fact, in view of the creation of new consonant clusters in the course of syncope, we might add that the phonotactic preferences of children seem to have little effect even in preventing the completion of sound changes that will cause them trouble.

4. *Conclusion*. In discussing three broad types of processes--consonant harmony, long word reduction, and cluster reduction--I have paid no attention to the many other processes involved in either child language, sound change, or both. Vowel harmony, for example, is a much more prominent feature of adult language than consonant harmony, but it seems to play a surprisingly small part in the acquisition data. Similarly, the interaction between vowels and con-

sonants probably accounts for the bulk of sound changes--
nasalization, palatalization, pharyngealization, and so on
all fall in this category. But again I have seen very little evidence of such effects in the child language data.
On the other hand, consonant deletion is a major process
for children, affecting as much as 50% of the lexicon for a
given child according to the tabulation I made in my consonant harmony study (the average was 17%, slightly higher
than that for consonant harmony). I believe it plays a
smaller role in sound change, but I have not collected data
on this point. Finally, there are of course context-free
substitutions that occur in both child language and sound
change, but as Drachman and Dressler have pointed out,
there are many disparities in the two types of data there
as well.

Quite aside from the question of the extent of parallelism between adult and child processes, it seems clear
that the role of such simplifications as reduction of clusters and long words is quite different in the two cases. I
leave it to Ohala, Labov, and others to elucidate the possible phonetic and social sources of change, but I would
like to point out that the constraint of clarity and maintenance of contrasts does not seem to weigh very heavily on
the young child, who is, after all, accustomed to speaking
largely of the here and now, in context, to familiar
adults. As Brown has put it, 'The child expects to be
understood if he speaks any appropriate words at all...'
(1973:65). Thus whether just a vowel or a vowel plus one,
two, or more consonants are omitted in cutting a long word
down to size is of little importance to the child, for whom
homophony is not an issue (see Vihman 1979). What does
pose a problem for the child is the burden placed on his
capacities for storage and retrieval of units of information
as his vocabulary increases exponentially (by literally
hundreds of words a month, in some cases). Here consonant
harmony, for example, can play a useful role in limiting
the bits of information per word that the child must store.
By the time these factors begin to fade--as the child reaches school age, speaks more often with his peers and with
strangers, and experiences a more leisurely rate of lexical
growth - the majority of his phonological adjustments have
been made. Though irregular aspects of the morphophonemics
of his language may take several more years to be mastered,
the processes we have been discussing are by and large no
longer a part of the child's productive phonology. Children, finally, do learn to speak like their elders, with
virtually no cases of residual deviation from the phonetic
norms by age eight (Templin 1957). Though it is of course
true that each child must 're-create' his language from the

start, the evidence seems strongly to show that the results of this re-creation are highly conservative. Innovations must be not only initiated but spread by adult speakers, whose offspring then duly learn to match what is to them the norm.

NOTES

*The entire conception of this paper owes a great deal to the many long and fruitful discussions I have enjoyed with Marlys A. Macken of the Stanford Child Phonology Project.

[1] It should be noted that Grammont (1902) is exceptional in that he presents both child language data (from a single pair of siblings) and historical data (from the Romance languages). Though the historical sound changes cited are selected with no attention to frequency of occurrence or pervasiveness in the language in question, the children's forms, at least, are scrupulously characterized in those terms, with an indication of the duration of the forms in the child's use as well.

[2] In the area of morphophonemic change some possible evidence supporting Kiparsky's position is adduced by Hooper 1978, who suggests—but stops short of attempting to demonstrate—a causal connection between the child language data and change as manifested in adult language.

[3] The sources used were, for English, Smith 1973 (Amahl), Leopold 1939 (Hildegard), and Menn 1976 (Jacob); for Spanish, Macken's unpublished data, collected as part of the Stanford Child Phonology Project: see Macken 1976 and 1977; for Czech, Pačesová 1968; for Slovenian, Kolarič 1959; and for Estonian, my own data on Linda (see Vihman 1971) and on my daughter Virve (see Vihman 1976 and 1978), as well as the data on my son Raivo (see Vihman 1979). All the children's names appear in Table IV. For further detail on the various sources used (aside from Raivo's data), the age of the children and length and methodology of the various studies, etc., see Vihman 1978: Table I.

[4] I include in this count only those cases where the stressed syllable is retained and the adjacent syllable is lost, regardless of whether or not an additional unstressed syllable is lost. Thus, in the case of first syllable stress, loss of first and second syllable is not counted, but loss of second and fourth as well as second alone is counted; in the case of third syllable stress, I count loss of first and second syllables.

REFERENCES

Bloomfield, Leonard. 1933. *Language*. New York: Holt, Rinehart and Winston.
Brown, Roger. 1973. *A first language: the early stages*. Cambridge, Mass.: Harvard University Press.
De Saussure, Ferdinand. 1959. *Course in general linguistics*. Ed. by Charles Bally and Albert Sechehaye. Transl. by Wade Baskin. New York: Philosophical Library. (First ed., 1915.)
Drachman, Gaberell. 1978. "Child language and language change". To appear in *Historical morphology*. Ed. by Jacek Fisiak. Berlin: De Gruyter.
Dressler, Wolfgang. 1974. "Diachronic puzzles for natural phonology". In *Papers from the parasession on natural phonology*. Ed. by Anthony Bruck, Robert A. Fox, and Michael W. La Galy. Chicago: Chicago Linguistic Society.
Grammont, Maurice. 1902. "Observations sur le langage des enfants". In *Mélanges linguistiques offerts à M. Antoine Meillet*. Paris: Klincksieck.
Halle, Morris. 1962. "Phonology in generative grammar". *Word* 18:54-72.
Hooper, Joan B. 1978. "Child morphology and morphophonemic change". To appear in *Historical morphology*. Ed. by Jacek Fisiak. Berlin: De Gruyter.
Kiparsky, Paul. 1965. *Phonological change*. Unpublished PhD dissertation, MIT.
_____. 1968. "Linguistic universals and linguistic change". In *Universals in linguistic theory*. Ed. by Emmon Bach and Robert T. Harms. New York: Holt, Rinehart and Winston.
_____. 1970. "Historical linguistics". *New horizons in linguistics*. Ed. by John Lyons. Middlesex: Penguin.
Kiparsky, Paul and Lise Menn. 1977. "On the acquisition of phonology". In *Language learning and thought*. Ed. by John Macnamara. New York: Academic Press.
Kolaric, Rudolf. 1959. "Slovenski otroški govor". *Jahrbuch der Philosophischen Fakultät in Novi Sad* 4.
Leopold, Werner F. 1939. *Speech development of a bilingual child, I: vocabulary growth in the first two years*. Evanston, Ill.: Northwestern University Press.
Macken, Marlys. 1976. "Permitted complexity in phonological development: one child's acquisition of Spanish consonants". *Lingua* 44.219-53.
_____. 1977. "Developmental reorganization of phonology: a hierarchy of basic units of acquisition". *Papers and Reports on Child Language Development* 14.1-36. (To appear in *Lingua*.)
Menéndez-Pidal, Ramón. 1949. *Manual de gramática histórica española*. Madrid: Espasa-Calpe. 8th ed.
Menn, Lise. 1976. *Pattern, control, and contrast in beginning speech*. Unpublished PhD dissertation, University of Illinois, Urbana.
Pačesová, Jaroslava. 1968. *The development of vocabulary in the child*. Brno: Universita J.E. Pukyne.

Paul, Hermann. 1888. *Principles of the history of language*. Transl. by H.A. Strong. London: Swan Sonnenschein, Lowrey & Co. (First ed., 1886).
Prokosch, E. 1939. *A comparative Germanic grammar*. Philadelphia: Linguistic Society of America.
Shevelov, George Y. 1964. *A prehistory of slavic: the historical phonology of common slavic*. Heidelberg: Carl Winter, Universitätsverlag.
Slobin, Dan Isaac. 1973. "Cognitive prerequisites for the development of grammar". In *Studies of child language development*. Ed. by Charles A. Ferguson and Dan Isaac Slobin. New York: Holt, Rinehart and Winston.
Smith, Neilson V. 1973. *The acquisition of phonology: a case study*. Cambridge: Cambridge University Press.
Stampe, David. 1969. "The acquisition of phonetic representation". CLS 5.443-454.
_____. 1973. *A dissertation on natural phonology*. Unpublished PhD dissertation, University of Chicago.
Sturtevant, Edgar. 1917. *Linguistic change: an introduction to the historical study of language*. Chicago: Chicago University Press.
Templin, Mildred C. 1957. *Certain language skills in children: their development and interrelationships*. Institute of Child Welfare Monograph No. 26. Minneapolis: University of Minnesota Press.
Vihman, Marilyn May. 1971. "On the acquisition of Estonian". *Papers and Reports on Child Language Development* 3.51-94.
_____. 1976. "From pre-speech to speech: on early phonology". *Papers and Reports on Child Language Development* 12.230-243.
_____. 1978. "Consonant harmony: its scope and function in child language". In *Universals of human language*. Ed. by Joseph H. Greenberg, Charles A. Ferguson and Edith Moravcsik. Stanford: Stanford University Press.
_____. 1979. "Homonymy and the organization of early vocabulary". Paper presented at the Child Language Research Forum, April 7th, Stanford University.

APPENDIX I

A selection of long words

		Adult model		Child	Stressed syllable	Omission
Czech		čokoláda	'chocolate'	koja:da	(1)	(first syllable)
		kolobežka	'scooter'	beška	(1)	(first & second)
English	A.	lawn mower		mɔ́:mə	(1)	(second)
		banana		ba:nə	(2)	(first)
	H.	automobile		ʔatobiə	(1)	(third)
		Mary Alice		meʔa	(2)	(second, fourth)
		pocket-book		babu	(1)	(second)
	J.	peek-a-boo		βika	(1)	(third)
Estonian	L.	elevant	'elephant'	van:	(1)	(first, second)
		kaelkirjak	'giraffe'	kaelki	(1)	(fourth)
		muusika	'music'	mu:si	(1)	(third)
	R.	aprikoos	'apricot'	apo:s	(3)	(second)
		artišokki	'artichoke'	asok:i	(1)	(second)
		siiruppi	'syrup'	sup:i	(1)	(first)
	V.	banaani	'banana'	ma:ni	(2)	(first)
		rebane	'fox'	eba	(1)	(third)
		unustas	'forgot'	unus	(1)	(third)
Slovenian	M.	metuljček	'butterfly'	túlc'ek	(2)	(first)
		ropotuljica	'rattle'	túlca	(5)	(first, second, fourth)
		ulica	'street'	úla	(1)	(second)
	T.	aeroplan	'airplane'	plán	(3)	(first, second)
		čokolada	'chocolate'	láda	(3)	(first, second)
		maškara	'masker'	más'ka	(1)	(third)
Spanish	J.	pelota	'ball'	péta	(2)	(second)
		cepillo	'brush'	píjo	(2)	(first)
		manejando	'riding'	maxánno	(3)	(second)

APPENDIX II

Sound change in Western Finnic

Key: Est = Estonian, Fin = Finnish, Kar = Karelian, Liv = Livonian, PWF = Proto-Western Finnic

Est.	hapneb	'sours'		Est.	maasikas	'strawberry'
Fin.	hapantuu			Fin.	mansikka	
Liv.	apandəb			Liv.	mɔ:škəz	
PWF	*happante-pi			Est.	naeris	'turnip'
Est.	jumal	'god'		Fin.	nauris	
Fin.	jumala			Liv.	naʔg:ərz	'potato'
Liv.	jumal			Kar.	nakris	

Est.	kange	'stiff'		Est.	sõge	'mad'
Fin.	kankea			Fin.	sokea	'blind'
Liv.	kaŋ:ktə			Liv.	soʔgdə	
PWF	*kankke-ta			PWF	*soketa	

THE FLUCTUATING INTENSITY OF A 'SOUND LAW'

YAKOV MALKIEL
University of California, Berkeley

There is scarcely any need to point out in tedious detail the fact that late-twentieth-century language historians and diachronically oriented linguists cannot possibly approach a type of shift in phonic relationship which once used to be called 'sound law', later 'sound correspondence', and still later 'phonological rule' with the same attitude as the remarkable generation of scholars that was active a century ago.* One of today's major front lines is the exploration not so much of the rise of such a change (e.g. the date of its earliest appearance, the interplay of its possible causes, a glimpse of its preliminary phases and initial stage, its concatenation with other changes) as its gradual containment past an all-time peak or crest, an initially minimal decline conducive, in the end, to major recession and, eventually, to possible extinction as a living force.

Even an observer equipped with only elementary knowledge of contemporary Spanish realizes that two rising diphthongs, namely *ie* /je/ as in *bien* 'well' and *ue* /we/ as in *bueno* 'good, kind' are of extraordinary importance in the smooth functioning of that language. Fleeting comparison of *bueno* with *bondad* 'goodness, kindness' suffices to point to an alternation of *ue* and *o* according to conditions of stress. In perfectly symmetrical distribution, one encounters *hierro* 'iron' beside *herrero* 'ironsmith'. This is, of course, not tantamount to saying that, assuming the word for 'ironsmith', absent from the vocabulary, were to be newly coined from *hierro* /jeRo/, all groups of Spanish speakers would inevitably hit upon *herr-ero*. Inasmuch as *-ero* continues to be a very productive derivational suffix, it is theoretically conceivable that, e.g. a child still in the process of learning who has not yet mastered the word *herrero* toys with *hierr-ero, on the model of *toro* 'bull': *torero* 'bullfighter', provided the diphthong's erstwhile strict limitation to the stressed syllable has meanwhile been relaxed or abolished.

We gain more arresting insights by adopting the historical perspective. Latin distinguished, in its inventory of phonemes, between /e/ and /ɛ/, and also between /o/ and /ɔ/. Spoken Latin, especially in rural environments, did not draw the line between the open and closed vowels exactly the way Classical Latin did. Thus, for the classicist the word for 'egg' is ō v u m. Conversely, the Romance comparativist, surveying such alleged offshoots of ō v u m as OFr. *uef*, It. *uovo*, Sp. *(h)uevo*, concludes that in provincial familiar parlance a new type *ŏ v u m, unattested in literary sources, cut loose from ō v u m and was allowed to prevail. For the purposes of reconstruction, only *ŏ v u m counts henceforth, on a pan-Romanic scale.

The initially striking parallelism between the configuration and the range of the two diphthongs has certain limits, once the provenience of these two sound sequences is closely examined, case by case. For all practical purposes *ie* indeed, almost invariably, reflects earlier stressed /ɛ/ = ĕ, so that the classic formula--that ancestral stressed /ɛ/ yields filial /je/ on Spanish soil--may be reversed with a minimum of risk; /je/ in an accented syllable ordinarily goes back to older /ɛ/. But the situation is radically different, and vastly more complicated, where the corresponding back vowel is involved. If the stressed /ɔ/ = ŏ of Antiquity predictably leads to /we/, the reverse fails to hold on the same scale, inasmuch as /we/ in a great many cases goes back to /oj/ = ō + i or ū + i, instead of /ɔ/. Thus, Sp. *fue* 'was, went' is an unmistakable reflex of f u i t., and Ptg. *foi* rather neatly embodies the transitional form.

When we repeat the truism that the change of ĕ, later /ɛ/, to /je/ and of ŏ, later /ɔ/, to /we/ occurred on a sweeping scale in the transition from provincial Late Latin to early Old Spanish, we imply that there were few additional conditions governing this transmutation. For instance, it did not matter (counter to the usual tendency in Romance) whether the stressed syllable ended in a vowel (which made it 'free') or in a consonant (which made it 'checked'): f ĕ / r i t 'he strikes, wounds' produced OSp. *fiere*, with a diphthong equally peculiar to its Old French and Old Italian congeners, much as p ĕ r / d i t 'he loses' gave rise to *pierde*, whereas in comparable sister languages a checked syllable was apt to prevent diphthongization. Witness for example OFr. *pert* < mod. *per(d)*, It. *perde*. Neither did it matter whether the word at issue was monosyllabic, oxytonic, paroxytonic, or proparoxytonic, so long as the syllable remained the carrier of the main stress, cf. OSp. *piértega* 'rod', from p ĕ r t i c a, or *muérdago* 'mistletoe' (Viscum album), from m ŏ r d i c u, connected with *morder* 'to bite' and flanking the straight postverbal *muerdo* 'bite, bit'. But the form of the auxiliary, inherently subject to variations of stress, was either *iet* or *es*, from *e(s)t* ; d o m i n u 'master', used as an independent word, was *dueño*, whereas, when reduced to a title and thus deprived of independent status, it shrank to *don*, mandatorily followed by a given name. On balance, with the rarest of exceptions, each borderline between monophthong and matching diphthong was traced very energetically. In this respect, Old Spanish diphthongization was at the opposite pole of the same process in Old Provençal, where it remained to the end strictly optional.

Nevertheless, certain neatly profiled limiting conditions did attach to the rules governing stressed ĕ > /je/ and stressed ŏ > /we/.

a) Uninterrupted oral transmission of the given form on native soil was an obligatory constraint. Neither learnèd words, propelled principally by Church Latin in medieval Europe, though occasionally reabsorbed into the vernaculars, nor words channeled through prestigious cognate languages, mainly Old French or Old Provençal, carry any evidential weight as counterexamples. The situation is highlighted by the sporadic appearance of doublets: learnèd *verso* accompanies vernacular *viesso* 'verse' from v e (r) s u, or of near-doublets: OProv. *Peire* 'Peter' (from P ĕ t r u) emerges in Old Spanish as *Per(o)*, while p ĕ t r a 'rock', following its own straight course, reaches the stage *piedra* 'stone'. Just why certain Latin words, in particular territories, survived in the vernacular or the learnèd layer, or in both, we do not yet know for sure. In the last analysis, such problems are lexical rather than phonological.

b) The concept of unstressed, specifically pretonic, syllable extends to such words--usually bisyllabic and typically titles or categorizers--as precede, or enter into, a proper noun, hence not only *don* vs. *dueño*, but also *Conde Fernán Gonçález* (elsewhere often *cuende* 'count' < c ŏ m i t e 'companion').

c) Where /ε/ from ĕ and /ɔ/ from ŏ immediately preceded some such palatal consonant as primary */λ/, somewhat later /ž/, at the early Romance stage, no diphthongization ensued. The near-consensus of opinion is that, through contiguity with such a consonant, Latin's originally open vowels had been closed--to /ẹ/ and /ọ/ respectively, neither subject to further change, well ahead of the diphthongization process, in which case the relevant starting points simply no longer were /ɛ/ and /ɔ/. Examples include OSp. *foja* /fožа/ 'leaf' (mod. *hoja*), from f o l i a, lit. 'leaves, foliage', via Proto-Sp. */foλa/ (cf. Ptg. *folha*), and OSp. *ojo* /ožo/ 'eye' (mod. /oχo/), from o c (u) l u (cf. Ptg. *olho*); also OSp. *reja* 'grate' < r ĕ g (u) l a and *teja* 'tile' < t ĕ g (u) l a (over against more conservative Ptg. *relha*, *telha*). By adding to our stock /j/ from /dj/, we obtain *hoy* /oj/ 'today' < h o d i e, lit. 'on this day'. It is puzzling that these very same adjacent consonants in Old Provençal apparently produced the opposite effect, namely that of provoking or facilitating optional diphthongization, as in *olh ~ uelh* 'eye'. Another surprise: the *ñ* for once followed its own separate course, as in *sueño*, whether we interpret it as 'sleep' (from s o m n u) or as 'dream' (from s o m n i u); similarly, *lueñ(e)* 'far away' < l o n g ē.

What I have so far presented is a maximally compressed synopsis of an enormous corpus of writings, of varying quality, which deal with the genesis of rising diphthongs in Old Spanish, until *ie* and *ue* reached the zenith of their development. There are numerous side issues pertaining to this initial evolutionary stage, e.g.: How does one account for the divergent developments in neighboring dialects (Asturo-Leonese and Navarro-Aragonese, say)? What were the earliest philologically admissible appearances of these diphthongs? Did *ie* actually precede *ue*? To what graphic representation did the scribes have recourse? What was the exact phonetic substance of the ancient digraphs-- did the second element, e.g. represent a closed, a neutral, or an open *e*, and did the stress ever, anywhere, fall on the first member of the sequence? Also, what is the evidence of assonances and rhymes, of the use of alphabets other than Latin, of words borrowed from and into older Spanish? All these discussions I shall omit, since my central commitment is to analyze the subsequent weakening of *ie*'s and *ue*'s powerful grip on the speech community.

For our immediate purpose it suffices to recall the major discoveries (or improvements upon earlier formulations) by Menéndez Pidal, which span the opening quarter of this century. Menéndez Pidal clearly demonstrated that, at the threshold of the literary period, the emerging diphthong *ie*, from ĕ, was in sharp competition with *ia*, of which there remain significant traces in the Asturo-Leonese domain, while *ue*, reminiscent of an Old French preference, was in keen rivalry with *uo*, to this day familiar from Tuscan, and, albeit on a minor scale, with *ua* (of which, once more, copious vestiges can be laid bare in certain

dialect areas, notably in Upper Aragon). This secondary
ua /wa/, a regional product of /ɔ/, must of course be
neatly distinguished from primary /wa/, inherited from
Latin as in *cuándo* 'when' and *lengua* 'tongue' and, in principle, common to all Peninsular dialects. In sum: Both
through their spread to virtually any kind of stressed
syllable and through the speedy eviction of *ia* by *ie* and
of *uo*, *ua* by *ue* in Castilian proper, the victors in this
struggle, namely *ie* and *ue*, emerged, somewhere around 1200,
as extraordinarily powerful and sharply profiled members
of the medieval Spanish sound system.

In numerous instances where *ie*, *ia*, *ua* sequences of a
radically different provenience happened to have sprung
into existence in a lightly stressed syllable, these sequences were ruthlessly eliminated, through secondary reduction in favor of the monophthong *e* or, less frequently,
a. Thus, g e r m ā n u 'brother' (beside g e r m ā n a 'sister')
and I ā -, I ē-n (u) ā r i u 'January' on the evidence of archaic charters, initially assumed the shapes of *yermano*,
-na and *yenero*, with *ye*, incontrovertibly, standing for
/je/; the crucial following stages resulted in the familiar
forms, absorbed into modern Spanish, *(h)ermano* (with an
unexplained, apparently whimsical, *h-*) and *enero*. Then,
the oft-cited contrast between the initial segments *catórze*
(mod. *catorce*) 'fourteen' and *quàraénta* (mod. *cuarenta*)
'forty' loses some of its outlandishness, if one remembers
that in the respective prototypes, the q u a- segment of
q u a t t (u) ó r d e c i m was in a pretonic, i.e. unstressed
or weakly stressed syllable, incompatible with a rising
diphthong after a certain cut-off point, whereas the q u a-
of q u a d r ā g i n t ā stood in a countertonic syllable, endowed by definition with much greater affinity to the
heavily stressed syllable. This hypothesis is confirmed
by the trajectory of OSp. *quàraésma* 'Lent', which issued
forth from q u a d r ā g ē s i m a 'fortieth'; witness the
repercussion of this state of affairs in Sp. *cuaresma*, as
against, say, Fr. *carême*.

We can now observe, throughout a period of neatly documented speech development, a gradual recession from this
all-time summit, in favor of monophthongal substitutes for
erstwhile diphthongs and, equally if not more important,
of a discernibly loose mutual conditioning between rising
diphthong and stressed syllable.

Such cases of secondary monophthongization (typically,
post-medieval) in Standard Spanish as have come to my attention are amenable, I think, to the following pattern of
categorization:

(1) Stressed *ie* mandatorily becomes *e* where it follows immediately upon one of the palatal consonants /λ/, /ñ/, /š/, /č/, /j/; also, in certain contexts, upon the vowel /i/; and it remains *e* even if the consonant that originally set off the movement conducive to this change loses its own palatality, as when /š/, somewhere around 1600, became /χ/. Thus one arrives, syntagmatically, at *dix(i)eron* 'they said' > mod. *dijeron*; *trax(i)eron*, var. *trox(i)eron* 'they brought' > mod. *trajeron* beside dial. *trujeron* (as against *fizieron* 'they did, made' > mod. *hicieron*). The rule does not hold after /ž/, cf. *cogiendo* 'catching', and fails to apply consistently after /š̌/ > /χ/, cf. *crujiente* 'crackling', OSp. *cruxieron* > mod. *crujieron*; but *condujeron* 'they led'.

(2) Stressed *ie*, in isolated cases, became *e* after word-initial *l-*, *n-*, phonemes which in the process, again syntagmatically, merged with /j/ to yield /λ/, /ñ/: OSp. *lievo* 'I carry' > mod. *llevo* (and, in its wake, also, inf. *llevar*, 1st pl. pr. ind. *llevamos*, in lieu of older *levar*, *levamos*). *Llevo* received support from *llego* 'I arrive', *lleno* 'I fill'.

(3) Through a morphological process rich in phonological implications, one of two rival types within the ranks of *-ir* verbs pushed back the competitor without completely overlaying it. The metaphonic *pedir/pido* model proved somewhat stronger than its diphthongizing *mentir/miento* counterpart, with the result that *siego* < s e q u o (r) 'I follow', *siervo* < s e r v i ō 'I serve' and a sprinkling of comparable verbs switched allegiance, reëmerging from the turmoil as *sigo*, *sirvo*. The noun *siervo* < s e r v u 'serf, servant, slave' was not affected by this reshuffling. The switch from *ie* to *i*, at least at the outset, must be interpreted paradigmatically.

(4) The hypocoristic-diminutive suffix *-iello*, *-iella* (from *-ellu*, *-ella*, as in m i s e l l u s 'wretched', based on m i s e r) began early to tend toward assuming the more advanced forms *-illo*, *-illa* under pressure from such rival diminutive endings as *-ico*, *-in(o)*, *-ito*; hence *camari(e)lla* 'small room', *menudi(e)llo* 'smallish'. The change gradually engulfed congealed diminutives, i.e. those no longer accompanied by their primitives, e.g. *Casti(e)lla*, lit. '[land of] small encampments, castles', as well as words into which the segments *-iello, -iella*, through sheer coincidence, entered as parts of their radicals: *si(e)lla* 'saddle, stool', later 'chair', from s e l l a. Again the change was paradigmatic.

(5) As part of an inflectional process, the preterital model *dieste* 'thou gavest' (etc.), from *dar*, traceable to

the so-called Low Latin dedī, stetī type, toward the end of the Middle Ages yielded ground to the *pediste* model, identifiable with the so-called weak type of the -īre verbs, e.g. fīnĭ(vi)stī, with the result that *dieste* itself was replaced by *diste* and that *bevieste* 'thou drankest', *comieste* 'thou atest' (from *bever*, *comer*) adopted the ending of *gruñiste*, from *gruñir* 'to grunt, growl, grumble' --one more paradigmatic change. Hence the extra-close association of *ie* > *i* with the following consonant cluster *st* and, through further extension, also with kindred *sp* and /sk/.

(6) Through interaction of (4) and (5), *ie* gradually began to give ground to *i* in approximately twenty nouns and a handful of toponyms and anthroponyms; among them *avi(e)spa*, from vĕspa 'wasp'. There developed a secondary dependence on certain contiguous consonants, or consonant clusters, e.g. /r/, /R/, the bilabials, and the labiodentals. Nevertheless, the phonetic change remained 'weak', as regards depth of penetration. *Fiesta* 'festival, holiday' and *siesta* 'afternoon rest', from fĕsta and sĕxta (hōra), respectively, resisted it; so did the Hellenism *pierna* 'leg'. Conceivably, the fact that there existed suffix-stressed derivatives clinched the matter in some instances. Morphophonemically, *pierna* in its relation to its satellites displaying the stem *pern-* made excellent sense: *pernada* 'kick', *pernaza* 'thick leg'. To reconcile these, and similarly shaped words, with more advanced **pirn-* would have required a new morphophonemic rule.

(7) By way of symmetry and, as it were, sympathy *ue* was affected by two waves of monophthongization, succumbing to neither. The structurally neatest parallel to *ie* > *e*, which we tagged as syntagmatic (see under (1) and (2)), was, obviously, *ue* > *e*, in the vicinity of a preceding (bi)labial as in *fr(u)ente* 'forehead'. But *prueba* 'proof' and '(s)he proves' were not allowed, except dialectally, to advance to *preba, so as to obviate the need for a new morphophonemic conjugational pattern, cf. the above remark on **pirn-*.

(8) In structurally tidy parallelism to *ie* > *i*, a change characterized as paradigmatic (see under 3), 4), and 5)), one discovers, if only vestigially, the change from *ue* to *u*. In dialect speech, *pues* 'thus, then' (from post blended with postea, witness Ptg. *pois*) may yield to *pus*, and *tuétano* 'pith, marrow' has to hold its ground against *tútano*.

(9) There has begun to develop a slight tendency, perhaps never before pointed out explicitly, to substitute monophthongs for diphthongs in nouns stressed on the antepenult.

This change still occurs but at rare intervals, only under a constellation of favorable circumstances. Thus, *retruécano* 'pun, play on words' is far too close to *trueque* 'exchange' and to the underlying verb *trueco/trocar* to drift toward **retrécano*; *jueves* 'Thursday' supports *miércoles* 'Wednesday'. But *piértega* 'rod' has been abandoned in favor of *pértiga*; OArag. *priéstamo* 'loan', which coexisted with OSp. *préstamo*, has disappeared without leaving traces. Perhaps the increasing weakness of *ie*, *ue* in this position is related to the absence of the slightest support from the ranks of verb forms.

(10) Finally, continued absorption of Latinisms, in the ranks of verbs, was apt, in certain contexts, to lead to further erosion of the diphthongs. Thus, vernacular *defiendo* 'I protect' flanked newly erudite *ofendo*, instead of medieval *agravio* 'I offend'; vernacular *tiendo* 'I tend', *atiendo* 'I pay attention to', *entiendo* 'I understand', etc. clashed with *pretendo* 'I claim'; vernacular *enfrento* 'I put face to face' disagreed with *confronto* 'I bring face to face'.

There thus occurred as many as ten neatly distinguishable categories of retreat from diphthongs in stressed syllables. All ten classes of secondary monophthongization could have been prevented, through analogical restoration or other pressures and therapeutic devices available to any vigorously reacting speech community. No such resistance ensued. We conclude that these are ten separate manifestations of essentially the same trend, away from the maximum use of *ie*, *ue*. Apparently the two rising diphthongs at a certain point began to lose their appeal.

Over against these numerous categories of debilitation of the two principal rising diphthongs in stressed syllables, to which we must at no time forget to add plain lexical attrition, through homonymic conflicts and cultural obsolescence, stand the instances of the complementary (or, if you wish, inverse) process, namely the gradual penetration of *ie* and *ue* into the less heavily stressed syllables.

(a) Posttonic *ie* and *ue* were probably at all times marginally tolerated in an obscure corner of the conjugational edifice. Consider the radical-stressed forms of the present subjunctive in the paradigm of certain *-iar* and *-uar* verbs: *acariciar* 'to caress', *copiar* 'to copy', which offer *acaricie*, *copie*. From medieval sources one can cite *apreciar* 'to assess', *apremiar* 'to harass'. Further relevant are the verbs in *-guar*, traceable to -f i c ā r e, such as *amortiguar* 'to deaden, muffle', *averiguar* 'to ascertain, find out', with present subjunctive members of the paradigm: *amortigüe, averigüe*. Independently, in the domain of the indefinite pronouns, *otrie* 'someone else' arose as a compromise between (nom.) *ôtri* and (obl.) *otrién*. Later on, a regional innovation, to wit *nadi* '(no) one', lit. '(no) man born', a transparent offshoot of *omne nado* equipped with the ending of q u ī 'who', was remodeled as *nadie*, in imitation of *otrie*.

(b) Midway between the heavily and the lightly stressed syllables one finds syllables known as countertonic, and here a good deal of wavering was tolerated, with the diphthongs slowly crowding out the monophthongs. A certain plant, obviously tough-fibered, is known as *quiebrahacha* 'breakax'; the 'groper in the dark' is called *tientaparedes*; and a 'marginal stop in the typewriter', unquestionably a neologism, goes by the name of *cierrarrenglón*.

(c) Because the rising diphthongs, from a certain moment still undetermined, began to sit well with the countertonic syllable, an effective technique was developed, chiefly in Peninsular Spanish, to preserve the diphthong in hypocoristic suffixal derivatives through use of an interfix, namely *-ec-*. The classic examples are *piececillo, piececito*, and *piecezuelo* 'little foot', from *pie*, and *piecezuela* 'little piece', from *pieza*; witness also *piedrezuela* 'little stone', *puentezuela* 'small bridge', *puertezuela* 'little door', *puertezuelo* 'small port', from *piedra, puente, puerta*, and *puerto*, respectively. The spread of this semantically empty, pretonic *-ec-* element clearly serves the sole purpose of strengthening the attachment of derivative to primitive, through avoidance of such allomorphic variants as **pedr-, *port-*, etc., demanded by the older rule.

Recent generations of speakers of Spanish, however, particularly those residing in the New World, have opened the gateway for the penetration of *ie* and *ue* into the pretonic syllables of all sorts of derivatives, so long as the corresponding primitives flaunt the *ie* or *ue* in a stressed syllable. Take *mueble* 'piece of furniture' as the starting point; the relevant adjective at present is *mue-* rather than *mo-blero*. For 'furniture factory' or 'furniture store' you are bound to hear *mueblería*, and the corresponding label for the 'furniture manufacturer or dealer' is *mueblista*. Cf. also the New World neologism *puestero* 'vendor, seller' (at a booth or stand), 'tender of livestock' (on a ranch), from *puesto*, as against *postor* 'bidder' (at an auction), from *puesta*, and many other, comparably intricate situations where the free interplay of diphthong and monophthong has been seized upon as a differentiation device, to avert any collision of homophones or any rise of polysemy.

What remains then, at present, of the power of the rising diphthongs *ie* and *ue*, so characteristic of the stressed syllables in early Old Spanish, is relatively little. The ranks of these diphthongs, tied to the accented syllables, have thinned out, through interaction of, at least, ten escape routes. Moreover, the tendential penetration of these diphthongs into other categories of syllables has diluted their original quintessence of stress-defined and stress-controlled sound sequences. The present-day situation can be briefly stated thus: *ie* and *ue* have preserved their neat status in conjugation; and their occurrence in pretonic syllables is still confined to derivatives whose primitives display /je/ and /we/ in stressed syllables.

NOTE

*A fuller version of this paper, with an apparatus of footnotes and a separate bibliography, has been reserved for the quarterly *Romance Philology*. A somewhat shorter companion piece is the note, 'The abandonment of the root diphthong in the paradigms of certain Spanish verbs', to appear in No. 5 of the new Italian journal *Incontri Linguistici*, set aside for a testimonial (ed. G. Francescato) in honor of Vittore Pisani.

LINGUISTIC REASONS FOR
PHONETIC ARCHAISMS IN ROMANCE

ROGER WRIGHT
University of Liverpool

It has been traditional to claim that the development of Romance is a special case within historical linguistics because of the coexistence of two distinct pronunciation norms during the Early Romance period, 'Latin' and the Romance vernacular of any area.* But it now seems probable that 'Latin' pronunciation as we know it today was an invention of the Carolingian Church at the end of the eighth century (Wright 1976a). The pronunciation of liturgical Latin was then standardized via the assignment of one specified sound to each written letter when reading aloud. Accordingly, if we want to continue believing the traditional idea of two distinct pronunciation norms in the preceding centuries, the belief will have to rest on linguistic grounds alone.

The argument is traditionally based on so-called 'learnéd' words, Sp. *cultismos*, whose vernacular development has not evolved as much as it might. The hypothesis is that this is specifically due to the use of these words by the educated classes in society, who were speaking Latin rather than the vernacular (cf. recently Macpherson 1975, Bustos Tovar 1974). Such words are thus 'exceptions' to previously established rules of change; Spanish *pienso* < p e n s o, for example, compared with *mesa* < m e n s a m, in which the nasal has gone; Spanish *flor* < f l o r e m, compared with the palatalized [λ] of *llama* < f l a m m a m.

Some words have survived virtually unchanged from Latin into Spanish, such as *canto* < c a n t o, which did not fall under the scope of any identifiably regular development in Castille. According to the rules, neither c a-, -n t-, nor the -o of the first person singular, change; so *canto* is regarded as regular, despite its similarity to the Latin. Nobody has worried about the comparative malleability of c a n t o in Northern France, where it underwent four sound changes that did not apply in Castille (>[ʃãːt]); these relative categories of statistical regularity are traditionally language-specific. There are, in fact, examples in Castilian of all the features of c a n t o changing; e.g. c a t t u m > *gato*, c a n t i o n e m > *canción*, s t o > *estoy*. We can claim *estoy* to be regular by asserting that this semi-vowel is regular in vernacular monosyllabic first person forms; we can preserve the regularity of *canción* by pointing to the conditioning of the following semi-vowel. Traditionally, exceptions are rehabilitated by specifying more sophisticated conditions (e.g., Wright 1976c). *Gato* is swept under the carpet as 'sporadic', although Corominas (1954-7) lists twenty-one comparable developments. *Gato* is thus considered irregular owing to over-evolution in the same way as *pienso* is owing to under-evolution. This is, however, merely a statistical truth; *canto* and *mesa* follow the majority, so *gato* and *pensar* are called 'irregular'.

Flor, however, traditionally called a *cultismo*, has not even got statistics on its side. Six Latin words with initial f l- seem to survive in Spanish; four preserve the cluster (*flor*; *flaco* < f l a c c u m; *fleco* < f l o c c u m; *flojo* < f l u x u m), one loses the f- entirely (*lacio* < f l a c c i d u m), and *llama* is the only 'regular' one. There are other cases in which the supposed 'rule' has several exceptions; supposedly anomalous forms can only be identified as such on the basis of prior identification of rules of change which they happen not to have undergone, and the assignment of regularity or irregularity is not as simple as the handbooks can make it appear.

Isolative change is almost unknown in Early Romance, and there is one general feature of conditioned changes that is of crucial relevance here: the fact that after the change, the old sound almost always survives in contexts unaffected by the conditions. This means that if, for any reason, a form happens to survive unaltered a sound change which we might have expected it to undergo, the form may seem to stick out like a sore thumb to philologists, but speakers of the time, synchronic phonologists of the time included, will never think of it as peculiar at all. The n̠ and s̠ of *pienso* are in themselves very common phonemes of late spoken Latin; the cluster even has moral support e.g., in *cansar* < c a m p s a r e, and other forms that preserve the nasal at a morpheme boundary, such as *enseñar* < i n s i g n a r e and *consolar* < c o n s o l a r i. *Pensar* does not seem obviously undesirable in the superseding phonological system.

'Exceptions' in historical linguistics are not usually 'exceptions' within the synchronic phonological structure of the language.

Wang (1969) suggested that sound changes do not normally apply to all the relevant morphemes at once, but spread progressively across the vocabulary morpheme by morpheme, i.e., by lexical diffusion. He is also skeptical of the value of dialect mixture as an explanation for exceptions. 'More often than not, linguists have used dialect mixture as an excuse for not producing evidence of a substantive nature' (Chen and Wang 1975; 256). Inventing hypothetical dialects, such as Latin as opposed to Early Romance before the Carolingian Reforms, seems even less adequate as a way of conveniently shunting aside cases of recalcitrance to our neatly posited rules. Wang's theory needs careful investigation, of course. However, if it is true that changes can peter out or be forestalled before reaching all apparently qualified items in the lexicon, then the problem of exceptions to sound change redefines itself as the investigation of the rationale behind the pecking order of items for the change.

The existence of such a pecking order has often been suspected. Consider, for example, the apparent doubling of the intervocalic consonant of Latin t o t a 'all' in Italy, Catalonia, and Northern France, giving *tutta*, *tota*, and *toute* respectively, compared with Spanish *toda*, where it voices regularly (Posner 1974). French, Catalan, and Italian speakers seem to have reacted against the voicing tendency by positively disqualifying this word from the conditions. In Northern France, v i t a and n a t a, for example, will have been early on the lexical list, since the [-t-] voiced (and has since disappeared: French *vie*, *neé*), whereupon t o t a saw the change coming and doubled the consonant, thereby preventing the voicing.

Samuels (1972:143) suggests several possible general reasons for reluctance to complete the extension of a sound change: there may be a desire to avoid taboo forms, or to remain transparently linked to a cognate outside the conditions, or, the operation of 'phonaesthetics' may be involved. Thus, English *swerve* may have avoided becoming *swarve because, Samuels suggests, *wir* is a symbolic syllable for circular movement (*twirl*, *whirl*). Onomatopoeic words may be similarly recalcitrant. But none of these seems quite sufficient in the case of t o t a. Perhaps it commonly attracted exceptional emphasis in view of its meaning.

Sometimes two Romance descendants coexist from one Latin etymon; e.g., *pienso* and *peso* from p e n s o, *mundo* and *mondo* from m u n d u m, *ración* and *razón* from r a t i o n e m. These are traditionally explained by saying that obviously the least evolved form comes from the Latin of the educated, and the most evolved from the vernacular. But they can be explained more rationally in another way (Wright 1976b). Since language change does not happen overnight, any event describable in retrospect as a sound change must at the time have been a case of free variation between the old and the new form. If both the forms survive, we have a pair of doublets. With polysemic and homonymic words there is a great advantage in having two forms preserved, in that the previous potential confusion can be thereby resolved. This happened with English *person* and *parson*.

Latin m u n d u s was homonymic, meaning both 'clean' and 'world'. Spanish has both *mundo* 'world' and *mondo* 'clean'. *Mundo* thus gets categorized as a 'cultismo', belonging to the speech of the educated. Latin p e n s a r e came to mean both the original 'weigh' and 'estimate, think'; all Romance languages preserve one variant with the nasal to mean 'think', and the other without it to mean 'weigh' (or 'grieve'). In both cases, the variation seems to have been exploited to help resolve potential ambiguity, and calling *pensar* and *mundo* 'cultismos' explains nothing at all. This device can be invoked to explain doublets of which even the less evolved of the pair is not particularly Latinate, such as *obra* and *huebra* from o p e r a, and even doublets of Germanic origin such as *ropa* and *roba*, supposedly from the same root *r a u p-, in which recourse to hypothetical Latin dialects is irrelevant.

Doublets are often thought to be clinching evidence for the coexistence of archaic and evolved pronunciation forms in the early centuries, but that, quite clearly, they are not.

The neogrammarians never expected morphological regularities of change to 'operate without exception' like sound laws. Thus, in practice, those forms that survive a morphological change unscathed have not been ascribed to the influence of Latin. For example, strong perfect forms that linger on, despite belonging to paradigms that are no longer productive, have avoided being called *cultismos* or 'learnéd', despite the general tendency to discard strong Latin forms in favor of analogous ones created regularly from the stem. Latin v i x i (from v i v o) survived as a strong form in Old Spanish *vísque*, but the weak form *viví* has now supplanted it. Latin d i x i (from d i c o)

developed with phonetic regularity to *dije*. This seems
difficult to explain in terms of phonetic context, or
semantic distinctions; both are very common ordinary words.
Yet I know of no scholar who has even considered calling
dije and other such strong perfects 'cultismos' ascribable
to the pressure of educated groups in society, and quite
rightly, too, for most of these strong perfects are of very
common verbs. Nor can we claim that morphological change
is, by its nature, likely not to be all inclusive; there
are no pockets at all, lexical or geographical, of, for
example, morphologically distinct neuter nouns, synthetic
present passives or vocative cases in Romance. Latin had
all these, Romance has none. These laws *have* operated
'without exception', more than is true of most sound laws.

The fact that explanations of retarded or evaded morphological change have no plausibility at all in a recourse to hypothetical Latin dialects in early Romance communities is good evidence against the usefulness of such explanations applied to phonetic changes, particularly in view of the fact that Latin grammars of the period 500 to 800 A.D. composed in Romance areas lay an inordinate amount of stress on morphological paradigms that have to be learnt by anyone learning to write, and say nothing whatsoever about pronunciation, so that dead morphology would indeed be accessible to the literate in a way that dead pronunciation would be quite inaccessible. Old fashioned morphology and vocabulary can be taken from books; old fashioned speech habits cannot.

The traditional view suggests that particular groups of people can resist sound changes generally affecting the rest of their community for up to a millennium. Surely, historical linguists outside the Romance field will regard this as ludicrous. Collinge, for example, takes it for granted that 'items ... of *high* incidence of use are among the most resistant to regular sound change' (my italics) Collinge 1978:71). In addition, the traditional view assumes that people necessarily pronounce sounds to correspond with every letter they write; that people who spell well necessarily speak in an archaic way; and that the 'pressure' of educated groups can hold back a sound change. This is supposed to have happened in the Early Middle Ages, with a very small literate community and no mass communications.

Let us try to visualize the traditional explanation in context. Were the mediaeval monks doggedly saying *pienso*, with the nasal consonant, and fiercely succeeding in getting everyone else to pronounce it too? If so, why were

they so weak as to fail in this determined effort whenever
the word meant 'weigh'? And why did they accept the de-
nasalized *mesa* of the common herd, without leaving us any
trace of a preference for *mensa? Monks had tables and
weights, after all.

Are we to visualize the Castilian monks being so determined to resist the palatalization of fl- that they re-
fuse to call flowers by anything other than the Latinate
flor? They were happy to change the gender from the Latin
masculine to the Castilian feminine, after all. If so, why
were the Italian monks able to preserve the original gender
and happy to palatalize fl- into Italian *fiore*? How did
the Castilian monks persuade the other ninety-nine per cent
of the population not to say the *llor that they are supposed to have been wanting to say instead? Why do they simultaneously say *llama* with no apparent qualms at all?
Monasteries had fires; the outside world had flowers; and
the traditional view is not only anomalous within historical linguistic theory, but implausible in historical context.

Comparative archaism of pronunciation has nothing in-
trinsically to do with education, literacy or illiteracy,
and the study of sound changes that have not applied to all
apparently qualified items can be carried out more success-
fully without inventing hypothetical 'Latin' dialects from
which to borrow them. Romance philologists may have to
refocus their idea of what is 'regular', but why not?
There are sensible reasons why a word may find itself towards the end of the queue in the lexical diffusion of a
change, and as Samuels says:

> In view of such possibilities, it would seem that com-
> pletely regular sound changes can be expected only as
> rarities. (1972:125)

Latin borrowings may come into Romance languages *after* the
advent of the Carolingian reforms into that community of
course, in which case they are not a miraculous conservative survival over a millennium but a revolutionary new
innovation based on the novel prestige of spelling pronunciations; such a case is Spanish *dulce* (Malkiel 1975). But
for the moment we can conclude that the linguistic phenomena that were once thought to necessitate a belief in the
existence of such a Latinate pronunciation norm before
these reforms can be explained better according to the
usual procedures of historical linguistics. Historical
linguists specializing in other fields need no longer regard this miraculous survival of Latin pronunciation

as established fact, for it is not. Bynon has said:

> There can be no doubt that both the dignitaries of the church and educated people in general used Latin as the normal means of communication throughout the area from a very early period. (1977:249-50)

In my view there is no doubt that they did *not*, and this traditional theory can now be discarded as a historical curiosity, comparable to the theory that space is ether.

NOTE

*This paper is a very condensed version of a chapter of a book at present in preparation, to be entitled *Late Latin and Early Romance (in Spain and France)*.

Bustos Tovar, José Jesús de. 1974. *Contribución al estudio del cultismo léxico medieval*. Madrid: Anejos del Boletín de la Real Academia Española 28.

Bynon, Theodora. 1977. *Historical linguistics*. London: Cambridge University Press.

Chen, Matthew Y. and William S-Y. Wang. 1975. "Sound change: actuation and implementation". *Lg*.51.255-80.

Collinge, Neville E. 1978. "Exceptions, their nature and place - and the Neogrammarians". *Transactions of the Philological Society* 61-86.

Corominas, Joan. 1954-7. *Diccionario crítico etimológico de la lengua castellana*, 4 Vols. Madrid: Gredos.

Macpherson, Ian. 1975. *Spanish Phonology*. Manchester: Manchester University Press.

Malkiel, Yakov. 1975. "En torno al cultismo medieval: los descendientes hispánicos de d u l c i s". *Nueva Revista de Filología Hispánica* 24. 24-45.

Posner, Rebecca. 1974. "Ordering of historical phonological rules in Romance". *Transactions of the Philological Society* 98-127.

Samuels, M.L. 1972. *Linguistic evolution*. London: Cambridge University Press.

Wang, William S-Y. 1969, "Competing changes as a cause of residue". *Lg*.45.9-25.

Wright, Roger. 1976a. "Speaking, reading and writing Late Latin and Early Romance". *Neophilologus* 60.178-89.

_____. 1976b. "Semicultismo". *Archivum Linguisticum* 7.13-28.

_____. 1976c. "Pretonic diphthongs in Old Castilian". *Vox Romanica* 35.133-43.

EARLY INTERVOCALIC VOICING IN TUSCAN

DIETER WANNER
AND
THOMAS D. CRAVENS
University of Illinois, Urbana-Champaign

Applying the recent theoretical concept of variable rule to the old problem of the treatment of intervocalic voiceless consonants in Italian, we intend to show that a preliterary variable voicing rule, motivated through circumstantial evidence, succeeds in resolving this apparent case of 'irregular sound change'.* The modern dialects of Florence and Central Tuscany seem to preserve Latin intervocalic consonants regularly as voiceless (in particular p, t, k, s). In part based on this observation, a typological classification of the Romance dialects into East and West Romance claims that to the north and west of a line La Spezi-Rimini, voicing of Latin intervocalic voiceless consonants is regular (v, d, g, z,), while to the south and east of the line -- including Tuscany and Central Italy -- they were preserved as voiceless.[1] However, the situation in Central Italy is not so clear-cut since Tuscan dialects, and thus the Tuscan-derived standard language, exhibit a considerable number of voiced items from Latin voiceless obstruents.

While Meyer-Lübke (1890:115-25) posited an accent-conditioned voicing rule which left too many cases unexplained, Merlo (1933) set forth the thesis that voicing is the sole indigenous outcome in Tuscany; this was rejected on the same basis of factual inadequacy. The materials of the AIS (Jaberg and Jud 1928-40) indicated that voicing was not native to Tuscany, the position argued earlier by Pieri (1901). Most notably Rohlfs (e.g., 1937, 1966:286-9,319) tried to reconcile with the facts the neogrammarian postulate of regular sound change (which also motivated the earlier attempts at solving the problem) by declaring that items with nonetymological voicing in Tuscan were northern borrowings from French, Provençal, or Northern Italy.[2] The argument is supported by the considerable northern political and cultural influence or domination of Central Italy beginning after the decline of the West Roman Empire. Hall (1943) modified this northern borrowing theory arguing that voiced items entered Tuscany through east central Italy as a result of the effective fusion of the Papal States under Innocent III (at the beginning of the thirteenth century). The Papal dominions (embracing Lazio, Umbria, the Marche, part of Emilia) would have served as conduit for the transmission of northern, especially Emilian, lexical items to Umbria and eventually to Tuscany. Though it can be assumed that some borrowing took place in this manner and at this time, its late date leaves unexplained the clear indications of voicing in Tuscany dating to the eighth century (cf. below).

The generally accepted explanation of the numerous voiced items in Tuscan continues to be that of (direct or indirect) northern borrowing. While the northern provenience of *some* of these items is defensible, a critical look at a rather comprehensive corpus of voiced Tuscan reflexes leaves many unexplained. Drawing from Pieri (1901), Holzheid (1947), and Rohlfs (1966), and excluding items with northern features other than the circular voicing issue, we have been able to identify just over one hundred words from all registers showing intervocalic voicing in modern Tuscan: e.g., *ago* 'needle' < a c u s, *spiga* 'ear (of grain)' < s p i c a, *budello* 'type of sausage' < b o t e l l u s, *sugo* 'juice' < s u c u s. Castellani's contention (1960:67,n.4; cf. also Tuttle 1977:608) that conscious imitation of northern prestige dialects in the Middle Ages led to the introduction of voiced items in Tuscan is weak in view of the presence of voicing in words other than cultural loans. Prestige imitation seems unlikely as an explanation for voicing in items employed in regular communication within those classes which, for socioeconomic reasons, were excluded from sufficient contact with speakers of the presumed prestige model. More important is the fact that the group of voiced items contains disproportionately more instances of voicing of k and t than of p, further undermining the hypothesis of haphazard borrowing of individual words; the most clearly Tuscan items were even further restricted to k, e.g., in toponymy. Thus, the preponderance of the voicing of k points to a *principled linguistic* cause for the voicing phenomenon in Tuscan.

Today the typologically unified dialects of Central Italy and Corsica present functionally identical allophonic alternations for voiceless stops. The dialects of Umbria and Lazio show 'lenited', i.e., lax and partially voiced [p̬], [t̬], [k̬], in word or phrase internal intervocalic position; thus [dík̬o] 'I say', [la#k̬ánna] 'cane', but [báŋko] 'bank', [iŋ#kánna] 'in cane' after a consonant. Corsican dialects of the northeastern section of the island obtain full voicing in the same environment: [dígo], [la#ganna]; but [báŋko] and [iŋ#kánna]. The greater part of Tuscany exhibits the well-known *gorgia toscana*, fricativization of simple *p*, *t*, *k* in the same position as before: [dîxo] or [dího], [la#hánna], but [báŋko], [iŋ#kánna]. All three dialect groups conversely change any consonant to a long segment after a final stressed vowel (or after a lexically designated set of unstressed particles); e.g., [perké#kkorréte] 'why do you run?', [da#kkwándo] 'since when'. Within each dialect group there are subdialects in which the relevant processes affect *k* more than *p* or *t*; in cases of categorical differentiation, only *k* is affected. Most recently Izzo (1972:98) has confirmed the much greater geographical extension of the spirantization of *k* than of *p* or *t* in Tuscany (cf. also Weinrich 1958:105-6), while earlier Bottiglioni (1926-27:46-55) established that Corsican voicing showed a greater southern extension for *k*, and Hall (1943:140) implies that lenition in Lazio affected the velar more widely than other stops (greater extension of borrowing area in his terms). The following rule schemata capture the functional unity of these synchronic variations in phonetic manifestation; [αF] stands for [+vcd] in Corsican, for [-tns, (+vcd)] in Umbria and Lazio, and for [+cont] in Tuscan.

(i) [+obstr] --> [αF] / V (#) _ (L) V

(ii) [+obstr] --> [+long] / [V,+str] # _ (L) V

Giannelli (1973) reports that the peripheral Tuscan areas of spirantization (where only *k* is affected) border immediately on dialects with lenition or lenition-voicing. The surroundings of Grosseto (SW Tuscany) appear to be in the midst of change since the lenited velar of the older generation is being replaced by recently introduced fricativization in the speech of the younger generations. Given the contiguity of (advancing) spirantization of *k* on the one side, and lenition-voicing on the other, Giannelli posits that lenition-voicing may at one time have been regular in those parts of Tuscany which presently only show spirantization; such modern voicelessness could thus be a secondary phenomenon following the reversal of an earlier allophonic lenition-voicing process. This view also agrees well with the typological dialect unity surrounding and including the spirantization of Tuscany, as described in rules (i) and (ii). In light of the voiced/voiceless uncertainty appearing from early Tuscan documents and (to a lesser extent) in the modern dialects, an allophonic voicing rule similar to (i) can now be postulated for early, i.e., preliterary

Tuscan; cf. (iii).

(iii) $\begin{bmatrix} +\text{obstr} \\ -\text{voice} \\ +\text{tense} \\ (!+\text{velar}) \end{bmatrix}$ ---> $\begin{bmatrix} \text{less tense} \\ \text{more voiced} \end{bmatrix}$ / V (#) __ V

conditions: variable with tempo, register (?)

The rule states that an unvoiced intervocalic obstruent, in particular a velar, becomes lenited and possibly partially voiced in intervocalic position either word internally or across word boundaries in those contexts where (ii) is not applicable. The more regular the voicing of the velar, the more expected it is that also *t* and/or *p* will be affected (by natural generalization of the phonological class) through the omission of [+velar]. As a surface phonetic process (iii) must have been variable over performance parameters, striving towards categorial completion with regard to the affected class and the phonetic result (full laxing/voicing). The Tuscan results can now be explained if we assume that rule (iii) ceased to operate in pre-literary Tuscan, before it had reached the stage of a categorial rule applicable to all segments in its phonological class, in all instances, in all environments, and throughout the lexicon. Due to its allophonic nature, in post-consonantal position (word or phrase level) rule (iii) had preserved the voiceless consonants. Thus in word initial position, the syntagmatically conditioned variation V# [C, lenited]X vs. C# [C, -vc]X allowed recovery of the surd, now invariable in all contexts after the cessation of (iii). Those word internal cases corresponding to the structural description of (iii) where voicing had not at all, or not yet consistently, become accepted (i.e., where [k̩] had not phonetically merged with [g] etc.) could give way to the still recoverable basic voiceless manifestations; wherever voicing had become regular the consonant was necessarily interpreted as underlyingly voiced in the absence of any voiceless variants.[3] The lack of voiced results in the verb morphology rests on the interaction of the phonological class limitation of (iii) (only *t* being relevant here) and/or on the contextual transparency of the consonant initial suffixes +*te*, +*tV* as underlying voiceless stops; but derivational suffixes with internal *t* (e.g., +*tade*, +*ada*) did not find such paradigmatic support. The few voicings of *p* are further complicated by the fact that the expected result *b* appears only in a few aphaeresized items (*befana* 'epiphany', *bottega* 'store') in the others turning into *v* (*riva* 'river bank', *vescovo* 'bishop'), which might be linked with the Early Romance fricativization of -*b*-. Given that in preliterary Tuscan -*b*- could only

derive from p through (iii), it must have allowed more
consistent reversal of voicing for p than for k or t,
contributing to the phonological class asymmetry of (iii).

There are various pieces of documentary evidence for
early Tuscan voicing.

(a) In the 13th and 14th centuries voiced forms are
frequently found for items which in other dialects appear
preserved as voiceless. This has been reported for Arezzo
(Serianni 1972), Monte Amiata (Sbarra 1975), even extending to Umbrian in Orvieto (Bianconi 1962); Pisa and Lucca
(Castellani 1952, 1965) etc. In each case k is most
affected. Each dialect thus will have reached a unique
combination of extension and intensity of voicing, while
the core of the examples remains more or less constant.

(b) There is considerable variation in the rendition
of Latin intervocalic surds vacillating between voiced and
voiceless symbolization, such as *recare/regare* 'bring',
botteca/bottega 'store' (Lucca; Castellani 1965:115-7),
luoco/luogo 'place', *riceputa/ricevere* 'receipt; to re-
ceive' (Monte Amiata; Sbarra 1975:57-8). This indicates a
linguistically effective alternation between the two categories, perhaps reinforced by the latinizing effect of the
death of rule (iii), rather than fully contingent, or even
semantically constrained, item by item borrowing.

(c) The formulation of (iii) includes fricatives as
well as the stops. While *f* is less relevant due to its
rarity (all Tuscan reflexes show preservation/restitution
(?) of the voiceless *f*; cf. Rohlfs 1966:203-4), *s* is known
for the same modern double *s* and *z* (Rohlfs 1966:281-4 for
a summary of facts and opinions); but the early Tuscan
voicing status is unidentifiable due to the indifferent
graphic representation of the two sounds as s. However,
the reflexes of Latin -s i̯-, [ʃ] and [ʒ] are of interest
(in spite of Rohlfs' defense of the exclusive voicelessness position, 1966:403-6; cf. also Tuttle 1977 for a similar position). With the alternate spellings *ci, gi, sci,
sgi* for both the voiced and voiceless sound (cf. *rasgione/
rascione* 'reason, rate' = [ʒ] from Galloromance z(i̯),
never *[ʃ]), Tuscan toponyms provide especially good evidence for such voicing. Castellani (1960), drawing from
Pieri (1919), has assembled relevant lists with alternations such as the following: *Baciano* < b a s i a n u,
Fuciano < f u s i a n u, *Suciano* < s o s i a n u; *Tociano* <
t u s i a n u, *Viciano* < v e s i a n u pointing to [ʃ]; vs.
Bugiano < b u s i a n u, *Fregiano* < f r e s i a n u, *Parugiano*
p a l l u s i a n u, *Tugiano* < t u s i a n u, *Vigiano* < v e s i a n u,
suggesting [ʒ]. Such differentiation of s i̯ in t u s i a n u

yields *Tociano* (Monte S. Savino, between Arezzo and Siena) and *Tugiano* (near Certaldo, between Siena and Empoli), both in areas of commonly recognized lack of (modern) voicing or lenition. For the toponyms *Viciano* (a southern suburb of Florence) and *Vigiano* (Borgo S. Lorenzo, Mugello) from v e s i a n u, medieval documentation suggests actual variation, however: Modern *Viciano* is quoted as *Viciano* in 1083, but as *Vigiano* in 1040; modern *Vigiano* is found as *Visciano* in the Latin Libro di Montaperti (1260) (cf. Castellani 1960:57 n.5). Again, the graphic duplication and confusion must rest on a real phonetic variability.

(d) Tuscan documents of the 7th and 8th centuries extend the voicing hypothesis considerably in time. In Latin documents from the archives of Arezzo, dating from 650 to 715, Aebischer (1961) identified recurring sonorizations before *r* (e.g., *consegratus* 'ordained', *saǰratus* 'sacred'). Similarly in 9th century documents from Lucca (including in the Codice diplomatico longobardo) voicing appears, again with *k* being predominantly affected: e.g., *Iagobo*, *altergationem* 'dispute'; *eglesiis* 'church', *sagramenta* 'sacraments', but also *probrietas* 'propriety'. The hypercorrection *Grecorii* (Lucca, 844) shows that for the linguistic awareness of the scribes, voicing was a surface phonetic process subject to (uncertain) reversal while writing in Latin. Given the low degree of classical correction of this chancery tradition, such instances of voicing as well as hypercorrection are to be expected if voicing is a process of the spoken language.[4]

We conclude from this rapid sketch of facts and arguments, intended to support a process interpretation of the sporadic sonorization of intervocalic voiceless consonants in Tuscan, that rule (iii) embodies the various factors responsible for producing the explicandum: Synchronically, rule (iii) of preliterary Tuscan is understood as a *variable rule* (variable frequency of application, variable intensity of modification, restricted phonological class constitution); diachronically in its effect up to the moment of its cessation as a process, (iii) describes a case of *lexical diffusion* (along the axes of the phonological segment and of the phonological class identity); finally in its metachronic impact (after its termination) it implies the *lexicalization* of its most advanced and consistent results of operation, thus another mirage of 'irregular sound change'. This interpretation of the data invalidates one of the two pillars of the division into East and West Romance (as already in Weinreich 1958:59-75); instead of this accidentally constituted simplistic typology, a componential categorization of the Romance languages

is needed. In order to prevent the variability concept
from becoming an empty device of diachronic description
(cf. 'analogy' in neogrammarian and psychologically oriented frameworks) any such claim must be supported by enough
indirect evidence establishing the process nature of the
problem at hand. In contrast to the empirical description
of a living language, such an historical argument cannot
have the value of proof. But continued research into
directly synchronic variability will improve the ability to
apply this concept meaningfully. The central relevance of
variability to real world linguistic change, present and
past, is firmly established (cf. e.g., Wang 1969, Chen and
Wang 1975, Weinreich, Labov and Herzog 1968, Labov 1971);
the understanding of its diachronic implementation needs
further case studies in the vein of the present paper.

NOTES

*The research results presented in this paper, and its oral presentation at ICHL IV 1979, have been made possible in part by funds provided by the Research Board and the Graduate College of the University of Illinois. Due to space limitation, the supporting data can only be introduced by way of references. Likewise, only the central publications will be mentioned which in turn contain the other relevant references.

[1] The other criterion is the preservation of s in Western vs. its loss in Eastern Romance, a trait problematical in its own right; cf. Wartburg 1971:29-41.

[2] The following considerations do not deny the existence of such borrowings; but not all voiced reflexes are eo ipso loans.

[3] The same type of argument was used in Weinrich (1958:133-34) to explain the phonemicization of the much more developed voicing process in traditional voicing areas (e.g., Northern Italy), where restructuring was conditioned by the consummation of the voicing process (phonetic merger of all original voiceless with voiced segments).

[4] This form of early voicing may indicate one of the origins of the process in the assimilatory context *obstr.* + *liquid*. -- The possible North Italian dialectal background of the notaries of Longobard administration centered in Pavia (also centralized?) would only invalidate this last point of evidence; we follow Aebischer 1961 in regarding these documents as relevant for the prehistory of Tuscan.

REFERENCES

Aebischer, Paul. 1961. "La sonorisation des occlusives intervocaliques en Toscane au début du VIIIe siècle d'après le témoignage de quelques documents longobards". *Estudis Romànics* 8.245-63.
Bianconi, Sandro. 1962. "Ricerche sui dialetti d'Orvieto e di Viterbo nel medioevo". *Studi linguistici italiani* 3.3-175.
Bottiglioni, Gino. 1926-7. "La penetrazione toscana e le regioni di Pomonte nei parlari di Corsica". *Italia dialettale* 2.156-210; 3.1-69.
Castellani, Arrigo. 1952. *Nuovi testi fiorentini del dugento*, vol. 1. Florence: Sansoni.
──── . 1960. "Il nesso 'si' in italiano". *Studi linguistici italiani* 5.97-135.
Chen, Matthew Y. and William S-Y. Wang. 1975. "Sound change: actuation and implementation". *Lg.* 51.255-81.
Contini, Gian Franco. 1960. "Per un'interpretazione strutturale della cosidetta 'gorgia' toscana". *Boletim de filologia* 19:263-81.
Giannelli, Luciano. 1973. "*k, p, t* intervocaliche in Toscana". *Atti e memorie dell'Accademia Toscana di Scienze e Lettere "la Colombaria"* 38 (NS 24).33-47.
Hall, Robert A. Jr. 1943. "The Papal states in Italian linguistic history". *Lg.* 19.125-40.
Holzheid, Sieglinde. 1947. *Die stimmlosen intervokalischen Verschlusslaute im Toskanischen*. Unpublished dissertation. Munich.
Izzo, Herbert J. 1972. *Tuscan and Etruscan*. Toronto: University of Toronto Press.
Jaberg, Karl and Jakob Jud. 1928-40. *Sprach- und Sachatlas Italiens und der Südschweiz*. Zofingen: Ringier (8 vols.)
Labov, William. 1971. "Methodology". In *A survey of linguistic science*, 412-91. Ed. by W.O. Dingwall. Dept. of Linguistics, University of Maryland.
Merlo, Clemente. 1933. "Il sostrato etnico e i dialetti italiani". *Italia dialettale* 9.1-27.
Meyer-Lübke, Wilhelm. 1890. *Italienische Grammatik*. Leipzig: Reisland.
Pieri, Silvio. 1901. "I riflessi italiani delle esplosive sorde tra vocali". *Archivio glottologico italiano* 15.369-89.
──── . 1919. *Toponomastica della Valle dell'Arno*. Rome: R. Accademia dei Lincei.
Rohlfs, Gerhard. 1937. *La struttura linguistica dell'Italia*. Leipzig: Keller.
──── . 1966. *Grammatica storica della lingua italiana e dei suoi dialetti*, vol. 1. Turin: Einaudi.
Sbarra, Siriana. 1975. "Documenti inediti dell'amiatino tre-quattrocentesco". *Studi di filologia italiana* 33.15-188.
Serianni, Luca. 1972. "Ricerche sul dialetto aretino nei secoli XIII e XIV". *Studi di filologia italiana* 30.59-191.
Tuttle, Edward. 1977. "Sociolinguistics and philology applied to an Italian phonologic asymmetry". In *The Third LACUS Forum*, 605-13. Ed.

by Robert J. Di Pietro and Edward L. Blansitt, Jr.. Columbia, South Carolina: Hornbeam.

Wang, William S-Y. 1969. "Competing sound changes as a cause of residue". *Lg*. 45.9-25.

Wartburg, Walther von. 1971. *La fragmentación lingüística de la Romania*. Madrid: Gredos, 2nd ed.

Weinreich, Uriel, William Labov, and Marvin I. Herzog. 1968. "Empirical foundations for a theory of language change". In *Directions for historical linguistics*, 97-195. Ed. by Winfred P. Lehmann and Yakov Malkiel. Austin: University of Texas Press.

Weinrich, Harald. 1958. *Phonologische Studien zur romanischen Sprachgeschichte*. Münster: Aschendorff.

THE TRANSITION PROBLEM:
LEXICAL DIFFUSION VS. VARIABLE RULES

JOHN REIGHARD
Université de Montréal

0. *Introduction*. In the data presented here - the change of [wɛ] to [wa] in Modern French - I would like to demonstrate a case of phonological change in which structural evolution of a variable rule and lexical diffusion take place at one and the same time.*[1] I also want to show the particular way in which an intermediate stage of the change takes on a powerful social function. In particular I want to show how the social marking associated with the change can be associated both with a structural stage of the evolving rule and with a stage of lexical diffusion. I will in addition have something to say about the relationship between the appearance of social marking on the ongoing change and the social conflict in eighteenth century France which culminated in the Revolution of 1789.

1. *The sixteenth century*. In the second half of the sixteenth century the majority of grammarians recognize only the pronunciation [wɛ], but the newer pronunciation [wa] is observed occasionally (e.g., in *bois* 'wood', *voix* 'voice', *disoit* 'said', *gloire* 'glory', *voile* 'veil', *trois* 'three', *mois* 'month', *fois* 'time', and *pois* 'pea').[2]

The variable nature of the rule can be seen from the fact that few examples occur at this time with the innovative pronunciation, as well as from the fact that not all grammarians observe the newer form, nor agree on which words it occurs in. In addition there is evidence already of lexical diffusion.

As far as the structural details of the rule itself are concerned, we may assume that it was a variable rule subject to a number of phonological constraints. Most examples have [wa] in a stressed final syllable, most often when the vowel itself is long; in nonfinal syllables [wa] is always long.[3] Thus we may write the following rule for the sixteenth century.

(1) $[wɛ] \longrightarrow \langle wa \rangle \quad / \quad \dfrac{}{\langle +long \rangle} C_o \langle \# \rangle$

2. *The seventeenth century*. For this period we have a great number of attestations of the new pronunciation, but it is useful to separate the grammarians of this period into two groups, which I will call the 'insiders' and the 'outsiders'. The outsiders consist of a group of grammarians, writing throughout the century, all of whom are either foreigners, or Frenchmen located somewhere outside of Paris. The insiders are not only Parisians, but are also typically active in Parisian intellectual or literary circles. Specifically this means that they have access to the literary salons, the Académie, or to the royal court itself, the three domains of activity where linguistic matters were not only extensively discussed, but where questions of correctness were ultimately decided. The attestations of the newer pronunciation given by the outsiders show clearly the extent of the spread of the sound change. Where these grammarians indicate the innovative pronunciation, it is entirely without evaluative judgement of any kind. In some cases, [wa] is given as the only pronunciation (e.g., by Lubin 1609, Van der Aa 1622, Mauger 1697, and Piélat 1700); in other cases specific examples are given (e.g., *roi* 'king', *miroir* 'mirror', *décrottoir* 'footscraper', *croix* 'cross', *bois*, *foi* 'faith', *loi* 'law', *moi* 'me', *toi* 'you', *droit* 'right').

The reaction of the insiders to the innovative pronunciation however is quite different. Here it is severely criticized, and in no uncertain terms. Beginning with Henri Estienne in 1582 [wa] is described as a pronunciation that can be heard in the speech of some court followers and in common Paris speech, unfortunately imitated by many people. It is then variously described by these grammarians as 'very corrupt' (Bèze 1584), as a 'fault even of Parisians' (d'Aisy 1674), as associated with 'crude and lazy people' (Hindret 1687), as 'very bad' (De la Touche 1696), and as a 'faulty pronunciation ... common even among respectable people in Paris, but which everyone admits as being faulty' (Buffier 1709) (Thurot 1966:357-8).

Examples given by this group include *bois*, *poids* 'weight', *poix* 'pitch', *pois*, *trois* 'three', *mois*, *noix* 'walnut', *voir* 'see' and *joie* 'joy'.

These forms show that the rule has generalized to final position, whether the vowel is long or short, and is apparently on its way to becoming categorical in that position, for some speakers at least.

(2) $[wɛ] \longrightarrow \langle wa \rangle \ / \ \underline{\quad} C_o \langle \# \rangle$

But once again there is considerable lexical diffusion, grammarians often disagreeing on whether particular words are pronounced [wɛ] or [wa]. There is one set of words which show up continually during this period, a subset of words formerly ending in a long vowel (e.g., *bois, trois, pois,* etc.), and these are all words which do not participate in productive morphological alternations. This fact suggests that for many speakers they have been reanalyzed, and are now simply listed in the lexicon with an underlying representation in [wa]. This, then, is the particular form that lexical diffusion is taking here. A subset of those words ending in a long vowel has undergone lexical reanalysis.

Notice however, that for many speakers the rule continues to operate as a variable rule. This means that the strong social stigmatization which is attached to the innovative pronunciation is in fact sensitive at one and the same time to the operation of a variable rule and to a lexical subset in which lexical diffusion has taken place.

3. *The eighteenth century.* In this period, innovative [wa] is accepted by some Parisian observers for the first time in a systematic manner: in final position by 1709 (Boindin) and before a final consonant by about 1750 (Dumarsais). Examples from the period include: *bois, mois, noix, pois, dois* 'must', *vois* 'see', *abois* 'at bay', *Génois* 'Genoan', *Suédois* 'Swede', *Liégeois* 'inhabitant of Liège'; *foi, loi, moi, quoi* 'what'; *joie, Troie* 'Troy'; *froid* 'cold', *toit* 'roof', *doigt* 'finger'; *avoir* 'have', *vouloir* 'want', *devoir* 'must', *pouvoir* 'be able', *voir; gloire* 'glory', *croire* 'believe', *boire* 'drink', *poire* 'pear'; *poivre* 'pepper'; *coiffe* 'headdress', *toile* 'canvas', *voile* 'veil', *moine* 'monk', *Antoine*).

Once again we have clear indications of lexical diffusion (especially, for example, with *boire, lavoir* 'washing room', *couloir* 'hall', *moine, Antoine,* and *poil* 'hair', all of which occur at least twice with different pronunciations recorded).

We can see then that the rule applies in a virtually categorical manner in all final syllables. These facts can be expressed as follows:

(3) [wɛ] ⟶ [wa] / ___C #

As far as the social evaluation of the innovative pronunciation is concerned, we find explicit acceptance of [wa] in all possible positions for the first time in 1751 (Dumarsais), in 1761 (Féraud), and quite unambiguously in 1805 (Domergue), just at the time of the French Revolution. Beginning about 1750 then, we may assume that for some speakers at least, all phonological constraints (and socal constraints) have been dropped from the rule:

(4) [wɛ] ⟶ [wa] / ___

However once again observers split into two groups: the progressives, who accept willingly the new pronunciation, and the reactionaries, who continue to reject it. Unlike the seventeenth century, when acceptance or rejection depended on whether or not the observer had access to aristocratic circles, in the eighteenth century we find both reactions among grammarians writing and living in Paris, and even among some very influential people. Among our reactionaries we find, for example, Antonini (1753), born in Italy, but who taught Italian in Paris for twenty-five years, and who published a grammar of French in 1753 (Thurot 1966:lxxxi); Restaut (1730), born the son of a fabric merchant, but who was a professor at the Collège Louis-le-Grand in Paris and who later acted as a lawyer in Parliament and on the King's Councils (Thurot 1966:lxxviii); and De Wailly (1763), born in Amiens, but who lived in Paris and who wrote a grammar of French which was adopted as a text by the University of Paris in 1765 (Thurot 1966:lxxxiv). Among these grammarians (including also Mauvillon (1754), Galmace (1767), Demandre (1769) and Delarivière (1799)), the newer pronunciation is either explicitly condemned, or simply not given, even for words which as we have seen, had been pronounced [wa] by a great many speakers for a considerable time.

Those grammarians who fully accept the new pronunciation, on the other hand, can in many cases be independently identified as progressives in the social or political sense. For example, Dumarsais (1761) was closely associated with the Enlightenment movement of the eighteenth century; he collaborated on that monument of eighteenth rationalism, the *Encyclopédie* of Diderot and D'Alembert, by contributing articles on grammar. Féraud (1761) was a Jesuit, and a professor at Besançon for many years. Finally, Domergue (1805) was an active and influential member of the Committee on Public Instruction under the Revolutionary Convention government (Cohen 1950:239).

Clearly the conflict between these two groups of grammarians centers around which form of speech is to be accepted as the standard. It is often claimed that [wa] was a popular form of speech and that its final acceptance as standard at the time of the Revolution was symptomatic of the changing power structures in French society at that time (cf. Cohen 1950:231, for example). In other words, according to this view, while conflict in the seventeenth century centered around aristocratic, as opposed to non-aristocratic forms of speech, in the eighteenth century, conflict centered around popular, as opposed to upper class speech.

However, there is considerable evidence that the new standard adopted toward the end of the eighteenth century was not that of popular speech, but rather that of the bourgeoisie. It is clear from the statements of the grammarians themselves that the newer pronunciation was widespread in Parisian society and by no means limited to lower classes, even in the seventeenth century (Thurot 1966:357-359). And as Domergue points out quite clearly in 1805, the older form [wɛ] was in fact normal in popular speech in the region just outside Paris. This observation is borne out quite clearly in the *Atlas linguistique de la France*, which shows that [wɛ] abounds even in the early twentieth century in the Ile-de-France region (as elsewhere in France) (Gilliéron and Edmont 1902-1910).

But in fact, all of this follows when we realize that the French Revolution consecrated the power and authority not of the popular masses - workers and peasants - but rather that of the land holding bourgeoisie and those with large financial interests (in the words of Balibar and Laporte (1974:11) this was a 'bourgeois democratic revolution'). The conflict that still went on in the eighteenth century between progressives and reactionaries surely symbolizes precisely that social conflict between the bourgeoisie and the aristocracy. We might say then that the change from [wɛ] to [wa] represents social pressure from below, but only in this very restricted sense. In fact the late eighteenth century conflict is more reminiscent of Bourdieu and Boltanski's model of the linguistic marketplace, and of the bitter conflicts which can arise among speakers of prestige dialects concerning precisely which forms are to constitute the standard for everyone (Bourdieu and Boltanski 1975:12).

NOTES

*This research was supported by a grant from the Ministère de l'Education de Québec, FCAC EQ-870.

[1] By 'structural evolution of a variable rule' I have in mind the kind of rule change described in Labov (1972). By 'lexical diffusion' I mean specifically the transition model presented in Chen and Wang (1975). See also Reighard (1977).

[2] All examples and references to earlier grammarians in this paper are taken from Thurot (1966).

In fact [wɛ] undergoes two changes: [wɛ]→[wa] as in *François* (proper name), *danois* 'Danish', and *froid* 'cold'; but [wɛ]→ [ɛ] as in *Français* 'French', *-ais* 1sg. imperf., and Canadian Fr. *frette* 'cold'. Only the first change is discussed in this paper.

[3] Length was a distinctive feature of all French vowels in all positions until the mid-seventeenth century, and is indicated orthographically by postvocalic s̱ (which was not itself pronounced), or by the circumflex accent.

REFERENCES

Balibar, Renée and Dominique Laporte. 1974. *Le français national: politique et pratiques de la langue nationale sous la Révolution française.* Paris: Hachette.

Bourdieu, Pierre and Luc Boltanski. 1975. "Le fétichisme du langage". *Actes de recherche en sciences sociales* 4.2-32.

Chen, Matthew Y. and William S.-Y. Wang. 1975. "Sound change: actuation and implementation". *Lg.* 51.255-81.

Cohen, Marcel. 1950. *Histoire d'une langue: le français (des lointaines origines à nos jours).* Paris: Les Editeurs Français Réunis.

Gilliéron, Jules and Edmond Edmont. 1902-1910. *Atlas linguistique de la France.* Paris: Champion.

Labov, William. 1972. "The internal evolution of linguistic rules". In *Linguistic change and generative theory,* 101-71. Ed. by Robert P. Stockwell and Ronald K. S. Macaulay. Bloomington: Indiana University Press.

Reighard, John. 1977. "The evolution of variable rules: a case of lexical constraints". In *Studies in Romance linguistics,* 96-109. Ed. by Michio Peter Hagiwara. Rowley, Mass.: Newbury Press.

Thurot, Charles. 1966. *De la prononciation française depuis le commencement du XVIe siècle, d'après les témoignages des grammariens.* Geneva: Slatkine Reprints.

LEXICAL ALTERNATION AND THE HISTORY OF ENGLISH:
EVIDENCE FROM AN URBAN VERNACULAR

JAMES MILROY
Queen's University, Belfast

Matthew Chen (1976:228) has commented that in the course of a linguistic change: A —> B, there is a stage during which A *alternates* with B.* This paper presents data from a low prestige variety of English which strongly suggests that the duration of the alternating stage: A~B, may be considerable; the issue of *residue* is naturally of importance here, particularly the manner in which residual word classes and individual residual lexical items may be preserved over a substantial period of time. In the first alternation discussed, we focus on a well-known difficulty in the history of English.

One of the most celebrated problems in English historical linguistics is the *MEET/MEAT/MATE* problem: the apparent merger in the sixteenth century of Middle English (ME) long 'open' *e* (the *MEAT* class) with ME long *a* (the *MATE* class), followed by what appears to be a reversal of this merger and subsequent coalescence of ME long open *e* with long 'close' *e* (the *MEET* class). This wholesale reversal of merger has always seemed puzzling, and various solutions have been offered (e.g. the influence of 'social dialects': Wyld 1936; differential functional load of the various classes: Samuels 1972). Recently, work by Labov and his associates on informant responses in experimental situations has suggested that realizations of phonemes can approximate each other closely without actually merging, and that such approximations can be interpreted by speakers as mergers, even though they are not (Labov, Yaeger and Steiner 1972, Labov 1974, Nunberg 1975). Thus, by 'the use of the present to explain the past', it can be suggested that the reported sixteenth century merger of *MEAT* with *MATE* was not a true merger but an approximation. The subsequent merger of *MEAT* with *MEET* then becomes less puzzling, though not yet fully explained. Detailed sociolin-

guistic work in Northern Ireland, investigating three
inner-city working-class communities in Belfast, can throw
some light on what the specific situation in Early Modern
English (E.Mod.E) may have been.

Labov (1974) considers that for modern English, the
conservative [e:] pronunciation for items of the *MEAT* class
is now a dead issue. This overlooks what should perhaps be
obvious: viz. that in some dialects, notably Irish forms
of English, the issue is by no means dead. The [e:] vowel
in *tea*, *sea* etc. is an Irish stereotype, found in the works
of Irish authors such as O'Casey and Synge. In rural dialects, this E.Mod.E class is to a great extent preserved in
such items as *wheat*, *weak*, *tea* (all with [e:]); and for Belfast a nineteenth century source (Patterson 1860) gives a
list of over a hundred items that then had the historic
[e:] pronunciation. In our investigation, speakers of the
working class vernacular have this [e:] vowel in (monosyllabic) items such as *beat*, *cheap*, *beak*, *peace*, *read*, *leave*,
steal and in the disyllable *decent*. Thus, in Irish dialects (including Belfast) we have direct access to a situation which had become irrelevant to Standard English by the
eighteenth century (Labov 1974). Examination of the present position in these dialects should therefore give us
some insight into the E.Mod.E situation.

Two questions arise. First: in what manner is the
present day merger between *MEAT* and *MEET* coming about?
Second: are tokens of the *MEAT* class with [e:] identical
with tokens of the *MATE* class? This question is of importance because it is clear that the *MEAT* class with [e:] is
a recessive or residual class, and that change is in progress.

The [e:] pronunciation in the *MEAT* class occurs in
Belfast urban vernacular only in the most casual informal
speech in intimate settings when members of closeknit social networks (Milroy and Margrain 1978) are interacting
with one another. Tokens using this pronunciation are only
accessible in any quantity to the fieldworker if very careful methods of access to the community are used. This pronunciation would not be accessible in urban speech to a
dialectologist using a formal questionnaire. From about
100 hours of tape we have so far identified less than 100
occurrences of *MEAT* tokens with the conservative [e:] pronunciation. When their attention is drawn to speech, informants transfer tokens of this class to the *MEET* class;
this is especially so in reading styles, in which informants cannot be induced to utter *MEAT* tokens with [e:].
Thus, in urban speech, the *MEAT* class is an alternating

class, and we are observing a late stage of lexical transfer or diffusion of *MEAT* items into the *MEET* class. There is no question of gradual phonetic approximation: it is a binary choice system with one alternant appearing occasionally in the most casual styles and the other when speech is more 'careful'.

The second question (are tokens of the recessive *MEAT* class identical with the *MATE* class?) is more difficult to answer, but preliminary results of work so far would appear to support Labov's argument that these two classes did not actually merge in the sixteenth century. For many rural and for some urban speakers, ME long a (and ai diphthong) items appear with a low-mid vowel [ε]. This is especially true in final position: items like *day*, *way* usually have [ε:], but closed syllable items such as *name*, *make*, *train* often occur with long or short [ε]. Our transcriptions from elderly rural speakers in S.W. Donegal suggest that the Great Vowel Shift has not been fully implemented there and that for many lexical items at least, a three-way distinction is preserved. Here, *meet* has [i], *wheat*, *weak*, *tea* have [e:], *name*, *place* have [ε:]. In Belfast, the three-way distinction is more difficult to establish, since, in the urban vernacular, reflexes of ME long a (*name*, *place*, etc.) have been raised to a high-mid or even high vowel with a centering glide. A chainshift mechanism would appear to require that the *MEAT* class should either merge with one of the other two classes or move out of the way. The ultimate proof that the two classes (*MEAT* and *MATE*) have merged or have not merged in Belfast depends on instrumental or quantificational evidence being produced; quantification and statistical analysis of the data have established that the phonetic distribution of *MEAT* items differs from that of *MATE* items to a statistically 'highly significant' degree ($p < .01$ by chi square test). The two classes have come very close together *without* merging--so close together that informants believe, when their attention is drawn to the recessive [e:] pronunciation in *MEAT*, that *MATE* and *MEAT* are 'the same'. In short, the slight distinction between these two is preserved only *below the level of consciousness*. When attention is drawn to speech, the residual three-way distinction is interpreted as a two-way distinction.

It seems entirely plausible to suggest that in E.Mod.E a similar situation may have existed. That is, the raising of ME long a brought about a situation where *MEAT* and *MATE* approximated, and at the same time a process of transfer of *MEAT* tokens to the *MEET* class came about. The lexical alternation involved in this seems in our Belfast study to be a very important phenomenon in the vernacular, and it may be suggested that it is a common property of nonstandard vernacular speech now and in the past. The phenomenon is not easily accessible by formal questionnaire methods, which tend to elicit single, unique forms for lexical items. Furthermore, identification of these alternations in a given present-day dialect may give us an insight into a particular kind of linguistic change in progress: a form of lexical diffusion (Wang 1969; Cheng and Wang 1973; Krishnamurti 1978; Toon 1978, etc.). In several alternating sets, we have been able to quantify the data (J. Milroy 1978). One of the most interesting of these is the (*pull*) set.

In Belfast vernacular there is no class corresponding to Standard English (St.E) short /u/, phonetically [ʉ], (as in *good*, *foot*), but a restricted lexical set (including *pull*, *bull*, *foot*) alternates between [ʌ], as in *cut*, *dull*, and [ʉ] as in *soon*, *pool*. That is, realizations of, e.g., *pull* merge alternately with the *dull* class and the *pool* class. The total membership of this set cannot be exactly predicted on phonological or historical grounds: whereas *would*, *took*, *foot* belong to it, *wood*, *cook*, *soot* do not. This alternation is an important and highly marked sociolinguistic variable, with the [ʌ] alternant carrying strong vernacular connotations and having clear symbolic value for speakers: they are consciously aware of it and remark on it. Quantification of the eighteen relevant items (about 1600 tokens) that occur in our data shows a clear 'covert prestige' pattern, with young males aggressively preferring the vernacular (and more conservative) alternant in spontaneous conversational style:

	Men 40-55	Women 40-55	Men 18-25	Women 18-25
Interview Style	12	29	43	12
Spontaneous Style	24	36	61	20

The (*pull*) variable: %[ʌ] alternant
TABLE I

These general figures, however, do not show that lexical items belonging to the alternating class are being transferred from the more conservative [ʌ] set to the more innovative [ʉ] set at differential rates. Tables II and III give the figures for individual lexical items, classified into two sets according to historical origin.

Certain generalizations can be based on these figures, as follows:

1. Disyllables are, in general, more resistant to transfer into the incoming [ʉ] class than are monosyllables.

LEXICAL ALTERNATIONS   359

(i) Items from M.E. short u (ii) Items from M.E. ō and other sources

	[ʊ]	[ʌ]	%		[ʊ]	[ʌ]	%
butcher	23	27	54	shook	40	1	2
bush	21	11	34	took	64	0	0
bull	27	14	34	foot	35	0	0
pudding	36	4	10	could	56	0	0
put	49	4	8	look	7	0	0
pull	34	1	3	would	41	0	0
				should	10	0	0
Totals							
b-items	71	52	42	*Total*	253	1	0.4
p-items	119	9	7				
Disyll.	59	31	39				
Monosyll.	131	34	21				

% occurrences of [ʌ] in reading styles
TABLE II

(i) Items from M.E. short u (ii) Items from M.E. ō and other sources

	[ʊ]	[ʌ]	%		[ʊ]	[ʌ]	%
bullet	2	8	80	football	5	4	44
pull	18	51	74	stood	10	7	41
full	17	15	47	foot	22	12	35
put	189	120	39	took	99	49	33
push	11	5	31	could	186	82	31
butcher	0	1	-	look	140	51	27
bush	1	2	-	would	453	88	16
bull	2	1	-	should	54	5	8
pudding	1	0	-	shook	0	1	-
Totals				*Totals*			
b-items	5	12	71	Disyll.	5	4	44
p-items	219	176	45	Monosyll.	964	295	23
Disyll.	3	9	75				
Monosyll.	235	191	45				

% occurrences of [ʌ] in conversational styles
TABLE III

2. Items from ME short u with initial labials are more resistant to transfer than are items from ME long ō and other sources.

3. Items from ME short u with initial labials are remarkably resistant to transfer even in reading styles (this may be affected by the ambiguity of the u spelling, as against *oo*).

4. Labial items with initial [b] are more resistant to transfer than other labial items.

But even when these generalizations are made, the fact remains that each individual lexical item seems to have its own unique probability of transfer from one class to the other. Notably, the item *pull*, which is not a disyllable and does not have initial [b], occurs in the vernacular alternant no less than 74% of the time, and is therefore remarkably resistant. It would appear that it is showing a tendency to remain behind as a *residue*.

In this case sociosemantic factors would appear to be involved. The item *pull* occurs frequently in casual speech as a slang term meaning, in effect, 'to beat up', as in 'I was [pʌld] for that', i.e. 'beaten up'. When it occurs in this meaning it is probably always an [ʌ] item. Our data from informal speech suggest generally that sociosemantic factors may often be involved in bringing about lexical residue.

In general terms, there is no doubt that the direction of change is from [ʌ] to [ʉ]. Evidence from the nineteenth century (Patterson 1860) shows that in addition to the items we have quantified, three additional items (*wood, wool, hood*) could at that time be realized with [ʌ]. These occur in our data only with [ʉ] and have clearly become categorical [ʉ] items in Belfast. Thus, we have a long term situation in which:

1. Certain alternating items have already been transferred to the incoming class;

2. Certain items alternate between the two classes;

3. Certain items may remain behind in the recessive class.

The items which remain behind are characteristically disyllables or polysyllables. The items *pulpit, pulley, woman* and *cushion* occur in our data as [ʌ] items only, and [ʌ] pronunciations for proper names like *Fulton, Fullerton* have been widely observed. There are thus strong indications that disyllabic items tend to remain behind in the conservative class, so that one can conceive of a future situation in which, e.g., *bull* may have been transferred to the [u] set, whereas *bullet* remains behind with [ʌ]. Such stabilization of the system, in which the alternation applies between monosyllables and disyllables, has not been achieved in this instance, but there are other alternations in which some stabilization of the system has been achieved. This is particularly clear in the case of 'short' /ɛ/ and 'short' /ɔ/. In these, a marked difference between a long mid vowel ([ɛ:, ɔ:]) and a low, short, front to central vowel ([a]) exists in, e.g., the following pairs of words (J. Milroy 1976; Milroy and Milroy 1978):

i) Monosyll. (mid, long)	ii) Disyll./polysyll. (low, short)
Ed	Eddy
Tom	Tommy
Prod*	Protestant
fell	fellow
ten	tenor
wed	wedding
mėss	message

*slang for 'Protestant'

TABLE IV

Our studies of the (ɛ) and (ɔ) variables (J. Milroy 1976, Milroy and Milroy 1977, 1978) have shown that linguistic change in progress moves away from [a] in the direction of the long mid vowels. Here as elsewhere, therefore, disyllables and polysyllables are resistant to change and preserve the conservative vowel. The result is that in most environments a regular alternation is set up between monosyllables (mid vowel) and disyllables (low vowel). This alternation is plainly phonetically conditioned.

On the basis of our study of the (*meat*) set, the (*pull*) set and of the /ɛ/ and /ɔ/ alternations, a number of general conclusions may be suggested.

(a) In vernacular speech, recessive or residual lexical sets can persist over long time scales.

(b) In-depth study of casual vernacular speech, as distinct from formal or standardized speech, can reveal linguistic changes in progress of a kind which reflect on probable vernacular changes in earlier stages of a language. The facts are not easily accessible by standard questionnaire methods.

(c) Vernaculars, as distinct from standard languages, may be rich in simple lexical alternations. The study of these may reveal long term processes of change by lexical transfer or diffusion.

(d) In the process of transfer, certain environments may be relatively resistant to change. In some cases this may result in stabilized alternation between, e.g., monosyllables and disyllables.

(e) There are some indications that true or permanent lexical residue may be conditioned by sociosemantic factors in addition to phonetic factors.

NOTE

*The research on which this paper is based was supported by a grant (HR 3771) from the Social Science Research Council, London.

REFERENCES

Chen, Matthew Y. 1976. "Relative chronology: three methods of reconstruction". *JL*.12.209-58.
Cheng, Chin-Chuan and William S.-Y. Wang. 1973. "Tone change in Cháo-Zhōu Chinese". In *Issues in linguistics: papers in honor of Henry and Renee Kahane*, 99-113. Ed. by Braj B. Kachru. Urbana: University of Illinois Press.
Krishnamurti, Bh. 1978. "Areal and lexical diffusion of sound change". *Lg*. 54.1-20.
Labov, William. 1974. "On the use of the present to explain the past". In *Proceedings of the Eleventh International Congress of Linguists*. Ed. by Luigi Heilman. Bologna: El Mulino.
Labov, William, Malcah Yaeger and Richard Steiner. 1972. *A quantitative study of sound change in progress*. University of Pennsylvania: U.S. Regional Survey.
Milroy, James. 1976. "Length and height variations in the vowels of Belfast vernacular". *Belfast Working Papers in Language and Linguistics* 1.69-110.
_____. 1978. "Lexical alternation and diffusion in vernacular speech". *Belfast Working Papers in Language and Linguistics* 3.100-14.
Milroy, James and L. Milroy. 1977. "Speech community and language variety in Belfast". Report to the Social Science Research Council. London.
_____. 1978. "Belfast: change and variation in an urban vernacular". In *Sociolinguistic patterns in British English*, 19-36. Ed. by Peter Trudgill. London: Edward Arnold.
Milroy, L. and S. Margrain. 1978. "Vernacular language loyalty and social network". *Belfast Working Papers in Language and Linguistics* 3.1-58.
Nunberg, Geoffrey. 1975. "A falsely reported merger in 18th century English". *Pennsylvania Working Papers in Linguistic Change and Variation* 1:2.
Patterson, D. 1860. *The provincialisms of Belfast*. Belfast: Mayne.
Samuels, M.L. 1972. *Linguistic evolution*. Cambridge: Cambridge University Press.
Toon, Thomas E. 1978. "Lexical diffusion in Old English". *Papers from the Parasession on the Lexicon*, 357-64. Chicago: Chicago Linguistic Society.
Wang, William S.-Y. 1969. "Competing changes as a cause of residue". *Lg*. 45.9-25.
Wyld, H.C. 1936. *A history of modern colloquial English*. London: Basil Blackwell. 3rd ed.

PRAGMATIC FEATURES
AND PHONOLOGICAL CHANGE

MARTHA LAFERRIERE
University of Massachusetts - Boston
and
Massachusetts Institute of Technology

The study of phonological variation and change in recent years has been concerned with the social factors within speech communities which govern the individual speaker's choice of linguistic variants. The empirical nature of these studies has shown that variable rules (Sankoff 1978) and other formulations must allow for an array of interdependent conditioning factors, attributes which make up the personal profile of both speaker and hearer: age, sex, ethnicity, race, occupation, education, class. None of these factors acts independently, but always in combination with at least one other factor.

The ontogeny of linguistic change lies in this very synchronic variation. Changes observed across several generations of speakers, as the work of Labov and others has shown, indicate that the same factors which condition synchronic variation also determine which variants will be carried through diachronically, and which will die out. Another finding of sociolinguistic research with relevance to linguistic change is that speech communities are made up of socially defined subgroups, often with overlapping characteristics. By examining the small details of social groupings as they relate to variation, that is, the designations which speakers use about themselves, their social groups, other social groups, their speech, and the speech of others, we can attempt to formulate some rules for change.

To describe the relationship between variation and change I will adopt a framework of *pragmatic features*. Like phonetic features, pragmatic features are identifying features attached to sound segments. Whereas phonetic features specify articulatory requirements of segments, pragmatic features specify the 'situational appropriateness' (Bailey 1973) of the segment with which they are identified. Pragmatic features relate articulation to the ethnographic requirements of communication, and may be situated in the conscious or unconscious speech behavior of the individual or his social group.

Pragmatic features are associated with allophones, or variants, of a phoneme. Most importantly, they are created by the consensus of the social group, which may be the entire speech community, or well-defined subgroups of the larger speech community. Thus a variant may have different pragmatic labels for different subgroups, although it may have a feature shared by all subgroups. For example, a variant may have the pragmatic feature 'working class' for all speakers, but it may, in addition, have the feature 'stigmatized' for one subgroup and 'correct' for another. A situation in which subgroups of a speech community have one different and one opposing pragmatic feature associated with the same variant is a situation of potential sound change.

A case of phonetic alternation in the Boston dialect (Laferriere, to appear) may serve to illustrate the role of pragmatic features in variation and change. In the Boston dialect, (and in all of Eastern New England), many words spelled with *or* have two variants. A sampling of these words includes the following:

form, normal, storm; short, quarter, forty, New York, orchestra, fork; orbit, order, landlord, organ, organization, George; orphan, horse, yours, north, orthopedic

One variant is the dialect phone, [ɒ], a low back slightly rounded vowel which I will refer to with the pragmatic feature 'local'. The other variant is [o], a mid back rounded vowel. I will refer to this variant as 'non-local', meaning that it is something other than the dialect form, and approximates an external standard. This standard is equivalent to what the dialect speaker thinks is standard, or correct, English, as may be seen in speakers' subjective evaluation of the two variants: pronouncing *short* as [ʃoᵊt][1] is referred to as 'putting the *r* in', whereas [ʃɒᵊt] is 'dropping the *r*'.

An empirical investigation showed that in general, there was a greater use of the local variant among speakers with less education, reflecting the association of [ɒ] with local, familial, and high-school oriented activity, and the non-local variant [o] with outer-directed personal contacts such as one makes at college or in a job where one associates with non-dialect speakers. In fact, one set of pragmatic labels that came from several subjects independently related the non-local [o] variant to education. The local [ɒ] was considered correct and acceptable in *speaking*, but the [o] form was the one which a person should use when *reading*. That is, one should 'put one's *r*'s in' (=[o]) when reading since they are there on the printed page. In speaking, however, the consensus was that it was too difficult, and somewhat unnatural, to use [o] in casual speech.

Education by itself, however, was not enough to define *or* variation, since some highly educated persons were also heavy dialect users, and others showed continuous alternation between local and non-local variants. The study showed that level of education, when combined with ethnicity, or subgroup membership, defined the pragmatic features of the *or* variable. I interviewed speakers of three ethnic groups, which are clearly distinguishable (in Boston) and which have long histories in the area - Irish, Italian, and Jewish. Jewish speakers considered the non-local form 'correct' and 'educated' and the local form 'stigmatized', implying 'uneducated' and even 'low class'. Both highly educated and less educated Jewish speakers applied this pragmatic labelling to the local variant. Many of the Jewish speakers also considered the local form to be 'Irish' (an interesting observation in that Italian speakers had a higher percentage of [ɒ] than Irish speakers). Most Jewish speakers in the study labelled the local form negatively, including those Jewish speakers who were [ɒ] users, but denied that they used it.

Irish and Italian speakers were the ones who applied the 'speaking' vs. 'reading' labels to the local and non-local forms respectively. Thus while all three groups recognized a pragmatic difference between the variants - roughly positive values for the non-local form and some negativity for the local form - the degree of negativity is what separates the Jewish speakers from the Irish and the Italians. The negative evaluations of the local form by these latter groups were much milder and less condemnatory than those of the Jewish speakers. The most negative evaluation of the local form from an Italian speaker was that it made one sound 'inner-city' as opposed to suburban. Highly educated Irish and Italian speakers who used the local form said that they tried to use the non-local form but 'slipped' occasionally.

While all Boston speakers recognized [ɒ] as 'local' and acknowledged that the two variants imply different things about the person using them, the degree of stigmatization of the local variant is different for different subgroups. For the Jewish speakers, 'local' implies 'uneducated', sometimes 'low class', and generally 'not our group' (i.e., 'Irish'). For Irish and Italian speakers, [ɒ] is also 'local', but when this feature implies negative features they are usually associated with level of education and imply nothing about class or ethnicity.

The split among ethnic subgroups in the assignment of pragmatic features to variants demonstrates clearly one function of socially conditioned variants - to establish group identity by keeping groups separate and unique. It is the nature of socially defined groups to maintain their separateness, especially in a competitive urban setting where group membership can often spell economic or political survival. As large immigrant groups, these three have been the most important ones in the economic and political history of the city over the last 100 years (Thernstrom 1973). As immigration continued, the groups staked out their turf and established their claims to nativeness in the city. The [ɒ] form of the *or* variable is a mark of local dominion. It is recognized as a feature of Boston speech by speakers themselves, as a sign of belonging, and the subgroups which use it without negative labels - the Irish and Italian speakers - are the groups that truly belong in the sense that they still possess their 'turf' (neighborhoods in the city), and control local politics. The Jewish subgroup also had its neighborhoods, but in recent years these have been Jewish in name only, most residents having moved to adjoining towns and suburbs. They have, in a sense, given up the struggle for city turf, leaving behind both the territories and the linguistic feature which would identify them as local.

As suggested, the pragmatic features which label socially conditioned variants also provide a framework for describing phonetic change. However, additional parameters must be considered. Two new designations for variants need to be introduced. An *active* variant is the one commonly used by a speaker or group. A *passive* variant is one which the speaker recognizes in all its social ramifications, but generally does not use. Over time, a phoneme may develop active and passive variants, each having a combination of pragmatic features: [active, local, stigmatized], [active, local, prestigious], [passive, local, stigmatized], etc. Diachronic change is defined as a change in the pragmatic feature system in a subpart of the speech community (since, as I have noted, different groups evaluate variants differently according to their need to identify with, or maintain

their separateness from, other groups). The mechanics of
change conform to the following basic pattern:

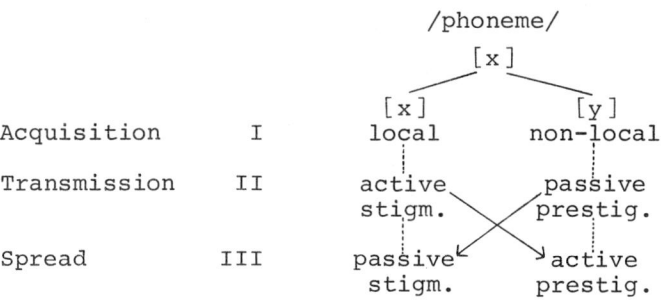

Acquisition	I	local	non-local
Transmission	II	active stigm.	passive prestig.
Spread	III	passive stigm.	active prestig.

   A phoneme is initially represented by a local variant
only. In the first, or acquisition stage of change, another, non-local variant comes to be associated with the
phoneme, usually through the exposure of a subgroup of the
speech community to some form of higher education. At this
stage the local variant is the active one, and the non-
local variant the passive one, for this subgroup. (Other
social subgroups may not even be aware of the non-local
variant.) No further features are associated with the
variants.

   At stage II, the transmission stage, the subgroup exposed to the new variant makes a decision, conscious or
unconscious, to incorporate the two variants into its system of social values. The group begins to consider the
local active form 'stigmatized'. The non-local, passive
form, which is now recognized but not used, becomes imbued
with prestige. It is important to note that, as seen in
the Boston study, the labelling of active and passive variants as stigmatized and prestigious respectively will occur
only if there is reinforcement of these designations by the
ethnic subgroup. If the group encourages the outer-directed, mainstream aspirations associated with the non-local
variant acquired through education, then younger speakers
in the group will tend to associate their own speech with
negative values.

   The sound change occurs in the third, or spread stage,
with the reversal of active and passive pragmatic labels.
At stage III, the subgroup passes on to younger speakers
the information that the variant which they use actively is
stigmatized, and the variant which they don't use but require their children to use, is correct or prestigious. If
this advice is followed, then the local stigmatized variant
becomes part of passive phonetic competence, and the non-

local prestigious variant becomes the active form.

This switching of active and passive labels between variants is illustrated in the history of the *or* variable. It was found that all older speakers (over 60) were heavy dialect speakers. Of these older subjects, only the Jewish speakers considered the local form stigmatized, although it was their active form. They are thus at stage II in the model of change. Younger Jewish speakers have made the active/passive feature switch (stage III). When they do use the local form it is only in casual speech, and with much less frequency than the other subgroups. Younger Irish and Italian speakers, on the other hand, are either at stage I, with no extreme pragmatic labels attached to the variants, or at an advanced Stage II, in which there is true alternation between the local and non-local variants. The younger Italian and Irish speakers are behaving exactly as did the Jewish speakers one or two generations earlier.

The history of the *or* variable indicates that a sound change may proceed across socially defined subgroups of a dialect population at different rates. An alternation may be in the variation stage with one group, while another group may have progressed to the stage of true change. Among Jewish speakers we can say that the completed sound change has produced two groups - the older dialect speakers and the younger 'standard' speakers - for this particular socially charged variable.

The linguistic behavior of the three groups reflects the shifting of pragmatic features - active/passive, stigmatized/correct/prestigious, reading/speaking - which each group assigns to the variants. It is therefore probably the case that in variation and change from above, as in the Boston case, it is necessary for speakers *as a group* to assign to the local variant features of negative social value, and to the variant of the mainstream culture (Thernstrom 1973) positive social values. This is the initial requirement which establishes the variation, and the condition necessary for variation to become change. The act of labelling in this manner is a means of establishing and asserting subgroup uniqueness through linguistic separateness.

NOTE

[1] The *or* allophones have a [ə] off-glide when they occur in monosyllables or in heavily stressed syllables.

REFERENCES

Bailey, Charles-James N. 1973. *Variation and linguistic theory*. Washington, D.C.: Center for Applied Linguistics.
Laferriere, Martha. To appear. "Ethnicity in phonological variation and change". *Language*.
Sankoff, David. Ed. 1978. *Linguistic variation: models and methods*. New York: Academic Press.
Thernstrom, Stephan. 1973. *The other Bostonians. Poverty and progress in the American metropolis, 1880-2970*. Cambridge, Mass.: Harvard University Press.

TONAL ACCENTS IN BASQUE AND GREEK

ALICE WYLAND GRUNDT
San Francisco, California

In his 1973 article Kiparsky investigates the traditional problem of whether Indo-European had distinctive contour accents or not. He points out that, logically, one may postulate that syllable-alternating accented languages like Sanskrit could have 'merged the countour accents by moving from a mora system to a syllable system for purposes of accent'; but, just as reasonably, one might assume that languages like Greek moved from a syllable-accented to a mora-accented system by means of vowel contractions. He tentatively concludes that pre-IE had phonologically predictable syllable accent on the last full vowel of the ending if possible, that this syllable accent became morphologically predictable on the basis of stem versus ending and weak versus strong cases by the time of IE proper, and that Greek reanalyzed the syllable-accent system into a mora-accent system which gave rise to the contour or circumflex accent (Kiparsky 1973:820ff).

This paper will argue that it is more plausible to assume that IE at all stages was a mora-based accent system and that whether or not a specific language developed contour accents as in Balto-Slavic, Greek, and Germanic depended on local conditions in the language in question. Evidence will be presented from tonal and stress accent developments in modern Basque dialects, showing that such development of contrasting systems presupposes a mora-counting accent in the protolanguage.

Ancient Greek accents are described by the Alexandrian grammarians as follows: The acute accent was characterized by a rise in pitch, the circumflex by a rise followed by a fall in pitch, and the grave had low pitch. The acute could fall on both long and short vowels, the circumflex only on long vowels or diphthongs in one of the last two syllables of the word, and the grave accent indicated no accent. Early papyri reflect the phonetic analysis of the circumflex by writing an angle over the vowel, formed by combining the acute and grave accent marks (Sturtevant 1940:95, 102). The accent was restricted to one of the last three syllables and could occur no more than four moras from the end of the word.

Kiparsky represents the circumflex accent by accenting the first mora of a long vowel or diphthong and the acute by accenting the second mora of a long vowel or diphthong. He is then able to show with his morphological rules the syllable accent alternation between stem and suffix in athematic nouns and the mora accent alternation on the long theme vowel in thematic nouns. However, his formulation entails an anomaly: the weak cases show a forward accent shift in the athematic nouns but a backward shift in the thematic nouns, an outcome which, Kiparsky comments, is 'just the reverse of what we might have expected' (Kiparsky 1973:800).

The marking conventions for accent which Kiparsky uses appear to have been formulated to reflect the contraction rules of Greek for vowels in hiatus in different syllables. In Greek vowel contraction, if the first vowel is accented, the resulting long vowel or diphthong has the circumflex; if the second of the two vowels is accented, contraction produces an acute long vowel or diphthong. But the accent occurs phonetically over the whole syllable. According to the Alexandrian grammarians, the contrast could be said to occur in the second mora since both the acute and circumflex are said to be rising at first and only the circumflex then falls. I propose to reverse the accent conventions and mark the circumflex in the second mora and the acute in the first mora. This could be done by marking both accents with a first mora acute and then the circumflex with a second mora grave. On the other hand, we could factor out the first mora acute in the circumflex and let an acute on the second mora represent a circumflex. If we do this, we can eliminate the anomaly:

Kiparsky (acute = vv́, circumflex = v́v)

	Strong cases	Weak cases	
Athematic nouns	pód + a	pod + ós	'foot'
Thematic nouns	phug + eé + n	phug + ée + s	'flight'

Alexandrian/Phonetic (acute = v́v, circumflex = vv́)

	Strong cases	Weak cases
Athematic nouns	pód + a	pod + ós
Thematic nouns	phug + ée + n	phug + eé + s

The surface phonetic or Alexandrian analysis reconciles the

accents of the thematic and the athematic nouns: both show
forward accent shift in the weak cases, thus suggesting
that morphological accent in Greek may be reducible to a
phonological base.

Some dialects of Basque show strikingly similar accent
patterns to Greek nominal paradigms. According to William
Jacobsen, who has exhaustively surveyed the available literature (1972, 1976), some Western Basque dialects have
tonal accents associated with noun plurals. The accents
are said to be falling in pitch in contrast to the unmarked
accent which is high, sustained or rising. Jacobsen reports that in Eastern Basque dialects of Souletin and Roncalese, a stress accent has developed, associated with the
plurals in Roncalese and with definite nouns in Souletin.
Jacobsen has reconstructed the paradigms for pre-Basque and
has shown that the final stress accent in Roncalese, which
contrasts with penultimate accent in other forms, correlates exactly with the loss of the plural morpheme marker
*-g- which was intervocalic in all plural forms except the
nominative plural. He explains the differing accent placements in Souletin and the western tonal dialects as redistribution of an accent which has become morphologized.

Penultimate word and phrase accent is widespread in
Basque and at least one scholar[1] has assumed penultimate
word stress for all pre-Basque dialects. Jacobsen, however, assumes penultimate word accent for the eastern
stress dialects only, and no word accent for the western
dialects. He explains tonal accent generation from the
shortening of the long vowels arising from the loss of
*-g-, even though other long vowel shortenings in the singular a-stems do not produce tonal accents. I think the
key to tonal accents in Basque, as in Greek, rests on the
contraction of two *syllables* into one syllable, not on
shortening. One of the contracting vowels must have carried a word accent before the loss of *-g- to generate
either a tonal or a stress accent.

I have argued elsewhere (Grundt 1977) that if the pre-Basque paradigms are reconstructed with the lost *-g-, as
in Jacobsen's analysis, and if one assumes that the penultimate mora of the pre-Basque word was accented, then the
accent alternations between stem and suffix that Kiparsky
proposes for IE are almost exactly paralleled and the tonal
accents are generated in the Roncalese pattern of stressed
finals. The distributional similarity to Kiparsky's formulation arises because the indefinite stem acts like an
athematic noun and the definite stems which add a definite
suffix -a- to the stem act like thematic nouns in Greek

(see Appendix).

In the a-stems which add the definite suffix -a-, we have the creation of a long vowel in both singular and plural definite forms. The alternating mora accent assigned by the accent rule in pre-Basque should generate circumflex accents and acute accents but, in fact, no accent contrast develops in the singulars: the accent is uniformly acute. This suggests strongly that pre-Basque was a mora-counting but syllable-accented language like Latin. After the loss of *-g-, the western tonal dialects became mora-counting *and* mora-accented languages.

The key to the diverse development of tonal and stress accents in Basque is the different results of the vowel contractions in eastern and western dialects after the loss of *-g-. In the east *-age-, *-agi- became -e- and in the west -a-. This difference meant that in the east word-final accent distinguished the plurals from the singulars and the nominative and ergative plurals remained segmentally distinct. These were the dialects where stress accent developed. In the west the contraction to -a- meant that nom. and erg. pl. and erg. sg. were segmentally identical and all had final syllable accent. Only tonal contrast could keep the categories distinct, and it was here that tonal accents became distinctive. It was also in these dialects that the tonal accent was redistributed, very often moving to the initial syllable of the word.

It is difficult to account for the development of mora-based systems in Greek, Balto-Slavic, Germanic and Latin if IE was not such a system. Sanskrit, Greek and Latin, like the eastern and western dialects of Basque, had different resources for maintaining their inflectional categories by phonological means. Greek accent is restricted to the last three syllables and last four moras of the word. Vowel contractions in these syllables could threaten the distinctness of the categories unless accents could contrast on the same syllable. Greek has suffered syncretism in its case system compared to Sanskrit and Latin: Greek has five cases, Latin six and Sanskrit eight. Latin has not simplified its possible finals as extensively as Greek, which permits only vowels, r, s, and n in final position. Sanskrit has also simplified its finals, especially with respect to allowable consonant clusters, but it permits final voiceless unaspirated stops as well as vowels, and it has the added advantage of a rich vowel alternation system and the freedom of accenting any syllable of a word. Thus, Sanskrit has a wider range of phonological mechanisms for maintaining its inflectional categories than do Greek and Latin. The implication is that a strict accent constraint fosters the development of tonal accents, while free accent does not. On this reasoning, western dialects of Basque would originally have had a more strict word accent rule than the eastern dialects; once the tonal accent became morphologized, the western dialects innovated by allowing free word accent.

To return to the Greek accents, one would like to find a single underlying phonological accent rule that would account for both circumflex and acute accents. Although Kiparsky considers the tonal developments in the Scandinavian languages secondary and not relevant to the Greek problem, it must be observed that the conditions for developing Tone II or tonal accent in Norwegian are the same as for Greek:

a) Haugen (1955) reports that in the Oppdal dialect of Norwegian a circumflex develops in the accented syllable when the following syllable loses its syllabicity, paralleling Greek vowel contraction: Norw. $b\hat{\bar{\imath}}t$ < $b\check{\imath}ta$ 'bite' $sk\hat{\bar{o}}n$ < $sk\acute{o}\text{-}en$ 'the shoe'; Hom.Gk. θαλασσάων, Attic Gr. θαλαττῶν (gen.pl.) 'of the seas'. Haugen's spectrographic evidence tends to support the subjective interpretation of these Oppdal circumflex vowels as overlong, i.e., containing three moras.

b) In Standard Norwegian accent retraction produces a Tone II in the first syllable and loss of length in the second, paralleling for instance the Greek first declension nominatives: Norw. $\tilde{a}vis$ < $av\acute{\imath}s$ 'newspaper' (Popperwell 1963: 116), Gk. πεῖρα < πείρᾱ (nom.sg.) 'trial, attempt'.

Based on the Oppdal evidence, we could assign three moras to the circumflex in Greek. If we revise our accent marking conventions and mark acute long vowels on the first mora and the three-mora circumflex vowels with an acute on the first mora and a grave on the second mora, we find an interesting pattern in words like πεῖρα and many others. The assumption of a simple word accent rule that accents the fourth mora from the end seems indicated. The pattern suggests that Greek circumflex accents actually conserve the number of moras in a word and act as a means of maintaining the phonetic timing of a word as it undergoes truncation. For example, in the paradigm of πεῖρα the number of moras following the acute accent remains constant at four moras, but with differing syllable distributions:

Nom.	πεῖρα	péira	ῠ̆ῠ̆ῠ̆ - v
Gen.	πείρας	péiraas	ῠ̆v - vv
Dat.	πείρα	péiraa	ῠ̆v - vv
Acc.	πεῖραν	péiran	ῠ̆ῠ̆ῠ̆ - v

This analysis suggests the reason for the loss of circumflex in Greek by the second century AD when Greek words were uniformly stressed on the penult: the circumflex or overlong accent must be unstable and a transitional phenomenon. The circumflex as a transitional stage is suggested by the forms of πλείων 'more' where it looks as if the word is changing from four moras to two:

Masc./fem.	πλείων	pléioon	ῠ̆v - vv
Neuter	πλεῖον	pléion	ῠ̆ῠ̆ῠ̆ - v
Alternate neuter	πωέον	pléon	ῠ̆ - v

Any new method of analysis--if it is any good--ought to offer insight into problems which it was not originally designed to explain. The proposal that circumflex accents do not merely indicate loss of syllabicity or duration but actually conserve moras suggests that both loss of syllabicity and second syllable shortening affect the rhythmical organization of the word in the same way. The mora patterning also suggests that the temporal structure rests on two-syllable units and their equivalents as well as on individual syllables. The πλείων example above, for instance, suggests that the word is distinctively made up of two syllables of two moras each and that its truncation most logically results in a temporal shape of two syllables of one mora each rather than a three-mora, two-syllable unit. We do find a three-mora, two-syllable unit in Greek in the regular comparatives of o-stems: before the endings -τερος, -τατος the final omicron of the stem is lengthened to omega if the preceding syllable is short but remains omicron if it is long: φοβερός 'fearful', φοβερώτερος 'more fearful', but πικρός 'bitter', πικρότερος 'more bitter'. The lengthening of omicron in these forms can best be explained by the requirement of maintaining three moras in the two-syllable unit and not by morphological or compensatory lengthening. The circumflex, then, represents a transsyllabic compensatory timing adjustment when the moras of a two-syllable unit undergo redistribution or truncation. For Greek accentuation, this explanation of the circumflex development supports the tentative assumption that the underlying Greek accent rule accents the fourth mora from the end of a word.

Considering the evidence presented, it seems more plausible to assume that IE languages are all underlying mora-counting languages but that this characteristic does not surface until the timing of the phonetic units--syllables, disyllables, and perhaps larger units--becomes disturbed by the loss of duration or syllabicity. Whether such phonetically developed circumflex accents become distinctive would then depend on what other means were available to the language to keep its categories phonologically distinct.

NOTE

[1] Jacobsen 1972:73 ft 10 cites and discusses Nils M. Holmer. 1964. *El idioma vasco hablado*. San Sebastian.

REFERENCES

Chase, Alston Hurd and Henry Phillips, Jr. 1961. *A new introduction to Greek*. Cambridge: Harvard University Press.
Grundt, Alice Wyland. 1977. "The inflectional accent in Basque and Indo-European". *Proceedings of the Third Annual Meeting of the Berkeley Linguistics Society*, 637-643.
Haugen, Einar. 1955. "Circumflex vowels in Norwegian". (English version of: "Tvetoppet vokal i Oppdalsmålet". *Maal og Minne*, Hefte 1-4: 66-78). Supplied by author.
Jacobsen, William H., Jr. 1972. "Nominative-ergative syncretism in Basque". *Del Anuario del Seminario de Filología Vasca "Julio de Urquijo"* 6.67-109.
Kiparsky, Paul. 1973. "The inflectional accent in Indo-European". *Language* 49.794-849.
Pharr, Clyde. 1959. *Homeric Greek*. Norman: University of Oklahoma Press.
Popperwell, R. G. 1963. *The pronunciation of Norwegian*. Cambridge: University Press.
Sturtevant, Edgar H. 1940. *The pronunciation of Latin and Greek*, 2nd Ed. Philadelphia: LSA.
Whitney, William Dwight. 1967 (1889). *Sanskrit grammar*. Cambridge: Harvard University Press.

APPENDIX

BASQUE: RECONSTRUCTED PARADIGMS

Rules:
1. Accent: accent penultimate mora of word.
2. ∅ → r/V + ___V (not definite suffix -a)
3. ∅ → e/C + ___C

Stems:
    Vowel stems
      a-stem: alhaba 'daughter'
      i-stem: mendi 'mountain'
    Consonant stem
      gizon 'man'

Indeterminate (stem + ∅ + case ending)

Nom (-∅)	alhába-∅	méndi-∅	gízon-∅
Erg (-k)	alhába-k	méndi-k	gizón-e-k
Gen (-en)	alhabá-r-en	mendí-r-en	gizón-en
Dat (-i)	alhabá-r-i	mendí-r-i	gizón-i

Definite (stem + -a- + case ending)

	Singular (-∅-)	Plural (-g-, -k#)
a-stem		
Nom (-∅)	alhabá-a-∅	alhabá-a-k
Erg (-k)	alhabá-a-k	alhaba-á-g-e-k
Gen (-en)	alhaba-á-r-en	alhaba-á-g-en
Dat (-i)	alhaba-á-r-i	alhaba-á-g-i
i-stem		
Nom (-∅)	mendí-a-∅	mendí-a-k
Erg (-k)	mendí-a-k	mendi-á-g-e-k
Gen (-en)	mendi-á-r-en	mendi-á-g-en
Dat (-i)	mendi-á-r-i	mendi-á-g-i
consonant stem		
Nom (-∅)	gizón-a-∅	gizón-a-k
Erg (-k)	gizón-a-k	gizon-á-g-e-k
Gen (-en)	gizon-á-r-en	gizon-á-g-en
Dat (-i)	gizon-á-r-i	gizon-á-g-i

Accent Patterns

	Indeterminate	Definite Singular	Definite Plural
Nominative*	pre-stem final	presuffix	presuffix
Ergative	presuffix	presuffix	post-stem
Genitive	presuffix	post-stem	post-stem
Dative	presuffix	post-stem	post-stem

*Also called Absolutive

APPENDIX (Cont'd)

INDO-EUROPEAN: Accent Patterns (Kiparsky 1973, p. 802)

Rules: a. Strong cases (Nom., Acc.) have presuffixal accent
       b. Weak cases (Gen., Dat.) have post-stem accent

Patterns generated by these rules:

	Singular	Plural
Nominative	presuffix	presuffix
Accusative	presuffix	presuffix
Genitive	post-stem	post-stem
Dative	post-stem	post-stem

But note accent pattern in Sanskrit consonant stems (parallels the Basque case):

Skt. pad- 'foot'

	Singular	Plural
Nominative	pá̄at	pá̄adas
Accusative	pá̄adam	padás
Genitive	padás	padá̄am
Dative	padé	padbhyás

ACCENT PATTERNS IN MODERN BASQUE DIALECTS (based on Jacobsen 1972) - plurals only:

	Eastern (stress = ´) *Roncalese*	Western (tonal = ˋ) *Guernica, Vizcaya* Older Speakers	Younger Speakers
Nom Pl	alhábak	àlhabak	alhàbak
Erg Pl	alhabék	àlhabak	alhàbak
Gen Pl	alhabén	àlhaben	alhàben
Dat Pl	alhabé, alhabér	àlhaba	alhàba
Nom Pl	gizónak	gìzonak	gizònak
Erg Pl	gizonék	gìzonak	gizònak
Gen Pl	gizonén	gìzonen	gizònen
Dat Pl	gizoné	gìzona	gizòna

Note: *-age-, *-agi- > -e- (Eastern dialects) - stress dialects
                    -a- (Western dialects) - tonal dialects

ACQUISITION AND DEVELOPMENT OF
"GASTARBEITERDEUTSCH"
BY MIGRANT WORKERS AND THEIR CHILDREN IN GERMANY

CAROL W. PFAFF
Freie Universität Berlin

0. *Background.* The presence of large numbers of foreign workers in Germany has given researchers a rare opportunity to test hypotheses about rapid, contact-induced language change involving languages of varying typological and genetic distance from German. 1977 figures show nearly two million workers--close to 10% of all persons employed--are from Turkey, Yugoslavia, Italy, Greece, Spain, Portugal, Morocco, Tunisia, and other foreign countries. Of necessity, these foreign workers have had to develop at least minimal competence in German. Many, especially those who intend to remain in Germany, have considerably more than minimal competence and are fluent speakers of varieties which differ to a greater or lesser degree from native German (cf. *Heidelberger Forschungsprojekt* 1975, 1978; Meisel 1977; Meisel, Clahsen and Pienemann 1979).

By 1975, children accounted for 20% of the foreign population. The proportion of children as well as their absolute numbers has since been increasing, as immigration from countries which are not members of the European Common Market is now limited to spouses and children of workers already in Germany. According to Stölting, in 1977 there were already approximately one million foreign children in Germany, with another million more potential child immigrants eligible under current law. Foreign workers' children acquire German under quite different circumstances from their parents, and some, born in Germany or immigrants at an early age, must be considered native speakers according to the criterion proposed by Bickerton (1977a:8) because their knowledge of German equals or dominates knowledge of their other language.

Certain aspects of the historical development of so-called 'Gastarbeiterdeutsch', particularly in the speech of adults, have already received considerable attention from linguists; for example from members of the *Heidelberger Forschungsprojekt* (1975, 1978), from Meisel and his associates in Wuppertal (1977, 1979), who have studied the speech of Spanish and Italian workers, and from Keim (1978) who analyzed the speech of three Turkish workers and their families.

In this paper I will first briefly review this work, then sketch and report preliminary linguistic results of a series of interrelated sociolinguistic studies of adults' and children's speech which I am conducting in West Berlin.

Early investigations of 'Gastarbeiterdeutsch', such as Clyne (1968) and Gilbert & Orlovic (1975), focussed on pointing out the 'pidgin' characteristics to be found in foreign workers' language, noting such features as zero copula, zero article, zero preposition, lack or overgeneralization of inflections, analytic constructions, and reduced lexicon.

This early work stimulated considerable debate about whether 'Gastarbeiterdeutsch' should be considered a pidgin, a jargon, or simply a phase in second language learning. This largely terminological issue has assumed less importance as theoretical views of pidgin/creole continua, expressed by Le Page (1977:222-3), Bickerton (1977b:52), and others, emphasize that in all cases we are dealing with processes rather than states or entities. Investigators including Schumann (1978) and Bickerton (1977b:64) note similarities between the pidginization and L2 acquisition processes, and Ferguson & DeBose (1977:117) see a pidgin as the output of verbal interaction between native speakers and foreigners in a contact situation. Concretely, they identify this output as broken language when used by non-native speakers and as foreigner talk when used by native speakers. The current view of pidginization as a process not fundamentally distinct from L2 learning focusses attention on two issues: the nature of the input and the process of acquisition.

1.0 *Input*. The linguistic input to foreign workers comes from three principal sources:

(1) the speech of native Germans,

(2) the speech of other foreigners, and

(3) the speech of the workers' own children.

1.1 *Germans' foreigner talk.* While both the *Heidelberg-er Forschungsprojekt* (1975) and Meisel (1975) found evidence of stereotypic 'simplification' in Germans' foreigner talk, these were by no means in general use by all Germans addressing foreigners, and Clyne's (1978) study comparing Australian foreigner talk to the speech of industrial immigrants found that these varieties differ systematically. These results suggest it is unlikely that foreigner talk has a significant direct influence on the development of foreign workers' speech, although it may well have an indirect negative effect on foreigners' attitudes, since this register is widely recognized by foreigners as 'simplified' and patronizing. The normal registers of local German dialects appear to have a much more significant role as primary linguistic data.

1.2 *Other foreigners' talk.* The second source of input, the speech of foreigners of other nationalities, was an essential factor in earlier formulations of pidgin/creole theory, e.g., Whinnom (1971), which suggested that the presence of at least two substrate languages was necessary for pidginization. Language contact among workers of different nationalities has not yet been systematically investigated. Spanish and Italian are close enough to permit communication without resorting to German, but speakers of the other languages must rely on their German. The extent of contact, however, varies. In the factory investigated by the *Heidelberger Forschungsprojekt*, nationalities are evidently mixed (1975:68-71). However, in other factories, such as those observed by Barkowski, Harnisch & Kumm (1978), workers are segregated by nationality. Similarly, contact among foreigners in housing and recreation varies. There is a certain amount of contact in shops operated by foreigners; however, such trade situations -- the epitome of the limited pidgin setting -- often require very little linguistic communication and may have negligible effect. A small proportion of foreign workers is active in political or business organizations which bring together foreigners of several nationalities. My observation in Berlin is that many, if not most, of these active workers speak near-native varieties of German with virtually no 'pidgin' features.

1.3 *Children's speech.* The third source of input to foreign workers' German, so far completely neglected *as a source*, is the speech of their children. In pidgin/creole or immigrant continua, the influence may flow in the opposite direction from language acquisition in a monolingual setting where parents' speech provides primary linguistic input to children and where language change can be seen as resulting from the children's construction of an optimal grammar for the adults' input. In the present situation, children acquire German in daycare centers, schools, and in the community, and use German with their older and younger siblings and often with their parents. Many parents who are eager for social integration make a point of speaking German with their children. For such families, the pattern of language choice is shift or mixture rather than diglossia or domain-specific compartmentalization.

Children's exposure to German in school usually involves more or less guided learning, but, depending on class composition and structure, may also involve considerable exposure to and unguided learning from other foreign children and foreign teachers. The present school policies and social attitudes have created a setting which may even be conducive to creolization, to a certain extent. Although foreign children are subject to the same obligatory schooling as native Germans, current policy restricts the proportion of foreign children in regular German classes to 20-50%, with the result that in areas of high concentrations of foreigners, where school populations may be 80-90% foreign, children are placed in so-called 'special classes' made up entirely of foreign children of various national origins. Even those children in regular classes with German children are often excluded from contact with them outside the classroom. Some children, of course, have extensive German contacts and friendships, often combined with weak ties to their native country, culture and language.

The linguistic result of these social forces has been described by recent investigators in terms of 'semilingualism' or 'Halbsprachigkeit', terms used to characterize children's lack of ability to speak either German or their mother tongue properly (Skutnabb-Kangas 1978). Some reports of semilingualism based on evidence of the children's nonconformance to the surface rules of the standard languages conclude that there are certain concepts that cannot therefore be expressed, but it is also possible that the children have developed alternative linguistic means for communicating the same information based on L1 models or on (possibly universal) creole patterns.

2. *Sociolinguistic studies in West Berlin.* Clearly, the situation here offers a wealth of opportunities for investigating language change in progress, and I am presently pursuing a series of studies in West Berlin, approaching the problem from several angles.[1] Among the

studies initiated to date are the following:

(1) Observation and participant observation of communication in public places, including shops, restaurants, hospitals, government offices, and public meetings.

(2) Conversations with adults interviewed individually or in small groups in casual settings in their homes, workplaces or recreation centers.

(3) Highly structured conversations with children and adolescents interviewed singly, using psycholinguistic elicitation techniques to investigate specific linguistic features.

(4) Paired interviews with children of different nationalities using two-person communication games which require them to solve nonlinguistic problems by means of questioning and answering each other.

In the remainder of this paper, I limit my discussion to a preliminary report of results from a study of the third type -- structured elicitation from individual children.

3.0 *Methodology*. In the study reported here, 57 children were interviewed: 23 Turkish, 8 Greek, 5 Yugoslavian, 2 Lebanese, 2 Spanish, 2 American, and a control group of 17 Germans.[2] With the exception of the Americans, who were interviewed in connection with a separate study of the John F. Kennedy School described in Kunsmann, Mühlhäusler, Pfaff and Portz (1979), all are residents of West Berlin districts which have a high proportion of foreigners, and all attend daycare centers or schools which serve a multinational population. Some of the foreign children were born in Germany, others arrived at an early age, others are recent immigrants who began school in their native countries. Individuals' age and length of residence in Germany are listed in the left columns of the Appendix.[3]

The interviews, which lasted 15-30 minutes per child, consisted of conversation with an adult interviewer who elicited social background information, personal narratives and a wide range of items of specific linguistic interest in the context of relatively informal conversation about a series of pictures. Data were evaluated using a revised and greatly expanded version of the Dialect Differentiation Measure, devised by Pfaff (1973, 1975) to investigate decreolization in Black English, and the Bilingual Syntax Measure developed by Burt, Dulay and Hernández-Chavez (1975). A more detailed description of the instrument is given in Pfaff (1979).

4.0 *Results.* The preliminary analysis of the responses shows that the children's speech forms a highly variable continuum, as would be expected. A summary of the results for some of the features which have been tabulated is given in the Appendix. This table is not meant to be an implicational scale -- children are listed by nationality, sex, and order of interview. The linguistic features, however, *are* partially ordered: the more 'pidgin' features are to the left and potentially 'creolizing' features to the right. In the middle are features of standard colloquial German (SCG) morphology and syntax.

4.1 *'Pidgin' features.* In contrast to studies of adult foreign workers, it is noteworthy that the speech of these foreign children -- even those who have been in Germany only a short time -- shows a very low incidence of features characteristic of 'pidgin' German. Only those children who arrived less than a year prior to the interview produce zero copula forms such as (1) to any great extent.

(1) *ich auch zehn* 'I'm ten too' TM7
    (Standard German: *ich bin auch zehn*)

and even these children sometimes have copula forms, though not always the standard ones, as in (2) and (3):

(2) *der sind* (SCG *ist*) *so dick* 'he is so fat' (of a 3 sg) YF1

(3) *die Fusse ist* (SCG *sind*) *oben* 'the feet are up' (of a 3 pl) YF1

Categorical or variable use of the auxiliary represents occurrence of *haben* or *sein* with past participles to refer to past events. Some children who omit AUX avoid perfective altogether; others use past participles -- notably in clause-final position -- but with no AUX as in (4):

(4) *und dann die Apfel schon runtergefall*[4] 'and then the apples had already fallen down' YF1
    (SCG. *...und dann sind die Äpfel schon runtergefallen*)

Many children generalize the auxiliary *haben* as in (5):

(5) *wir ham gekommt* 'we came' TF1
    (SCG. *wir sind gekommen*)

Sein is never generalized as a perfective AUX.

Perhaps the most stereotypic 'pidgin' feature, the use of infinitive forms in the place of main verbs which would be inflected for person/number agreement in the standard, is almost totally absent. One of the rare examples is given in (6). Note that a standard first singular inflected form also occurs in the same sentence:

(6) *ich schreiben* (SCG. *schreibe*) *schon Hausarbeiten und dann ich spiele schon jetzt* 'I write my homework and then I play' YF1

4.2 *Word order*. Turning now to word order phenomena, the columns SVX XVS VSX M...INF/Aux..PP and Subord...V in the Appendix, we note that, in contrast to the adults analyzed in the *Heidelberger Forschungsprojekt* and Wuppertal studies, German word order does not appear to pose much of a problem for these children. In the three cases where German requires verb last -- subordinate clause, participle after auxiliary and infinitive after modal -- an implicational relationship is found. Standard word order in subordinate clause implies standard order of participles and infinitives, as for TF1, paralleling Clahsen's findings for Spanish and Italian adults (Clahsen, 1979). That is, examples like (7) are found for children who correctly place participles and infinitives at the end:

(7) *Weil sie ist dick*[5] 'because he is fat'. TF1
 (SCG. *weil er dick ist*)

TF1 appears to be in the process of acquiring the verb last rule for subordinate clauses; she does not apply the rule in (7), but does so in (8), repeating the postsubject occurrence at the end:

(8) *weil hier ist zu schmutzig ist's* 'because it's too dirty here' TF1
 (SCG. *weil es hier zu schmutzig ist*)

Colloquial native German includes a number of verb-first constructions in declarative sentences as in (9) and (10):

(9) *kann ich nicht* 'I can't'.

(10) *weiss ich nicht* 'I don't know'.

which apparently are the result of deletion of a preposed object *das* 'that'. Surface structures of this type have been acquired by those children who have '+' in the VSX column. It appears that some foreign children generalize verb first order to sentences which would not be grammatical in colloquial German and which can not be derived as deletions of preposed elements, such as (11) and (12):

(11) *hab ich Schwester. Zwei habe ich Schwester* 'I have sisters. I have two sisters'. TM9
 (SCG. *ich habe Schwestern. Zwei Schwestern habe ich*)

(12) <u>weiss</u> ich das nicht   'I don't know that'. TM13
(SCG. ich <u>weiss</u> das nicht or das <u>weiss</u> ich nicht.)

4.3 *Morphophonemic alternation.* The German of these children is morphophonemically simpler (more regular) than colloquial native German. Some notion of the incidence of regularized verbs, e.g., *esst* for *isst* (3rd pr. sg. of *essen* 'eat'), *gekommt* for *gekommen* '(has) come, arrived', as in (5) above, and plurals, e.g., *Vogel* for *Vögel* 'birds'. *Füssen* for *Füsse* 'feet' is given in the columns IRREG VERB and PL in the table. Cases marked "H" are generalizations of plural forms for singular or doubly marked plurals like *Vögelkinder* for *Vogelkinder* 'baby birds'.

4.4 *Analytic constructions.* It has often been noted that pidgin/creole continua characteristically develop analytical marking of case and tense/aspect categories. In the present study, a significant proportion of foreign children used analytic, prepositional marking of the recipient indirect object rather than the inflectional dative of colloquial German, producing sentences like (13) and (14):

(13) *der bringt <u>zu seine Kinds</u> Futter*   'she brings food to her children'. TM11 (SCG. *sie bringt <u>ihren Kindern</u> Futter*)

(14) *die will so geben <u>bei die Kinder</u> schon die Essen* 'She wants to give the food to the children'. YM3 (SCG. *sie will schon das Essen den Kindern geben*)

Possession and part/whole relationships are analytically marked by prepositions as in (15) and (16):

(15) *den Fuss <u>von der Tisch</u>* 'the foot of the table'   TF10 (SCG. *der Fuss <u>des Tisches</u>*)

(16) *<u>von der Hose</u> die Ärmeln* 'the sleeves of the pants' <u>TF10</u>   (SCG. *die Ärmel <u>der Hosen</u>*)

or by postposed analytic possessive pronoun plus noun as in (17) and (18):

(17) *Vogel <u>sein Kinder</u>*   'bird's children'   TM9 (SCG. <u>*die kinder des Vogels*</u>)

(18) *auf dem Stuhl <u>seinen Fuss</u>*   'on the foot of the chair' TM9   (SCG. <u>*auf dem Fuss des stuhls*</u>)

or both as in (19):

(19) *die <u>von den Frau seine Tochter</u>* 'the woman's daughter' TM9   (SCG. *die Tochter der Frau*)

Meyer-Ingwersen et al. (1977:182-93) suggest that such constructions might be expected on the basis of transfer from Turkish syntactic structures which are parallel, but it is also possible that they are present in dialectal native German, in which such forms are attested. They did not occur in the speech of any of the German control group, however.

4.5 *Lexical expansion.* Finally, the data provide evidence of certain semantic extension or lexical progression (Hancock 1979) processes characteristic of the development of pidgin/creoles from a limited lexical inventory. For example, (20) illustrates a semantic extension of *Haar* 'hair', which is probably spontaneously coined and idiosyncratic:

(20) *Herbst? Dann die Apfel geht alles weg und die Blatter geht auch weg dann hat der Baum keine Haare mehr.*

Fall? Then the apples all go away and the leaves go away too, then the tree has no more hair. TM9

Another example is the semantic extension of *gehen* 'go' to express 'becoming' as in (21) and (22). This, however, is less idiosyncratic than the extension of *Haar*, and occurs in more than one child's speech.

(21) *mit Wasser geht dein Füsse nass* 'his feet get wet with water' TM1

(22) *die geht ja gross* 'it gets big' GF2

5.0 *Concluding remark.* These preliminary results demonstrate some factors about foreign children's use of German. Obviously a great deal remains to be done. Such studies, however, promise to pay off handsomely in terms of our increased understanding of historical language contact and pidginization/creolization processes.

NOTES

[1] In this work I have been fortunate to have the cooperation of a number of foreign and German students and colleagues at the Freie Universität Berlin who have assisted in making initial contacts, interviewing, transcribing and tabulating data. I would like to acknowledge the efforts of A. Agyül, S. Breede, B. Bröskamp, T. Cybulski, P. Feiser, A. Gotowos, F. Klien, W. Krenz, S. Lucas, H. Offenbächer, B. Sedello, and C. Wetzel. Renate Portz collaborated with me in devising the elicitation procedures and Ulrich Steinmüller kindly facilitated access to one of the schools as well as providing stimulating discussion of the problems. I am grateful to M. Wagner and U. Bacher for their cooperation in arranging interviews at the Hunsrück-Grundschule. None of these people have seen this paper or are in any way responsible for my interpretations.

[2] However, tapes of 2 Spanish, and 3 Greek children had not been transcribed at the time of writing and are excluded from the analysis.

[3] Studies of adults have found age and length of residence in Germany to be less significantly correlated with level of proficiency in colloquial German than are such social/psychological factors as contact with Germans and desire to remain in Germany. These factors are also integrated into the interviews for the present study (see Pfaff 1979) and will be reported in subsequent papers.

[4] Nonstandard form of the past participle (*runtergefall* rather than *runtergefallen*) is not significant here. The salient mark of perfective here is the infix *-ge-*. Dittmar (1979) notes that for Spanish and Italian adults, the adverb *schon* 'already' appears to function as a perfective marker. This does not seem to be the case for children, who frequently use *schon* in clear nonperfective contexts as well, for instance YF1's use in (6) in response to a question of what she habitually does after school.

[5] Nondifferentiation of gender in personal pronouns (*sie* (fem. sg.) rather than *er* for the masc. sg. referent in (7)) is a characteristic variable of foreigners' German. As indicated by (13), which has *der* (masc. nom. sg.) and *sein* (masc. poss. sg.) referring to a feminine subject, this feature is not stabilized.

REFERENCES

Barkowski, Hans, Ulrike Harnisch and Sigrid Kumm. 1978. "Deutsch für ausländische Arbeiter". Linguistic Colloquium, Freie Universität Berlin.

Bickerton, Derek. 1977a. *Change and variation in Hawaiian English, vol. II: Creole Syntax*. Final Report NSF Project No. GS-39748.

⎯⎯⎯. 1977b. "Language and language universals". In Valdman (ed.), 49-69.

Burt, Marina, Heidi Dulay and Eduardo Hernández-Chavez. 1975. *Bilingual syntax measure*. New York: Harcourt Brace Jovanovich.
Clahsen, Harald. 1979, "Psycholinguistic aspects of L2 acquisition: word order phenomena in foreign workers' interlanguage". *Wuppertaler Arbeitspapiere zur Sprachwissenschaft (WAS) 2.54-79.*
Clyne, Michael. 1968. "Zum Pidgin-Deutsch der Gastarbeiter". *Zeitschrift für Mundartforschung* 35.130-9.
_____. 1978. "Some remarks on foreigner talk". In Dittmar et al. (eds.) 155-62.
Dittmar, Norbert. 1979. "Ordering adult learners according to language abilities". Intervention Paper presented at the Conference on Theoretical Orientations in Creole Studies, St. Thomas, Virgin Islands, March 28th-31st.
_____, Hartmut Haberland, Tove Skutnabb-Kangas and Uif Teleman (eds.). 1978. *Papers for the First Scandinavian-German Symposium on the Language of Immigrant Workers and their Children.* Roskilde Universitetscenter.
Ferguson, Charles A. and Charles DeBose. 1977. "Simplified registers, broken language, and pidginization". In Valdman (ed.), 99-125.
Fox, James. 1977. "Implications of the jargon/pidgin dichotomy for social and linguistic analysis of the Gastarbeiter Pidgin German speech community". In Molony et al. (eds.), 40-6.
Gilbert, Glen and Maria Orlović. 1975. "Pidgin-German spoken by foreign workers in West Germany. The definite article". Paper presented at the International Congress on Pidgin and Creoles, Honolulu, Hawaii.
Hancock, Ian F. "Lexical expansion in creole languages". Paper presented at the Conference on Theoretical Orientations in Creole Studies , St. Thomas, Virgin Islands, March 28th-31st.
Heidelberger Forschungsprojekt 'Pidgin-Deutsch'. 1975. *Sprache und Kommunikation ausländischer Arbeiter.* Scriptor Verlag.
_____. 1978. *The unguided learning of German by Spanish and Italian workers. A sociolinguistic study.* Paris: UNESCO.
Hymes, Dell (ed.). 1971. *Pidginization and creolization of languages.* London: Cambridge University Press.
Keim, Inken. 1978. *Gastarbeiterdeutsch. Untersuchungen zum sprachlichen Verhalten türkischer Gastarbeiter.* Tübingen: TBL Verlag Gunter Narr.
Kreuzer, Helmut, Wolfgang Klein, Rul Gunzenhäuser and Wolfgang Haubrichs (eds.) 1975. *Sprache ausländischer Arbeiter,* Heft 18. *Zeitschrift für Literaturwissenschaft und Linguistik.*
Kunsman, Peter, Peter Mühlhäusler, Carol Pfaff and Renate Portz. 1979. "A study of bilingualism at the J.F. Kennedy School". Paper presented at the Deutsche Gesellschaft für Sprachwissenschaft, Tübingen.
Le Page, Robert. 1977. "Processes of pidginization and creolization". In Valdman (ed.). 222-55.
Meisel, Jürgen. 1975. "Ausländerdeutsch und Deutsch ausländischer Arbeiter. Zur möglichen Entstehung eines Pidgin in der BRD". In Kreuzer et al. (eds.), 9-53.
_____. 1977. "The language of foreign workers in Germany". In Molony et al. (eds.), 184-212.

_____, Harald Clahsen and Manfred Pienemann. 1979. "On determining developmental stages in natural 2nd language acquisition". *Wuppertaler Arbeitspapiere zur Sprachwissenschaft (WAS)* 2.1-53.

Meyer-Ingwersen, J., Rosemarie Neumann and Matthias Kummer. 1977. *Zur Sprachentwicklung türkischer Schüler in der Bundesrepublik.* Vols. I and II. Kronberg/Ts: Skriptor Verlag.

Molony, Carol, Helmut Zobl and Wilfried Stölting (eds.). 1977. *Deutsch im Kontakt mit anderen Sprachen/German in Contact with other Languages.* Kronberg/Ts: Skriptor Verlag.

Pfaff, Carol. 1973. *A sociolinguistic study of Black children in Los Angeles.* Unpublished Ph.D. dissertation, UCLA.

_____. 1975. "The process of decreolization in Black English". Paper presented at the International Conference on Pidgins and Creoles. Honolulu, Hawaii.

_____. 1979. "A sociolinguistic framework for research on incipient creolization in 'Gastarbeiterdeutsch'". Intervention Paper presented at the Conference on Theoretical Orientations in Creole Studies. St. Thomas, Virgin Islands, March 28th-31st.

Schumann, John. 1978. *The pidginization process: a model for second language acquisition.* Rowley, Mass.: Newbury House.

Skutnabb-Kangas, Tove. 1978. "Semilingualism and the education of migrant children as a means of reproducing the caste of assembly line workers". In Dittmar et al. (eds.), 221-51.

Stölting, Wilfried. 1978. "Teaching German to immigrant children". In Dittmar et al. (eds.), 99-110.

Valdman, Albert (ed.). 1978. *Pidgin and creole linguistics.* Bloomington: Indiana University Press.

Whinnom, Keith. 1971. "Linguistic hybridization and the 'special case' of pidgins and creoles". In Hymes (ed.), 91-115.

APPENDIX FOLLOWS
(p. 394 + 395)

APPENDIX

Realization of selected semantactic features in foreign children's German

Key

In general:
- **+** means categorically present
- **−** means consistently absent (or nonstandard)
- **x** means a variable

For BECOME:
- **G** means *gehen*
- **W** means *werden*

For IRREG VERB and PL:
- **X** means both standard and nonstandard forms occur, but for different lexical items
- **H** means pl. form used for sg.

For IND OBJ:
- **X** means uninflected or nonstandard inflection, with no prepositional marker

	Age	Years in G	COP	AUX	per/no AGMT	SVX	XVS	VSX	M...INF AUX..PP	Subord...V	IRREG verb	PL	IND OBJ	BECOME
TM1	9		+	+	+	+	+		+	+	−	x	x	G
TM2	10		+	+	+	+	+	+	+	x	x	−	x	
TM3	11	5	+		+	+	+		+	x	+	−	für	
TM4	10	10	+	+	+	+	+	+	+	+	+	−	zu	
TM5	10	3	+							−		+	x	
TM6	10	5	x		+				+	+	+	+		
TM7	10	½	x		−							−	x	
TM8	9	½	x											
TM9	10	8	+	x	+	x	x			+	−	−		G/W
TM10	11	10	+	+	+	+	+	+	+	+	+	+	zu	W
TM11	15	7	+	+	+	+	+		+	+	+	+		
TM12	13	8	+	+	+	+			+	+	+	−	zu	W
TM13	5		x		+	+		+	+		+	−	für	W
TF1	10	8	+	+	x	+	+		+	−	−	x	zu	G/W
TF2	10		+	x	+	+	x	+	x	+	+	−		

"GASTARBEITERDEUTSCH" 395

APPENDIX (Cont.)

	Age	Years in G	COP	AUX	per/no AGMT	SVX	XVS	VSX	M...INF AUX..PP	Subord...V	IRREG verb	PL	IND OBJ	BECOME
TF3	11		+	+	+	+	+	+	+		+	x	x	W
TF4	12	6	+	+	+	+	+		+	+	–	+	von	G/W
TF5	11	6	+	+	+	+	+	+	+	x	+	x	zum	
TF6	10		+	x	+	+	+		+		–	+H	x	W
TF7	9	4	+	+	x	+	+	+	+	x	–	x	zu	W
TF8	13	5	+	x	x	+	+		+	x	–	x	+	W
TF9	9		+	+	+	+	+		+	+	x	+	für	W
TF10	12	5	+	+	x	+	+	+	+	+	–	+	x	W
GM2	12	12	x		+	+	+			x	x	–	zu	G/W
GM3	9	3	+	+	+	+	+		+	+	–	+H		G
GF1	11	4	+	x	x			+	+	x	x	–		
GF2	9	3	+		–	+			+	–	–		x	
GF3	9		+		+	x	+		+	–	x	–	+	
YM1	13	½	x		+				+	–	+	+	+	
YM2	13	7	+	+	+	+	+	+		x	x	+H	bei	W
YM3	6	2	+	x	–	x	x		+	x	–	–	+	W
YF1	12	1	x	+	+	+	+		+	+	–	+	+	
YF2	5	5	+		+	+			+		+	x	zu	
LF1	12	1½	+		+				+		+	–	für	
LF2	13	2	+	+	+	+	+		+		–	x	zu	W
AM1	10	1	+	+	+	+			x	+	–	–	zu	W
AF1	9	3	+		+	+			x	–	–	–	zu	W

PIDGINIZATION AND FOREIGNER TALK:
CHINESE PIDGIN RUSSIAN

JOHANNA NICHOLS
University of California, Berkeley

Chinese pidgin Russian is attested in two principal areas: the border city of Kjaxta, where it arose (attested in 19th-century sources: Čerepanov 1853, Timkowski 1825, Maksimov 1864, V. P. 1849, Ščukin 1850; see also Neumann 1966, Fox MS); and Manchuria, where it was used until the mid-20th century in Russian settlements (it is recalled by many emigrés in this country).

A third variety spread to the indigenous Manchu-Tungus tribes of the Ussuri area. It is well documented in ethnographic and geographic accounts (Margaritov 1888, Lopatin 1915; UK, DU, ST, SA) and in fiction works (PU, PK, Ud, BR). The Ussurian materials indicate a distinct dialect, one showing clear substratal influence from the Manchu-Tungus languages. This suggests secondary pidginization, and gives the Ussuri dialect considerable importance for the general study of pidginization. Furthermore, it gives us the only solid evidence on how this pidgin was transmitted and locally adapted.

Unfortunately, the materials are difficult to use. The primary source is from literary works (Arsen'ev's books: UK, DU, ST, SA), and a literary corpus, even non-fiction, obviously requires special interpretation. In addition, crucial sociolinguistic information is lacking. The corpus may reflect active distortion by Arsen'ev himself, a Russian who knew one Manchu-Tungus language at least passively. Alternatively, it may represent the adaptations of the protagonist, a Manchu-Tungus speaker who had learned the pidgin from Russians and/or Chinese.

My analysis involves a point by point comparison of the Ussurian corpus with samples of literary stereotypes representing the nonnative Russian of various Siberian ethnic groups. This analysis is an exercise in the methodology of interpreting literary sources of pidgins; but the results also shed light on the nature of simplification in Russian, and have interesting implications for the origin of Chinese pidgin Russian.

The entire corpus surveyed can be subdivided, on purely formal evidence, into three distinct kinds of texts. *Chinese pidgin Russian* (CpR) proper is most clearly represented in the Arsen'ev works and reflected fairly consistently in PU, less so in PK, Ud, VT. An example is:

(1) *Moja doma netu. Moja postojanno sopka živi. Ogon' kladi,*
    I house neg.   I   always   mt(s) live fire put

   palatka delaj -- spi. Postojanno oxota xodi, kak doma živi?
   tent   make   sleep   hunt   go how house live
   (UK:12 Nanai speaker)
   'I don't have a house. I've always lived in the mountains. I make a fire, put up my tent, and sleep. If you're always hunting, how can you live in a house?

Conspicuous features include: loss of Russian inflection; use of the Russian imperative form for most, but not all, predicate stems (in (1), *živi, kladi, delaj, spi* are Russian imperatives; *xodi*, with initial accent, is a truncated indicative form); and the use of Russian possessive forms instead of personal pronouns (*moja* 'I, me' is Russ. 'my', fem. nom. sg.; for the complete paradigm see Neumann 1966, Nichols 1977).

Broken Russian includes utterances with grammatical errors, usually in inflection. This definition subsumes CpR proper, although below *broken Russian* will be used to refer to sources other than Arsen'ev. Broken Russian may include some CpR elements, but need not. Examples (2) and (3) have no pidgin features:

(2) *Čum idi, moj čum. Gosti.*
    tent go my tent   company (ZM 28: Yurak Samoyed)
    'Come into my tent. Come and visit.'
    (Russ. *Idi v moj čum. V gosti prixodi.*)

(3) *Kogda tvoj   lavka   otkroetsja, a?*
    when your(masc) stall(fem) opens   (DP 53: Ostyak)
    'When does your stall open, eh?'

(2) lacks prepositions and has only fragmentary syntax. (3) has masc. *tvoj* modifying fem. *lavka*. Broken Russian with CpR elements was found in RO, ZK, BR (and the defective CpR of PK, Ud, VT, DM is grouped here also); broken Russian without CpR elements, in ZM and DP. Broken Russian with CpR elements often generalizes the imperative as the sole

form of the verb, producing forms such as *mogi* 'can, may' (PK 365), cf. CpR *mogu*; or *xoti* 'want' (Kurosawa's film Dersu Uzala, in a passage not taken from Arsen'ev), cf. CpR *xoču, xyči*. *Mogi* and *xoti* are unanimously rejected by pidgin speakers.

Simplified Russian is Russian without actual grammatical errors, but distinctive in its simple syntax, word order, lexical infelicities, etc. Principal sources are ZM, TMD, IPK, exemplified by:

(4) *Sovsem   ušel.   Pozabyl staruxu.   Ty   tože   takoj.*
    completely left   forgot   old woman you also   that kind

    Vyros -- v gorod ušel. Tajgu   brosil.   Xudoj   paren'.
    grew up to city left   taiga   gave up   bad   guy
    (TMD 20: Evenki)
    'He left for good. Forgot the old woman (=speaker). You're like that, too. Grew up -- left for the city. Gave up the taiga. Bad boy.'

(5) *Sovsem   prixodi. Malo oxotnikov stalo.   Budeš'   v*
    completely   come   few hunters   left   you'll be in

    tajge, Avdo spokojno umret.
    taiga, A.   in peace will die   (TMD 20: Evenki)
    'Come for good. There aren't many hunters left. (If) you're in the taiga, Avdo (=speaker) can die in peace.'

Note the unvaried choppy sentences, absence of subordinating conjunctions and particles; in context these passages contrast sharply with the native Russian of the interlocutor. In:

(6) *Začem sejčas? Utro   budet,   togda   pojdem.*
    why   now   morning will be   then   we'll go   (TMD 16: Evenki)
    'Why right now? We'll go in the morning.' ('...Morning comes, we'll go.')

note again the absence of conjunctions and particles, and the replacement of Russ. *utrom* 'in the morning' by a paratactic clause.

The broken Russian corpus is not consistent. (7) is a typical example:

(7) <u>*Moja*</u>   *ne ponimaj,   čto   ty govoriš.*
    I   neg understand   what you say   (2D 159: Yakut)
    'I don't understand what you're saying.'

The first clause is broken Russian with the pidgin elements *moja, ponimaj*; the second clause is pure Russian. (8) shows one instance of nonagreement, one mispronunciation, and one nonstandard verb form (*pobegiš'* 'you'll run off', cf. standard *pobežiš'*) which may be a dialect trait rather than broken Russian:

(8)   *Vrys'*   *pobegiš'*,   *i to,*   *xolera,*   *nastignet* ...
      at a trot   you run   even so   (invective)   catch up

     Nisjavo-o,   *bol'šoj*   *voda*   -- *ryby*   *mnogo!*   *Promyšljat'*
     nothing   big (masc) water (fem)   fish   lots   fishing

     pojdem.
     let's go   (DP 4: Ostyak)
     'Run off at full speed, and even so it will catch you, the bastard (=flood water). Doesn't matter (mispronounced), high water (no agreement) -- lots of fish. Let's go fishing.'

In other respects the utterance is fluent, lively colloquial Russian that a foreigner might envy. We may conclude that in literary texts occasional errors symbolize the broken nature of the entire passage. Typically, the individual's first appearance in the novel or story is marked by the most broken Russian.

    The author may be putting his own simplified, broken, or pidgin Russian into the mouth of his character; if so, we are dealing with foreigner talk in the sense of Ferguson 1971, Ferguson & DeBose 1977. If the actual speech of a non-Russian is being faithfully reported, then we have broken language (ibid.; note that here *broken language* is the term of Ferguson & Debose, while *broken Russian* is a particular style as defined above). It may be assumed that works of fiction display foreigner talk, since the utterances have been made up by the author; while nonfiction contains broken language, since the conversations were real, However, the nonfiction works usually follow by several decades the actual events recorded, and much may have been forgotten; and the fiction works were all written by men who lived in the places depicted and who therefore may well be rendering broken language rather accurately.

    The more conservative assumption is that the texts represent at least foreigner talk; they may also represent broken language. To claim that they do not reflect foreigner talk would be to assume a perfect memory on the part of each writer. Furthermore, several properties listed below are consistent with the assumption of foreigner talk. No evident formal property distinguishes the fiction from the nonfiction works; i.e., no formal property appears to be diagnostic for foreigner talk vs. broken language. In the absence of evidence to the contrary, I assume the properties documented below characterize Russian foreigner talk.

A statistical survey of available texts produced the results summarized below.

Morphology. Loss of inflection characterizes pidgin and broken Russian as against simplified Russian. Specific categories are tabulated below.

Property	Example	CpR=	broken R	Simplified R
noun case, preposition	1,2,6; 9 10 (below)	lost*	lost*	retained
adjective agreement	3,8	lost*	lost*	retained
polite plural (Russ. *vy*)		lost	lost	lost
verb agreement	all	lost*	variable**	retained
tense		lost*	variable**	retained
aspect		lost*	variable**	retained
marked moods (conditional, etc.): text frequency		zero	zero	zero

* Contextual restrictions, see below.
** Lost in broken Russian with CpR elements; retained in other broken Russian.

Inflectional forms are nowhere randomly mixed; inflection is either lost or preserved intact. Loss is signaled by use of a single invariant form, usually nominative of nouns, imperative of verbs. Loss of case and preposition is inconsistently reflected in texts, as mentioned. There is a pattern to the inconsistency. Loss is typical in the following, highly accessible, syntactic relations:

(a) subject (relevant to adjective agreement only);
(b) direct object, as in:

(9) *Karagasok ezdil, bol'šoj načal'nik iskal.*
    (place) went   big   boss (nom) looked for
    (DP 27: Ostyak)
    'I went to Karagasok, looked for the big boss.'

(c) subject of inverse predicate (dative in standard Russian), as in:

(10) *Baba   ego sovsem   ploxoj: skoro rožat' ej...*
     wife(nom) his completely bad(masc.nom) soon give birth her
     (DP 5: Ostyak)
     'His wife is in very bad shape. She's due to give birth soon.'
     (Russ. *babe* (dat.) *ploxo* (undeclined predicative).)

(d) locative expression with verb of location or motion, as in (1), (2), (9), and (17) (below).

Other, more oblique relations are most often properly inflected. In broken Russian without CpR elements, loss of inflection is limited to nouns and adjectives. (The latter pattern agrees with my own (unsystematic) observation of the imperfect Russian of Soviet ethnic minorities: verb morphology gives few problems, while cases are not infrequently incorrect.)

Syntax. The relevant features are shared by all three types: subordination is rare, parataxis usual (1, 4-6). SOV and Verb-Aux order are typical, and substantially increased relative to native Russian speech in the same texts, cf. (1) and:

(11) Ryba <u>lovi ponimaj</u> tože <u>netu</u>.
 fish catch know how (Aux) also neg (Aux) (UK 12: Nanai)
 '(I) don't know how to fish, either.'

(12) Naša skoro balagan <u>najdi est'</u>.
 we soon cabin find Aux (UK 16: Nanai)
 'Soon we'll come to a cabin.'

Anaphora. Zero anaphora is much more frequent than pronominal anaphora (1, 4, 5, 11). First, and occasionally second, person singular pronouns are replaced by names or nouns in some simplified Russian texts (IPK, TMD; e.g., (4-5)).

Lexicon. All three styles use evidential or inferential expressions. All texts use Siberian Russian inferential *odnako* 'I guess, probably', as in:

(13) Vot, <u>odnako,</u> moja olen' pošel.
 Voilà my reindeer went (ZK 189: Even)
 'There goes one of my deer, I guess.'
 'That must have been one of my deer.'

CpR also uses parenthetical *moja dumaj*, lit. 'I think', in roughly this function (standard *po-moemu* 'I'd say'). All three styles use titles of address, often exotic or eccentric ones, for Russians (*bojjo* in (16) is an Evenki term of address):

(14) Spasibo, <u>kapitan</u> -- šibko spasibo!
 thanks captain very much thanks (DU 169: Nanai)

(15) Nado ubivaj amba, <u>komissar!</u>
 have to kill tiger commissar (PK 381: Nanai-Udehe)
 'We've gotta kill that tiger, sir.'

(16) *Ja dumala, zabyl, bojjo.*
    I   thought   forgot   (TMD 15: Evenki)
    'I thought you'd forgotten, my friend.'

All styles show reduction of synonymy. Broken Russian reduces the complex system of Russian verbs of motion (two aspect oppositions, classificatory oppositions reflecting motion by foot, vehicle, etc.) to one or a few forms. The following sentence:

(17) *Ty   Moskva,   naverno,   idti   budeš'.*
     you   probably   go (by foot) future   (BR 224: Nanai)
     'You'll probably go to Moscow.'

shows *idti*, in Russian 'go (by foot)', used of a vehicle trip. (The interlocutor's response uses *poedu* 'I'll go (vehicle)'.) CpR uses *xodi*, which in Russian denotes multidirectional motion by foot, in all contexts except that *uexal*, in Russian 'has gone, left (vehicle)' means 'gone, no longer here'. Russian uses a number of verbs in the expressions 'put up a tent; pitch a tent'; in (1) the simple verb *delaj* (Russ. *delat'* 'make, do') is used instead. Lexical prefixes may be removed from verbs: (1) shows *kladi* 'lay (a fire)' for Russ. *ras-kladyvat'*. The CpR corpus has only *ogon'* where Russian uses *ogon'* 'fire' and *koster* 'bonfire'. The wealth of Russian intensifiers is largely reduced to *sovsem* 'completely' and *šibko* 'very' (Siberian dial.).

All three styles, then, share losses of Russian grammatical elements. What makes genuine CpR distinctive is a number of specific additions and substitutions. In addition to the special pronoun forms *moja, tvoja*, etc., CpR has a distinctive lexical stock, e.g., *karaběi* 'steal'. Ussurian CpR has innovated a verbal inflectional category based on evidentiality (Nichols 1977; the analysis given there is incorrect in detail, but does indicate a systematic category). Another innovation is the frequent use of a marker of parataxis in the second of two clauses, as in:

(18) *Ogon' i   voda   propadi   -- togda vse   srazu   koncaj.*
     fire   and water   disappear   then   everything at once   finish.
     (UK 200: Nanai)
     'If it weren't for fire and water the world would come right to an end.'

Manchu-Tungus influence is reflected in the use of specific types of reduplication (Nichols 1977); the evidential category may also be Manchu-Tungus (Nichols 1979). Manchu-Tungus words are occasionally used. In general, CpR differs from mere broken Russian in having a norm: systematic verb categories, a complex VP structure, unpredictable lexicalized verb stem forms (Nichols 1977).

Discourse. Examples of connected discourse are, in simplified Russian, (4), (5), and:

(19) (Russian: I'm lost.)
    (Evenki: Did you cross little creeks?)
    (Russian: A few times. Why?)

Pošto	xudo	dumaeš'?	Kuda	eti	rečki	tekut?
why	badly	you think	where	these	creeks	flow

(Russian: Into the Nepa)

Po	nim	nado	idti.	Rečki	privedut	na	reku	Nepu.
along	them	should	go	creeks	lead	to	river	N.

Po	nej	zimov'e	najdeš'.	Vse	sovsem	prosto.
along	it	winter hut	you'll find	everything	completely	simple.

(TMD 10: Evenki)

'Why can't you think clearly? Where do these creeks flow?' ...
'You should follow them. The creeks will lead you to the
Nepa river. Along it you'll find the winter cabin. It's
all perfectly clear.'

An example in CpR is (1). Discourse in all three styles -- CpR, broken Russian, and simplified Russian -- is strikingly uniform. There is little superfluous use of language: all utterances are informative, many didactic. Complete sentences, and complete paragraphs, are used. This is in sharp contrast to normal (literary) dialogue, which abounds in fragmentary utterances, interruptions, tag questions, feedback devices. Rhetorical questions are frequent in lieu of, or as introduction to, answers. Utterances never take the form of an abstract summary of an issue; they are grounded in concrete events.

    Several of the grammatical properties are motivated by discourse properties. The preference for parataxis over subordination points to an overall tendency to maximize assertion and minimize presupposition. The use of a clause (*utro budet* 'morning will come') rather than an adverb (*utrom* 'in the morning'), in (5), has much the same effect. The absence of marked moods from the corpus is connected with the loss of subordination: the conditional, modal uses of the imperative, etc., are used primarily in subordinating constructions. The use of evidential and/or inferential markers such as *odnako* must also be related to the discourse prominence of assertion in these texts.

    The pragmatic and discourse properties may be summarized as an overall strategy: make your assumptions explicit; give the evidence. This strategy follows from the particular type of interaction depicted in these works.

Typically, the non-Russian is wise, almost infallible; the Russian is out of his element, thus ignorant, although possessed of technological marvels. The two individuals have vastly different background knowledge and assumptions; and the purpose of most of the discussion is to explain the non-Russian's assumptions and knowledge. Frequently the Russian asks a question whose answer is so obvious to the non-Russian as to warrant a rhetorical question as comeback: How can you not understand? (UK and DU, frequently); Why can't you think right? (19). This situation, with its attendant pragmatic and discourse features, is characteristic of fiction and nonfiction works alike. It presumably reflects the set of attitudes which the Russian brings to the (Siberian) contact situation.

Conclusions. There are two aspects to simplification of Russian: implementation of a distinctive discourse situation; and loss of inflectional categories and lexical complexity. These are accompanied by the appearance of SOV order and sometimes a distinctive lexical stock. The latter traits are not connected with simplification but reflect historical accident: the northeastward expansion of the Russians involved Siberian Russian dialects meeting SOV languages whose personal pronouns resembled possessive pronouns (thus *moja*, *tvoja*, etc.).

On the basis of the text survey, the major properties can be hierarchized: discourse properties < SOV order < loss of noun and adjective inflection < loss of verb agreement < use of *moja*, etc. < loss of tense < loss of aspect. CpR is the extreme development. This hierarchy represents degrees of knowledge of the basic stereotype, thus degrees of 'proficiency' in foreigner talk. The study of literary stereotypes, then, has suggested a way of integrating CpR into the normal spectrum of Russian styles. This approach is compatible with an assumption that the contribution of the Chinese to CpR in Kjaxta was not so much the nature of the pidgin as its stability. The same assumption accounts for the distribution of CpR elements in my corpus: although they dominate in areas where the Chinese were established, they are depicted as being used throughout Siberia: on the upper Kolyma (ZK), some 1500 miles northeast of the Ussurian area; and near the Urals (RO), a good 1600 miles west of Kjaxta. The same features characterize Russenorsk, used along the White Sea; and traces are even found in Soviet prison camp speech (Galler 1977 s.v. *karabčit'*, Galler & Marquess 1972:38, 78-9). If pidgin elements are today an organic part of the range of literary stereotypes, they may always have been part of foreigner talk. The study of literary stereotypes, then, supports the hypothesis that CpR goes back to an early Russian-Uralic or Russian-Turkic contact language (Kozinskij 1974) and/or to an ancient tradition reflected in (genetically related) Russenorsk (J. Fox, MS and personal communication).

REFERENCES

Čerepanov, S.I. 1853. "Kjaxtinskoe kitajskoe narečie russkogo jazyka". *Izvestija Vtorogo otdelenija Imperatorskoj Akademii nauk*, 2.10.370-1.
Ferguson, Charles A. 1971. "Absence of copula and the notion of simplicity: a study of normal speech, baby talk, foreigner talk, and pidgins". In *Pidginization and creolization of language*, 141-50. Ed. by Dell Hymes. New York: Cambridge University Press.
_____, and Charles E. DeBose. 1977. "Simplified registers, broken language, and pidginization". In *Pidgin and creole linguistics*, 99-125. Ed. by Albert Valdman. Bloomington: Indiana University Press.
Fox, James. n.d. *Russenorsk: a study in language adaptivity*. Ms. Stanford University.
Galler, Meyer. 1977. *Soviet prison camp speech: a survivor's glossary*. Supplement. Hayward: Soviet studies.
_____, and H. Marquess. 1972. *Soviet prison camp speech: a survivor's glossary*. Madison: University of Wisconsin Press.
Kozinskij, I.Š. 1974. "K voprosu o proisxoždenii kjaxtinskogo (russko-kitajskogo) jazyka". As reported by A.N. Golovastikov, Ju. X. Sirk, *Izvestija AN SSSR, Serija literatury i jazyka*. 34.1.94-6 (1975).
Lopatin, N. 1915. *Leto sredi oročej i gol'dov*. Vladivostok: Tipografija i cinkografija "Dalekaja Okraina".
Maksimov, S. 1864. *Na vostoke. Poezdka na Amur (v 1860-1 godax)*. Saint Petersburg. Tipografija "obščestvennaja pol'za".
Margaritov, V.P. 1888. *Ob oročax Imperatorskoj gavani*. Saint Petersburg. Tipografija Imperatorskoj akademii Nauk.
Neumann, G. 1966. "Zur chinesisch-russischen Behelfssprache von Kjachta". *Die Sprache* 12.237-51.
Nichols, Johanna. 1977. "Chinese pidgin Russian in Siberia". Paper read at LSA winter meeting, Chicago.
_____. 1979. "Syntax and pragmatics in Manchu-Tungus". *CLS* 15.
Ščukin, N.S. 1850. "Čaj i čajnaja torgovlja v Rossii". *Žurnal Ministerstva Vnutrennyx Del* 30.4.69-91, 30.5.195-211.
Timkowskii, Egor. 1825. *Reise nach China durch die Mongoley (1820-21)*, part 1. Leipzig: G. Fleischer.
V.P. 1849. "Rasskazy kjaxtinskogo starožila (stat'ja II)". *Moskvitjanin*, 1849: 5 (July 17th).5-15.

SOURCES

BR Lidin, Vladimir. *Bol'šaja reka.* Tri povesti, 175-310. Moscow: Sovetskij pisatel', 1967.

DP Kolyxalov, Vladimir. *Dikie pobegi.* Moscow: Sovremennik, 1977.

DU Arsen'ev, V.K. *Dersu Uzala.* Moscow: Gosudarstvennoe izdatel'stvo geografičeskoj literatury, 1960.

IPK Šeludjakov, Aleksandr. *Iz plemeni kedra.* Moscow: Sovremennik, 1972.

PK Aramilev, Ivan. *Putešestvie na Kul'dur.* Rasskazy oxotnika, 361-98. Moscow: Sovetskij pisatel', 1951.

PPT Bytovoj, Semen. *Poezd prišel na Tumnin.* Leningrad: Sovetskij pisatel', 1951.

PU Fadeev, Aleksandr. *Poslednij iz Udege.* Sobranie socinenij, 2.151ff. Moscow: Xudož. lit., 1959.

RO Aramilev, Ivan. "V gostjax u Mansi". *Rasskazy oxotnika,* 137-50. Moscow: Sovetskij pisatel', 1951.

SA Arsen'ev, V.K. *V gorax Sixotè-Alinja.* Moscow: Molodaja gvardija, 1937.

ST _____, *Skvoz' tajgu.* Moscow: Mysl', 1966.

TMD Kuzakov, Nikolai. *Tajga -- moj dom.* Moscow: Mysl'.

Ud Aramilev, Ivan. *"Undèxe".* Rasskazy oxotnika, 420-25. Moscow: Sovetskij pisatel', 1951.

UK Arsen'ev, V.K. *Po Ussurijskomu kraju.* Moscow: Gosudarstvennoe izdatel'stvo geografičeskoj literatury.

VK Lidin, Vladimir. *Velikij iti tixij.* Tri povesti, 5-172. Moscow: Sovetskij pisatel', 1967.

ZK Bronskij, B.I. *Na zolotoj Kolyme. Vospominanija geologa.* Moscow: Mysl', 1965.

ZM Simčenko, Ju. B. *Zimnij maršrut po Gydanu.* Moscow: Mysl', 1975.

CONCLUDING STATEMENT

PAUL KIPARSKY
Massachusetts Institute of Technology

The following comments are substantially as given during the conference in response to the papers orally presented there and summarized in the abstracts (see LLBA Supplement 3, 1979). I have not seen any of the written versions and my contribution had to be written up directly after the conference before the final list of papers submitted to the editor and appearing in the proceedings was available.

* * *

If healthy progress in a field means bringing increasingly rich and specific data to bear on increasingly comprehensive and articulated theories, then historical linguistics appears to be in good shape.* Old-style pretheoretical cataloguing of uninterpreted observations as well as metatheoretical pleas and manifestoes have given way to systematic inquiry, reflecting considerable agreement on what the issues are and what sort of evidence is needed to settle them.[1] Even the five years since our first meeting in Edinburgh seem to have brought some classic issues closer to their resolution, and opened up new topics not long ago considered intractable, such as variation, diffusion, and syntactic change, to name three that were prominent in our program. What emerges from this work is a picture of multiple causation and complex interaction of conditioning factors governing change, themes to which the papers and discussion at the conference reverted again and again. Accordingly, we were not offered panaceas but contributions to an eventual integrated theory of linguistic change, yet without any illusions that such a theory is just around the corner as yet.

What might be the components of that prospective theory? Especially three have figured here.

The *acquisition* of language was the special topic of the last session. Solberg reported on her large-scale field study that reaffirms the relation between processes of child phonology and potential sound change. Vihman on the contrary cautioned that such common substitutions in early stages of language acquisition as consonant harmony are rare as sound changes. Her point, while well taken, may be answered by theories which take into account the role of the speech community in filtering out the most salient or dysfunctional mutations from the pool of variants arising in the transmission of language, and which operate with the child's reanalysis of the acoustic material (rather than purely with articulatory substitutions). Such a perceptual mechanism of sound change, discussed here by Ohala and Greenlee, Hombert, and Herbert, is certainly not implausible in view of the patent importance of reanalysis in morphology (cf. Andersen) and syntax (Pepicello).

The *structure* of language was invoked in a number of papers on the implications of aspects of grammatical theory for language change. A paradigm case was Steele's proposal of a highly constrained theory of the Auxiliary in Universal Grammar whose predictions carry over as limits on possible syntactic change. Iverson noted that his and Houlihan's Markedness Constraint on phonological rules also predicts certain limits on possible sound change. We saw how syntactic change can be conditioned by and thereby reveal grammatical structure, such as the distinction between lexical and transformational processes (Horrocks) or the animacy hierarchy (Comrie). The apparent typological anomaly of the English diptotic nominal case system led Janda to the idea that the genitive was at some point in English reanalyzed as a phrase-final pronominal element. Holman's discussion of 'typology as a regulator of change' also belongs here.

There were also two papers which reversed the argument. Campbell and Ard took the position that unversals have to be relativized to change: we can countenance 'exceptions' to universals as long as we can find historical causes for them. Some sufficiently constrained notion of 'historical cause' is obviously necessary to keep this from being a permanent escape hatch which renders the notion of a 'linguistic universal' vacuous. But if they are right, we face a number of fascinating questions. Are there two kinds of universals - the kind that can be 'stretched' by historical processes, and the kind that sets fixed boundary conditions on the historical processes themselves? Or is there some more complex resolution, perhaps partly random, of the clash between 'universal' constraints and changes that threatens to break them? In any case, relativizing universals to history would have far-reaching consequences. It would in effect break down most of the remaining autonomy of synchronic linguistics. Of course, de Saussure's idea of the absolute mutual independence of synchrony and diachrony has already been eroded, partly by the idea of dynamic synchronic variation and partly by the idea that structure can control change and that change is therefore diagnostic of structure (both formulated by Jakobson and developed respectively in recent sociolinguistic and generative work). The historical relativization of universals would imply something more drastic: that the theory of grammar could not *in principle* be discovered from strictly synchronic evidence, since there might be no way of making the proposed distinction between mere tendencies and true universals violable only by historical processes (unless the latter kinds of universals can be identified by some independent, structural considerations, as might be the case for example if they turn out to be identical with so-called markedness principles).

Bailey enlivened the panel discussion by going even further and rejecting the whole idea of synchronic linguistics out of hand. I have to disagree with him if he really means to throw out the hard-won Saussurian insight that the role of an element in the linguistic system is something in principle absolutely independent of its historical origin. Without the fundamental concept of restructuring we can understand neither system nor change in language. In all other respects, however, I do think the separation of synchrony and diachrony is useless and simply tends to get in the way.

Our third main theme has been the grounding of change in the *use* of language: pragmatics, discourse, function, and society. A functionalist viewpoint came up in Mithun's interpretation of syntactic change in Iroquoian, Christoffersen's analysis of Old Norse word order, and Wheeler's work on inflectional morphology. O'Neil made a case for the interesting claim that literacy does not merely extend 'processing capacity' but has had structural efforts on English syntax. And the problem of pragmatics and discourse and its relation to structure was latent in a series of contributions tracing general tendences of change associated with particular grammatical categories: Hopper on passives to ergatives, M. Harris on demonstratives to definites, Greenberg on prepositions to postpositions via 'circumfixes', Comrie on 'inverse' verb forms, Jeffers and Zwicky on clitics, Lord on serial forms of 'take' developing into case markers. The claim that such general tendencies of morphological and syntactic change must be rooted in 'the elementary speech situation' (Kuryłowicz 1964: 240) was borne out in several of these studies.

What we heard on lexical diffusion provided more evidence to modify the picture of sound change randomly spreading through the vocabulary that the early articles by Chen and Wang projected (cf. Chen 1972, Chen and Wang 1975). What goes on is apparently something rather more interesting and narrowly circumscribed. For one thing, all the papers were able to demonstrate at least some patterning in the diffusional process, with certain kinds of environments showing more frequent and consistent implementation of the sound change, that is behavior of the sort that is found in variable rules. Secondly, in many cases it is possible to provide an explanation for *why* certain conditions favor the spread of the rule and others resist it. This is an area which is particularly rich in multiple causation: the interaction of phonetic factors, frequency, social factors, to mention those which mainly came out in contributions by Reighard, Dumas, Milroy, Malkiel, Laferriere, Dworkin, Wright, Hathaway, and Wanner and Cravens. And thirdly, all the cases of lexical diffusion discussed here involved *neutralization* rules. Neutralization rules are rules whose output could be synchronically derived from some other independently existing source, and whose lexicalization therefore would not complicate the grammar by adding new underlying segments, unlike the lexicalization of subphonemic variants, which would complicate the grammar. So the voiced stops in Tuscan (Wanner and Cravens) are *phonemic*, as are u and $\wedge$ in Irish English (Milroy), a, e and $ö$, k^h and g in Bavarian (Hathaway), wa in French (Reighard), long and short e and a in French (Dumas).[3]

If these three points hold up in general, then we would have to conclude that a theory of lexical diffusion is unnecessary, because the process can be accounted for in the narrower limits of the theory of variable rules together with normal assumptions about lexicalization of non-alternating output forms where simplicity requires it. The picture would then be as follows: newly added phonological rules in a language are variable rules whose application is favored or impeded by a variety of multiple interacting conditioning factors. Wherever possible, their most consitent outputs are liable to become incorporated into the underlying representation. On this interpretation, then, it is just this selective progressive lexicalization of the output of neutralizing variable rules that constitutes lexical diffusion. As a corollary, reversing the argument in the unclear cases would then supply us with evidence on the character of underlying representation: lexical diffusion is evidence of lexicalization.

Several papers brought out interestingly how analogical innovations in morphology and syntax (such as the loss or generalization of rules) can develop by selective diffusion processes resembling those found in sound change. Saltarelli argues that certain syntactic transformations in Romance have generalized along a relational hierarchy. According to Seiler, the dimension of 'individuation' defines a possible path for processes of change. Klenin noted the generalization of the Russian accusative-genitive case marking rule in a series of 'morphological quanta'. Klein demonstrated an intricate variation pattern in the distribution of 3rd person clitic pronouns in Spanish, governed by grammatical, pragmatic and social factors. Jansen showed how Left Dislocation in Dutch was selectively retained and grammaticalized where it best fit the canonical sentence pattern of the language. In A. Harris' analysis of the stepwise loss of Psych-Movement the attested intermediate stages turned out to be just those which are inherent in the logically possible ordering of the transformational rules.[4] Gerritsen's Dutch data supported the implicational hierarchy earlier put forward by Canale on the basis of English. It is rather clear, in fact, that such stepwise though orderly generalization is the norm rather than the exception, a fact which the theory of change must address itself to.[5]

An important suggestion towards explaining these facts is the idea of Naro and Lemle (1977) that some factors that control stepwise diffusion can be interpreted as special cases of a single dimension of *saliency*. An innovation progresses through the system beginning with the least salient circumstances, where saliency is a function of how different the old and new forms are phonetically, how monitored the speech is, and (I would like to add, how frequent the form is) and how much the innovation deviates from the canonical syntactic or phonological pattern of the language. This accounts for the well-known tendency for 'small' morphological alternations to be leveled out before 'big' ones, for innovations to progress relatively further in informal speech and marked morphological categories, and for 'structure preserving' effects, all traceable to the patterned selection imposed in language use on the structural variation arising in language acquisition. The character of syntactic and phonological change would accordingly be determined by the complex interaction of structural and functional factors.

Beside its quantal implementation, another problematic feature of analogy has been the curious blend of 'deep' and 'surface' properties which it exhibits. How do we reconcile the cases demonstrating control of analogy by abstract phonological and morphological structure with the cases where analogy complicates the grammar by projecting a 'wrong' surface regularity? Largely in order to deal with this problem, a series of additions have been proposed to the evaluation measure: transparency, paradigm conditions, the alternation condition and similar constraints on abstractness, recoverability (Kaye 1974, 1978; Gussmann 1976; Eliasson 1975, 1977; Kenstowicz and Kisseberth 1977), preferred identity of deep and surface patterns (Hale 1973). They are all unlike the purely *formal* simplicity measure in that they involve the relation between *surface forms* and something else, either rules (transparency), other surface forms (paradigm conditions), or underlying forms (Alternation Condition, recoverability, deep-surface canonical matching). Moreover, they have been tacked on mainly on the basis of historical evidence and their synchronic validity remains suspect.

Others have rightly tried to modify the theory of grammar so that the right predictions about change are made *directly*. Natural Generative Grammar and Upside-Down Phonology, though very different theories, both succeed in reducing some of the above problematic types of 'surface' analogical change to simplifications, at the price of building the superficiality into the grammatical analysis of the language itself. But aside from synchronic problems, these theories have trouble with the sorts of analogical changes that do reflect deeper features of linguistic organization.

The more promising line seems to be to view such changes as 'false analogies', that is, as forms projected by the optional grammar based on a restricted set of data at an intermediate stage of language acquisition which are *retained* even though they do force a complication in the final grammar based on the full data. Latin *honor* is the best guess for the nominative singular if just the oblique paradigm *honōrem honōris* etc. is under consideration, but creates a complication if retained in the face of the more peripheral datum of *honestus* coupled with the $s \rightarrow r$ rule needed for *flōs flōris etc*. In this way complexity can arise in the learning process even if learners always make the simplest projection, as long as we assume that they may internalize their own 'wrong' outputs. It is possible (though not necessary) to make the additional, logically independent assumption that learners are stuck with their own 'wrong' *analyses*, as Andersen (1973), McCawley (1975), and others have suggested. The mechanism can be postulated even if the learner is assumed to restructure freely so as to always have the optimal grammar for the part of his language that he controls. The active adoption of learners' innovations by other speakers is of course a likely contributing factor.

The idea, then, is that the sorts of analogical changes that have been ascribed to transparency, paradigmatic leveling, etc. are actually simplifications too, in that they are generated by the simplest grammar for the subset of data in the purview of learners at some stage of language acquisition. It is perhaps only the unmotivated carryover of the idealization of instantaneous language acquisition from formal grammar that has blocked this rather obvious picture of analogical change, which allows the interpretation as a simplificatory process to be maintained while resolving the apparent paradox that it can nevertheless complicate the grammar.

This then is one direction in which the 'pluralistic' approach called for by Beade can profitably be taken. Language acquisition and language use cannot be idealized away from the theory of change as they can from formal grammar, nor smuggled in disguised as structure, as has happened in generative work. The theories of grammar, language acquisition, and language use have to be considered as interactting subsystems in the explanation of change. Hence, while analogy is a simplificatory process, consideration of the actual process of language acquisition and the interaction of the individual with the speech community implies straightforward mechanisms by which grammars acquire complexity through 'partial' and 'false' analogy.

While this has the happy effect of vindicating a purely formal evaluation measure, it means by the same token that we cannot take change as direct evidence on structure. The inferences about synchronic grammars based on change (and *a fortiori* on acquisition data) will have to be rethought. Arguments for constraining abstractness, for transparency and other principles are based on historical facts which from this standpoint can be explained purely within the richer theory of change that we require in any case. Change cannot supply simple litmus tests for structure, though a more judicious use of historical evidence will undoubtedly be an ever increasingly important source of grammatical insight.

NOTES

* This work was supported in part by a grant from the National Institute of Mental Health (Grant Number MH 13390-12).

[1] The neogrammarians and Schleicher did not share such essential common ground, and I cannot therefore follow Koerner in ascribing to them the same 'paradigm'. Looking beyond the techniques of comparative grammar that he mentions (not to speak of technicalities such as the use of the asterisk) we see how different were their whole ways of 'doing' linguistics. The neogrammarians and other contemproary innovators explicitly disagreed with such representatives of the older (Bopp-Schleicher) tradition as Curtius about the very *goals* of comparative grammar, as documented in Kiparsky (1974). Schleicher's biologism was scarcely the main issue: most comparativists never took it very seriously and it appears to have been a dead letter by the time the neogrammarians appeared on the scene.

[2] The material in their papers raises interesting structural questions too. It seems to me that Christoffersen's data on main clause surface word order actually *confirms* Heusler's and Diderichsen's verb-initial theory as far as *deep structure* is concerned, for this allows the simplest derivation of all possible Old Norse word order patterns. Only an optional Topicalization rule is needed then, while both a Verb-second and a Verb-first transformation would be required *in addition* to Topicalization if SVO was taken as basic. The reason SVO is more common than VSO, OVS, etc. in *surface structure* might be that subjects are relatively likely to satisfy the pragmatic conditions for topicalization.

[3] The lexical diffusion of tense æ before certain consonants in New York and Philadelphia studied by Labov and his associates might be a case where outputs of variable non-neutralization rules have become lexicalized. However, it remains to be cleared up what role the 19th century prestige pronunciation of 'broad a' words like ask, which clearly was phonemic, played in the history of this tensing process. Bybee-Hooper calls my attention to her argument for lexicalization of the output of the (non-neutralizing) $s \rightarrow h$ rule in certain Spanish dialects (1978).

[4] If, as appeared to be the case, the intermediate 'dialects' have no independent existence of their own but overlap with the initial and final stage of the syntactic shift, an alternative analysis suggests itself: assume no Psych-Movement rule but different deep structures for *Me liketh X* and *I like X*. The change would then be a restructuring of the *underlying* configuration and the intermediate cases would not represent any well-defined dialect but hypercorrections by speakers of the innovating dialect attempting to use the older impersonal construction. It seems that Extended Standard Theory actually *requires* such an analysis and thereby *predicts* the marginal character of the mixed intermediate constructions - another example of the historical consequences of structural theories.

[5]Allen, who was unable to attend, announced a contrary case, of a rule which generalizes across the board where one might have expected a series of intermediate stages.

REFERENCES

Andersen, Henning. 1973. "Abductive and deductive change". *Lg*. 49.765-93.
Bybee-Hooper, Joan. 1978. "Child morphology and morphophonemic change". *Buffalo papers in linguistics*, 1(2).38-34. To appear in *Recent developments in historical morphology*. Ed. by Jacek Fisiak. Paris and the Hague: Mouton-DeGruyter.
Chen, Matthew. 1972. "The time dimension: contribution toward a theory of sound change". *Foundations of Language* 8.457-98.
Chen, Matthew and W. S.-Y. Wang. 1975. "Sound change: actuation and implementation". *Lg*. 51.255-81.
Eliasson, Stig. 1975. "On the issue of directionality". In *The Nordic languages and modern linguistics* 2, 421-44. Ed. by K. H. Dahlstedt. Stockholm: Almqvist and Wiksell.
_____. 1977. "Inferential aspects of phonological rules". *Phonologica 1976*. Ed. by Wolfgang Dressler. *Innsbrucker Beiträge zur Sprachwissenschaft* 19.
Gussmann, Edmund. 1976. "Recoverable derivations and phonological change". *Lingua* 40.281-303.
Hale, Kenneth. 1973. "Deep-surface canonical disparities in relation to analysis and change". In *Current Trends in linguistics*, 13.
Kaye, Jonathan. 1974. "Opacity and recoverability in phonology". *Canadian Journal of Linguistics* 19.134-49.
_____. 1978. "Recoverability, abstractness and phonotactic constraints". To appear in *Phonology in the 1970's*. Ed. by D. Goyvaerts.
Kenstowicz, Michael, and Charles Kisseberth. 1977. *Topics in phonological theory*. New York: Academic Press.
Kiparsky, Paul. 1974. "From paleogrammarians to neogrammarians". In *Studies in the history of linguistics; traditions and paradigms*, 331-45. Ed. by Dell Hymes. Bloomington: Indiana University Press.
Kuryłowicz, Jerzy. 1964. *The inflectional categories of Indo-European*. Heidelburg: Winter.
McCawley, James. 1975. "Acquisition models as models of acquisition". In *Proceedings of the 1974 NWAVE Conference*. Washington, D.C.: Georgetown University.
Naro, Anthony and Miriam Lemle. 1977. "Syntactic diffusion". *Ciencia e Cultura* 29.259-68.

INDEX OF NAMES

A Ackerman, F. 15
   Aebischer, P. 344, 345
   Agyül, A. 390
   Ahlqvist, A. 2, *107-14*, 107
   Aissen, J. 183
   Aitchison, J. 207
   Alberg, L.A.H. 124
   Alexandrian Grammarians 371, 372
   Allard, E. 124, 126
   Allen, C. 2, 417
   Amin, W.O. 162
   Andersen, H. 6, 49, 74, 97, 253, *285-301*, 285, 410, 414
   Anderson, S.R. 151, 152
   Antonini, abbé 353
   Antonsen, E.H. 117
   Anttila, R. 12, 196, 273, 274, 278
   Ard, J. 4, 410
   Aronoff, M. 207
   Arsen'ev, V.K. 397, 398, 399
   Aub-Buscher, G. 195
   Avanesov, R.I. 297

B Bach, E. 181
   Bächer, U. 390
   Bailey, C.-J.N. 4, 29, 35, 364, 411
   Balibar, R. 353
   Barkowski, H. 383
   Baugh, A.C. 79
   Beade, P. 1, 415
   Bedir Khan, E.D. 155
   Behagel, O. 123, 124
   Bélanger, M. 194, 196, 197
   Bello, A. 76, 84
   Bender, M.L. 38, 39, 42, 45, 46
   Beniak, E. 4, *193-98*, 194
   Benveniste, E. 152
   Bergin, O. 108, 109
   Berlin, B. 19, 20
   Berlin, E.A. 19, 20
   Bever, T. 266
   Bèze, T. 350
   Bianconi, S. 343
   Bickerton, D. 381, 382
   Binchy, D.A. 108, 111, 112

Bloomfield, L.   287, 303
Boendale, van   139, 145
Boindin, N.   351
Boling, B.   108
Boltanski, L.   353
Bopp, F.   416
Bottiglioni, G.   341
Bourdieu, P.   353
Boyce, M.   161, 162
Braune, W.   116
Breede, S.   390
Bresnan, J.   208
Bretkūnas, J.   261, 269
Bromlej, S.V.   299
Bröskamp, B.   390
Brown, R.   315
Brugmann, K.   181
Brunner, C.J.   161
Brunot, F.   197
Buffier, C.   350
Bulatova, L.N.   299
Burt, M.   385
Bustos Tovar, J.J. de   331
Butler, M.C.   167
Bybee Hooper, J.B.   4, 299, 316, 416,
Bynon, J.   6
Bynon, T.   5, *151-63*, 336

C   Cable, T.   79
Calvano, W.   183
Campbell, L.   1, *17-26*, 22, 23, 24, 97, 410

Canale, M.   4, 123, 126-30, *193-98*, 194, 196, 197, 413
Cardona, G.   152, 153, 161
Carlton, T.R.   254
Castellani, A.   340, 343, 344
Čerepanov, S.I.   397
Čerkasskij, M.A.   7
Cerulli, E.   237
Chafe, W.L.   221
Chen, M.Y.   183, 333, 345, 354, 355, 412
Cheng, C.-C.   358
Chomsky, N.   137, 181
Christie, W.M.   3, *47-51*, 50
Christoffersen, M.   2, *115-21*, 411, 416
Cinque, G.   141
Clahsen, H.   381, 387
Clyne, M.   382, 383
Cohen, M.   352
Cole, D.T.   212
Cole, P.M.   271
Collinder, B.   37
Collinge, N.E.   335
Comrie, B.S.   5, 151, 253, 410, 411
Contini, G.F.   346
Coromines, J.   278, 332
Coseriu, E.   61, 285
Cowan, H.K.J.   37, 38
Cowgill, W.   102
Cravens, T.D.   5, 412
Cuervo, R.J.   74, 76, 84

INDEX OF NAMES

Curtius, G. 416
Cybulski, T. 390

D Dahl, O.C. 215
d'Aisy 350
d'Alembert, J. le R. 352
Daukša, M. 261, 269, 270
Dawkins, R.M. 33
De Bose, C. 383, 400
Debrabandere, I. 144
Delarivière 353
De la Touche 350
Demandre 353
de Rooij, J. 134
de Saussure, F. 53, 303, 411
De Wailly, M. 353
Diderichsen, P. 117, 416
Diderot, D. 352
Dik, S.C. 148
Dillmann, A. 235
Dittmar, N. 390
Domergue, U. 352, 353
Dover, K.J. 208
Drachman, G. 305-08, 315
Dressler, W. 110, 111, 305, 315
Dulay, H. 385
Dumarsais, C.C. 351, 352
Dumas, D. 5, 412
Dworkin, S.N. 3, 412

E Edmont, E. 353
Eliason, S. 414
Enkvist, N.E. 120

Ernout, A. 181
Estienne, H. 350

F Fairbanks, G.H. 37, 270
Féraud, J.-F. 352
Ferguson, C.A. 21, 234, 236, 382, 400
Fieser, P. 390
Fitzgerald, J.J. 58
Flier, M.S. 299-300
Fokkema, K. 124
Fourquet, J. 115-16, 118
Fox, J. 397, 406
Francescato, G. 330
Friedrich, J. 100, 105
Friedrich, P. 118, 119, 208, 240, 260
Frisk, H. 208

G Galler, M. 405
Galmace, A. 353
García, E.C. 61, 66, 68, 73
Gary, J. 184, 271
Gerritsen, M. 2, *123-36*, 144, 147, 413
Gianelli, L. 341
Gilbert, G. 282
Galliéron, J. 353
Givón, T. 123, 126, 146, 223, 229, 251, 253
Goddard, I. 21
Gonda, J. 223
Gotowos, A. 390

Gougenheim, G. 184
Grammont, M. 303, 316
Green, J. 229
Greenberg, J.H. 2, 17, 22, 37,
    41, 76, 78, 80-83, 85, 97,
    118, *233-41*, 243, 245, 411
Greene, D. 109, 111-12
Greenlee, M. 6, 410
Gregor, D.B. 225
Grevisse, M. 193, 195
Grinaveckis, V. 264
Grundt, A.W. *3*, *371-79*, 373
Gulsoy, J. 278
Gundel, J.K. 137
Gussmann, E. 414
Gvozdev, A.N. 290, 300

H Haas, M.R. 22, 221
Haiman, J. 227
Hale, K. 414
Hall, R. A. 27, 28, 71, 244,
    245, 340, 341
Halle, M. 288, 304, 305
Halliday, M.A.K. 104, 119
Hammarström, E. 124
Hancock, I.F. 389
Hardwick, C.S. 55
Harnisch, U. 383
Harris, A.C. 4, *165-71*, 165,
    168, 413
Harris, M.B. 2, *75-86*, 75, 76,
    82, 83, 411
Hasan, R. 104, 119

Hathaway, L.H. 5, 412
Haugen, E. 123, 375
Heidelberger Forschungsprojekt
    381-83, 387
Henning, W.B.H. 159
Herbert, R.K. 4, *211-20*, 212,
    215, 410
Hernández-Chavez, E. 385
Herzog, M. 61, 67, 211, 345
Hetzron, R. 241
Heusler, A. 116, 416
Hindret, J. 350
Hjelmslev, L. 53
Hockett, C.F. 245
Hofmann, J.B. 181
Holman, E. 1, *7-16*, 15, 410
Holmer, N.M. 377
Holzheid, S. 340
Hombert, J.-M. 4, 410
Hooper, J. B. see Bybee
Hopper, P. 5, 134, 411
Horrocks, G.C. 5, *199-201*, 410
Houlihan, K. 410
Hudson, G. 216
Hutcheson, J. 215

I Istrina, E.S. 255
Iverson, G.K. 3, 410
Izzo, H.J. 341

J Jaberg, K. 339
Jacobsen, W.H. 373, 377, 379
Jakobson, R. 53, 55, 59, 243,

286, 287, 294-96, 299,
304, 411
Janda, R.D. 3, *243-52*, 250,
410
Jansen, F. 2, 134, *137-49*,
131, 146, 413
Janson, T. 223
Jeffers, R. 2, 211, 218, *221-
31*, 223, 411
Johnson, D.E. 271
Jud, J. 339
Justeson, J.S. 1, *37-46*, 46
Justus, C.F. 2, *97-106*, 100,
104

K Kähler, H. 215
Kahr, J.C. 223
Kangasmaa-Minn, E. 13, 14
Kaufman, T. 34, 35
Kay, P. 19, 20
Kaye, J. 414
Keenan, E. 146, 184, 271
Keim, I. 382
Kelly, F. 110
Kelly, R.C. 226
Kenstowicz, M. 414
Kent, R.G. 153
Kiefer, F. 115, 118
King, R.D. 259
Kinkade, M.D. 21
Kiparsky, C. 176
Kiparsky, P. 6, 273, 278, 297,
304, 305, 316, 371-73,

375, 379, *409-17*, 416
Kisseberth, C.W. 414
Klein, F. 2, *61-74*, 63, 71,
74, 390, 413
Klenin, E. 3, *253-57*, 255,
256, 413
Klingenheben, A. 236
Koefoed, G. 273
Koelmans, L. 144
Koerner, E.F.K. 1, 416
Kolaric, R. 316
Kooij, J. 134
Korhonen, M. 7
Korsakas, K. 269, 270
Koster, J. 142
Kozinskij, I. Š. 406
Krapp, G.P. 247
Krause, W. 117
Krenz, W. 390
Krishnamurti, B. 358
Krysin, L.P. 297
Kumm, S. 383
Kummer, M. 389
Kuno, S. 109
Kunsmann, P. 385
Kuryłowicz, J. 181, 199, 201,
205, 412
Kwofie, E.N. 6

L Labov, W. 61, 97, 211, 259,
315, 345, 354, 355-57,
416
Laferriere, M. 4, *363-69*, 412

Laigonaitė, A. 263
Lange, O. 9
Langendoen, D.T. 266
Laporte, D. 353
Larsson, C. 117
Lass, R. 1
Latta, F.C. 213
Lehmann, W.P. 97, 100, 105, 117, 223, 260
Lemle, M. 413
Leopold, W.F. 316
Le Page, R. 382
Lescot, R. 155
Leslau, W. 234-36
Leumann, M. 181
Li, C. N. 116, 151, 147, 221
Lightfoot, D. 181, 196, 197
Lopatin, N. 397
Lord, C. 3, 411
Lubin, M.A. 350
Lucas, S. 390
Lüdtke, H. 83
Lyons, J. 56

M Mac Canna, P. 111
Mac Coisdealbha, P. 109
Macken, M.A. 316
Mackenzie, D.N. 154, 156, 161-63
Macpherson, I. 331
Maher, P. 4
Maksimov, S. 397
Malkiel, Y. 5, *321-30*, 336, 412

Mamet, M. 217
Mańczak, W. 3, 299
Mann, O. 156, 157, 161
Marckwardt, A.H. 247
Margaritov, V.P. 397
Margrain, S. 356
Mariner, S. 71
Marquess, H. 405
Matejka, L. 299
Matuzevičius, E. 269
Mauger, C. 350
Maurer, F. 124
Mauvillon, M. 353
McCawley, J.D. 414
McCone, K.R. 108
McNeill, N.B. 20
Meid, W. 108
Meillet, A. 27, 28, 29, 181
Meinhof, C. 219
Meisel, J. 381, 382, 383
Mel'nikov, G.P. 9
Menéndez-Pidal, R. 310, 324
Menn, L. 304, 316
Merlo, C. 339
Meyer-Ingerwesen, J. 389
Meyer-Lübke, W. 339
Miller, D.G. 176, 179, 181
Milroy, J. 5, *355-62*, 358, 360, 361, 412
Milroy, L. 356, 360, 361
Mithun, M. 4, *87-96*, 97, 411
Mougeon, R. 4, *193-98*, 194, 196, 197

INDEX OF NAMES

Mourin, L. 275
Mühlhäusler, P. 385
Muller, H.-F. 184, 186
Mustanoja, T.F. 244, 247, 249
Muysken, P.C. 148

N Naro, A. 413
Neff, K.J. 5
Neumann, G. 397, 398
Neumann, R. 389
Nichols, J. 6, *397-405*, 398, 403
Norberg, D. 184
Nunberg, G. 355
Nyberg, H.S. 240
Nygaard, M. 116
Nyman, M. 15

O Offenbächer, H. 390
Ohala, J. 6, 19, 23, 315, 410
O'Neil, W. 1, 411
Orlović, M. 382
Ornée, W.A. 124, 134
Otanes, F.T. 216
Otheguy, R. 73
Ožegov, S.I. 297

P Pačesóva, J. 307, 316
Palionis, J. 270
Panchvidze, V. 168, 169
Patel, P.G. 266
Patterson, D. 356, 360
Paul, H. 303

Paulitschke, P. 237
Paunonen, H. 7, 14, 24
Peirce, C.S. 53-58
Pepicello, W.J. 5, *175-82*, 177, 183, 223, 410
Perlmutter, D.M. 165, 183
Pfaff, C. 1, *381-95*, 385, 390
Piélat, B. 350
Pienemann, M. 381
Pieri, S. 339, 340, 343
Pisani, V. 330
Popperwell, R.G. 375
Portz, R. 383, 390
Posner, R. 333
Postal, P.M. 183
Powell, J. 21
Praetorius, F. 236
Prokosch, E. 310
Pulgram, E. 3
Pulles, J.A.M. 124
Pullum, G.K. 271
Pyles, T. 244, 247, 249

Q Querido, A.A.M. 75
Quine, W.V. 57

R Radford, A. 184
Raman, C.F.J. 103
Real Academia Española 73
Reichelt, H. 152, 161
Reighard, J. 5, *349-54*, 354, 412
Reklaitis, J.K. 3, *259-71*, 260,

269
Restaut, M. 353
Riškus, J. 269
Rohlfs, G. 339, 340, 343
Ronconi, A. 184

S Sadock, J.M. 271
Šalčiutė, A. 269
Saltarelli, M. 4, *183-91*, 183, 190, 413
Samuels, M.L. 333, 336, 355
Sankoff, D.E. 363
Sapir, E. 7, 21
Sapir, J.D. 85
Sbarra, S. 343
Schachter, P. 216
Schiefner, A. 168
Schleicher, A. 416
Schmidt, K.H. 107, 162
Schuchardt, H. 27, 28
Schumann, J. 382
Schwyzer, E. 181
Ščukin, N.S. 397
Sedello, B. 390
Seiler, H. 3, 413
Serebrennikov, B.A. 11
Serianni, L. 343
Shapiro, M. 57
Shapiro, M. 1, *53-59*, 57, 299
Sherzer, J. 21
Shevelov, G.Y. 310
Silverstein, M. 35
Simons, P.J. 145

Sims-Williams, N. 161
Širvydas, V. 261, 269
Skutnabb-Kangas, T. 384
Slobin, D.I. 310
Sluckis, M. 269
Smith, N.V. 316
Solberg, M.E. 6, 410
Sommerstein, A. 75
Stampe, D. 304-05
Statha-Halikas, H. 153
Steele, S. 6, 221, 229-30, 410
Steiner, R. 355
Steinmüller, U. 390
Stellinga, G. 124, 140
Stennes, L.H. 85
Stephens, L.D. 1, *37-46*, 46
Stern, G. 57
Stockwell, R.P. 123, 126, 127, 133, 134
Stoett, F.A. 133, 140, 148
Stokes, W. 107
Stölting, W. 381
Strachan, J. 107, 111
Sturtevant, E.H. 303, 372
Swadesh, M. 38, 44
Szantyr, A. 181

T Tegey, H. 151, 162
Templin, M.C. 315
Thelin, N.B. 299
Thernstrom, S. 366
Thomas, F. 181
Thomason, S.G. 4, *27-35*, 32,

INDEX OF NAMES

34, 35, 198, 273
Thompson, S.A.   116, 147
Thomson, A.I.   253, 254, 256
Thurneysen, R.   111
Thurot, C.   350, 353, 354
Timkowski, E.   397
Toon, T.E.   358
Traugott, E.C.   123, 131, 244, 247-49
Trubetzkoy, N.S.   243
Trudgill, P.   4
Trumpp, E.   239
Tsiapera, M.   5, 218
Tuttle, E.   340, 343

U Umbrasas, K.   269
   Unbegaun, B.O.   256
   Ureland, P.S.   117, 123, 134

V Vaillant, A.   79, 80, 85
   Valkhoff, M.F.   32
   Van Boendale   139, 145
   Van den Berg, B.   126, 134, 148
   Van der AA, B.   350
   Van der Kallen, M.   124, 126
   Van Ginneken, J.   124, 126, 134
   Van Kersbergen, G.C.   131
   Van Maerlant   139, 145
   Van Riemsdijk, H.   141, 142
   Van Tiel-Di Maio, F.   184
   Vendryès, J.   181
   Vennemann, T.   118, 123, 125, 126, 299

Verdam, J.   148
Vihman, M.M.   6, *303-20*, 305, 315, 316, 410
Vincent, N.   273
Vinogradov, V.V.   297
V.P.   397

W Wackernagel, J.   229
   Wagner, H.   107, 109, 111
   Wagner, M.   390
   Wang, W.S.-Y.   183, 333, 345, 354, 358, 412
   Wanner, D.   5, 221, 225, *339-47*, 412
   Wartburg, W.v.   345
   Wasow, T.   202, 203, 207, 209
   Watkins, C.   97, 108, 110, 199, 200, 223, 228
   Weijnen, A.A.   126, 133, 134
   Weinreich, U.   27, 31, 32, 61, 97, 211, 345
   Weinrich, H.   341, 344, 345
   Wessén, E.   123
   Wetzel, C.   390
   Wheeler, M.W.   5, *273-83*, 276, 278, 411
   Whinnom, K.   28, 34, 383
   Wilbur, R.B.   219
   Winner, J.   134
   Wolfram, W.   97
   Woodcock, E.C.   181
   Wright, J.   250
   Wright, R.   3, *331-37*, 331, 332,

334, 412

Wyld, H.C. 247-49, 355

Y Yaeger, M. 355

Z Zwarts, F. 141, 142

Zwicky, A.M. 2, 213, *221-31*, 221, 224, 227, 230, 245, 411

INDEX OF LANGUAGES

A Afrikaans 32
   Akkadian 105
   Alawa 306
   Algonquian 21, 24
   Amharic 45, 233-37
   Anatolian 223
   Arabic 237, 241, 306
   Aramaic 83
   Austronesian 211, 214-20, 227
   Avestan 152, 161, 240
   Aztec 23

B Balochi 240
   Baltic 314
   Balto-Slavic 371, 374
   Bantu 211-14, 217-20
   Basque 371-79
   Belorussian 254
   Black English 385
   Bolia 217
   Bulgarian 79, 80

C Caspian 240
   Castilian 61-74, 325, 332, 336
   Catalan 188-89, 275-78, 333
   Caucasian 162
   Cayuga 88

   Celtiberian 110
   Celtic 107-14, 228
   Cherokee 87
   Chinese Pidgin Russian 397-407
   Chinook Jargon 34
   Cholan-Tzotzilan 22
   Chukotian 240
   Chumash 306
   Corsican 341
   Cushitic 234
   Czech 305-20

D Danish 117, 123
   Diola 85
   Dutch 123-36, 137-49
      Cape Colony Dutch 32

E English 45, 46, 47-51, 84, 98-
      106, 111, 123-36, 137, 148,
      165-71, 194-98, 207, 208,
      221, 225, 243-52, 260, 305-
      20, 333, 355-62, 363-69,
      385-95
      Old English 78-80, 84,
         123-36, 165-67, 243-
         52

Middle English 166-67,
    247, 355-62
Early Modern English 49-
    50, 247-52, 356
Estonian 227, 305-20
Ethiopian Semitic 234-41
Ethiopic 236
Evenki 399-407
Ewe 227

F Finnic, Western 310-20
Finnish 17-16, 24, 314
Flemish 141
Fogny 85
French 77-86, 187-91, 193-98,
    229, 323-24, 325, 333, 339,
    349-54
    Canadian French 194-98
Frisian 123-24, 131-36
Fula 82, 85

G Gafat 236
Gallo-Romance 343
Gascon 226
Ge'ez 235-37
Georgian 45
German 84, 123-24, 131-36, 225,
    381-95
Germanic 78, 117, 123, 126,
    310-11, 314, 334, 371-74
Greek 33, 101, 175-82, 199-209,
    223, 226, 371-79
Guarani 306

Gurage languages 236
Gurma 81

H Harari 235, 237-78
Hausa 233
Hittite 97-106, 223-24
Hmong 222
Hua 227
Huron-Wyandot 87

I Icelandic, Old 116-17
Ibero-Romance 61
Indic, Old 152-53
Indo-European 28, 34, 40-41,
    76, 98, 101, 105, 153,
    228, 230, 240, 270, 273,
    371-79
    see also Proto-Indo-European
Indo-Iranian 151
Indonesian 214-17
Iranian 151-63, 233-41
Irish 107-14, 226, 228-29
Iroquoian 21, 25, 87-96
Italian 81, 83, 187-91, 197,
    322, 333, 336, 339-47, 383

J Japanese 20, 104-05
Javanese 306

K Kurdish 151-63, 238

INDEX OF LANGUAGES

L Lappish 7
   Latin 30-31, 75-86, 101, 152-54,
      175-82, 183-91, 221, 223,
      244, 248, 269, 310, 313,
      322-27, 331-37, 339-47,
      374, 375.
      Church 323
      Classical 229, 322
      Vulgar 229, 322
   Lithuanian 259-71
   Livonian 311, 314
   Luganda 212, 218

M Maβeta 214
   Madurese 227
   Makah 221-24
   Makonde 213-14, 217-20
   Malagasy 215
   Manchu-Tungus 397-407
   Mayan 22
   Miao 222
   Minjan 239
   Miwok, Lake 43-46
   Mohawk 88-95

N Nanai 398-407
   Navaho 45, 306
   Nitinat 21-24
   Nootkan 21
   Nordic 114, 123
   Norse, Old 115-21
   Norwegian 115-21, 123, 373

O Oneida 88
   Onondaga 88
   Ormuri 239
   Ossetic 238, 239
   Ostyak 398-407

P Paiute 306
   Pamir languages 239
   Pashto 227, 230, 233-41
   Persian 152-63, 238, 240
   Pipil 23
   Pitcairnese 32
   Polish 269
   Portuguese 188-91, 197, 218,
      227, 322, 324, 327
   Proto-Indo-European 43-45, 46,
      115, 117, 123, 233-24, 226,
      268
      see also Indo-European
   Provençal 323, 339
   Pukapukan 20

R Remo 45
   Romagnol 225
   Romance 30-32, 76-86, 183-91,
      197, 222, 225, 229, 322,
      323, 331-37, 339-47
   Rumanian 30-31, 81, 188-91
   Russenorsk 34, 405-06
   Russian 58, 79-80, 254, 260,
      285-301
      Chinese Pidgin Russian 397-407

S Sanskrit 223-34, 226, 306, 371, 374, 379
   Scandinavian 79, 115-21, 123-36, 375
   Semitic 233-41
   Seneca 88
   Serbo-Croatian 230
   Slavic 30-31, 222, 253-57, 310-20
   Slavonic 79-80, 85
   Slovenian 304-20
   Spanish 23, 61-74, 77, 81, 83, 84, 187-91, 197, 222, 229, 305-20, 321-30, 331-37, 383, 385
   Sumerian 105
   Sundanese 227
   Swedish 123

T Tagalog 216-17, 222, 227, 230
   Tadjik 238
   Talysh 239-40
   Tat 238-40
   Tigre 235-38
   Tigrinya 235-37
   Turkic 1, 11
   Turkish 227, 238, 285-95
   Tuscan 339-47
   Tuscarora 88-96
   Tuscarora-Nottaway 88

U Udehe 402-07
   Udi 165-71
   Ukrainian 254-55
   Umbrian 343
   Uralic 406
   Uto-Aztecan 229

V Voltaic 81

W Wakhi 239
   Walbiri 230
   Welsh 225
   Wolof 82
   Wyandot 87-96

Y Yaghnobi 239
   Yakut 399-407
   Yucatecan 22
   Yurak Samoyed 398-407

INDEX OF SUBJECT MATTER

A abduction 58, 74
accent 371-79
accusative-infinitives 175-82, 183-91
acquisition of language 285-301, 303-30, 321, 381-95, 410, 415
adaptive rules 285-301
additive change 285-301, 305
adpositions 233-41
affixes 7-16, 44-45, 211-20, 225, 233-41, 243-52, 273-83, 321-30
analogy 66, 273-83, 345, 413-15
analyticity 248, 388-89
anaphoric pronouns 76-86, 402
animacy constraints 103, 254-57
arbitrariness 37
archaisms 331-37
article, definite 75-86
asyndeton 100
AUX 414

B backgrounding *see* foregrounding
Bergin's Law 108
borrowing 194-98, 340
broken language 382-95, 397-407

C case 7-16, 61-74, 151-63, 165-71, 175-82, 183-91, 200-01, 233-41, 243-52, 253-57, 259-71, 374-79
case roles 89-96
causatives 184-91
child language *see* acquisition
circumfixes 233-41
classifiers, nominal 211-20
clefting 91-94, 105, 107, 111
clitics 61-74, 154-63, 221-31, 243-52
cohesion, clausal 98, 119-20
color universals 19-20
comparative reconstruction 27, 35, 37-46, 234
complementation 92, 97-106, 175-82, 183-91, 193-98
compounds, verbal 199-209

consonant cluster reduction 311-314
consonant harmony 305-06
continuity,
    change as aspect of 53-59
    of transmission 27-35
creolization 27-35, 383-95

D declension *see* case
decreolization 33
definiteness, marker of 75-86, 92-93
deixis 66-74, 85, 101
deletion 100, 290
    see also Equi-NP, Raising
determiner 76-86
dialect *see* variation
diffusion 412
    areal 21-22
    lexical 183, 331-37, 344-47, 349-54, 355-62
    paradigmatic 183
    syntactic 183-91
diglossia 384
discovery procedures 37-46
discourse functionality 197, 253-57, 404-05
doublets 331-34
drift 87-96, 269

E emphatic function 89-96
Equi-NP 197-80
ergativity 151-63, 168-71

evidentials 403-04
evolutive change 283-301
exbraciation 124-36
exceptions 17-26, 331-37
explanation 17-26, 47-51, 415
extraposition 246-47

F family tree model 29
focus fronting 89-95
foregrounding 89-95
foreigner talk 382-95, 397-407
functionalist approach 8-16, 48-51, 61-74, 87-96, 115-21, 253-57, 263-69, 411
functional load 355

G Gastarbeiterdeutsch 381-95
gender 62-74, 101-06, 249
generalization 246, 305
genetic relationship 27-35, 37-46, 233-41
grammaticalization 253-57
Great Vowel Shift 49-50, 357

H heteroclitic stems 101
Humboldt's universal 196, 273

I iconicity 12
imperfect learning 30, 303-04
impersonal passive *see* passive
implicational relationship 234, 387

indexicality 12
infinitival complement *see*
    complement
inflectional categories 326-27
innateness 305
innovation 253-54, 304
internal reconstruction 180
intonation 141-13
inversion *see* movement rule
irregular sound change 339-47

K Keenan-Comrie hierarchy 189

L learnéd vocabulary 331-37
    left-dislocation 137-49
    leveling 415
    lexical change 199-209, 323
    lexical complexity 382, 402-03, 405
    lexical diffusion *see* diffusion
    lexical rules 199-209
    lexicalization 344, 412
    literary stereotypes 397-407
    locatives 199-209
    loss, of rule 165, 171

M markedness 110-11, 243, 410
    merger 355-62
    metaphor 57-58
    metathesis 227
    metonymy 57
    mora 371-79
    morphological change 7-16, 75-86, 186, 211-20, 221-31, 233-41, 243-52, 259-71, 273-78, 285-301, 326, 334-35, 401-02
    morphological cycle 222-23
    morphophonemic rules 285-301, 306, 338
    movement rules 165-71, 200-09
        and entries under word order

N natural change 27-35, 198
    number-marking 249

O object marking 253-57
    optimalization 9-16
        see also simplification
    orthography 248-49

P particles 199-209, 222, 245
    passive 51, 151-63, 176-82, 184-91
    perceptual strategies 10, 50, 87-95, 211-20, 259-71, 273
    personal pronouns 61-74, 75-86, 243-52
    phonetic change *see* sound change
    phonological change *see* sound change
    phoric usages 100-06, 139
    pidgin languages, pidginization 27-35, 392-95, 397-401
    portmanteau forms 225-27

postpositions 98, 233-41
pragmatic strategies *see* functionalist approach
pre-complementizers 97-106
preposed elements (prepositions, preverbs) 98, 199-209, 233-41
presupposition 89-95
production 47-51
pro-forms 222
   see also anaphoric pronouns, demonstratives, personal pronouns
prosody 306
Psych-movement 165-70, 413, 416

R raising 178-80, 183-91
reanalysis 66, 133, 183-91, 211-20, 226-27, 243-52
recoverability 414-15
reduction, phonological 306-20
redundancy 47-51
referential meaning 62-74
regular sound change 331-37
reinterpretation *see* reanalysis
relations, grammatical 165-71, 189-90
relative clauses 90, 123
relativizer 98-106
relexicalization 211-20
residue 355, 360
restructuring *see* reanalysis
rhythm 119-20

S saliency 413
second language acquisition 382-95, 397-407
second position 134, 144, 210, 222
semantic change 53-59, 61-74
semilingualism 384
semiotics 7-16, 53-59
signs 53-59
simplification 273, 304, 383-95, 398-407, 415
   see also optimalization
social factors in language change 61-74, 297, 336, 340, 349-54, 355-62, 363-69, 381-95
sociosemantic factors 360
sound change 17-26, 48-50, 186-87, 248-50, 276, 303-20, 321-30, 331-37, 339-47, 349-54, 355-62, 363-69, 371-79
sound symbolism 37-46
speech community 281, 363-69, 410
spelling pronunciation 336
split, of category 206
standard variety 63, 339-47, 352, 364
stereotype 356
stress 259-71, 303-20, 321-30, 349-54, 371-79
stylistic variation 288-301, 331-37

subject agreement 166-71, 180
syllable structure 7-16, 306-20, 371-79
symbols, nature of 54-59
symbolism 7
synchrony, role of 17-26, 411, 415
syncretism 253-57, 263, 273-83, 374-79
syntactic change 87-95, 97-106, 107-12, 115-21, 123-36, 137-49, 151-63, 165-71, 175-82, 183-91, 193-98, 199-209, 233-41, 243-52, 259-71, 386-89, 402

T teleology 57-58
tense, compound 123-36
thematizing 51
tmesis 108
tone 371-79
topic, topic shift 91, 116-21, 126, 141-49, 157-63
transitivity 187-91
transparency 414-15
truncation 286-301
typology 7-16, 17-26, 97, 107-12, 116-21, 189, 243-52

U unaccusative 165-71
uniformitarian principle 132
univerbation 228
universals 17-26, 97-106, 107, 410-11
universal grammar 410

V variable rules *see* variation
variation 97-100, 193-98, 288-301, 339-47, 349-54, 355-62, 363-69
verb inflection 273-83, 285-301
verbs of motion 193-98
verbs of perception 193-98
vernacular speech 61-74, 322-30, 331-37, 355-62
vocabulary increase
  in children 315
  in language change 57

W weight, of clause 120
word order 97-106, 107-14, 115-22, 123-36, 137-49, 158-59, 165-71, 233-41, 244, 259-71, 387-88
  see also topic shift

OHIO UNIVERSITY LIBRARY

Please return